The Free Musics

Jack Wright

Cover image, design and layout by Barbara Upton and Larry Deitch
Photo by Ugo Boscain

Spring Garden Music Editions
www.springgardenmusic.com

ISBN-10: 1537777246
ISBN-13: 978-1537777245

For Grant Strombeck
Chicago drummer and video artist

CONTENTS

Foreword

It makes sense that Jack should write this musico-anthropology of free music. Not as historian or memoirist, and certainly not as self-promoter, but as the voice of an active musician even now working directly inside the subject matter of this book.

In the more than three decades that we've been friends I've always known Jack as a sax player with a refined and hugely expansive language. And as a writer. A critical-thinking essayist in the discussions and writing around free improvisation. At times, a de facto conscience.

He's also always been vigilant in networking as an integral extension of playing free music. His performing career is consistently at the service of connecting and empowering others in free-playing activity. He enacts a sense of community between far-flung locales both here and abroad. A veteran musician, grassroots proponent for a music-making endeavor whose validity is proven by its near-total absence from the music-industrial complex. For Jack "just playing" is more than just playing the music.

In the course of extensive travel, playing countless gigs outside the commercial spheres, he has been able to function not only as advocate and exemplar but as a kind of explorer, a scout, "The Johnny Appleseed of Free Improvisation," as I called him back in the 80s. Cultural reconnaissance of free playing's outposts. Mapping the nature of free playing itself as well as of free players and our milieux.

In *The Free Musics*, as in his ensemble playing, Jack focuses on others more than himself. Not just on other musicians but on the free musics themselves, which, like music-making generally, are regarded as a cultural outsider.

This book is not intended as a "story of free playing" type of history, though it speaks as a musicologically sound narrative. In fact it's more like a diagnosis of the placings and movements within and around that history, which of course extends into the socio-political situation of musical freedom and its role in our civilization as we know it today.

Suffice it to say that "The Free Musics" is more than simply a book on free music. It's also a crucial treatise, a news report, a weather forecast, a network of dialectics, and a theoretical work of encompassing urgency.

-----Davey Williams, Birmingham

Preface

"Free" joins two musical genres at the hip, free jazz and free improvisation. They have taken up little room in the cultural landscape but have raised questions at the core of the meaning of music. In North America they have implicitly challenged the primary social function of music in our time: to establish a stable center of enjoyment and a buffer of relief between people's inner lives and the daily reality they face. They are often designated as art but have been in tension with the most accepted meanings of art.

"Free" is commonly expected to provide happiness, yet it was also one of the keywords of the disturbing and critical modernist approach. Composers stripped music of the guarantees that helped it stabilize and normalize people's lives. Boosted by an irreversible advance called Progress, they abandoned the idea of a ruling tradition for art music, which had dictated what is to be done so that music would be recognized as music. The wide rejection of modernist music, combined with the rise of popular musics, has led to plural "musics," deflating the modernist progression to the position of one tradition among many. To defend a line protecting music from the totality of organized sound is no longer of importance for the social order. Sound can evoke fear and insecurity—noise--which does not guarantee universal enjoyment. That cat is out of the bag. On the other hand, if all sound *can* be music we are in a more effective consumer situation of choosing which sounds make us feel safe and avoiding others.

The *approach* of the two free musics in their origins is what I will be calling "free playing." It faced people with sound they could not comprehend as music, and it still has that potential. Cultural backing reassures us we are human, and this it lacks. Intentional sound-making released from the bag of pre-determined musical order is no more reassuring than the world we live in. The free musics and their originary approach have come to us through the historical process, which is none other than ourselves. To get past the now-pacified consumer forms of free musics to the central experience they promise--first of all for the players--is what I attempt to do in this book.

Free jazz and free improvisation had their origins in the turmoil of the sixties, when "free" was on the agenda of both dissident politics and unsettling art. At the same time the word has been the master harmonizing term of American ideology, which attempts to justify "our way of life" at home and the extension of market relations into every nook and cranny of human existence. At least in the US, free is starkly divided against itself, and cannot shake off the ambivalence.

To implicate "free" in any art-making opens the door to unruly desire. Art is first of all a doing, an intransitive verb missing from the vocabulary, a space of absence that evokes questioning: What are you doing? What will you do? Reduced to art*works* however art is a noun promising fulfillment: it's been done, time to put it to use. To consider desire fulfilled and attained allows it to be possessed in object form, whether a CD box set on the shelf or a bulging folder of internet links. Art so understood suppresses the suffering of lack and conflict that constitutes the desiring subject. Active searching is bypassed; the excess and ambivalence of desire is forever deferred. The imagined resolution is compulsively relived as the background of life that music has been for some time. Musics that open to desire and conflict are reified and available as commodities and reliable discourse, and that shuts the door.

Pointing people towards the open door, then shutting it, is what the most familiar ideas surrounding art boil down to. For desire to be turned into pacified beauty for some and cathartic release for others is what the social order is responsible for achieving. It is not desire that does that. Once evoked historically, culturally, and personally, it does not automatically suck the life out of itself. It's the fear of the depths to which desire might take us that produces the effort to shut it down through satisfaction. Those depths have been called chaos, which the social order barely contains; promising to do so is part of its reason being. To the extent that we internalize the social order as the superego of authority, we are its subjective analogue, and desire is what we humanize and contain. The bait of fulfilling desire makes us receptive to art, but its guards, institutional home, and media remind us to keep our distance if we want desire to be stable and functional. The collateral fear is that the guarantees designed to protect us from ourselves and each other will fall apart. We lift up our eyes to the world outside of entertainment and art and get a glimpse that, lo and behold, that is already happening. The need for music to suppress this awareness is stronger than ever.

One way to deal with the presumed threat is to project the ineradicable disorder in our psyches onto something external. This is the age-old recourse to scapegoating—there's the evil; build a wall and put it outside the culture. Another approach seems the reverse, but merely follows later on--turn those who once embodied the threat into revered icons. Harmless now, they are welcomed back. Spectators will introject into their psyches the images of those who then *represent* desire, even more perfectly than the actual artists ever did. Those represented are then distanced from their own activity. Frozen where they once embodied art in motion, they are mere names, shells emptied of the "it" of desire. As icons they stand guard against spectators' desire, with no way to join them. We are mortals to these gods; the golden age is past and we bow to relics.

Ideology and institutions that wall people off from desire provide relief, so most are tempted to go along. It seems foolish to think one can sustain the drive to the depths, an overwhelming, oppressive mess. Where desire will lead is unpredictable, and how it will shake us is what our reasonably ordered lives cannot know. To be free in this sense is to be a loose cannon. It looks attractive when projected onto icons, but when we are both the cannon and the ship it wreaks havoc. To welcome desire, to let it swirl and spin and crash around, we will find, if only buried under mounds of regret, there is no safety for the self.

Free jazz has become a subgenre minimally supported by a music world whose larger job is to maintain stable and distinct taste categories.[1] Its advocates consider it a marginalized extension of jazz, which itself is promoted as achieved freedom. "Jazz means Freedom" appeared first in the Cold War, was sustained through the construction of Classic Jazz in the 80s, and is affirmed today in the huge edifice of jazz education. Present free jazz sends out hints and sparks of what it once meant to offend the dominant culture. It draws in many whose politics deny the meaning of achieved freedom and instead assert it as emancipatory promise. However the strength of free jazz rests on reproducing a fixed and even hyperreal image of the earlier age. Musicians are overshadowed by the iconic, resurrected figures of the sixties, forming a niche for the disaffected that says "we're holding on." Whatever the political intentions of the players, the social order has accommodated them, as if to say, "free" no longer means trouble-making.

Free improvisation on the other hand has never functioned as even a marginalized option in American culture. Those not presented as jazz musicians don't do this for a living, with one possible exception.[2] Its public insignificance has prevented professionals from adopting it as more than incidental to their main task. Lacking effective public definition of the term's meaning, it is commonly merged with free jazz, the large body of experimental music, or noise music. Its origin is in Britain beginning in the sixties, and its cultural strength is still there and on the Continent, though contested and weakened since the turn of the millennium. In the states it has been be-low the media radar ever since its appearance in the mid-seventies, and mu-sician interest in it has fluctuated. In both Britain and North America it de-veloped out of a context that included both jazz and composed experimental music, and has always shown evidence of the dialectical engagement of these two established categories. A few American players identify fully with it, but do so without market and institutional support or committed audience, fac-tors essential for considering it even marginal.

Ongoing and ineradicable desire cannot be contained in genres or hybrid musical categories. The radical act for listeners would be to join up with those wandering outside the stockade of authorized culture and stock, pre-dictable emotional responses. Authenticity then is key to determination, but a slippery word. If we are not to be trapped in the essentialism of genres ("jazz is…"), or in worship of icons pedestaled out of reach, how can we be sure? What does it mean to cross the line; can we handle the implications? What conceptions and institutional walls must we undermine before their mystifying power crumbles? Desire pursues what we disavow but cannot consistently resist, leading us to wonder: Why am I doing this and feeling this? We imagine it possible to become the full subject of music as player and as listener, but what must music be for that to happen? Desire is the un-known that will take many forms; it roots its way into all corners of existence and behavior and is not confined to music. If it is ongoing it spirals without boundaries, ever inching towards what John Coltrane called "the crux." One thing for sure; it does not find any boundary marked "freedom."

Sound produced by desiring subjects gets sorted into results, assigned a value, packaged and marketed. The conviction on all sides is that initiatives to break away from processed music are futile; it's been tried, with inevitable relapse. This book intends to be a starting point that hasn't been tried, an analysis of the conflicted relations of the musicians, their playing and inten-tions, the music world, the audience, and the social order. When this is fully grasped, the unraveling of the present situation will have already begun.

I am an American saxophonist, playing freely improvised music exclusively since 1979, based in Philadelphia and touring extensively since the early 80s. I am a working musician, a phrase that today covers both the regularly em-ployed performer and those for whom playing and performing is their cen-tral focus of life. For me this also includes the search and selection of partners and gigs most interesting to me, ad hoc sessions, experimental work on the instrument, writing, reading widely, and thinking in dialogue with the playing. In the end, simply playing is the keystone, without which the arch collapses.

When in the late 80s it seemed that free improv had become permanently underground, many active practitioners were discouraged, including myself. By late in the decade some were subordinating free playing within a larger repertoire, but I had no other musical interest. I went into relative retreat from the competitive East Coast scene, abandoning Philadelphia for Boulder Colorado in 1988, though returning twice yearly, with annual tours to the Bay Area. Then in the late 90s a new crop of improvisers appeared, boosted by internet communication. In 2003 I moved back to the Philadelphia area, where I had earlier established Spring Garden Music in a house I still owned, and which I now filled with musicians. I realized that if I wanted to take advantage of the resurgence I would have to be somewhat in tune with the political economy, which I'd earlier ignored. I must at least pretend that I was the entrepreneur of my music or miss out on the expanding movement.

After several years of organizing tours, promoting myself and partners, I fell into a crisis and began to pull back. I had become involved with some musicians more concerned for their earning power than what we were playing. My own activities were little different from those seeking better paying gigs and more audience, which my Boulder retreat confirmed was not what music meant to me. My initial playing-desire had arisen out of the traumatic period of my thirties, during the 70s, not career desire. I needed to think through how to relate to the music world and to professionalism in general if I did not fit the entrepreneurial type. As a good organizer I could do it, but the aim to increase recognition and reward was repulsive to me. My true joy was to discover what is authentic strictly for myself.

I began to see how I and my partners are situated in the world, as well as others playing a music that is both improvised and falls outside the marketplace, sometimes called "outside" music.[3] The bulk of such music has some compositional, pre-structured element, which enables it to be identified with a known category. In contrast those I play with intend to be free of prior structures; our art is contained in the momentary act of playing. When we are grouped with experimental, jazz-based, or individually-styled performance musics our distinction is lost. How can we properly understand *ourselves*? What are the terms we are expected to comply with, and how did this situation come into being? Since playing as we do offers no financial self-sufficiency, what could be our motivation?

Like many others outside media comprehension and attention, we avoid the terms of cultural acceptance but at the expense of cultural irrelevance. The marketplace pounds it into us that our music is not good enough for public purchase, and the institutions that fund music have consistently avoided anyone who cannot promise pre-existent form and stylistic homogeneity. We rely on our association with each other for support and only occasionally draw curious outsiders. When this situation is taken for granted over time it can negatively affect our playing, for although any music can grow apart from an audience, the world is ultimately our context. Frustration with an underground existence and the internal pressure for personal success can yield a crisis. Expectation of recognition takes over and locks in an attractive style. That was once my own bitter experience, and is commonly the case with others.

Free music cannot be written but reflection on it can feed back into the playing. In the late 80s I had examined free improvisation as a form that was the negation of composition and superior to it. I abandoned the project, realizing I had created abstractions detached from the musicians and the wider world, which pressures all spontaneity into fixed forms, as it had my own. In defending the abstraction I was defending myself against humiliation, at a time when my trust in own playing had broken down. Instead I turned to a writing project of self-exploration that ended in a book I showed to a few friends, *Shaky Ground* [1995], and continued to revise.[4] With my plunge into full-time organizing around 2000 I experienced for the first time the struggle of musicians to create a place for themselves. Now I've had sixteen years of that, and I'm reinforced by my earlier book project to carve out a confident space of critical self-awareness. In *The Free Musics* my earlier writing and study projects have found enough resolution to be published.

The immediate stimulus came from an invitation to present a paper at the 2011 Guelph Jazz Festival Colloquium in Canada, which was focused on music improvisation. I was surprised to find that the (academic) participants showed no interest in developments within free improvisation. Ajay Heble, the director of the event and the larger Guelph project, suggested that I submit a paper for their online journal, but there was much more to explore than could be confined to an article. Besides, my interest was not academic, and I didn't want to start down that road.[5]

The Free Musics broadly generalizes the approaches available for the players and the conditions under which they choose what to play. This is not a study of the names assumed to represent these musics but of the general situation for all the players--their relation to what they do, to the market (commercial and funding), to listeners, and to each other. Unlike most of the other arts, almost all writing about musicians is hagiography, of little use for these questions. It is assumed that the great, culminating period of all music was the sixties, which was the end of historical change and possibility. To defend the sixties legacy is then all we can do with it. This may be academically suitable but blocks artistic growth, which needs a flexible relation to the past.

Distinct approaches to playing are commonly reduced to the identities of name musicians, whose relation with the demands of the music world is bracketed off. The very decision of musicians to become visible by achieving careers and playing styles is inseparable from the larger political economy and its increasing need to identify and frame "advanced" artists. Those the media promotes today are only a small portion of all those competing for attention. Both are outweighed by an even larger number drawn into music and performance in the past two decades who have no interest in entering the race. Among the latter are those who, asked what they do, will say "free improv." Outside the hierarchy of ranked players and forming a loose collectivity all their own, they are the unacknowledged challenge to the structures that determine musical significance for the spectacle.[6] Since those structures are a continuing evolution, the present cannot be interpreted correctly without unearthing the past, with eyes open to the changing conditions for musicians.

This study attempts to provide insight into the subjectivity behind a kind of playing that alienates all but a few. To this end I ask what music can be for the free improviser. For us art is a way of knowing through our sensuous activity, which resists conclusive understanding and is unending. Ultimately no interpretation satisfies, only playing into the dark room of what we can't know is there. Those who can imagine something beyond the score, genre, or prepared aesthetic will approach music as a blank tablet on which to write experience not known to be musical. In interrogating playing as that act, this study will be aiming at the raw subject of subjectivity itself.

The present moment of making sounds is completely open in what it can be, even with no vision of a different future. The past can be retrieved from centennial celebrations, predictable festivals, academic biographies, and quasi-religious worship. These create a false sense of continuity, identity, and completion, yielding an image of us following in larger footsteps, while they only take us around in circles. Even those of us who give limited practical assent to the music world can withdraw from it long enough for an examination and re-balancing, a recovery of self from what the world asks of us.

Some in Europe have come to see free improvisation as old hat, non-controversial, and even superseded, given its long, continuous life there and the hierarchy of its old guard. In North America music with some trace of "jazz feeling" is still considered the limit of improvisation and beyond the range of even scholarly examination. Foreclosed in principle is any new path. However the discontinuity and subterranean existence of free improv has made it a new discovery for successive generations, today even in some universities. The initial grounding of the free musics in the experience of free playing holds a critical potential. The once-loose cannon still has weight and wheels to roll out of position on the deck, as the sea that holds us all gets rockier by the day. That prospect, which is the mobile and unpredictable edge of culture, is rarely experienced; to sharpen that edge is inseparable from my cognitive project here.

The media of the music world, with which every musician must deal in order to play in public, continually trumpets our society's supply of art and hides its efforts to rank and tailor it to its specifications. Of all the arts of our culture, music is what penetrates most lives and so has the most direct route to the psyche. The social order so depends on it that hardly any critique dares to penetrate beyond its humanistic guarantees, which makes music the primary accompaniment to "the American way of life." It has been most subject to taming, yet is also periodically the most resistant, breaking through with dissonance only to be recaptured and re-harmonized. Art-maker and world cannot be pulled apart; not even art for art's sake achieves that. As the established world seeks to make art fill the needs it defines, art is torn. So is the artist, the inescapable creator-subject, who then must find a voice to express that the contractual relation is not working out. That voice comes through implicitly in the music, and explicitly in words it is my voice here.

What I once wrote in 1983 to proclaim my first recording still holds:

> **What I want is this**: a music that is the appearance in the world, the reality, of feeling, of desire, need, contradiction. I want a music deep into the present time, how we truly exist now, music which defines us and gives us the future we deserve. I want a music done for the love of playing, which for this reason has to exist, is surrounded by its exist-

ence. A music of intense pleasure, polymorphous, naïve, risking itself for its own sake. This music is here for us and won't deceive our hopes if we give everything to it.

~~~~~~

A brief definition of some terms is in order. The best known contemporary titles, *free jazz* and *free improvisation*, are identities commonly recognized by musicians and some listeners. These forms are specific and go beyond simply playing something that isn't written down. They are not transhistorical; not only were they created at a specific time but they have changed in meaning *over* time. Free Jazz (capitalized, as it was at the time) will refer to its originary period from roughly 1960 through the early 70s, when it was considered a movement whose primary locus was New York City. What is performed today I will reference in the lower case as "free jazz," a recognizably jazz-based idiom patterned after some of the originators, and since the late 80s a stabilized genre. As in the later sixties, free jazz might be called "energy music," experienced as hard-driving and expressive.[7]

Free improvisation is a title used so loosely and infrequently in North America as to be useless except for its practitioners' self-identification. In this study it will refer to the music played by all those who engage it seriously, whether as their only music or along with other options. It lacks a definable sound, since it is understood that any move one makes is acceptable and other players must work with it one way or another. In terms of results it has been called "non-idiomatic," since neither jazz nor any other music is its necessary reference, nor does it have any *particular* emotionality, as free jazz does. It was first championed by British musicians, where it is now a musical genre represented by those whose playing is far more consistent than would be expected, given the implication of the title. The media-prominent Europeans assumed to play under its sign are soloists, whereas here improvisers with a solo identity are commonly identified as jazz musicians. Here it has had a trajectory increasingly distinct from free jazz, though an underground tension between the two has persisted. There are maybe three hundred musicians who would say they play free improv occasionally, and a minute number that does this as their exclusive focus. On witnessing it as a performance, free improvisation would today be called music but is not recognized as a kind of music clearly distinct from others.[8] The ratio of audience to player-performers is probably lower than any other musical category, making it virtually a private music; frequently the performers outnumber the listeners. Wherever significance it has is not in numbers.

9

Improvised music that often goes under the name of avant-jazz will not be part of this study. This is a more precise term than "avant-garde jazz," a phrase that began with bebop, often covered Free Jazz, and was subject to change. Avant-jazz is more aligned with straight-ahead (mainstream) jazz and its audience than is free jazz, though both presume a legitimate place in the jazz tradition. There are also some jazz musicians who actively push at the boundaries of jazz and at times do improvise quite freely, though that is difficult to sustain given their standard-jazz audience and commitment, which demands a return to trademark jazz feeling. On the non-jazz side of the fence, I will also be largely ignoring the bulk of what is called today "experimental music," far broader than its usage by John Cage and other composers would indicate. Free improvisation is often submerged under that name, which includes composition (often called "new music"), sound art, field recordings, and improvisation of specific aesthetic parameters and solo styles prepared in advance.

What I'll be calling *free playing* is not a musical form and has inspired no public or academic discourse, but it is common among North American musicians who call their performed music free improvisation. My use of it is specific: it will signify an approach to playing that is more verb than noun. It is pure praxis; it can be discussed but is not a theory or guideline to be taught and followed. It names the idea and experience of playing rather than performed results, and originates most often in private sessions, unmoored from the performance ritual. There the players' engagement is at stake and not the response of the music world, market, or audience. Free playing denies abstract form, model, or style, for the sake of the concrete. Each instance is its own form, in contrast to playing whose identity is subsumed under a pre-existent form. Less ambiguously than visual art, music is what the world hears and identifies as such; whether free playing is so identified is irrelevant to the activity. In the instant and irreversible moment of making sounds it raises the question, to what extent has the player accepted an internalized guide and judge, or even unconscious habits. The experience can be exciting, as "free" often implies, but the extent to which specific players explore the infinite options is another matter. Achievement is inherently problematic. Players' understandable wish to provide something meaningful for non-participant observers easily leads them to reproduce their playing as spectacle, under contract to please others, a social-psychological pressure particularly strong among Americans.

Free playing is the approach historically and musicologically in the background of free jazz and free improvisation, their hidden link. It exposes the gap separating human beings at play from musicians functioning as entertainers. It is available for musicians who acknowledge the current dead-in-the-water state of improvised musics and wish to move out of it, as well as those who care little about the world of music and want to take playing to its highest level.

---Jack Wright, December 2016

Part I. Jazz and Free Jazz

1. Jazz as the Prehistory of Free Musics

The following discussion of jazz and Free Jazz concerns professionally-oriented musicians, those who intended to make a living from playing music. Roughly through the 70s it was taken for granted that "musician" referred to a professional, or someone aiming to become one. This limited focus will change when I turn to American free improvisation, which attracted non-career players and contributed to a basic shift in the social production of music.

"Jazz" is an abstraction said to have a real existence yet with borders that have long been contested. Jazz is immersed in the murky waters of authenticity claims, an "it" subject to judgment over who and what is to be included and thereby validated. Into the seventies critics and many fans were asking "what path should jazz take?" This is not their concern today; it has apparently already taken its path. Even when some presented jazz as a *ruling* tradition with a defined essence for all time, they were contradicted by the strong assertion of jazz pointing to its future, what I will call an *open* tradition. The latter was more in tune with the practice of the musicians considered most prominent in jazz history. The ruling tradition follows writing, whose authority is the letter of the law; the open tradition follows the oral aligned with the spirit, a great strength and attraction in black culture and the true ground of jazz improvisation. These two have ever been in contention, with the oral facing the absolutism of the prosaic, written word, the medium of interpretation and publicity.

Anyone involved in jazz was liable to oppose the new, only to adopt it a few years later, with no reason to apologize; they had simply moved to where the "it" of jazz was going. The conception of jazz somehow existing in its future meant it was in the hands of what the players decide to do, minute by minute. Without the assumption that tradition is open, the sixties "New Thing" cannot be understood as a useful and assertive label competing for attention and acceptance. Those who favored a kind of playing from decades past could not ignore what some current group of jazz musicians had come to, if it had a live, performed urban presence, with a handful of followers and interpreters eager to fight for it and secure its future. To be marked as a jazz aficionado or critic was to participate in this flexible identity and take a position on the new arrival.

Jazz was affirmed as a being that is alive and therefore threatened with extinction, which could come through any commercial acceptance that diluted and betrayed the musicians' intent. The outcome was never secure. Fans wrote impassioned letters and a few became critics, who identified and promoted their partisan version of jazz. This is part of what kept it alive. It was "Jazz is in movement—and it's going *here*" or "Jazz is fine right where it is." Behind every condemnation of newly appearing developments in the postwar period, in fact what made them noticeable, was the assumption of some, and for others the fear, that the new would displace the old. In still-modernist sixties America irreversibility was thought inevitable; the past belonged to the past. What today would be considered marginal then had the momentum of the new behind it, assuming it came from professional musicians. Hence the vitriol, the debate, the jazz wars, as they were called; it was a fight over the body in motion known as jazz. Only later did the title refer to an essential core with a multiplicity of subtitled and hybrid genres extending forever into the future, with the possibility of jazz taking a different path foreclosed.

In the twenties it was associated with the more literary Harlem Renaissance—"Black Manhattan"; the first time that urban whites took black writers seriously they were also entranced by jazz. Both were thought to be progressive, a word variously defined and with its own evolution. The new was ephemeral fashion but also referred to a concept of human betterment and fulfillment. This meaning was borrowed from the Victorian past but used against its culture and morality, a freeing of eros from straight Victorian propriety. Since proper society thought itself already progressive, "modernity" was contested, with resistance coming from those who thought "jungle music" regressive. Progressive also implied that lines would be drawn *within* jazz, which began to appear in the thirties. The newcomers (called "modernists") advocated swing over "sweet" popular music, and also diverged from the traditionalists, who felt that true jazz had come to an end in the later twenties.[9] With the rise of bebop out of the heart of swing in the early 40s, jazz was identified not only as progressive (the changing and relative) but increasingly as a middle-brow art form, the spiritual absolute of secular culture. Whether people liked or despised it, bebop was "the new," and those opposed to it were dubbed "moldy figs," as the 20s traditionalists had been called earlier. Bebop was the first sign of a jazz avant-garde, and although it reigned only a few years it took jazz further down a path bound to be internally conflictual. For it to be art meant an upgrade from entertainment, yet art in its modernist version was inevitably problematic and unstable for audience, critics, and for the players.

What I've been describing as jazz is what concerned fans, critics, managers, club owners, academics, the record industry, and of course the musicians, who were not the subjects but the objects of the discourse. The concept of a ruling tradition for jazz was something specifically constructed, and has been useful to the music industry, musicology, and educators. The narrative follows a perceived continuity from one serial historical moment to the next, with each one the crucible of the next and yet continuing to challenge the new thing. Yet for musicians, tradition referred to a common, living bond between the loose collectivity of interdependent musicians past and present, and it distinguished them from others. That continuity had its origin not in the music world and its narrative but had its own existence that spanned generations of new paths. Scholars normally merge musicians into that music world as if their survival needs and their musical activity coincided. While musicians depended for their livelihood on pleasing the jazz world and audience, they had musical interests beyond economic survival and their identity as recognized musicians. To that extent they were artists, though confined to the entertainer role.

Committed critics interpreting and debating jazz, and devoted fans making judgments and purchases, presumed that adventurous jazz musicians were aiming to extend the meaning of jazz, keeping jazz vital and fulfilling. This doesn't describe the motivation and activity of the players. Some of the most prominent even said they were just musicians and not *jazz* musicians, and so were not confined to a commercial title or its destiny. Many didn't limit their interest to jazz but listened and borrowed widely, insisting that they were full artists who explored freely.[10] Yet the job market offered black musicians no other place to go but jazz. That whites had lucrative options for conventional playing (classical, studio work, vacation resorts, etc.) was a factor weakening the full engagement of many with jazz and its new directions. At times the players themselves had to make use of titles to get an audience, as musicians have always had to do where there are multiple, competing offerings. Their historically validated expectation at the time was that at least the jazz world would have to deal with them, and possibly catch up to where they were going.

A version of progress and innovation came directly out of musicians' relations with each other. From the beginning of jazz popularity in the 20s through its heyday they listened to each other carefully and picked up on each other's solos in a way that led to both individualization and advance. Building on and away from the other's move, they made their own irreversible as well, and this would stimulate the next move. They "signified on" each other, a practice that came directly out of black culture and is still evident in rap. It can be called serial innovation, but only if the new idea was adopted by others and displaced what came before. On a larger scale of change, small-group jazz, which had been the rule in New Orleans jazz, reappeared in the late 30s but as a concert group, and caught on as an alternative to the big swing bands, which never crisscrossed the country again. Initiated by band leaders, it offered the musicians a break from commercial dance music, which many had come to despise. A few then picked it up as the vehicle for their new way of playing, soon known as bebop. And so on, a lineage of historical progression.

The interdependence of musicians was strongest when they were located close to each other, competing for the same gigs and mutually available for recording and private sessions with each other. Here is the link of jazz and New York City. Players moved there not just to make a better living but to be part of this collectivity and accepted as peers. From the mid-forties through the sixties specific musicians self-consciously created new forms, approaches, and groupings that impacted each other. Debate and controversy about whether to follow a direction followed, inspiring some to forge their own versions of the new. No one could stand apart from what others were doing. They went to each other's shows with the thought that if they liked what they heard they'd give a call the next day and set up a session. Peers were often welcomed to sit in (I remember it still in the early 80s; you didn't go to a jazz gig without taking your horn and possibly sitting in on the last set.) This practice ceased when club gigs gave way to the formality of full concert settings. The hierarchy of respected peer musicians was tight, with still some degree of "cutting" out those who lacked facility on their instruments, yet it seems to have loosened up a bit from the later fifties onwards, with the onset of Free Jazz. Self-policing their ranks was necessary if musicians were to have any independence from the music world and record industry, always eager to do the selecting. Leaders could pick "sidemen" who were relatively unknown, chosen strictly for where the leader wanted to go musically. Probably all jazz musicians had some formal training, but were not tied to it; their growth was private study, sessions, and gigs with mentors who attracted them on musical grounds.

Jazz as an art form began with an audience obeying the rule of concert music to sit down instead of dancing. The shift was controversial and came gradually, but opened up the option of dispensing with danceable speed and rhythm (or what that meant at the time). Art in the modernist sense was thought to be intellectual, which meant that people paid for it out of their "serious" as opposed to "having a good time" pocket. Bebop was borderline serious, the first such direction to have a name, as expected of modernist avant-gardes. Also expected of art was that it would both attract and repel, which it did, yielding antagonism between fans and critics as well as within the collectivity of jazz musicians. As art, jazz was soon called progressive or modern jazz, followed by cool jazz, West Coast jazz, hard bop, soul jazz, and then the titles with the greatest attraction/repulsion, Free Jazz, New Black Music, and Fusion. All these forms can be seen as evoking public controversy concerning taste and authenticity; what is specific to the musicians is that they were debated among themselves.

To demand that the most adventurous postwar playing be treated as art, to create more latitude for their musical choices, and personally to withstand a mountain of abuse, musicians had to attract attention as *concert* and not social-function musicians. It put them on the same path of challenge as all postwar art, and that might leave them no financial ground to stand on. Yet they could not imagine that the loose collectivity of peers and its economic base in live performance would come to an end. They were proud to have a degree of autonomy, yet their ability to perform depended on the white jazz world—the sympathy of critics, particular club owners, and the changeable opinions of fans. Celebrity provided little protection in the long run. They played what they were moved to play, but under conditions not of their making.

The paradox of jazz as art form in the American sixties was that given the progressive faith no one wanted to be left behind, "stuck in the past," yet art has never been able to wipe the slate clean. The NY Experimental Avant-Garde (John Cage, et al.) did at times present that picture, priding itself on innovation and rejection of the past as if it were like painting, the "tradition of the new." Modernist critics presumed the necessity of new flowering, but audiences essential to jazz balked and could not be ignored, given its commercial base. Jazz was thought to be indivisible but in contention, not a variety. Moreover the new was not a completely open field. Specifically black jazz musicians, who as improvisers were the prime *musical* source of jazz, could not imagine turning their back on the collective suffering of black people, especially in the age of burgeoning Civil Rights, nor dispense with the open and oral nature of their tradition. Musicians identifying with the sixties New Thing attempted to recover and sustain their roots to black popular culture, which much of fifties jazz music world had obscured in the rush to satisfy the growing middle class (and middle-brow) thirst for art. This complicated the effort to have it considered a form of serious, avant-garde art, which trusted new concepts of spontaneity but not the spontaneity of feeling that is essential to all popular culture.

Jazz music has had at least this one consistent attribute and link to popular culture: it must express and evoke concrete feeling that in the end moves an embodied collectivity of people and not just a sum total of spectators. Jazz was a delicate balance of surprise that threatens--even the 4/4 time mildly disrupted by syncopation--and feeling that recovers and expands. A style that merely represents such feeling is a fake, and not good enough, and the audience for jazz prided itself on separating the wheat from the chaff. It must be fresh, which contributed to the progressive character of jazz since the originally fresh would inevitably become stale. The avant-garde high art of the New York School directly opposed attachment to music through direct, committed feeling, which it perceived as regressive, cloying sentimentality. This was precisely what jazz could not do without. This "surplus lyricism,"[11] as Fred Moten has called it, was the backbone of jazz musicians' livelihood, threatened when audiences could not find it in the new directions. "Make us feel the way we did when we first heard you" is not something the Experimental Avant-garde audience or critic would demand. What some audience called difficult and abstract in the music of the jazz avant-garde was because they were unprepared to accept a fresh, immediate, concrete form of passion or feel the subtlety in it, the expansion of feeling that was the musicians' project. To others, confusion was a drawing card for Ornette Coleman's group, when in April 1960 it was advertised as "a quartet that is capable of going in one ear, out the other, and leaving utter confusion in between."[12]

Jazz in its prime was no more stable than life. If life is what *could be* life, no more a real line than the horizon, then jazz was what *could be* jazz.

The Free Musics

Since the 80s jazz has been dominated by the spread and proliferation of jazz culture—popular courses in jazz history; mass media attention and use in upscale commercials; the proliferation of highly-schooled musicians acting as their own promoters; repertory imitation of every historical style; state and wealth-institution funding and credentialing of "the best"; promotion as the triumph of the liberal consensus; the keystone of the arch of Black achievement; a music industry focused on icons; an established and closed canon of players and recordings; the shift of music jobs from performance to teaching; vastly expanded jazz scholarship; and jazz hybrids of global culture found throughout the world. There is no longer a collectivity of jazz musicians capable of resisting this expansion, at least there is no effective vehicle for their expression. Scholars write of long-past jazz in the present tense eliding the difference with the actual present, which no one claims to be as musically interesting as the past. In the present climate, when jazz is treated as an accomplished fact, no media voice imagines that a jazz-identified musician will add anything to jazz history.

2. Sixties Free Jazz

There is no critical and comprehensive study of Free Jazz, one that would bring into relationship the early origins and changing interests of musicians, its musical challenge, its thread in the social and political fabric, audience and critic reaction, and the economic survival and psychic needs of musicians.[13] What I do here is chronological but not that study, rather a sketch some of these factors, pointing to a larger understanding of the phenomenon, specifically emphasizing the situation of the musicians.

It was the unprecedented destructiveness of WWII that cleared the ground for musicians dependent on the public marketplace to undermine many common conceptions of their trade. Without aiming to do so, they were also reacting to cultural homogenization with an alienation found here and there in the other arts that was given concretely new form.[14]

The public, and therefore limited, record of playing in the freeform direction includes tentative moves that did not end up as instances of Free Jazz but nonetheless indicate the coming boldness. Recording opportunities were rare. Decent recording equipment belonged to the studios, and the dates were offered by producers, who only paid for what they thought would sell. The first freeform playing made publicly available was done in 1949 by the blind pianist Lennie Tristano and his circle of players, some his students. On the last day of sessions for the album *Intuition* they ventured a step beyond the bebop they ordinarily played, then still at its height. With no song form or repeated melody and only a vague meter, it was only held together by a steady beat, contrapuntal interaction, jazz (swing) rhythm, and standard instrument timbre. There is nothing sloppy about the playing; it's as precise as if they were playing a rehearsed composition. Yet as never before, in order to make their playing choices musicians had to—and must have wanted to—listen closely to what the others were doing, a work of collective engagement that foreshadowed the most contemporary free playing. Those few minutes indicate they must have been doing this in sessions for a while, and probably continued it. As for the album, these short pieces were one-offs they would not have called "the new thing." They don't sound like Free Jazz or today's free improv, but would have had knowledgeable jazz audiences scratching their heads.

To drop their assumptions of how to make music was something players did for themselves; their professional job was to entertain. Although it wasn't strictly bebop, it carried forward the postwar inclination towards spontaneity and erratic behavior that bebop initiated. Spontaneity, or impulse, motivated an artistic culture that reacted against the enjoyment-culture of postwar consumerism. A thoroughly militarized society sacrificing for the war machine was being transformed into peacetime consumption. This dynamic set up the condition for receptivity later to Free Jazz, viewed as the epitome of spontaneity. As never before, it meant musicians would place themselves firmly *ahead* of the music, their imagination prior to the results.

Of the Tristano circle the most out-going and well-known was alto saxophonist Lee Konitz,[15] with many more attracted to him as a locus for exploratory sessions. Tristano himself, like the jazz avant-garde later, refused commercialization as best he could, even ostracized those who did not obey his strictures. This early free playing took place in insular sessions rather than club dates competing for space in NY. Its precision makes it sound like European avant-garde chamber music, except for the instrumentation. Its influence on fifties jazz was minimal and was associated with Gunther Schuller's attempt to create a Third Stream music, an effort to create an avant-garde music that would negotiate between European composition and jazz.

Similar to that playing, but at a slower pace was the 1962 release by reed player Jimmy Giuffre (*Free Fall*, with Giuffre on clarinet, pianist Paul Bley and bassist Steve Swallow). This sounds equally modern-contemporary and composed, yet except for some schema of solo passages and organization as distinct pieces it is completely free-improvised. Free Jazz was by then in full swing but it makes no appearance here, despite Bley's prominence in that scene and the fact that Giuffre was frequently booked opposite Free Jazz groups. *Free Fall*, a strictly studio anomaly, was probably judged lacking in swing or drive, thus outside jazz altogether rather than the outside *of* jazz. Contributing to this judgment, in the 50s the music of Giuffre and other white players such as Dave Brubeck, Gerry Mulligan, and Paul Desmond had been lauded in the mainstream press but dissed by many, including some critics, as inauthentic "white jazz," often considered *too* intellectual in the common binary with "gutsy," such as hard bop.[16] In a split that had not appeared during swing, white musicians were seen as beholden to polite

European art culture, and blacks were assigned to American popular culture, two versions of art in a competition that is still playing itself out. *Free Fall* was an indulgence possible for established musicians to do what probably no one thought would sell. The system of media-prominent names ensured that at least costs would be covered. Though it doesn't sound like Free Jazz, the playing was driven by the same desire to move into the open field Free Jazz had by then made public.

Critics led the cognoscenti in believing they would be the first to recognize true art, in advance of cautious audiences. They expected New York City to be the birthplace, so they missed Hal Russell in Chicago, whose trio one night in 1959 spontaneously started dropping parts of jazz that felt encumbering. Free playing was their private invention and had little public resonance, despite Chicago being the home of the principal jazz magazine, *Downbeat*.

In NY Charles Mingus pushed the often reluctant musicians of his Jazz Workshop into new territory by way of his explicit ideas. He was the best-known experimenter with jazz forms and set the tone for later group free-playing. The novel concept of a workshop was a space somewhat outside commercial pressures and a step beyond pure rehearsal, where musicians are presented with a score and not an experiment. NY composer Edgar Varese led private sessions of jazz musicians in 1957, including Mingus, recordings of which have surfaced only recently.[17] These sessions come close to the density of Free Jazz soon to come, with everyone blowing together, at times sounding like individuals practicing runs and licks. Varese began with the musicians' free material he would ask them to repeat, thus making it into a loose, player-based composition. This is at least evidence of what was possible for some outside their commercial work. Around that time, NY musicians often said they were "playing free" when in sessions they abandoned what they normally played on gigs and did something of their personal invention.[18] What resulted might be useful material to perform, or judged too "far out" and just for fun, an activity for off-duty professionals. As such it would have been irresponsible for them to be so adventurous in public, since it would disturb club-goers, most of whom took the music for granted and chattered through it.

Free Jazz proper, as a period in the jazz narrative, did not begin until someone who many thought lacked the technical basics of jazz, Ornette Coleman, came on the New York stage in fall 1959. Free playing that had been waiting in the wings of private sessions and in Los Angeles now commanded attention in what was considered *the* art-culture capital. Coleman and three partners he had led in his direction took responsibility for it, shaping it as a distinct musical approach, and offering it up for judgment.

In this early period "free" did not mean random or formless, otherwise it would not have been allowed to appear publicly enough to stir controversy. Like bebop, what free referred to was compositionally framed distinct pieces invested with standard-jazz elements such as repeated melody or fragments, accepted timbre, pulse, and an uninterrupted stream of playing. Literally speaking, if it was jazz it could not be free, if that word betokens a totality. "Free Jazz" was a manifesto that overstated its challenge to form for emphasis, at a time when "freedom" was a distinctly provocative word in its political, philosophical, and personal meanings. "Free" was a keyword for opposite sides of the political fence, implying anti-communism, since Communism was considered enslavement, and also meaning emancipation from whatever enslavement one has experienced, including segregation, censorship, and a conformist lifestyle. The word could be contested: who is really free? Privately it could also indicate a transcendent feeling that might arise in many situations and that no one can contest, least of all oneself. It then bears a different kind of commitment, a dream one experiences more compelling than everyday reality.

I will be using "Free Jazz" for the direction that began to take hold in 1959 and continued until around 1970, despite the use of other terms and its greater significance after 1965 and usage today. Its origin was Ornette Coleman's bold recording of that name (*Free Jazz: A Collective Improvisation*) released in 1961 on the prestigious Atlantic label—two quartets of parallel instrumentation improvising at the same time in a general jazz style and sound within a roughly prepared framework. "Free" appeared in "free form," the term musicians commonly used among themselves and rarely as a title, as in "he went to the so-called free form thing," which indicated an approach rather than a publicity claim or a form of music.[19] My wider interest is in free playing and the role it had in various musical directions. Despite differences, there is something "free" about them all, linking today's free playing back to jazz and the black heritage.

Coleman's entry to the NY scene in 1959 had been arranged by critics and sponsors over the heads of the musician community. Prominent musicians in attendance generally dissed him, ostensibly on musical grounds but also because he was an outsider to the NY hierarchy, and because they resented the interference of the (white) critics. One would expect Coleman's musicians to be ostracized, yet their approach attracted many of their NY peers who absorbed his approach over the next several years. Some were emboldened in their earlier experimenting, as if the avant-garde-style shock of Coleman gave them the validation they had been lacking, a space that seemed to be opening in other parts of the culture as well. They couldn't ignore his presence, not because his music was selling well, but because playing more freely made sense to them in the context of the times and their own evolution. At the same time, the acceptance of someone outside the apprentice-mentorship system of the NY collectivity of jazz musicians spelled the eventual doom of the control it had had over its membership.

Free Jazz was an experiment in large-group free playing, something not attempted again in public form for several years, so as a title for that early period it is something of an anachronism. The music of the jazz avant-garde[20] early on was more commonly called "the new music." The publicity title was often the "New Thing," which Coleman himself seems to have preferred, due to public misunderstandings inherent to "Free Jazz."[21] New Thing indicates nothing aesthetically or racially specific; it could encompass all those experimenting with jazz forms, white and black. It associated them with modernist innovation, which was about form rather than "anything goes." It could include many who weren't playing freeform, such as George Russell, whose Lydian Concept was going the rounds among musicians. New Thing did not raise any particular musicological or political specters, so it was useful for attracting audience.[22] The poet and critic Amiri Baraka saw it as comparable to bebop and expected it to displace the old. Lacking the musicological unity of bebop, its "thing" was vague, but it was the spirit of a new direction summed up in the names of musicians who seemed on the track of something significantly different from what came before. It was exploratory compared to hard bop, which was criticized as formulaic and "commercial," the curse word of the day. For someone like Steve Lacy, whose identification in the sixties with jazz was total, free playing was in the air for a certain period (until 1967 for him) as something musicians had to check out, and then having plumbed it to their satisfaction could dismiss.[23]

Coleman had a profound and irreversible impact even on those who resisted his music. Musical self-determination and the orientation of musicians to each other in making music developed behind the scene, in rehearsals and discussion. Coleman wanted them to listen in the moment rather than follow what the score literally told them to do. For instance, the professional norm was for the leader to shape the music as he wants it, and instruct the bassist accordingly. Contrary to that, he told his bassist Charlie Haden to make up the harmony himself, which made the player a shareholder in the composer role and somewhat displaced the leader.[24]

As this kind of listening/playing extended to all Coleman's players it released them as music creators with almost equal responsibility. He rehearsed a group in L.A. for his 1958 album "Something Else!!!" (exclamation points in the original) and changed the composition at each rehearsal, even on the recording date. This ignored the usual progression from rehearsal to perfected piece, which, outside the latitude of the jazz soloist, had been standard for *all* musical production.[25] He may have done this without conscious intent, but he apparently didn't feel inhibited by the conventional practice. His players would have to listen, roughly follow the score, *and* depend on their own initiative, a kind of forced confusion. He insisted on this over his partners' objections; they had to believe in Coleman's vision beyond what they felt was right.[26] This brought the *rehearsal* more in line with the leaderless private *session*. These two modes of off-stage playing had usually been carefully distinguished, maintaining the separate roles and integrity of skilled professional and self-motivated creative artist. Coleman transformed the rehearsal into a means for making musicians flexible and open to a variety of possibilities, to think creatively in the widest possible way in the moment. This brought musicians in direct contact with each other rather than mediated through the leader.

Since the twenties there had been a firm distinction between musical director/score-provider/paymaster and hired player who executed his will on pain of dismissal, a master-servant pattern of leaders hiring soloists and sidemen to do the leader's selected and often self-composed music. For those under Coleman's tutelage the players led themselves, progressively dispensing with chord progressions and later even with time-keeping. The musical director had brought the players to the point where he could withdraw—and they'd still get paid. This led to the possibility of a group choosing its own members, without a leader financially in charge. Here began the radical shift to players as mutual partners of each other, even friends, as Lacy said. This arrangement would be in tension with the industry standard of sidemen and leader, who negotiated the contract for the gig or record, got the most credit in the press, and got paid extra, often double.

Free Jazz made public a collectivity of equal musicians, whose relations with each other were directly to each other. This move occurred precisely when jazz had achieved recognition as an art, usually considered an elite form. The emancipatory shift extended jazz as an improvisational music:

now *every* jazz musician is an improviser, not just the leader-selected soloist. To weaken the formal leader-employee relationship raised the rank and file musician to a position where their intelligence and consciousness was called for. Henceforth it was up to each one what to play.

Around the same time European and American avant-garde composers were scoring pieces that specified sections for orchestral musicians to improvise freely. They too were being offered emancipation; they would not have done it spontaneously. They were never enthusiastic about it, and the composers followed the wider culture in dropping the improvisational aspects of their work when the spirit of the times shifted. Improvisation had been associated with radical change, for which the wind was no longer blowing, and the musicians went back to their role as realizers of marks on the page. Improvisation is by nature a voluntaristic act on the part of players, which is at the heart of its distinction from composition. To be instructed to improvise, and when or how to do so, is not to be in command of it oneself. Orchestral musicians were not internally motivated to improvise; to force them to do so was not just an embarrassment but an act that violated their sense of vocation.[27] On the other hand, jazz was constituted by a push and pull between composed form and improvised content. Whereas Coleman's initial players were at first resistant, they and others quickly came to welcome the change and built it into their self-conception, for their music was already improvisatory.

Looking ahead for a moment, Coleman's initiative was crucial for free improvisation to evolve soon a few years later in Britain, where musicians had been absorbing American developments along with their own self-assertive motivations. Free improv would presume a self-selected, at times almost arbitrary, grouping of musicians rather than the band concept of a leader-determined entity. In commercial jazz, leaders continued to audition sidemen and exercise aesthetic control, yet the direction of collective responsibility for the music pointed a different way. It would soon manifest as "collective improvisation," which the writer Amiri Baraka would relate back to African tribal music, and some British free improvisers would conceive as a kind of open society. This inverts the normal schema of musical production: composer to leader to performers, all subordinated efficiently to create something that will be received as good music. The re-ordering put the playing ahead of the music; whether it is "good" or not is not ensured by following the production procedure.

Merging musicians into the collectivity of an ensemble and empowering each as a co-creator initially went hand in hand, but they would have separate fates. The culture was geared to favor the soloist, and the music economy, increasingly since the big band era, had room for only a few to perform live music for a living. This meant it was the soloist that was to triumph over the ensemble. The prominent singular name would bring Free Jazz close to the standard band concept after all, led by the star soloist who "fronted" the band, an apt word. Not only collective free playing would suffer but also the larger collectivity of all jazz musicians was weakened, as workers facing a music world of bosses and interpreters, leading to the entrepreneurial musician of today. Moreover, past its origins, this empowering, emancipatory experience would be impossible to repeat, since it had already been absorbed and taken for granted by musicians. Later free jazz would not provide that freeing act to establish its claim. And lacking the promise of following an adventurous vision, commitment would not play such a part in the formation of groupings.

To generalize broadly, NY Free Jazz of the early to mid-sixties extended outward from the fundamentals of fifties jazz, continuing much of bebop language.[28] Its jazz identity was strongly asserted in obvious references to earlier jazz, such as the song frame and in the scalar arpeggios of solos. As in straight-ahead jazz a rhythm section provided the steady base for "lead" instruments, long assigned the role of providing the main track for listeners to follow. The pace was usually set for the whole piece and maintained by the rhythm section, with the drummer providing a metronomic beat in 4/4 meter disguised under individual specializations. Lead instruments jointly played a composed melody or "head" before launching into relatively free playing, often recalling traces of the melody. A piece would often return to the head in the middle and always at the end, with the final ending stylized to be recognized as such. Each song was expected to be distinct, and while longer than bebop tunes (which in the days of 78 records were limited to three minutes), they were still relatively short. The standard jazz solo format was still unquestioned, with lead instruments taking turns for relatively set periods of time. Recording engineers were experienced in jazz and brought soloists to the front of the mix, so they were heard against a background and not all musicians at an equal dynamic level.

The most obvious difference was that chord progressions in the solos were replaced by a tonal center, often so buried as to be unnoticed. Coleman scored chord changes initially but dropped them when he started playing with the drummer Ed Blackwell in 1960. The way had been prepared by

Miles Davis and John Coltrane, who introduced modal playing, rocking back and forth between only two chords closely related, which opened up the options for improvisation beyond fast-changing and difficult progressions. It lacked the analytic complexity of bebop's elaborate chordal options, so in this sense the playing was both simpler and freer. Coltrane's solos might have been strange for audiences but that was balanced by the more accessible modal form, a shift contributing to the increased focus on the individual soloist over the piece of music and direction coming from the leader. At the same time modal playing was a step towards deskilling jazz, since less formal learning was required in order to participate at the ground level—just learn two chords and you can improvise on Miles Davis' "So What."

Deskilling is however a misnomer; it's really the progressive shifting of players' skill orientation. Gaining a wider range of impulses and responses to the situation rose in value over knowledge of the code and ability to reproduce the forms that identify jazz and hold the bulk of audience. This wider knowledge was now largely individualized in the hands of the musicians, giving them a stake outside the code. "What I can get away with"—violation of the code—shifts to the outright "I play what I feel, directly from my experience." This promised total subjectivity: my musical identity is whatever I feel like playing, and feeling can go literally anywhere. "Freedom" as spontaneous impulse had gone so far in the postwar consciousness that it came to mean not new elaborations of the code but large scale abandonment of it. The focus on the moment is in tension with the internalized code and therefore with easy judgment of the result; it is impossible to do both at the same time. The player is split between being in the heat of the moment and allowing a space for the internal and external judge to find it musically satisfying. The gain is cognitive but not what musicology can handle. Its rational framework can only chart results: the code and improvised variations on it, not when players ignore the code and take the experiential moment as their starting point.

Chord progression for instance is a rational sequence aimed at predictability; musicians are expected to follow it with a precise limit on how far to go, stretching the code but not breaking it. When the chart and pulse say the chord has changed, the music must register that. To prioritize the moment is to create a space in which potentially it's the code that is on the outside, to be referred to not as master but as contingent possibility, along with others. In Free Jazz the internalized and collective superego of the code came up against the individual will to deny its power, a typical sixties phenomenon, for this dynamic could be found elsewhere, as in the emergence of rock music. To lean towards contingency required a subjectivity that could resist the wider, more predictable path laid out for professional jazz. "Mastery" was poised to take on a new meaning.

More than any other sixties art form jazz musicians faced this split, and were divided from each other by it, as were audiences, a tension more exacerbated than during bebop. When the hierarchy of respect depends on maintaining the code, certain players are favored, and those who diverge are considered inadequate—the initial judgment against Coleman. When respect shifts to the latter the hierarchy is threatened with inversion—the last shall be first. The code is policed by the music world and by those musicians wary of diverging from it. When so-called sloppy musicians like Don Cherry are sought-after and moving up the charts, the code-followers are seen as lacking the confidence to go out of bounds and even perhaps envious. "What's in a name?" in a situation where the top dogs are scrambling to show that they're up to the challenge, and they adopt some of the new adventurous language. This dynamic led to a situation that was snowballing. It was all fully competitive, with musicians aware of their economic fate, yet for a time it shifted what was considered musical experience and contributed to the wide-open gate of the sixties. When people reacted to Free Jazz as chaos, this topsy-turvy inversion is part of what they had in mind.

Without any clear harmonic movement it was more difficult for listeners whose ears were attuned to what had come before. Specifically, the common way people listened to music (and still do) was to follow its form without knowing they were doing so, participating by anticipating what comes next. They had learned to follow bebop by enjoying the novelty of how pitches are arranged differently in the same chords, a listening mode not found classical or popular music. With an audience and players both following the chord changes it would seem they were following each other. The soloing of the new music frustrated that experience, for there was no linearity to follow, only the frame of composed head to remind one that it was a piece of music. It expanded on the direction towards soloist freedom that had begun with Louis Armstrong in the 20s and at the same time seemed to be mocking that past.

As for instrumentation, an important innovation that began with Coleman was the elimination of the piano as a necessity. It had had the function of maintaining the harmonic structure that lead instruments would follow, as well as the fixed pitch of the tempered scale, since the piano tuning was standard. Freed from the piano, the bass, which lacks the frets of a guitar, could adjust to any eccentric intonation of the lead player. Here and elsewhere, learning to play with another player became more subjective; you weren't just playing the same tune. Most noticeably, the leads (usually sax and trumpet) could become far more "expressive," a problematic word that connotes here the whim of the player. Using standard fingerings but modifying the pitch easily with their embouchure, their intonation could be far removed from the tempered scale, extending where the slide guitar could go. Audiences were accustomed to the tempered scale as the straight line that got bent; now without the piano to hold the others to the pitch musicians were seen to run wild. The "free" of Free Jazz meant more individualist expression but at the expense of accusations of anarchy, musicological innovations that violated norms of how to listen to music as well as play it.

This was all still tentative; an evolving of musical consciousness. In *Archie Shepp and the NY Contemporary Five*, recorded in Copenhagen in 1963, the lead players--Don Cherry, trumpet, with John Tchicai and Archie Shepp on saxophones—are more sidestepping jazz conventions than repudiating them. They push, stumble and insert interruptions in what seems like a rush to find what they can only barely imagine, but at the same time flouting their resistance to precision, what best showed technical ability. For this Cherry was especially criticized by some, while others considered it refreshing, the very flavor of the avant-garde insult to taste. There is still a clear split between rhythm section (Don Moore, bass; J.C. Moses, drums) and solo voices, allowing occasional drum and bass solos. For the bass to be scored with a solo was an upgrade, an innovation of Charles Mingus, and was now a regular feature of Free Jazz, which finally provided at least a solo space for all instruments. The solo is still the core, as in bebop and fifties jazz. Each piece is blocked out as a composition, with heads in unison or in harmony (though sometimes a mockery thereof), with solos of pre-arranged order but of rough length rather than cycling through and counting 32-bar choruses. The other lead instrument occasionally jumps in for short spurts, perhaps spontaneously, which was rare in bebop. Each piece is a short tune, a few by Coleman and Thelonius Monk that were covered show what sources this avant-garde was drawing from. The pace is set, with loose time-keeping drums of shifting rhythms, and a pulse-keeping walking bass line. Coleman refashioned the rehearsal, but unlike free improvisation, this music is prepared to go a certain way.

From our seat in the future these musicians and those in tune with them are now legendary for having pushed the boundaries, but on such a map others soon went further. The players' psyche has a role here, where each move is a unique step and cannot be rescinded. No one goes farther than they will risk; finding that limit is psyche, the subjectivity of the subject. You're being exposed to what you don't know is in you to play. That is at the same time excitement and terror, just as it is to go somewhere completely alone, an irrevocable historical act continuous with the western explorers who thought they were discovering the world. Why should anyone do that? The act is often masked by bragging and posturing, and stepping into the dark is partly why these musicians gathered together collectively. Hearing another take a leap off a cliff one night excites the rival to leap from higher up. That was a unique historical situation, difficult to comprehend as something we might find today. It favored and reinforced the bold, but they didn't simply fit their environment. On some level those who were bringing contingency into the playing had to deal with the unpredictability of the Fates they were evoking. We can learn and duplicate their music now, but are not peers with them unless we too throw caution to the wind — out in the open, where witnesses are ready to judge.

After the flurry of attention and controversy over Coleman's NY appearance and album died down, Free Jazz seemed to have stabilized as a public issue. However, the musicians who were absorbing it increasingly formed a collectivity of mutual influence, discussion, and groupings. They were led especially by Archie Shepp, trumpeter Bill Dixon, and pianist Paul Bley, who in sessions, choice of partners, and recordings modeled their structures and playing after Coleman. The way had been prepared by the relative openness of the scene to new players in this period. The initially negative reaction to Coleman shifted to mutual acceptance and the integration of generations, without which a second wave, as it has been called, would have had little chance to grow and find an audience. A musician who had been isolated by the strangeness of his music, Cecil Taylor, asked the unknown Steve Lacy to record in 1956, and was always on the hunt for partners regardless of their lack of name recognition. John Coltrane responded to the 20-year-old Shepp in 1957 without having even heard him play.[29] The door was already half-open to newcomers when Coleman blew the hinges off. A collective then gathered as an avant-garde, eager to make a scene together and driven to create a greater public presence for what would become a cause, like others in the air.

These players were ready to ignore the commercial platitude that audiences would come on the basis of expectations of what they would like to hear. Bassist Alan Silva:"I don't want to make music that sounds nice…"[30] In 1965 Drummer Sunny Murry proclaimed, "this is the music of our era, no matter how much they hate it."[31] Unlike more profitable musical directions such as hard bop, those who took the Free Jazz direction did not refer back to a fully established identity, concept, style, or even familiar names of musicians consistently committed to it. As time went on, Coleman was an honored elder but distinct from the spirit that was evolving, in which players were released to go in directions he had not envisioned. For one writer close to this period, "The ever-incomplete definition of the 'thing' … leaves a freedom of appreciation and active, constructive participation, not only to the individual who is most obviously participating, but to the observer."[32]

This "thing" was unstable, its identity unclear. It was different after Bill Dixon's "October Revolution in Jazz" performance series in 1964, when a wide number of musicians of the new music were emboldened by an overflow audience.[33] Free Jazz was an experimental working-out, in a decade when process confronted product in every art form. Process *means* "this is changing, watch out." Artists were drawing and crossing lines in the sand people hadn't ever been aware of, and in New York they found a small but promising audience of spectators for their offensive acts. Whatever it was, Free Jazz later permitted a unified critique under its name, implying the existence of thus-titled musicians, who intended to play under it and contribute to it. But this is retrospective; what coalesced under the name was steadily coming into being from one session and project to another, in an era when everything seemed increasingly up for grabs. As never before or since, professional artists were asking themselves "how far can I go?" in a context where they knew they would face significant resistance. They even made music *because* of that resistance, enjoying and gaining strength as it snowballed. (Think of the contrast with today—what professional musician would be emboldened to go further by *resistance*?) This is what it felt like to be a self-determining avant-garde, with no institution nominating them for the position. They were making art at a time when going out on a limb posed a real risk of defeat--the end of one's only livelihood—but that's what art *was*.

Part of the reason Free Jazz can't be pinned down from one year to the next was the broad drawing power the freeform approach had among musicians. While today, for past and current critics Free Jazz is summed up as the work of a handful of icons, more likely a majority of those affected did not record, nor did their names find their way into print. Coltrane's producer, Bob Thiele of Impulse Records, told critic Frank Kofsky, "if we had signed everyone that John recommended, we'd have four hundred musicians on that label." [34] Given Coltrane's musical inclinations we can assume many of these were playing freeform. With most living close by each other in the East Village, this music was happening not only on occasional recording dates and concerts but more frequently in relatively open, unrecorded sessions. Some were casual events in coffee houses, where sitting-in by a walk-in unknown player was frequent. From the outset Free Jazz was limited by personal financial need; many dropped in and out of it depending on whether paying gigs and audience were available. If all this is taken into account it is unreasonable to limit Free Jazz to the hierarchy of stars.

In mid-1965 the premier jazz musician and commercial leader (besides Miles Davis), saxophonist John Coltrane joined the younger players with his recording of *Ascension* and gave Free Jazz a new direction. This album was the watershed that inaugurated the second wave. It was no longer a peripheral affair of outsider rebellion to be absorbed over time but a serious threat to the heart of jazz conventions. Comparable to Coleman's *Free Jazz* in its controversial impact and collective improvisation, *Ascension* included many of the new generation and caused a split in the musician ranks and jazz world. Some critics had put Coleman in the field of European atonal music and abstract expressionism, a relatively aesthetic move. Coltrane's *Ascension*, with eleven musicians all playing at the same time, and only the loosest composition, was called the "Battle cry of the Black Revolution."[35]

Albert Ayler, who was not in *Ascension*, had had a strong influence on Coltrane. He had already begun a revolution in saxophone playing when he entered the scene in 1964 (his first real impact in the states). His rough timbre was created by making a vocal sound while playing--"speaking through the horn." Critics called it honking, animalistic, unsophisticated, and inappropriate for the audience to whom jazz had been marketed until then. Indeed the saxophone style was borrowed from popular music--the forties rhythm 'n blues saxophonists, who often thrilled crowds with this and acrobatics down on the floor. The sixties players inspired by Ayler were self-conscious artists and so did not go in for full theatrics, but the threat of unmitigated emotive engagement was there. He added high-pitched cries from above the normal range and multiphonics, a plethora of indistinguishable, non-tempered pitches, like Janis Joplin's visceral screams unleashed to mass youth audiences right at that crucial period. Ayler crossed the line of vulgarity and visceral Dionysian release by bringing this into Apollonian avant-garde art. This took Free Jazz beyond the interpretation of linear innovation and contemplated art object to become an invitation to excess.

Audiences and critics were challenged first of all by the sound: full-out passionate, physical, fast playing, with a steady high volume, a dense swarm of notes, and often multiple voices at the same time. Musicians broke away from most of the remaining ties to European-based music, widening the field of how a piece could be structured as well as approaches to each instrument. Crucial to the shift was that drummers dropped their key role of time-keeping. Sunny Murray said he had discovered it, now imitated by others — the contagion expected of jazz musicians.[36]

Also associated with second wave Free Jazz was the broken boundaries of the performance ritual and so of conceptions of music, risking audience antagonism for the sake of the playing itself. Without time being "kept"— under guard, as it were--music could appear continuous with life itself. The containing ritual structure of entertainment (a time and place for everything) was threatened. The LP, with its maximum of about twenty minutes per side, had expanded the concept of a proper attention span, but live performance was an opportunity for musicians to determine that limit themselves. The ritual frame required not only individual songs but sets of forty minutes or so, which clubs required to provide an interval for people to buy more drinks. (That is the origin of the set, incidentally, and short by hours of what many cultures consider the limit of audience musical reception.) Coltrane felt free to violate that. His club dates followed the highbrow art form of concerts, where audiences squirmed and then left when they've had enough. However with him the soloist is a long distance runner in a race as long as life, coming to a stopping point only when he had "said all he had to say." Coltrane's way of saying it all made his solos breathless, without a pause, and could either take the listeners' breath away, entranced out of clock time, or leave them with a feeling of overwrought exhaustion. He practiced long hours of scalar exploration, building the kind of physical stamina equal to the task of getting to the depths of feeling. The audience and musician that stuck with it had to be committed to the music with an assertive, uncompromising spirit.[37]

If Coltrane was an extremist, it was in assuming that jazz is an open tradition, which can be bent to the players' musical needs. To say whatever you needed to say was only what every jazz musician would have considered their fullest right, even when they agreed to follow the ritual performance limits. This is where "getting down to the crux," as Coltrane put it, became speaking the truth. One's subjectivity is sought in the moment of playing, even though it ends up as art object. This is more possible in music than any other art form, because more easily disguised, though some postwar abstract expressionists (deplored as "angst-ridden" — too subjective) came close. In terms of musician-centered music, to play what your truest self *needs* to play, rather than "good music," leaves the musician's social role behind. The art audience of that day often had one foot out the door, a tension the musician received as the incentive not to pull back but to go deeper — don't win everyone over, *make them decide, divide them*. For those who walk out, the authority of the musician is weakened, the performance frame and player's aura of no avail. Or maybe they're stunned: "What happened?" which no media, no other can inhabit and exploit.

Later saxophonists influenced by Coltrane did something similar with the breathless solo. The British saxophonist Evan Parker's tour de force circular breathing and incredible speed has at least this density and all-out energy, leaving no space unfilled; any empty space is like dead air on the radio, a blank one is obligated to fill. Someone criticized me in the 80s for always playing to the end of each breath, with no interest in breath that wasn't functional to sustaining the energy. That practice was typical of Free Jazz, but neither I nor Evan Parker would have gone over the usual time limit of the set. The concept of saying all one has to say, and extending that beyond the patience of the audience, had by then been swallowed up by the reestablished performance contract, from which it has not emerged.[38]

Critics thinking in terms of formalist innovation would see Coltrane's long solos as courageously breaking the rules. That makes them an avant-garde duty, when rather they were long because he abandoned himself to intensely joyful excursions. His arrangement with himself, known as the psyche, wouldn't tolerate interrupting that for the audience demand for comfort. His solos were like sexual pleasure which only a life-threatening fire could interrupt, not a phone call from people reminding him of his responsibility to them. Formalism has made artist autonomy a service to art history — here it would be jazz history — to avoid the charge of self-indulgence, aka self-motivation. According to the promotional ideology of high art, a handful of geniuses, by nature responsible to humanity, escape the ritualized and everyday demands of the social order, a functional balancing act limited to the stage. Some artists take their media preeminence to mean just that kind of service, but it is meaningless for those fully immersed in play.

Coltrane and Ayler were judged to have gone too far, but the critique missed the continuity with earlier jazz and other, more popular black traditions. Ayler's outrageous passion was almost always framed by a conventional form, such as his childlike or church-based melodies, including bits quoted from earlier pieces. Coltrane had long been working on intricate scales, and his posthumous *Interstellar Space* of 1967 was a musicological expansion from his tour de force of bebop-based fast chord changes, "Giant Steps," which he had come to feel was just an exercise.

The players in both *Ascension* and Coleman's *Free Jazz* album were undeniably jazz musicians, yet critics painted them as outsiders, cacophonous or ecstatic depending on their point of view. A shift is definitely evident, for *Free Jazz* was a collective improvisation of individual, identifiable soloists, whereas *Ascension* gave the impression of a mass, a swarm of wild Dionysaics you either join or run away from. Part of that effect might come from different studio engineering, meaning that engineers were found who could conceive jazz differently, with soloists emerging from the mass rather than standing apart.

Coleman's group may sound comparatively restrained, like its native LA environment, but its initial challenge was perceived as hot--disruptive and potentially divisive. At least it confused the tendency of the fifties to identify "hip" with "cool." If to be cool means to be hip, the most advanced and latest on the scene, then music that created a hot reaction was the new cool.[39]

Free Jazz would now indicate those in some solidarity with a radical approach, but it was an energy and not a form or organization. The heat and energy *felt* political. As the black struggle heated up—by mid-1966 Stokely Carmichael's "Black Power" was the new agenda—"free" meant something more militant and urgent than voter registration and desegregation. The musical direction was enhanced when in 1965 Leroy Jones (who became Amiri Baraka in 1967), renamed the new music the New Black Music and allied it with the Black Arts movement.[40] This was highly significant since he had been the chief published critic backing and interpreting the Free Jazz movement. He and others located their organization (the Black Arts Repertory/Theatre or BART/S) in black Harlem, a wild dream, since the taste of Harlemites was for popular music, far removed from the bohemian and arts-oriented East Village. The cultural-nationalist Black Avant-Garde, a name he initiated, was never so unified as the collectivity of NY avant-garde composers, the New York School (John Cage, Morton Feldman, Earle Brown, Christian Wolff and others). But the BART/S leadership took a far bolder position, for they sought the full unity of black artistic culture, specifically music, theatre, and literature, with the task of bringing it to the ordinary black person ("We want a black poem. / And a Black World").

The Free Musics

With a grouping of musicians taking their music as a movement cause, "New Thing" covered too much. A "new thing" cannot be unified, for any kind of playing coming down the pike can be *the* new thing; the title doesn't even specify it as jazz. Only by becoming something of a form can a music be identified apart from the players, which means, like bebop earlier, it can be learned and adopted by others and embraced by many—as it is today. The "New Thing" also did not register that the leadership and almost all players were black. Baraka's concept, in line with Black Nationalist politics, took leadership to mean exclusivity, the premise that blacks alone—and none of Norman Mailer's "white negroes'--could achieve greatness in this music. Not surprisingly, by the later sixties the relation of many black to white avant-garde musicians became more problematic.

To relate this to previous history: some black bebop musicians had claimed to be playing a music too fast and difficult for white imitators, hoping to hold a patent on it they never had with swing. It was a playful/serious game of intimidation and challenge, for it was as absurd to think that whites were genetically lacking in such dexterity as to think blacks could not be intellectuals. It was grounds for the accusation of inauthentic "white jazz," and akin to the argument that to play jazz you had to have "it," a je ne sais quoi that was in black hands. White musicians would have to grant the truth that jazz could only have arisen from those despised in a Jim Crow or de facto segregated country of that time. If jazz is to become an art form, the bebop-pers were saying, it had to be recognized as a *black* art form, a correction to a Benny Goodman anointed as the King of Swing. The musicological challenge of bebop was partner to that of authenticity. Jazz was returned to its black roots at the same time it was moving ahead in European modernist terms.

White musicians would have to take off their hats if they wanted to enter the room, that is, recognize that it was the black aesthetic to which they submitted their musical lives. It's as if the black musicians were saying, "If you want to eat at our table then abandon the illusions white society permits itself." Once that's accepted they would fully share the meal. Bebop speed was a challenge, and set the pace for young whites attracted to jazz. Fast playing while following the changes was the basic skill to master (I found this out as a young player in the late fifties); creativity was built on that. It was limited musically, since simple fast playing is not particularly imaginative--runs up and down on the saxophone are easy and become the most conventional. At least there was something to be mastered as a step to inclusion in the ranks.

This is what happened; it would be blacks who invited whites into their bands and not Benny Goodman sneaking Teddy Wilson into his party. "White jazz" of Dave Brubeck may have gotten national press but was not the hip scene. The fifties through the early period of Free Jazz was the integration period for much of that scene. Even before Rosa Parks refused to give up her seat to a white person, black jazz musicians were inviting whites to join them, choosing them on their merits, just as whites would hire blacks without fanfare. Musical interest, with an understanding of the political/racial implications, motivated Goodman and later the black musician-leaders, such as Miles Davis and Sonny Rollins. It was the musicians--ahead of the institutions and politicians of segregated society–who prefigured the social movement to come.[41]

Post-*Ascension* Free Jazz by contrast had no in-principle bar to whites on the level of skill, such as speed or complexity, no achievement test to legitimate them. For the second wave imported form was minimal, leaving the field wide open and any limitation of participant players would limit the music. The exclusionary insistence on black-only groups—whether formal or informal—that began with Baraka's Black Avant-garde concept (Sun Ra preceded him in this requirement for his Arkestra), was a test that provided no challenge to technique; there was nothing whites could do to legitimately engage those peers on an equal basis. Taking off their hat in recognition that they'd caught the bug of the black aesthetic was not enough.

Exclusion was a contradiction to the music, yet it was not the actuality of Free Jazz as far as race was concerned. Not only Coleman rejected Baraka's nationalism but also Albert Ayler was not in line with it beyond rhetorical hints; neither hesitated to play with whites as full partners.[42] Even Archie Shepp, the musician most in step with Baraka's nationalism, continued to perform with whites (such as Roswell Rudd). Musical interest trumped politics and black solidarity a good bit of the time.

This should not be construed as a triumph of liberal integration over separatism; the dilemma was real and unavoidable. Black liberation could not be limited to acquiring civil rights. Like all political goals it engaged the internal question of consciousness, which is collectively accessed through culture. If jazz is an expression of black artistic culture, and only blacks can liberate themselves from a music world that wants to keep them entertainers, then it makes sense that blacks would assert their artistic ownership. That meant to subordinate the position of whites, who had more favorable relation to employers--commercial studio work and cushy summer resort gigs, from which blacks were commonly barred. Nationalists rejected white liberals, accused of benefiting from their race, who wanted desperately to escape the accusation by being part of the problem. In telling blacks that only they can liberate themselves, Malcolm X and Baraka would have to say the same to whites — your race limits your consciousness. Black hatred of these whites cannot be taken on face value, since it was for the sake of their mission of consciousness to blacks, to become clearly visible to themselves. The problem was in the realm of practicality. Writers can do it, since they work alone, but the playing of music is collective. If your interest is to get the best musicians for your musical conception, then to refuse to audition whites who are the obvious choice would be to put black consciousness ahead of musical imagination. Both interests are understandable; together they were contradictory.[43]

The contradiction is crucial to understanding the rejection of Free Jazz, a turn that was not predictable in the early period. In the fast-paced turmoil of the sixties, one day's radical became the next day's liberal, with a loss of political credibility. Some white critics used Coleman to indicate the acceptable (MLK-integrationist) alternative to Coltrane and the more black-culture-oriented second wave. Malcolm X's assassination was Feb. 21, 1965, and for many blacks (such as Baraka) it was the moment of decision to split the former scene. Coltrane's *Ascension* was a mere four months later, "a torch that lit the free jazz thing" according to saxophonist Dave Liebman. One critic said it was "fire music," meaning emotionally hot and engaged or even incendiary, as in James Baldwin's threatening "The Fire Next Time" (1963). Others called the more militant Free Jazz not just the musicological "anti-jazz" but "hate music," accusing it of expressing anger. Musicians who wanted to bring the social struggle of blacks into the music world saw themselves as target. The white audience wanted to hear it as music but could not; they wanted a music free of the rage of that mid-sixties moment, and the two could not be disentangled.

Musicians such as Max Roach, Abbey Lincoln, and Bill Dixon had earlier expressed political support for radical black activists, but the mid-sixties "energy music" was not theirs.[44] This title joined the physicality of the playing and the sonic impact on listeners, as well as distinguishing it from early 60s Free Jazz, which was not so charged as "Black Music." However titled, the image of black rage suddenly appeared, unleashed from music world control, a door being opened that led to many other doors, a Pandora's box that could not be closed. To boldly dispense with so many conventions was modernist musicology, Coleman's innovation. However, to do so in a fully commercial form of music, which unlike other art music depended on popular appeal, hinted at disruption that was social in its implications. It was a revolt of the entertainers against their minstrel past, who had moved beyond demanding simple acceptance as artists in their own sphere. If they had been feted, funded, and formally dressed as serious artists on stage with the New York School, their music framed and critiqued as high-brow concert music, it would not have stirred up white fears, but that was inconceivable. ("Serious music" is the literal translation of the main classical tradition, German Ernstemusik, as in "earnest"). When avant-garde jazz musicians finally *did* receive this treatment it was long past the period of turmoil, after the demons had been put back in the box.

Spontaneity had seemed benign, useful and submissive to the music world and had even enabled its fifties expansion. Almost overnight it revealed itself as the dark reality of psyche, exceeding the bounds of reason and leaping three-dimensionally out of the frame of entertaining performance. The desire found in the artful moment of free playing showed its colors as sublime experience—attractive and repulsive at the same time. Art is trusted to be a safe distance from the self until the chasm is opened; all hell breaks loose and people are threatened with falling through what turns out to be a very thin crust.[45] It was the threat of enslavement to dark forces, which could only arise from that part of the population that had historically known slavery. They appeared to be finally reaping vengeance, not through overt violence but worse, through a riot of sound that escaped the confines of music and could not be suppressed by the military.

"Breaking the rules" was the officially recognized and rewarded domain of avant-garde high art--the New York School and contemporary European composers.[46] It was the achieved freedom that ideology positioned against Soviet control over artists. John Cage was a scandal to musicology, the proper home of which was high art, but he was no threat to the divisions of the social order. In the early 60s this order included such slow-paced and regulated racial integration that it would never arrive unless it was pushed hard, with the threat of violence (whether non-violence could have done it was mooted by history). Then and today what is dubbed "art" in the most officially respected sense is given the longest leash of any public activity, but the the second wave black avant-garde were considered poachers on that territory. In a segregated world they hinted at the core American dilemma, as it had been called, the contradiction of democratic ideals and social reality. After the break with non-violent integration, the wildest music was coming from blacks who could not be easily seen as upwardly mobile to the middle class—the hope of integrationists--and who were militantly dedicated to the music over the safest path to career reward, conventional jazz.

Their intent betrayed the modernist iconoclasm of breaking rules set up by the patriarch--the slammed door and "I'm going my own way now," with dad sighing his annoyance at the adolescent. That can go on interminably, always another rule to break, hence the conceit of modernism. Instead this new music was the more intimate insult of the one who has left and returns only to say "Not only do I not need you but I'm *permanently* outside your understanding of me," that is, not the hipster version. Mystery, which beginning in the 19th century was the key to the uniqueness of music among the arts, is thereby revealed as embedded in the deepest and most troubling cultural fault line. Here were black entertainers saying to the respected social order: "The mystery that excites and disturbs is not yours, it's over here." This was a more brutally assertive rupture than hippie alternative culture then in the making, always on the verge of a mature adult return and accommodation. It is captured in Baraka's declaration of an a priori ontological difference between a black and white self that is then an epistemological break, and like other such absolutes comes across as a conversation stopper.[47]

Black musicians seeking their freedom from music industry standards and asserting themselves as artists in their own right were not widely applauded, as they would be by today's self-satisfied left-cultural politics. Jazz had dominated the popular charts not long before, and so there was at least the implied question, absent from funded high art--what if all blacks took "being free" seriously? While among the white avant-garde composers there were serious conflicts, their disputes did not have the consequences outside musical concerns that existed for Free Jazz, where being free seemed to encourage revolt, even for those who were only aware of such music. In the dominant conception of Europeans, authentic art might be produced by individuals who are poor, but not by those identified with a vocal and rebellious underclass that resists assimilation. For the provocative "Free Jazz" to be used as a label was to say, just as Civil Rights was amping up in militancy and changing its name, "We're going to be free, dig it or not!"

We're dealing here with a crucial conjuncture of politics and musicology in a decade of such conjunctures, without which "Free Jazz" is an oxymoron. Since jazz is understood as improvised within a pre-given structure, Free Jazz could only be self-contradictory, at best a compromise. Yet for so much jazz that was merely unconventional to acquire that title correctly stresses a collective assertion—the will of a new jazz generation to be free from musical constraints enforced by the commercial system and reinforced by the common habits of jazz musicians, which is an external and internal struggle. With "free" taken as an imperative verb it even means to emancipate jazz from its associated music world. Those on a path of independent organization took that seriously, such as Dixon in 1964, and apparently where Coltrane was headed just before he died.

Given that, the second wave move can also be viewed as a class issue, the appropriation of the music by the immediate music-makers (in Marxist terms, "expropriating the expropriators") rather than leaving it to the composers' contractual relation with the music world. The most influential free-oriented black players were more interested in music than politics, yet musical self-determination sailed ahead on the wave not only of black self-determination but class interest. In retrospect we can join them with others moving towards a more egalitarian situation for musicians—at least a more favorable hierarchy. To see class struggle here would be to universalize the meaning of the cultural-political break, to interpret it as part of the wider process by which *all* players would eventually come to insist on their experience. Without this, parallel to rock's insistence, DIY and its social ramifications would not be around today. It is not inconceivable to link white non-professional garage bands on a path to punk DIY independence with the black avant-garde on a path that threatened their professional status as jazz musicians.

Most players who had a public voice denied that anything political was intended, where "political" conventionally meant an explicit public stand, such as Black Power. However context is important in perceiving the musics import: post-colonial American blacks engaged with nationalism knew they were struggling alongside Africans to redefine culture for themselves against European control. Although Coltrane did not discuss this as others did, his study of non-western musics was a step in this direction.[48] His long form solo and scalar explorations were informed by a Indian high art music, to which he listened intently. Here musical need for a wider vocabulary and canvas was answered by the rising tide of validation for non-white culture. Coltrane's emancipatory move, like Picasso's sixty years earlier (African masks on European women), participated in the shift from the white man's fantasy burden to the reality that humanity is not a moral scale but is exemplified by every human being. Henceforth no art or mentality is to be condescended to.

To consider a music that has no text as expressing an emotion with political meaning is a clear case of projection. Some openly adopted a racial politics, but even that would not clinch their music's meaning, as art often reveals to interpreters aims other than its makers' political views. Music is more fictional than any novel; it is the audience and critics who read into it what they want. Some listeners heard rage and protest in Free Jazz, but some of Beethoven's music can be called raging, which people find stirring rather than evoking fear. Unlike the images of visual art that are of unavoidable meaning ("Guernica") and pointedly political, non-verbal sound by itself cannot be pinned to political intent. This is why, when theorists today speak of the politics of art, they ignore purely instrumental music, thus tacitly dismissing its avant-garde as politically irrelevant or even regressive. And it is, following a short-sighted pragmatic view that takes politics as a direct line between act, in this case the artwork, and result.[49] Yet far more than visual art, the music that people select represents their chosen identity, a good part of which today implies a unified political and life-style opinion. It depends on what one *wants* to hear, identity's echo, and doesn't need an act of listening, which can go in many directions besides securing an image for oneself.

"The personal is the political" was launched by feminists in 1970, but it was preceded by a general shift in what political was to mean henceforth. One could now *be* political, meaning to have a politicized (left) consciousness and therefore identity, especially when achieved through an awakening, as in the Christian-Islamic tradition. (It took a longer time for the right to be able to do the same on such a large scale, and then in opposition to the unified identity the left had created.) Political opinions were no longer held strictly on pragmatic or utopian grounds but indicated an identity that implied a variety of behaviors and life choices. This merger of politics and life is so pervasive today that we can hardly imagine a time when a political statement was judged on its own worth apart from the person. To sort out its positive from negative effects, such as the common subversion of political argument by ad hominem references, would take us far afield from the present topic. For our purposes here, spiritual and political implications were wedded to expansive musical form, which deeply affected the nature and later reception of the iconic status of its most prominent figures.

"Spiritual" is cultural meaning for a collectivity as well as signifying a personal life choice. The merger (or confusion some might say) relates to the sixties resurgent dream of collective and individual transformation, of which the consciousness-raising of second-wave feminism and later New Age inner search were diverse offshoots. When Free Jazz began to be called energy music, it signified a unified musical, political (activist), and spiritual identity, which did not exist publicly prior to 1965. Alan Silva's earlier statement illustrates this, and it will be found throughout the writings of John Sinclair of the later sixties, those of Ayler, and certainly Baraka. Anything that can call itself "the movement," such as the white identity today, refers back to the collective solidarity, empowerment, and freshly raised consciousness which Christianity inaugurated and our culture tends to honor.

For Coltrane to "go down to the crux" was not political in any usual sense.[50] Yet for an artist to put this forward while increasingly disregarding his commercial audience opened a path for jazz outside secularist art, which had supposedly freed itself from Christianity, including Coltrane's cosmic universalism. Modernist formalism, the predominant framework used to interpret the advances of jazz as art, recognized the biography of the artist, usually messy and alien to middle-class morality, but isolated it from the artwork. It resisted—even feared--the psychic impact of art, arguing for an aesthetic experience of spectators beyond the turmoil of the artist's life. The sublime was thought to irreversibly advance the critic/spectators' (Kantian) aesthetic taste and interpretation, while keeping their hands clean. Coltrane and Albert Ayler both presented their work as an extension of their private experience yet it transcends them and reaches out to any who would hear their incantations. In so doing they exchanged modernist purity for expression direct from the soul to the Source, introducing a different persona from that found in the promotional blurbs common to jazz albums and interviews.

That Source is not benign. In the later Coltrane, music is not protected by the Apollonian triad of rhythm, melody, and harmony, conventions that Charlie Parker had affirmed. Ornette Coleman had these cultural guarantees literally beaten out of him when he was young, and resurrected himself on a new plane. In Coltrane's struggle with the pleasure of drugs, as if he inherited and achieved what Parker could not, he beat himself up and arose in a new place. In both cases biography was of great significance for their playing. An artist transformed by such struggle creates work where the personal negatives to which most succumb, such as the need for approval and resentment, are transmuted into forms that teeter on the abyss. In *A Love Supreme,* whose chant and liner notes no critic was allowed to alter, Coltrane affirms music as the singular God fully in control of his life. The album was widely applauded, as if he was referring to the Christian God, and moral good had triumphed once again. However within that God, whose song Coltrane had become, were the seeds of an ascension that would undermine that interpretation. It was recorded in December 1964, and six months later he made *Ascension*, the supposed battle cry of the black revolution.

Coltrane went *down* to the crux, meaning the pit of chaos and terror, where the demonic reigns, usually suppressed by Christian peace and harmony.[51] The crux was the shaky ground of the social order. There the deepest meaning of jazz improvisation is revealed as a drama of the rebellious dark unconscious against above-ground civilized goodness. Jazz seemed dislodged and would have to find a new balance. The final act of the ritual drama might not be the reassurance that above-ground culture demands of artists. In the darkness where the Judeo-Christian sky God can locate no code to validate them, musical formulae and style lose their civilizing function and meaning. Their subjectivity is at stake; idealized artistic autonomy is truly tested, and they don't pass through art-making without scars. The assurance that musicians can rest on their laurels, satisfied with their legacy, is belied by their continued struggle, which culture would rather see pacified as "experimentation." Artists whose desire can't be satisfied cannot be dressed up as the pride of the culture. They cannot leave their listeners in peace. The natural consequence is social hell, to which they are banished.

Here the personal precedes the political. In the wider American culture the honoring of personal spiritual experience had not been extinguished, so it could conceivably still validate personal questing. Presumably anywhere the artist goes would test the limits of art, including the modernist taboo on the personal. *A Love Supreme* was accepted as avant-garde jazz, a musicological violation and advance; at the same time it bridged the gulf to popular musics, which were then uncovering layers of subjective experience for public consumption. When personal motivation is not subordinated to advancing a progressive agenda, the subject is liberated even from the rational structures expected of the modernist sensibility. Some whites were prepared to hear this call and acknowledge it—this black man opening his depths through music was speaking for them too. Then when *Ascension* came close on its heels (though not released until 1966), the personal expanded into the social radicalism of a mass joined in sound. As intimate expression his music was lauded; as a collective expression it was "something else" beyond what Ornette Coleman had envisioned in his album title.

Increasingly Free Jazz musicians were living on shared commitment rather than a secure career future. People squeamish about strong assertive egos should remember that to make the kind of conscious moves that might destroy a career relies not on a applauding fans but commitment and arrogant self-belief. This was epitomized by Coltrane, Ayler, Cecil Taylor, Archie Shepp and others, at a time when they were publicly available to be heard and judged by an urban audience. By the mid-sixties it seemed to a significant number that America was going through some kind of revolution, which is unavoidably a traumatic experience ("not a dinner party," as Chairman Mao said). A large segment of people were making choices accordingly. "Which side are you on," was the question--either go deeper, pull back in terror, or sit confused and ineffective in between. The era that destabilized many gave hope to others for the first time, a break from the endless passage of time. In times of crisis only inner and outer division seems possible; later the sides will be taken for granted or dismissed as contingent. The claim that musicians are exploring freely can be made at any time, as it is often today. But to stake oneself on a direction that pleases few and provides little reward depends historically on times when either confusion and conflict are felt as present and unavoidable, or people have the will and hardness to create such a situation. Then exploring is not a private venture and decent career move but an act that opens the future, a screen on which to project dreams.

What most writers have failed to deal with adequately is that for many musicians and followers jazz was a kind of secular religion, and Free Jazz was no exception. One study of jazz from the sociology of religion perspective, and one coming from New Jazz Studies recognizes this.[52] Both are useful, but the investigators' safe, scholarly distance makes the players' motivation look like a regressive blind spot, not something the reader might share. Jazz writers during its prime were born-again fanatics, who proselytized for their cause and vilified opponents. Writers of the current generation have also chosen their area of interest subjectively, yet they owe so much to the academic world socially and ideologically that their personal motivation is hidden beneath the pretense of objective scholarship. For all the current interest in Free Jazz, including interviews, no one is examining their collective situation and perspective back then. The serious study of Free Jazz has not begun; perhaps the conclusions are feared.

First-hand musician anecdotes clearly demonstrate the relevance to jazz of the sociology of religion. For young white Chicago players in the twenties, commitment to one's initial experience was as strong as in any genuine religious conversion. Suddenly an entire world is opened and they cannot go back without suffering loss and the guilt of betrayal. In the sixties, mentors suggested free playing to the newly arrived (such as Cecil Taylor to Sunny Murray); the mentored seized upon it as revelation and ran with it. The bulk of record buyers today will see their Free Jazz taste choice as one among several, quite unlike the musicians then. Like converts, some sobered up later and could not connect with their earlier passion, while others kept the faith.

The personal reached in the crux of conflict becomes the universal, the challenge to the world. In the words of Albert Ayler: "The music that I am playing, this is what keeps me going in life. Right now my imagination is beyond civilization. I believe I am the prophet...This is the only way that's meant for musicians to play. All other ways have been explored."[53] Today anyone saying "This is the only way" would be ridiculed as a megalomaniac, at best intolerant. That is how icons are thrown out of reach. Ayler did not make promotional statements but spoke articulately and persuasively from his core identity with "the music," as some jazz musicians still call it, almost bowing the head. For instance here again, after speaking with great respect of Sidney Bechet: "We try to do now what musicians like Armstrong used to do: their music was joy. Beauty appeared in it. It was this way in the beginning, this way it shall be in the end. One day everything will be as it should be."[54] The "spiritual unity" Ayler advocated in the name of peace and love opened a can of worms that, in his apocalyptic view, could not be put back — it was beyond the range of what culture could assimilate. Many listening to Ayler in that period—like myself in 1967 hearing Coleman live for the first time—would hardly call his music beautiful and peaceful, but for a time he was riding a wave and oblivious to rejection.

At the height of the movement devotion was ascetic to the point of denying the supposed object of career musicians, material success, for as long as possible. For the committed, personal survival need was inessential to the life of the music. Moreover, common to so much music is the refusal to put it into words, since "the music" is a deep subjective and collective experience.[55] John Sinclair was one of the true believers, not alone in thinking the new music was of social and personal emancipatory significance, even questioning whether a particular musician was a true revolutionary.[56] At the same time, as common in Western/Islamic history, fierce commitment can be problematic, easily leading to a dead end that will block its expansion of form.

An exploratory music might seem to accord with the optimistic advance of secular enlightenment, yet for jazz there was a core of resistance, and Free Jazz did not violate it. The mantra of jazz musicians was: music is first of all about concrete, experienced feeling, and audience taste agreed. To imagine a future emancipated from old attachments would then put that "jazz feeling" under suspicion. Musicological rule-breaking can be schematized—just how many rules are broken and how logical is their succession. The progressivist excitement generated by this comes across as the trampling of so-called sentimental attachment, and can thrill the most modernist segment of the audience. Early Free Jazz could accommodate this model, but the second wave was built not on such advancement but on the boldest expression of feeling. Here was the more insistent conflict: how far can the feeling of musicians go before they violate the performer contract with the audience—to represent *their* feelings—and instead take the audience places they fear to go.

The sixties expanded feeling beyond its presumed and legitimated limits. Free-floating eros, to which the birth-control pill was the real and symbolic door, threatened relationships based on standard conceptions of love— marriages dissolved. Free love fit well with Freudo-Marxist demands of the fifties (Herbert Marcuse et al.) as well as the French Surrealist and Situationist aim to transform everyday life, of which they considered sexuality a major part. It joined free music as unstoppable, unleashed eros, which the Establishment considered a unified threat, even as ad agencies exploited it.[57] Resistance even encouraged its advocates—fucking, as well as blowing wild music, was thought to be messing with "the system" and creating a new, collective, utopian future. Any act based on feeling that goes against the grain of defended culture and morals contributed to an activist politics of culture, whether it was articulated as such or not. Even when it crashes the next day, it has been articulated, it happened, it is the historical process that we not only inherited but still are continuing. New shifts are inevitable.

When does the witnessing of strong feeling resonate with people to the point of both frightening them and making them self-aware, and when does it become background music at a cocktail party or a gallery show? Was Lady Day not excessive, did not the feeling spill over from the record into the listener's heart, isn't that what listeners longed to hear, rather than to calculate the liberties she took with earlier jazz singing? Extend this same ear to the music of John Cage, in the modernist tradition of scandalizing bourgeois audiences by breaking the rules. Listening for one's true feeling-reactions would reveal a mixture, contradicting his romantic philosophy of the health and goodness of sound. At a time of exuberant feeling he built a wall of fear (my tendentious opinion!) against the sensuality of new commercial music of the time. This was not only jazz. Music called "popular," beginning with rock and roll, was escaping the adolescent demographic and becoming "of the people"—adult culture. The context Cage preferred was high art, which would make his more chaotic pieces assimilable as *intellectually* difficult, outside the range of bodily reactions like disgust and enthrallment.

As with the Coltrane pieces that jazz radio stations select, the repertoire of today's resurrected Cage includes only those pieces that are relatively serene and therefore meet the criterion of accessibility. The selection of one's portable musical environment is as emotionally protective, as if one was advised in advance how to avoid trouble. To control what goes in one's ears is an attempt to order peace of mind in a world that is now, as it was from the Depression to the Bomb, screaming "disaster ahead."

While critics and audience debated Free Jazz as a public music, playing free was an immediate private issue for NY jazz musicians, a choice they felt faced with. Steve Swallow, who played freeform with Jimmy Giuffre in 1962 (*Free Fall*), had reservations by 1965, just as Free Jazz entered its new phase: "Interviewer: Does anyone play without 'givens'? Swallow: No. I'd say no. [Those who try to do so] are limited by their unwillingness to recognize limitations." They rely on habit, "a way of doing something that hasn't been *transcended*." They do it because they're addicted to it, and "the best music I know of has progressed beyond the whole apparatus of *wanting*...I think most of the music that's advertised by its players as 'free' music, is self-involved music to an unhealthy degree: ego music."[58] Swallow echoes John Cage's criticism and shows their common attraction to Zen Buddhism, but this is coming from a practicing improviser, the figure Cage dismissed in favor of the composer in charge. Swallow's argument here is rich in moral superiority over desire and emotion. It brings up the argument that later was raised against free improvisation, that we must humble ourselves to our limitations rather than allow affect to lead us beyond them.

Swallow had been taken to task for playing with Art Farmer, a relatively straight-ahead player, and in response he says: "There's a strong feeling among the young people [Swallow himself was 24 at the time!] who play the new music that financial reasons are the only ones for doing anything else."(p. 73) He criticized those committed to playing only the new music; his approach was to learn from many situations, to develop his craft as a bass player. Like jazz musicians at the time he did not rely heavily on institutional training, but the distinction he makes shows the gulf between the straight-ahead and new music players, one which jazz education would later exploit. The masters of craft know many things and have a versatile strategy, always able to present themselves as capable, while the others know only one big thing. However deep they go into it they will not be the ideal jobbing musician. In that fertile period the two were thrown together and had to deal with each other as competitive approaches, whereas today the versatile players trained in all the historic styles are fenced off from the committed free jazzers, many of whom don't even try to improvise on jazz tunes.

In a further criticism, Swallow recognizes the validity of new music players who make no concessions to the audience, and points to Cecil Taylor as an example. (In 1962 Taylor abandoned conventional tunes and the song form, and was playing free within his own structures.) When Taylor has trouble making his way financially, Swallow says, he should not be unhappy with the results, feeling hurt and wronged by society. Swallow never mentions race as a factor, that for white musicians like himself rejection was not amplified by race, so they were unlikely to feel it with the same personal intensity. His focus on the practical consequences of a musicological choice ignores the employment advantages white musicians still had to tide them over between gigs taken for artistic reasons. His comment however points to a weakness in the position of some of the black avant-garde, who merged their anger and resistance to racism with their musical commitment. To the extent their specific way of playing had become a badge of honor, to question it on musical grounds would be to slide back on their commitment to a racial politics. They had a built-in reason to avoid criticizing their work internally, as artists do when they are no longer satisfied with it. This contributed to free jazz later becoming frozen in place as a style that communicated commitment that one could only be for or against.

To the extent that Free Jazz had acquired a rough form it had its limit case. This is exemplified by the Free Form Improvisation Ensemble, in a 1966 recording that did not appear until 1998. Alan Silva was on double bass, Burton Greene on piano, Gary William Friedman, sax, Clarence Walker, drums, and John Winter, flute, all sounding like accomplished musicians with obviously strong jazz backgrounds. Greene later called it "the first total free improvised open communication music,"[59] "free form compositions"; only one piece seems to begin with a short composed line, and it's not repeated. Otherwise, the only sign of jazz form is that the players are given solo space. Much of the playing is driving, hinting at second wave Free Jazz, but a sudden break in pace appears, and parts where a musician drops out unexpectedly. Greene goes inside the piano, common for Experimental Music but very unusual for anything that would have been called jazz.[60] These aberrations put the group outside Free Jazz, however slightly, more of a bridge to British free improvisation than other playing that has come to light.

3. Collapse of the Free Jazz Movement

Had it followed the pattern of modernist advancements, Free Jazz would first be attacked as a violation of essential form and the radicals would hold firm. For modernists a new direction was not meant to please the widest audience but first of all the artists; the later accusation of artist elitism was built-in. "One doesn't *like* free jazz, one realizes one fine day ...that it *is*," similar to Sunny Murray's forceful statement: "this is the music of our era, no matter how much they hate it."[61] Eventually a growing number of audience and critics would absorb and positively interpret it. They would identify what immediate contemporaries had been deaf to, and eventually the radicals would be vindicated. It would achieve a place in jazz history like bebop and be the ground for further developments.[62] But what Baraka and others expected went unrealized. It was defeated as the next step for jazz, and—similar to the other arts at the time--that ended the pattern by which *any* irreversible "next step" could be made. It was one of the hinges that portended the shift between the break-out of postwar modernism from its shelter into the larger culture, and the stability of the postmodern.

The active movement of Free Jazz can be broadly dated from 1959 to the early 70s, with the peak of disturbance occurring for only about three years, mid-1964 through 1967. *Downbeat*, though published in Chicago, covered the NY phenomenon as *the* major controversy of the period. By 1967 it had reached its height of public attention, record contracts, occasional large crowds, and even the capitulation of some prominent critics who had opposed it. It looked like it was on the road to integration into what the word "jazz" meant, but it still had not enough audience to sustain it commercially, and the critic support it had could not be maintained against audience rejection. If "the way to learn how to make music is to find an audience," as Paul Bley said (referring generally to the individual musician), then this movement was doomed.[63] By 1970 its strongest critic-supporter Amiri Baraka was trashing two of the very musicians he had advanced, Ornette Coleman and Albert Ayler, as having betrayed their earlier advances. He also implied that the movement was unable to win the hearts of those he thought should be the core audience for black musicians—the black populace.[64] With this he turned against the renunciation of popular appeal that had ruled avant-gardes since they first appeared.

Bursting with unpredictable energy, Free Jazz made it difficult for the music world and audiences to settle on any overarching conception and identity of jazz, and to feel secure that they were listening to the genuine article. "What's in a name" pressured jazz to be one entity, not irrevocably divided. Given this anxiety over the being of jazz, for that identity to become the new "shape of jazz to come," as promised by Coleman, was the only possibility for its further growth. Yet in the total corpus of music in its short life, everything from the Black Avant-garde added up to very little recorded music and very few followers.[65]

The economic factor was symptomatic but crucial. The effort at a collective structure to sustain employment for avant-garde jazz musicians, a union Bill Dixon spearheaded in late 1964 (The Jazz Composers Guild), began to fall apart after several months. Decisions were by consensus, common to grassroots civil rights and New Left groups, which meant interminable discussion about music, race, and economics. Like all radicals they were deeply engaged in face to face talk and argument about what they called the "nitty-gritty," which covered much outside of music. Members agreed idealistically to take no jobs at venues or record contracts which denied the same to others in the union. If their music was to be the future they would be in high demand, and players would make a decent living from it. They began to back out of the agreement when faced with the reality of their individual financial situations. That was their short-term but necessary option, given their preference to seek steady work only as musicians, and specifically jazz gigs of their musical direction, for which Swallow criticized them. Also, and more significantly, it was in 1967 that clubs began turning to rock music, which drained the economic base of all jazz musicians' lives. They lost the next audience generation to an emotive popular music rooted in black culture. A slump had come earlier with bebop, but was followed by its transformation into a middle-brow art form. This time around the very ground of jazz popularity was eroding, and it was still too current to be turned into nostalgia or an educated classical taste.

Since John Coltrane's turn to Free Jazz had given the movement a respected leader, the effect of his death in July 1967 cannot be minimized. It was almost the death blow to the mid-sixties direction, a symbolic periodization for those writing the narrative, and it sealed the fate of those who had ridden his coattails. Albert Ayler, the immediate inspiration for Coltrane's turn, was pressured to overcome his controversial image, besides being personally motivated to move on to more commercial musical forms. The praise and income the musicians had gotten from a few faithful fans and critics was not enough to keep their spirit alive.[66] Several packed their bags for Europe, giving Free Jazz a second chance, but since Continental Europeans weren't respected back home for their popular taste, they couldn't return in triumph.

The jazz avant-garde faced opposition from the music industry that was cautious about supporting it. Their recordings are now considered iconic, but little attention is given to the conditions under which they were produced. All jazz musicians had to submit to "the man" — record producers, managers, promoters, and critics--and this substantially affected how far they could go in their music. After Coltrane died they had no one rooting for them in the music world, no funded festivals sprinkled around the country as were appearing in Europe, no state agency to back them. The musicology of recorded Free Jazz depended at least partly on what the bosses permitted. After 1967, Ayler's record company prevented him from using drummer Milford Graves because of Grave's reputation as a militant.[67] And what would have happened if Albert Ayler's manager had allowed him and his brother to play (and presumably record) with British musicians as they wanted to do, instead telling them it would be "bad for their image" to do so?[68]

It was the jazz avant-garde that led the struggle against clubs whose interest in jazz depended on the bottom line, and against the record companies that had turned jazz into an enterprise financially more beneficial for them than for most musicians. This was the very industry that today profits from the respect for that era's rebels.[69] Their criticism of the bosses was common shop talk at the time and a bond between them as exploited workers, but the bosses determined who got recorded and whose music would get to the stores and be promoted. They often expressed contempt for the jazz press as well, yet knew that the Downbeat Poll boosted or lowered their market value, on which they depended for performance and recording gigs. Like today's professionals, they knew how far they could go in media situations where their bread and butter was on the line, but they retained a self-respecting hostility to the hands that fed them.

The musicians weren't making enough to sustain their lives, but in that era professionalism made it demeaning to take other jobs to make up the difference. The alternative was self-organization and entrepreneurship, such as the Jazz Composers League, Coltrane's efforts towards the end of his life, and Milford Graves' independent label. This had unintended consequences.

It was commonly understood at the time that the legitimacy and prestige of professionals rested on focusing all their energy on their specialized expertise, and that the judgment that mattered most would come from their peers. Just as no outsider could tell a mechanical engineer how to do his job, professional status protected the autonomy of musicians against outside interference. No musician could be validated as "among the best" without this; that was the internal nature and functioning of the hierarchy. Anything besides playing music was to be handled by those talented and capable in those other tasks. Yet there's something quite American in wanting to become one's own boss. In fact that was the future for the most challenging nonconventional music, which was soon to be thoroughly de-professionalized, in that earlier, precise sense of the term. The musicians may have considered it an emancipation, yet it was also a defeat. Their scarce financial resources and time were taken away from playing and put towards concert production and publicity, record promotion and labels. This rebellion ironically aided the majors by getting them off the hook of musician pressure. The music industry would be free of any obligation or personal motivation beyond what their cost-accountants were badgering them about. The solidarity and shop-talk griping by exploited musicians would be replaced by the positivity required of entrepreneurs, who are believed to be the architect of their own success.

Some critics blamed Free Jazz for the general decline of jazz popularity, but the controversy surrounding it coincided with the rise of high-amplified music. Jazz was acoustic (the guitar was merely amplified acoustic), and as the folkies had found out, no form of jazz could compete on the level of amplified rock, followed soon by the celebrity-prone, mass audience hybrid, jazz-rock, which accorded with the music industry's expansion of the youth market. The blurred line between art and popular culture was aided by the massive appeal of the Beatles and then rock to an older and even art-oriented generation, such that the claim of jazz as an art form had stiff competition. This affected what clubs were willing to offer (the drinking age in NY state was 18 until the 80s), and clubs were the mainstay of most jazz musician, not recordings. Jazz had long been tagged as commercial, and despite musicians claiming they were "just playing music," their fortunes followed the charts for their assigned category. Free Jazz players fully conformed with the self-critical edge known to postwar jazz, and didn't aim to replace jazz with something else. They had a huge impact on Miles Davis and the musicians he hired, who also made the boundaries of jazz difficult for its original fans. However, the cool-hip backdrop generated for Davis's free-floating solos was something intense Free Jazz couldn't compete with. It was being superannuated by greater accessibility, just as abstract expressionism had been a decade earlier by pop art.

The musicological challenge cannot be separated from the changing strategy of the record companies. In the fifties they targeted the prosperous white audiences, who were challenged by the nagging question that their buttoned-down life was missing something. Male consumers especially wanted as smooth a ride in their music as in their cars and fantasized sex lives. Harmonically cool jazz of the mid-fifties jazz renaissance provided a supportive background, whereas everything coming from the jazz avant-garde was a bumpy ride — for white and non-white listeners alike. Yet the commercial rise of Davis and Coltrane above the conformist background showed that maybe a few bumps were needed to hold interest. The inability of Free Jazz to repeat this pattern of sales leadership meant re-thinking the strategy.

Sales for Free Jazz were as weak as for the NY School of John Cage and other composers, but institutions legitimated the latter as artists, who did not need buyers to prove their entitlement. They had hesitant support from what was then called the Establishment, whom they could pressure into providing funds from time to time. They fed on small in-group enthusiasm boosted by publicized scandal but were soon to receive university favor, and the promise of reward unifies the hopeful allies. Free Jazz on the other hand would today certainly qualify as avant-garde, but it went unnoticed by those critics most engaged in avant-garde promotion and analysis.[70] They weren't invited to tour the big universities across the country, as was John Cage. On the contrary, Free Jazz lacked the financial promise that would have persuaded more musicians to follow it. It was even generated by division, where politics, culture, and music as personal expression were intertwined.[71]

This was a player-advocated music of an integral community that played sessions regularly, not merely the individualized voices the world wanted to hear. This community was an outcast defender of its artistic status at a time before "outcast" was appropriated and recuperated as marginalized and worthy.[72] Commercially-based performers are entertainers under contract to at least attempt to reach the audience. In the collectivity of jazz musicians, decisions of what to play depended on hearing each other, being inspired to follow or invent for oneself, and assuming that others would do the same. Players were both self-determining and proud to lead others. To a greater extent than any other public music they were playing *for each other*. Critics and audience however expected the musicians to play *for them*-- after all they were paying the bill. Without intending to, Free Jazz exposed the commercial support system undergirding the very existence of jazz, such that henceforth "Jazz Means Freedom" would have to ignore them. Jazz was not alone here. What growth in acceptance and numbers today cannot hide was part of a much wider shift in how art is understood in relation to audience and the wider world, and how those dedicated strictly to creative work are treated.

The association of Free Jazz with the Black Power movement, Black Culture and separatism was also detrimental to its sales figures. Revisiting that earlier discussion, Amiri Baraka saw black musicians in general as "the lowest class of Negroes,"[73] in fact more authentically representing black people than writers, whom he felt were compromised by both white *and* black middle class culture. This was an intentional slap in the face to those who could not appreciate jazz if they thought the musicians were in a class with dishwashers. Baraka and others later in the Black Arts Movement faced a dilemma. They wanted to unify blacks on the basis of their cultural and historical distinction from whites, yet to advance with the boldness of an avant-garde was a move of European (white) origin. Their aim *as artists* was to break out of the curse of presumed difficulty derived from Modernism, yet to do so *as blacks*, by gaining an audience among the black populace for an end run around white resistance to the black avant-garde. In material terms this failed; the earlier black audience for jazz had declined and the new generation wanted soul music in their lives. In that case, at least for the moment the black avant-garde could only survive under the terms of the music industry and institutions it had opposed.

Black Nationalism urged the unity of black people; whites took that unity as a literal fact rather than largely the dream of a handful of writers and organizers. In those days of urban rebellion the shift from civil rights to an overt demand for power and armed community self-defense, this music translated as unassimilable politics, as "difficult" as its musicology. It rose on a tide increasingly radical, and by 1968 its inability to gain more of a foothold in the established world was shared by the more radical white political dissidents. Significantly, conductor and composer Leonard Bernstein, who epitomized the liberal high art music establishment, attended the initial Coleman performance in 1959. Thereafter he paid no attention to Free Jazz, yet he threw a donation party for the Black Panther Party, which aimed to arm the black communities.[74] Musical radicalism, which had no weapons but sound, could not be bent to the needs of radical chic.

In the minds of granting agencies the association of music with racial politics would add to the reasons for refusing the funding available to other, similar but white groups of artists. Some of these were more openly political, in a countercultural and explicitly anti-war direction. They held political and cultural positions more plausible to the media; even if vilified they got attention.

Comparison to the poetry scene is striking. Many of the musicians shared the same few blocks of the Lower East Side and were reaching similar café audiences. Unlike the black musicians, the poets were shifting towards audience engagement: "The avant-garde is less about change in the arts than it is about genuine experimentation in social relations."[75] Poets may have initially thought their audience would widen, as did the avant-garde jazz musicians, riding on the expectation that cultural change in their direction would follow persistent commitment.[76] Through press attention to their politics and provocative language, not to their poetry, the scene was lifted out of obscurity. The NY underground poets were frequently jailed for obscenity and their public readings shut down by police, all of which got a NY Times notice as sensational news, publicity the musicians never had.

Their poetry had broken with literary tradition by following the European counter-tradition, which provided a clear target in New Criticism, dominant in publishing and academia. This made them look like a bona fide manifesto-waving avant-garde facing an entrenched Establishment. With open readings they were easily strengthened by new recruits, whose scribbled thoughts over morning coffee qualified as poetry, a contrast with the musician community, which demanded instrument skills from its members. Technology also came to their aid; the mimeograph revolution begun in the fifties allowed poetry to escape the publishers' grasp, as print-on-demand does today. It was a far cry from the high-tech recording studio musicians had to depend on. While originally the poetry scene was vociferously anti-academic, anti-competitive and egalitarian, soon poets were selectively siphoned off by the universities. This carried them into a phase where the expected cultural and social transformation could be indefinitely delayed. As obscenity became legally disregarded their Cause was winnable within the emerging postmodern paradigm of pluralistic toleration.

No matter how upsetting was the Downtown music scene of the New York School, performance ("happenings"), and the avant-garde of poetry and dance (the first art to be explicitly called "postmodern"), they all profited from being what the media, government and critics felt obligated to comprehend and appear somewhat sympathetic to. On one hand they ("the Establishment"), like music educators at the time, feared the situation would get out of hand. On the other hand, their ranks were divided. The major media were dealing with a revolt of their own successor generation, which they couldn't dismiss wholesale, whereas they could not imagine a black avant-garde except as an external social/musical threat, which, given the liberal cant that "to understand is to forgive," *should not* be comprehended. At best writers covering the arts for the largest publications could ignore it rather than bring it up for debate. As for the bulk of the poets, after being chased out of coffee houses they found a home in St. Marks Church. For a crucial two years beginning in 1966 federal funding was obtained for the Poetry Project, although it was earmarked for social work with youth (which they mostly ignored). Followed by other grants, the Poetry Project is still in existence, whereas the collective projects of the sixties avant-garde jazz community were rarely funded and did not survive.

As important as was the opposition of some critics to Free Jazz, its association with Black Power, and the lack of institutional and record company support, the collapse of Free Jazz cannot be attributed solely to these. Earlier mentioned was the importance of feeling as a component of jazz. When players are more concerned with expansion of feeling than musicological advance, the music gets to be called "self-indulgence" and "masturbatory." That reaction is a fearful act of purification that slices off deep desire, need and feeling from the music. What was allowed success was in part what philosopher Herbert Marcuse called "repressive desublimation," when the dominant culture finds that passionate expression can be rendered harmless through careful framing and interpretation. The spontaneous feeling of Free Jazz ran into the fear that unleashed eros will tear us apart. As free love became normalized and commodified as routine casual sex, Free Jazz faced the same shutting down. The vision that feeling could break the mechanisms of the social order had to be abandoned.

On another front there appeared the shift of audience from critical art to popular culture, a sign of emergent postmodernism, touched on earlier. Through the fifties and early sixties there was a middle class of philistines, who dismissed the new art out of hand ("my kid coulda done that"), but also a younger public that wanted the philistines to get their comeuppance. Those who flooded the October Revolution in 1964, staged not in the club scene but around the corner from Columbia University, had a modernist temperament and education. They were primarily white, liberal arts/college–educated, and from "permissive" middle class families. They took the humanities seriously and thought it related to life: "art yields more truth than any other intellectual activity."[77]

This audience had imbibed the literary complaint against civilization, honoring from a distance irrational Dionysian joy and release, the heart of darkness to which Joseph Conrad's hero Kurtz had been driven. The image of the "crazy" jazz musician tantalizing Norman Mailer's "white negro" (1957) was in the air; perhaps the most authentic art would come from the despised, who held a dark secret. Jazz had originally gained its place at a time when "the primitive" had been discovered as an argument against Victorian social order. Dancing wildly to "jungle music" represented the challenge of the pleasure principle to the reality-based work ethic. Whites who wanted release from the taboo projected their unconscious on black musicians and imagined themselves dancing around the flames in an African village, even when the musicians were safely white. Later, when bebop tore off the white mask and forced the recognition that jazz was a black art form, whites who had mimicked Kurtz's "The horror! The horror!" could feel that to consume jazz and blues balanced against the rationalistic order. At the same time it demonstrated they were unprejudiced, on the right and rational moral side of history.

The middle-brow press, which had given the abstract expressionists and then the beats their attention, encouraged and shaped this college-educated public. (Researchers into 21st century politics accused of racism please take note; poor whites were considered uneducable white trash.) Despite popular anti-intellectualism, the broad faith in Progress was strong enough to protect many elites—scientific, educational, and artistic—who openly denied the validity of mass public taste, opinion polls, and common sense opinions. The avant-garde contributed to this image of the artist by ostracizing those who "went commercial" or "went Hollywood" as inauthentic. Meanwhile the everyday social order was loose enough for interstices that enabled artists to survive--stores that kept a tab, ways to skip out of debts and responsibilities, and cheap rent. The image of artist as bohemian rebel served the better-heeled youth of the early sixties.

Past that time the cartoon of whites being boiled in the African village pot was no longer funny—it was the liberals' goose that was being cooked. Those committed to what was increasingly called "the revolution," thought to be inevitable, also feared it for not knowing what form it would take, perhaps including their own apocalyptic death. Those rising against civilization were blacks targeting white stores; this was close to home for the white spectators. In the midst of this Free Jazz, seemingly off the leash, appeared as the return of the repressed--vengeance on the social order and contempt for helping-hand liberals. To link the orgiastic music and the collective violence of the burning cities gave a sinister twist to the modernist belief that "art and not ethics constitutes the essential metaphysical activity of man."[78] Those attracted despite this still had to face the gulf of distance. Musicians were a class apart, professionals who lived a precarious life; all the audience could do was buy records, go to concerts.

Later-sixties Free Jazz was looking for an audience at a time when those attracted to a wild experience could find it in a different new thing, rock. Here lyrics and volume expressed a more engaged and demanding, larger and less elite demographic. Instrumentals borrowed heavily from the authenticity-based blues revival earlier and jazzed the core harmonics and beat. While rock was a music *for* the mass, *Ascension* was *of* the mass, with solo voices submerged and then emerging as if buoyed up and fully dependent on the others. Coltrane's phalanx of musicians, joined as no orchestra had ever been, signified musicians standing in for humanity. This was a working model of how bodies can relate and create, a musical version of the populace joined together and conscious of what they were about. Free Jazz could only appeal through unamplified, direct individual musical experience and hard choice, available mostly on records and not reinforced by mass appeal. The mass that rock heralded was unified electrically by amplification, McLuhan's virtual global village. They broke down the fences to concerts but were worshippers of heroes from their own ranks who, like Janis Joplin, told them to be non-conformists. They believed they were; henceforth the postwar nonconformism of a few evolved to become a mass consumer taste.

In addition to the industry shift to the popular side of music, the economic division of white artist and black entertainer was still in full force. Free Jazz musicians' body of work might be art but their function was still entertainer. They were as far from the taste of the jazz audience as French cubism initially was from the art-buying public of its era, but they had no angelic patrons (like Gertrude Stein and her brother) to sustain them over the long haul. Nor did they have a powerful "discoverer," as Bob Dylan had found in John Hammond, only a handful of fans, critics and producers who ultimately had to go with the flow of audience rejection. They were more truly "on their own with no direction home" than the author of those lyrics.

Their option, to cast themselves as a modernist avant-garde, proved to be problematic for improvisers. Continental Europe was the birthplace of Modernism, and under it scores were often confined to a drawer, paintings were sold cheap and re-sold dear thirty years later, but even wet they had the aura of a material thing, a work of art and an imaginary posterity. For artists to assume that few would like their work was an incentive; they were even expected to create for Art alone. What the middle class didn't like immediately was still given a reserved space; the avant-garde might know something the unsure public had yet to learn. The French might laugh at their intellectual class but then posthumously named streets after them, which encouraged the next generation. Scorn, disgust, and critical and popular invective was the prelude to later critical and institutional acceptance.

This part-mythical trajectory was nothing like the market obsolescence Free Jazz faced. Poor musicians who at times went hungry couldn't wait for it to kick in. Many had day gigs, but to legitimate a "bread" gig without a sense of shame was still waiting for the DIY performer, who doesn't hanker after artist legitimacy. The prized work of Modernism was far removed from the mostly unrecorded performances at an East Village coffee shop. European composers survived providing scores of interest only to the next generation of avant-gardists and a few musicologists, whereas once played, the music known as Free Jazz would be gone forever and could not pay the rent today. That was the cynical side of what "spiritual" meant; an empty substitute for what you could take to the bank. Free Jazz had only a few years before record companies concluded it was not going to work, which was their reasonable decision. The record and club business depended on people buying the music *now*, and after testing it too many people ran for the exit.

Not until the mid-sixties did baby-boomers begin making significant demands. The popular keynote was "relevance," the demand of youth for their taste to be patronized and commodified. The upheaval in the academic world eventually contributed to this: under the guise of anti-elitism a new consensus was to be established. Early sixties New Left radicals had condemned liberal academics as aloof from political reality. As some of the later radicals entered academia they made a similar charge against those who refused to think in terms of popular taste and the consumer market. That would include sixties NY avant-gardes, for whom Pop Art was a joke on consumerism (which, as it *became* popular culture, backfired on them). They flaunted their distance from the American hinterland, suburban complacency, and mass produced culture. After all, the majority culture and populace had supported the American War against Vietnam through the sixties, and to resist that war was the firm political position of the artists. It wasn't until the early 70s, as the result of a vocal and disruptive minority, that a majority came to oppose the war, enabling a shrewd politician like Tricky Dick Nixon to begin withdrawal. Only then was it possible to proclaim "the people" and popular culture as holding the higher ground. An avant-garde that resisted them was unworthy of support and attention, if not passé. Like other aspects of the counterrevolution, the academic populists got to call passé those who once thought *they* were the future. Whether it was collapse or transformation of the various artistic and political movements, it was across the board.

What happened with Free Jazz was an early sign of the decline of New York as the home and shelter of modernist musical advance, and beyond that, of the general assumption that a true cultural center must find a place for radical challenge. Such a center has always been defined as a spot on the map for whatever goes beyond mass taste, historically the role of cities. The rise of private, digitally dispersed, abstract listening, among other things, seems to have finally doomed this to a myth lacking any real substance.

Gradually the ranks of the sixties musicians engaged in free form playing in New York were depleted, and by the early 70s all but a few had dialed down their wildness and turned to more conventional forms.[79] The move to Europe was ironic for those who scorned the European contribution to jazz structures, but at least in France of the late 60s, at the height of its revolutionary period, they found some immediate response and financial support. Francophone North Africa, a heritage of the former French Empire and a strong presence in France, was partly the reason for ex-pat black Americans to choose France; also in 1969 the French BYG Actuel label invited them to record, although this boon was as short-lived as in the states.

In the diaspora a few were picked up by mostly high-priced, liberal east coast colleges as authentic avant-garde artists, hopeful to attract liberal students.[80] Some, such as Steve Lacy, said they had gone as far as they could go, nothing more worth doing in this direction, so for them the abandonment was voluntary; they had other options. The communal solidarity that had nurtured them and integrated new players was largely reduced to personal relationships, with a huge dose of bitterness for some.[81] Then as now romanticized tragedy is thought the natural fate of black avant-gardes (as earlier, "cursed" French poets); they must die in order to be rewarded with immortality. "Bird Lives" (which I saw graffitied on a wall near my high school in 1955) indicated the earlier death of the bebop era, mourned partly because it had triumphed as a conventional style.

By the mid-70s the most visible survivor of the sixties movement who still played in the same direction was Cecil Taylor. Though his performances were scattered, in his fame and continued presence on the scene he summed up and concentrated the past for the public that had known it. Besides occasional appearances by him and a few others, recordings from the sixties inspired those just coming into free playing, like myself. Yet in sharp contrast to today, it was near-impossible to find players open to free playing.[82] A Canadian film made in 1981 (*Imagine the Sound*) contained anecdotal remarks and short clips with some of the principals from the sixties—Bill Dixon, Archie Shepp, Paul Bley, and Cecil Taylor—but only Taylor was playing outside the usual jazz format.[83] The loose compositional structure of Free Jazz and the solo format could be duplicated, as could the playing styles, but the time of bringing new ideas to the table was past.

Diaspora is not death. There were strong individual exceptions, who have contributed to the fortunes of current free and avant jazz. Cecil Taylor taught in a variety of situations for short periods and influenced many of those currently playing today. On the strength of his reputation he could pull together ensembles that included non-students wherever he went to play his compositions, in which periods of free jazz were scored. Bill Dixon and Milford Graves taught at Bennington College and created a small cadre of students, who with other such students seeded groups playing today. The strongest organization to come out of the sixties that advocated for the jazz avant-garde was the Creative Music Studio (CMS), a school headed by vibraphonist Karl Berger. It lasted for fifteen years at Woodstock NY (1971-1984) and has since been revived and received funding. It offered paying students workshops with the most prominent sixties players and attracted a generation of younger players eager to identify with the avant-garde legacy. The CMS direction was not freeform playing per se but jazz-structured improvisation of original compositions. One went to CMS either as a student or one of the stars, not as a peer, or even potentially one, as were the newcomers such as Archie Shepp in the earlier days.

Free jazz continued as a musical style in small Manhattan venues and lofts, attended by some earlier converts and cognoscenti but less accessible to the general public. Seventies Loft Jazz included some Chicago Art Ensemble musicians, otherwise participants were mostly new to the scene.[84] The end of Free Jazz visibility and conflict did not keep musicians from moving to New York to inhabit its original home. Their numbers were not insignificant, some getting to play with remaining sixties jazz and Free Jazz musicians, but the context of their playing had radically changed.

The collapse of Free Jazz as a movement helped clear the path for a time when *every* music had to be popular if it was to provide its musicians with a sense of legitimacy. That meant they must find an audience that consumes only what it is comfortable with, which excludes the shock and ambivalence the earlier avant-garde provoked. To get more people coming in the door would be the work of musicians with the right attitude and aura, stabilized playing patterns, and marketing that characterizes it attractively, matching up each music with an appropriate audience.

4. Free Jazz in Revival

The late 80s and early 90s was a turning point for the kind of playing found in the second wave of sixties Free Jazz. With only a few of the musicians from that earlier period still committed and performing, most would be relative newcomers. Keeping the faith with Free Jazz had been the tone of the 70s loft scene, which by the next decade had disappeared. Given the new political climate and generational change in the 80s, the remaining musicians could no longer align with rebellion, only its symbolic form. Free jazz became part of the resistance to the counter-revolution that was so eager to suppress the sixties memory. Public performance and recordings would continue as a genre in its own right rather than a movement *within* jazz. Only then could it gather commercial strength in this climate. Growth would depend not on the small older audience committed from the sixties but one with only an image of that music, to which it was attached for current cultural and social-political reasons. The merging of musicians and audience interest around a common playing style was the only way for free jazz to become a national phenomenon outside the jazz music world.[85]

Fundamental to the revival in NY were the efforts of William Parker and his wife Patricia. Parker, the native New York double bassist, learned music from jazz musicians in the informal mentoring tradition. He has been active in the NY avant-garde scene since the early 70s, having doggedly maintained his free playing along with large group compositions. These had been the especial practice of avant-garde jazz musicians, following Coltrane's *Ascension* and earlier "schools" such as Lennie Tristano's and Charles Mingus's. The driving energy music of the sixties became the core aesthetic of the Vision Festival that William and Patricia organized, still going strong today after twenty years (2016). The revival returned a few of the survivors from the sixties to a performing life and broadened to include some of the white avant-jazz scene. The musicians have not followed the dictates of sixties black nationalism but relied strongly on the spiritual and cultural side. Audience support was boosted by record companies that began to reissue earlier Free Jazz as well as unreleased material gathering dust in their storerooms.

The revival in New York was augmented a decade later by something similar in Chicago, which would reach national media attention via a young white reed player, Ken Vandermark, the son of a prominent critic. Unlike the struggling free jazz musicians in NY, and those of local Chicago fame earlier such as saxophonist Fred Anderson (who nurtured much of the scene) and Hal Russell (and his NRG Ensemble), Vandermark was boosted by a $265k "Genius Grant" in 1999 from the Chicago-based MacArthur Foundation. He reinforced Chicago free jazz by bringing especially prominent Germans to Chicago. Of all the Europeans it was they who had most imbibed the earlier NY jazz avant-garde and had gained media legitimation beyond the original enthusiasts. Other continental Europeans were also welcomed into Chicago free jazz, far more than New York, which as the original home of Free Jazz favored its own musicians.

In order to advance the free jazz project it has been defined as broadly as possible; the limit has been jazz. The Vision Festival has been its gathering point, and it defines what it does as "a disciplined disregard for traditional boundaries."[86] To disregard is to go out; to be disciplined is to stay firmly within, a bounded freedom; free jazz sits in the middle of a contradiction. "Tradition" here is what Classic Jazz has defined; what the musicians turned into their own tradition was free jazz, to disregard which would have been self-contradictory. It would have no characteristics, obviously untrue. To break boundaries has been the general claim for the non-conventional arts since the 80s, the most important sign of allegiance to the sixties past. The discipline is two-fold: externally to survive, internally to maintain the characteristics of Free Jazz as the core aesthetic and home base. In a blind listening test the original and later versions are very similar, yet musicians creating it new in a tumultuous period, when free and straight-ahead were mutually subject to pressures, are in a different situation from those following a now-conventional model. The relation to the world, the very meaning of the music in its context, is not going to be the same. [87]

A style continuous from the 70s until the present can be abstracted apart from that of individual players. Following straight-ahead jazz, instrumentation is acoustic, at times altered by electronics but no invented instruments, computer electronics, or pre-recorded sounds. As with most jazz and popular musics, lead and backup (rhythm section) are usually distinguished, the latter constant and the lead taking long solos, with rhythm section players often taking individual solos while the leads are silent. As with small-group jazz the focus is on the soloists, not the composition; in free jazz the latter is minimal, yet performances aren't composition-free jam sessions. A piece is the length of a set, as with the later Coltrane, not one tune among several. Usually there is a basic structure framing the piece but not a key that continues into the solos, and it often lacks the ABA form of even Ayler's pieces. Compositions are one-offs, not tunes popular with audiences that other musicians would pick up later. At times playing might come close to non-jazz free improvisation, a blur of notes that seems purely textural, but then convention rules. For instance beginnings and endings are intentionally clear, as common to all musics whose implicit aim is performance.

Intensity of the playing is the standard, and requires every instant to be filled with sound. For the saxophone, Coltrane's later sound and upper range is honored and his hard-blowing style is common for other instruments as well. Players are trained in the so-called "real" notes of Western acoustic instruments based on fingerings any music teacher would approve, with occasional overblowing and growling as embellishment. Drums are essential for maintaining pulse, usually overlaid and hidden but still needed to create the forward drive expected of free jazz. Playing volume ranges from moderate to loud, but never to the level of highly amplified noise music, and virtually no slow, quiet playing, which for most audience would signal a drop in intensity.

From the above it should be clear that free jazz bypasses the first wave of sixties Free Jazz, a distinction that needs some elaboration. Musicians of most genres aim to play close to what they perceive audiences will understand and be able to judge. Sometimes they can teach audiences new things to listen for, but are expected to reassure through markers of the genre. Especially during the first wave, standard technique and the jazz code were the presumed ground for the hierarchy of respect from beginners to masters. The audience would have absorbed that code, the chords and structure that underlay those sophisticated harmonic flights, hence the shock—and thrill-- of hearing them violated. So much of bebop had been ironic or parodic twists in relation to its past and to popular tunes. Just as a joke falls flat outside a cultural background, one cannot catch that irony without knowing what is being ironized. Musically, Coleman was just as interested in pitches as the bebop players were, and among the audience for early sixties Free Jazz were expert listeners who "got" the twisting he was doing. Those of the first wave like Don Cherry took care to bend strings of pitches in unique ways; an audience would be impressed today, but most would lack the ears to delight in the nuances.

By the late 80s that earlier audience was largely gone, and without it players have had no reason to pursue the skill and playfulness of the early Free Jazz era. Why bother with all that learning if it falls on deaf ears? the musician might say. Second-wave playing can largely be imitated as a style without it. "Notey" playing often qualifies to get praise, where any pitches are equally good so long as they come fast and furious. That was not true of the late Coltrane (especially *Interstellar Space*), where every pitch gives the feel (to my ears) of precisely what it should be (Coltrane: "If we only knew the right notes..."). What is copied is not his huge harmonic vocabulary and inventiveness but the emotive quality and drive, as if the musicians are like him in reaching beyond their limits. There are obviously some very skilled free jazz musicians, whose choices tease the ears into rapt attention, but to please those critical early sixties ears would be far more challenging than today's.

Why did free jazz musicians not begin a third wave of Free Jazz, instead duplicating what had come before? The general answer is that conditions differed from the 60s as well as the early 80s. The rebellions of the 60s were replaced by resistance to the counter-revolution of the 80s, and all media-dependent, career-worthy art has had to adapt to neoliberal and postmodern conditions. To help explain this, the situation of more acceptable, "mainstream" jazz must be taken into account, for it had come out victorious in the contest over the identity of jazz.

To deter the leftist politics precipitated by the earlier dissident generation, Reagan advocated for an uncritical image of America, which involved a denunciation of sixties cultural initiatives. Musical radicalism in the form of Free Jazz was one of those, and was now confronted with a strong opponent in the form of a reformulated and resurrected mainstream.

As a promotional and polemical term "mainstream" implies resistance to fashion. In the postwar forties, it referred to small groups that avoided bebop improvising and continued in the swing style. The term indicated authenticity and popularity at a time when swing was actually losing its market. The clever term, like Reagan's "Heartland America," connotes the will of a majority, but is actually only one demographic among others. Marketers attempt to pair each with an appropriate music. Mainstream also implied that its content follows a consistent ruling tradition, which presumes a stable audience taste over time, but as an industry term the content has changed with the decades. In the sixties it was no longer swing, but then-conventional club music that had incorporated bebop, its former antagonist. It was under heavy assault from critics who supported the avant-garde, the effect of which was far wider than its admirers. In the seventies mainstream referred to acoustic jazz that resisted fusion and the avant-garde both. Today "mainstream" has entered the vocabulary as a widely-applicable adjective, since there are now multiple musics, each with its most homogenized and commercially successful center, which gets promoted as its main stream. As such it's no longer necessary to claim that a mainstream follows a ruling tradition. There can even be a mainstream avant-garde, whatever cops the prize of the greatest respectability.

By the late 70s, with sixties radicality now as a passé underground style, the record industry had reorganized its priorities. One target was the upward-mobile segment that had adopted liberal, multicultural politics, an expanded version of those earlier attracted to radical chic. Like the earlier sixties blues and folk audience, it was seeking progressive social meaning and cultural authenticity. That was the market for the new mainstream, now with a content defined even more aggressively as the full and exclusive meaning of jazz. It was the most respectable jazz, to be sure.

As a phenomenon of postwar culture the search for authenticity is the hope to escape the anxiety of living in a world where the pieces don't fit nicely together and disturbing emotions are quick to surface. Solace is found in a constructed, bowdlerized past; as with the media and high school treatment of American History it can be politely called a "usable past." It is meant to be bought and bought into such that American culture is perceived as the triumph of goodness rather than trauma and violence, traces of which are ignored or treated as evil that has been almost completely stamped out. The constructed authenticity is henceforth *the* tradition, sanctioned by a narrative that will send an unequivocal message of progress.

For those who needed to recover from the disturbing sixties, and their own youthful exuberance, there was a project to enshrine jazz as the most genuinely American music *and* the one that represented the American racial "other" in the light most favorable to patriotism. For this the title Classic Jazz was promoted, which later critics more accurately called "neo-traditional" jazz.[88] "Classic" assimilates jazz to the European tradition but is even more ruling and inflexible. Its canon of entries implies that jazz lacks present creative initiatives, only loyal re-creators and sustainers, suitable for a middle class audience eager to think itself educated. "Classic" Jazz is a narrative that begins in the erotic desire and physical energy of a disfranchised people and ends up satisfying the image of a well-ordered society.[89] "Neo-traditional" would indicate that what goes under the title is a partisan opinion, and not the broad agreement that "classic" implies. I will mostly use the first since it is better known as a specific project, while "neo-traditional" is the more general trend, which could be applied to several other musics today as well (rather than "classic" rock, for instance).

Besides being cultural capital for a progressive and educated audience, Classic Jazz also appeared to converge with black demands for official respect. Jazz musicians who came across as the real deal could act as examples for a compliant audience. This they could not have done for the aficionados of the earlier generation, who would often take the magazine critics—and the musicians--to task. For those who expected music to be part of their present, changing experience, Classic Jazz would turn them against jazz.

An even greater market for jazz was an audience quite uninterested in authenticity or jazz history, preferring instead an entertainment music highly produced and shorn of anything jarring or lacking full melodic continuity. For them the industry created smooth jazz, led by a white sax player, Kenny G. Jazz-identified musicians still consider him an inauthentic fraud and worse, a usurper for taking the market lead.[90] Unlike the bowdlerizers of Classic Jazz, he and his audience had no resistance to the post-production manipulation and synthesized sounds common to other popular musics. The irony often present in jazz improvisation, and the intelligence and originality of complicated chord changes found in Classic Jazz was lost on this demographic.

The two-fold refashioning of the market was a makeover of jazz (later came the proliferation of jazz hybrids, equally detested by Classic Jazz defenders, further marking them as purists). What had earlier been a contentious whole now bore separate titles and audiences that could be served separate dishes. Classic jazz would be heard as serious art music and the other as light entertainment, the two split as never before--one music for the classes, another for the masses. The "jazz wars" would henceforth be fights over pieces of the pie rather than factional struggles over the to-be-determined future of jazz. Industry and institutional backing for Classic Jazz was so strong that the opinions of older musicians, those who had created its content but were alienated by the new formulation, had no outlet or effect on sales or funding. There was no room for new musical ideas or even many of the older ones, as had been possible when the intra-active collectivity of players had some authority that the music world recognized.

The chief creator of Classic Jazz was trumpet player Wynton Marsalis. Finding a welcome home in Manhattan at the Lincoln Center, the locus of the European classical tradition since 1962, Marsalis and the writer Albert Murray initiated a series of concerts in 1988, following years of preparation. His configuration of jazz was later reinforced for a mass audience by documentarist Ken Burns in his 2000 PBS series *Jazz*, whose main commentator was Marsalis, joined by musicians and critics who seemed to agree with the neo-traditional thesis. One was Stanley Crouch, an earlier advocate of both Free Jazz (he had been a drummer) and Black Nationalism, and later equally vociferous as a turncoat against his earlier positions on the black avant-garde. The film narrative meant to set in stone the borders of jazz and to close debate. Marsalis often repeated how "American" jazz was, designed for pluralistic democracy, as if opposition to his view could only be racist. The grit and turbulence of jazz was swept under the rug, turning it into a luxury commodity and eminently teachable to every new generation, without having to re-work the lecture notes.

In content, Classic Jazz was a repertory of successive musical styles intended to encompass the origins of jazz up through the sixties, the decade of its presumed demise. The construct was politically and aesthetically selective, with the new sixties initiatives positioned as the decline. Unlike earlier jazz styles that competed with each other (New Orleans Jazz, Swing, Bebop), Classic Jazz was presented as the inclusive narrative that transcended all the others, the final version of jazz, which would preserve it forever as its definitive, scholarly bio. It pictured jazz as a story made from whole cloth, with the most recent movements torn off for ruining the design. Free Jazz an aberration, effectively resurrecting the charge that it was "anti-jazz." A companion to the neo-con philosophy around the same time, it was a counter-attack on the sixties, seeking to establish a clear line between truth and falsehood, good and evil. This rejection was no novelty, for it followed the views of a large portion of the sixties jazz audience, which had felt betrayed by its most honored heroes. Targeted also was the "electric period" of Marsalis's bête noire, trumpeter Miles Davis, the foil for his main hero, Louis Armstrong. Davis' *Bitches Brew* (1970) had offended many of the jazz audience and critics for crossing the acoustic line, as well as the genre and color line into rock music territory.

Classic Jazz identified the other main betrayer of audience taste as John Coltrane, the quintessential jazz artist for searching and developing new ideas. While Davis had moved towards the broad plain of mass commercial appeal, Coltrane was thought to have gone too far in the opposite direction, towards the thin edge of the avant-garde. In each case Marsalis split their legacies between authentic and inauthentic periods. The rebuke to Coltrane contradicted the practice of jazz musicians since bebop. To go "out" musicologically had been an imperative, and previously no limit had been defined. The true "nature" of jazz is nature itself, the chthonian depths of the crux that defies Apollonian reason and order, and weaves improvised, ephemeral webs like Coltrane's matrices in his final work that be cannot unfolded — inexplicable and mystifying. The rejection of Davis' later development was less of a contradiction, however, for it upheld the belief common even to Free Jazz that jazz could only be acoustic. Also, it had become taboo to follow mass taste, as presumably electric instrumentation did, especially to mess electronically with the sound of an acoustic instrument, as Davis did. The mainstream depended on the concept of a solid middle ground. Both men had challenged the jazz audience of the center, and it was that which Marsalis hoped to restore and back up with extensive rhetoric, organization, and support from cultural authorities and the jazz industry.

For the sixties player and audience a question could be raised whether a highly commoditized artist, who had needed the music world to help construct an image and build an audience, had a right to betray that investment. It would be like mocking the industry with one's strong fan base as a weapon. For Davis it was no problem, for it fit his persona as an uncontrollable rebel. And while some fans left, the jazz industry could present him now as crossing over to a wider audience, making him an even more profitable source of revenue. As for Coltrane, what kind of record contracts would he have gotten had he lived beyond 1967, given the situation of Free Jazz at that point?

Jazz at its height appeared to be an autonomous art at the whim of its most renowned artists; the music world would have to adjust. Revenge would come later, with the formulation and establishment of sobered-up Classic Jazz. That lesson has been absorbed: professional musicians of succeeding new generations (including avant jazz) are far less successful as commodities, yet they avoid taking such bold steps as their predecessors. The image of mediatized artists as autonomous has been sustained, though redefined, for they have no such license as Coltrane or Davis to define the potentially sprawling "it" of jazz.

At a time when the star of neoliberalism was ascendant, those aiming to make jazz safe for a unified commercial/state/educational sponsorship wanted to bury the artistic challenges of the sixties outside the walls, with no Antigone to mourn them. Free Jazz may have appeared dead in the water but for Marsalis and his colleagues the sea was only becalmed; it still haunted jazz. This is evident in the flashes of vindictive comments Burns included in his film, where ressentiment, Nietzsche's word for the weakness of moralists, rules. Marsalis' argument echoed modernist critics to the extent of thinking art is essentially form progressively evolved by geniuses, but for him form is not discovered anew in each aesthetic experience but is historically given. Like "America," it stands outside the immediacy of present experience. Modern art sought to make things about which we cannot know until after they appear (Theodor Adorno's aphorism). Marsalis would go the opposite direction, to purify the jazz identity, such that we can know exactly what it is. This would justify a jazz police qualified to guard the borders and check credentials. Marsalis claimed to validate "jazz in every form that it can be played," leaving out free-form playing, which he took to mean a formless blob. Also, although for him jazz is a form of improvised music, he distinguishes it from "improvised music." This put Free Jazz and its inheritors in the same boat with free improvisation that might have no anchoring jazz elements, thus muddying the distinction for the sake of the purity of the key signifier, jazz. (A decade later, free improvisers who thought they could purify themselves of the sexual juiciness of jazz would end up with the dry toast of experimentalism.) He also borrowed the same post-modern and neocon shibboleth "elite" to characterize his enemy, with himself on the side of the presumably oppressed people.[91]

Classic jazz improved the situation for some performers and led to the huge growth in jazz education, under whose regime normative jazz has survived. These institutions hire straight-ahead players, most of whom in their youth probably dreamed of being full-time performers. That Classic Jazz excised the sixties also helped stabilize the larger American culture in preparation for an unprecedented consumerization of art, and this impacted the remnant of sixties avant-garde musicians. By the time neo-traditional jazz was on the rise the avant-garde originators were no longer challenging those of the parent jazz tradition or each other. Cordoned off, it seemed there was nothing more to do in the free direction without stepping outside the main body of jazz. Anthony Braxton was the limit case in the 70s, an eccentric first hailed by critics looking for the next new voice of advanced jazz, but he moved away from identification with the jazz world to find a unique place of his own. What was possible for him at the time was to be the individualist artist without obligation to represent a titled music. Over time that position would be generalized, a figure not sharing in a collective movement but working as one's own boss, whose fortune depends on extra-musical abilities, contacts, and image.

Marsalis' formulation prompted a strong reaction from some scholars, who initiated a new critical Jazz Studies, demanding that at least the questions of jazz history and its relation to culture remain open.[92] For his *Jazz Among the Discourses* [1995], Krin Gabbard, a jazz trumpet player himself, collected those who took this direction. They came not from the music schools or journals but from English departments, where cultural critique was most likely to be found. Soon thereafter, Ajay Heble initiated the Jazz Festival and Colloquium at the University of Guelph in Canada, and a studies program there, "Improvisation, Community, and Social Practice." To the extent these scholars have engaged the present situation they have strongly backed the free jazz revival along some of the same lines as neo-traditional jazz. For them it is a progressive social practice, emphasizing its continuity with older jazz rather than examining its musicological tension with it. The academic interest follows the small but significant audience that has grown for free jazz, to which it has contributed with biographies similar to those of Classic Jazz figures.

As I approach the present era a general comment is in order: To portray the historical and social limits of our situation is like throwing a monkey wrench into the machinery of many who are actively creating music. Some are my own music partners, who would say they are just playing the music they love and not specifically free jazz. They share the feelings that motivate their playing with others, and that's a powerful, hidden incentive for what they do. I apologize to them, but ask them to recognize that even music that follows the banner of freedom is made under conditions that change over time. To live within an active movement that doesn't know its future, and to honor it as one's musical standard and limit—these are two different things. Where could free playing take us today? is an absurd question once we recognize that the situation of Free Jazz musicians is not ours today. To examine those different conditions sympathetically yet critically releases us to restore internal movement to Free Jazz, a true honoring of their spirit.

For musicians to assert their freedom from many musical norms in the sixties marked them publicly as rebellious, at a time when that distinction had an audience to be reckoned with. They paralleled other avant-gardes, who all appeared as transgressors, which power would punish if it could not manage and incorporate them. Twenty-some years after that moment had passed the rebellious spirit could be represented in a form that threatened no one. Once turned into a normative music for a particular demographic, the risk of transgression that musicians earlier faced collapses. The music gains in stability and predictability, lending itself to niche market creation where the originators failed. Rebellion becomes incorporated into the range of available musics as the *permanent* outside of jazz—Free Jazz recuperated in the form of a proxy.[93] With it stabilized, those following it can feel it represents their stubborn resistance to the present order, honoring it as if Free Jazz is still standing tall against a world of rejection.

The immediate post-war version of artist rebellion was collective and snowballing, not the teenage rebel without a cause who resolves into an atomized adult consumer. Rebellion is only a social threat when it arises in frustration with what is perceived as a static and oppressive collective situation, which the rebels believe their action *can* change because on some level it *is already* changing and provoking reaction. To change that perception to one of fluidity and toleration is the corrective to it, for it appears that the rebellion has achieved its goals. In music new faces appear as avatars of the old gods, or at least as worshippers in the same pews as the consumers. A musician might have gone off the straight road, thinking to carve a path for others, but comrades appear only given a general spirit of frustration and belief in their dream world. If the music world authorizes a niche for an avant-garde "rebellious spirit," then frustration will be systemically channeled and disruption will be illusory. The respected and rewarded artist will still be the one who struggles for a better world, but on that world's laid-out terms.

Calling Free Jazz musicians the Black Avant-garde had not been intended to help them gain acceptance among (primarily white) jazz fans. It only did so in the mid-70s, after the fires had gone out and nationalism among blacks had peaked. The identity then became a positive signifier for some college youth, who didn't know they were hearing a remnant of survivors. The nationalist view of Free Jazz put it on a path where, if it failed to become the successor to earlier jazz innovations *or* gain a recognized position within the black community, it would be isolated. Between a rock and a hard place is exactly what happened. On the one hand, the black populace had little interest in it, on the other, the militancy of the sixties black-cultural position ended up aiding eighties neo-traditionalism, which portrayed its truncated version of jazz as representing *the* achievement of black people. Given the political shift between these periods, which few could have predicted, neo-traditionalism had the power to exclude from its pantheon as wreckers and haters of jazz precisely the next agency of jazz re-invention, Baraka's Black Avant-garde. Adding insult to injury, Marsalis threw the "elite avant-garde" in the garbage bag with "improvised music," which would include (European) free improvisation, meaning that Avant-garde was not black enough. This defines "elite" as whatever the populace, in this case blacks, find difficult to accept. Like the neo-cons, who finally triumphed in the 2016 election, Marsalis embodied the powerful wolf in the sheep's clothing of populism.

Jazz musicians who had not been part of Free Jazz had no effective means to resist Classic Jazz; though it cut them off from their peers, it seemed to laud them. The tilt of musicians' heads to the applause meter is their endemic weakness. Taking action fell to those most stung by the exclusion, those dedicated to sixties Free Jazz. To defend it required organizing concerts of all those like-minded and rallying those resisting the Marsalis effort. It also meant promoting figures from the storied past, an outsider parallel to the neo-traditional canon that would show that Free Jazz had survived. To hold that past in reverence meant to treat the earlier figures as absolute models, an inspiration to later musicians if not their very reason for entering the jazz field. In the later context however their earlier role would be transformed. In their day they had encouraged young musicians and each other to go beyond their limits and create the future. They had occupied roughly the same dissident cultural space as the sexual revolution, rock music, the New Left, and all the proliferating anti-war, Civil Rights and liberation movements. Now their iconicity referred to the bygone past. To advance down the same path seemed foreclosed by the sound defeat before: "Let's not try that again."

This direction had already attracted the recording industry. As for other sixties phenomena and Classic Jazz, the market value of the icon, now permanently enshrined, was not lost on it. Along with CD technology and an audience prepared to imbibe the past would come a flood of re-releases and discovered tapes. These ventures would be more profitable than the risky first ones, which besides low sales always had studio costs to cover. For some musicians and audience, their own past was fed back to them, better than ever, a reassurance that sixties values survived despite repression.

What now achieved value could not be a music of exploration, truly and affirmatively "something else," outside the felt boundaries of entertainment. For the time of Coleman's album that would be what psychologist Jacques Lacan called "surplus enjoyment," or *jouissance* (also the word for sexual coming, not unlike the gizzum of "jazz"). What goes beyond pleasure does not extend it but is unpredictable and therefore not necessarily pleasant, art that can evoke disgust and trouble. This alone has the chance to change the horizon of what is possible. It cannot be satisfied by entertainment categories but dissolves their commoditized form. This is what drives musicians out of any niche, ghetto, or private playing and onto the most public stage that will allow them to proclaim their defiance, and it drove Free Jazz in its time.

To our ears today Coleman's early music has strong roots in the genres--blues, gospel, and modern, even fifties cool jazz. Unable to hear this at the time, many were shocked and violated, while others thrilled at its radicality--and at how upsetting it was to *others*. We cannot reconstruct those ears or the music's divisiveness. Over time musicians, audiences, critics, and the record industry sorted themselves out. "Jazz," came to include this and exclude that as a fixed line, and powerful institutions adopted that model as most consistent with their purposes. Jazz became an historical event that was untouchable and inflexible. It ceased to be living history, which depends on the tensions of the present tense—*here is our situation now*. The iconicized rebels were no longer any kind of threat; they were deprived of the pathway to the audience that had once debated how to listen to them. Defeated, they had at least succeeded in frightening people into silencing their message.

In returning to the marketplace as a classic form, free jazz would have to create and inhabit a visible space (market, reputations, funding, academic acceptance, loyal audience) in harmony with the social order. The belated victory was possible on the assumption that it would not encourage the recurrence of the earlier disruption. Given attachment to the norms of what is marked as "outside" turf, one can then only take a rebellious *stance*, an image frozen in place like a tableau vivant of the gods. It cannot encourage actual assault on the fortress, for which the word "success" is always problematic.

That stance is today bound up with one's reputation as culturally marginal. It is how all dissent gets characterized, stabilized, and validated in a society defined as heterogeneous —dissent is tolerated as a marginal difference others respect without having to consider. Here difference refers not only to marketing demographics and minimal musical individuality but also to antagonism and political value. It's the new isolationist version of the liberal social compact: you can ignore me—and the music that expresses my identity--if I can ignore you. Reputations built on mass acceptability are called the mainstream, and those built on a marginality must remain marginal to be validated. It can be abandoned only at the risk of losing those of one's audience who feel that support for the margin is a moral-political virtue. However, whoever *must* represent the vanguard (a marginal art culture) cannot *be* it. That is the box neoliberal pluralism has created to confine the flowing, juicy spirit, with a place for everyone and everyone in their place. For Free Jazz it is a pyrrhic victory to win a market and lose the snowballing forward movement of the original players. The avant-garde moment will have passed--no fault of the current players, it's just the changed situation.

The name "free jazz" persists as a music one can envision continuing forever as a self-standing model, the umbilical cord to the bulk of the jazz audience having been cut decades before. Classic Jazz was now the City Hall you can fight but not beat. A jazz club is a competitive business; it might bow to the projected audience numbers of a famous free jazz musician but not to those who do much the same thing and lack the drawing power, which then does not reside in the experience of live music. To the duality of Classic and smooth jazz, presented as the test of authenticity vs. commercial appeal, is added a few years later a jazz known as the outside to both. It would be a parallel but marginal institution if it was to have a public place at all.

Endless musical growth—*jouissance* beyond manufactured pleasure--is what mid-sixties Free Jazz advocates knew to be fully within the jazz tradition. They were the resurgence of the jazz spirit. Whether the limits of jazz were reached back then cannot be settled apart from questions of what it means then to participate in a tradition. The free jazz revival claims to stand within the tradition, but the effective concept of that tradition blocks it from creating anew *from within*, which would have been understood when the jazz audience was vulnerable to "The New Thing." Today's free jazz faces being delegitimized as a betrayer of the now *ruling* tradition's stable norms, such that it would also rightly be called neo-traditional. It is unreasonable to expect or demand present claimants to a ruling tradition to push the outer edge of their freedom, when they must also defend themselves against tacit charges that they don't belong in the *true* jazz tradition. Further down the road (which the sixties avant-garde did not have to face), what would happen if the claim to be dynamically expanding the meaning of jazz were to challenge the constraints of formulaic *free* jazz?

Going beyond is now an object of representation—which means at one remove from the real movement of "going beyond." Its current representatives have either already done this or have learned the playing style and need go no further, the air let out of the tires. To claim to still be jazz when tradition is adhered to through conformity, free jazz must curb internal challenges, yet unconsciously, for to do so openly would violate the image that they are actively pushing the edge. Since its origin in the late 80s, this has been the dilemma. Its contract with the music world and audience says it must represent far-out jazz, the difference the mainstream requires and cannot claim for itself. This forces anyone committed to the adventurousness of Free Jazz into cultural homelessness. The space outside the marketed and media-recognized "outside" would have to be a marginality beyond the margins, which is an anomaly and cannot be located on the cultural map. Without explicitly making the claim, the unrecognized outside would be loyal to the earlier, open version of tradition, not a dock to be firmly tied to but a shore to push off from that adventurers need and use to get in motion.

Apart from a few individuals, the older player community could not be restored, but free jazz could be staged as an avant-garde that refuses to die.[94] The changing configuration of the market comes in here. Earlier, for a new and unknown product to become accepted—first by the mass media, which built the stage for the receptive sixties public--it had to be imagined as both challenging and capable of making the present offering seem obsolete. This worked when the record industry could profit from sidelining the old. Jazz musicians had a precarious position, just a product the industry was pushing for the moment, in which it had a stake only until the market changed. Resurrected free jazz, however, needed something more stable: a remnant of older musicians who felt their music could still appeal to people; an audience of equal stubbornness locked into that sixties past, what the Europeans call "the 68er's"; plus a young audience convinced that the past was more vital than the present. This would not have resonated when chaos seemed to winning; rather when the idealized fifties (of neo-conservatives) was ascendant and the idealized sixties were on the defense.

For the upcoming generation, only repeating the past model would work; there would be no alternate route. Given that limitation however, anyone who plays the stylized version can say they play free jazz. It can be picked up by newcomers without their heroes urging them to go further out, nor straight-ahead players complaining that they don't follow the rules because they can't, nor is there the unstable relation to the social order and potential accusation of being antagonistic to the public. For a culture that has imbibed the value of the simulacrum, to provide the same image of passion in every performance will replace the sixties passion that came from pushing against real barriers. "Fire music" becomes merely "fiery."

"The sixties" is still the symbolic expression for a major traumatic event; even suppressed it had laid a seed some feared would sprout again. (In 2007 Nicolas Sarkozy came to power in France with the promise to end "the spirit of 68" for good.) The sixties experience that could be effectively marketed depended on what its advocates imagined was possible under new circumstances. The field looked wide open, for onto the neo-con counterrevolution Reaganism had piggy-backed neo-liberal celebration of the open market. The market could accommodate anything that would compete in production and sales, so it could not hinder Free Jazz from blooming again. However, as a movement it had risen on a tide, which now had turned; this is a zeitgeist perception on the level of myth but nonetheless widespread and effective. Not only the cynics said "change" was now headed the other way; those especially clued into the urban arts culture knew it. The sixties progressives and its younger allies now felt they must dig in their heels for the long haul with no thought that the tide would ever turn back.[95] To find support a cultural avant-garde had to be re-built as advancing *with* the social order rather than against it. Impossible to ignore, the earlier avant-gardes could be honored only if they were historicized and theorized as contributing to a present society that was advertised as advanced. Against their original intention and even that of the revivalists they would function as an antidote to hidden discontent and boredom.

In a cultural climate of reaction against the presumed sixties excesses, the music world's consolidation of genres made player-initiated innovation inconceivable. This was explicit in the classicized jazz of Marsalis but hidden in its mirrored other, free jazz. If you perceive yourself entrenched and surrounded on all sides it would be foolhardy to send out an avant-garde patrol; rather, conserve and reinforce your defenses, maintain commitment. This is a novel position for those labeled avant-garde. Historically it has been perceived as taking bold action, a few who advance so others can follow…or maybe they don't; at least the artists haven't set a limit to where they will go next. The avant-garde's alienation from commercial concerns (their claims of autonomy) allowed them to address universal human existence rather than concrete needs, which is rather the market's function to fill. Once genre became a wholly commercial formulation, concretely defined by the needs of targeted demographics, the earlier avant-garde rejection of limits to their direction was no longer feasible. The re-shaped avant-garde became as stable as its audience bargained for.

Continuous to our period today, jazz and free jazz is neither be internally challenged nor open to external stimulus and intervention. Those of the audience reaching outside the box are given another box to play in—if jazz doesn't satisfy your itch then free jazz is prescribed. A move today as radical as *Bitches Brew* would simply fall into a different genre and not raise a stink. For free jazz in particular, the form will be elaborated by new representatives, but to go outside it by abandoning key ties with its ancestor--the steady stream of notes, heavy drive, emotive expression, or the soloist focus--would question the musician's loyalty. To take even John Coltrane's last recordings as a place to jump off *from* would be to jump into the abyss. In a situation that is pluralistic and friction-free, all options can be pursued, so long as they stay within self-policed borders. That will help prevent the kind of controversy that leads to questioning the broad schema of the past three decades.

Sixties Free Jazz audiences knew they were hearing something absolutely current, and the players drew from other forms of black culture still current. By the 80s free jazz did not have currency, nor was there any such pretense. It was for the sixties-experienced generation to remember, and for the young to get a hint of the emancipatory spirit they'd missed; for both a form of resistance to the door closing to that spirit. Despite its presumed leftist politics it met the conservative drift of politics with its own conservative strategy. While the neo-cons froze an image of the fifties as their ideal of normalcy, free jazz did something similar for the sixties. It could not help but become ahistorical—unbending in the face of changing time, which is the covert enemy of all stability.[96] Meanwhile, the neo-cons could put on a progressive face by accusing the 68'ers of nostalgia and telling them to "get over it."

The huge respect bestowed on Free Jazz musicians is something of a trap for them. Comparison can only reveal the revivalists as unoriginal epigones, turning originality into a negative value. Today's free jazz playing may bring an audience to cathartic Dionysian release, but it lacks the impact of a live Ayler performance or a 90 minute immersion in Coltrane, with their insistence on "something to say" and the incorporation and surpassing of their own and others' earlier work. The spectator-performer relation has changed. No performer today would risk the audience's impatience with a solo that went beyond standard duration. Even if today's performers were true replicas of the past, audiences are not prepared to receive them. Once upon a time musicians commonly and openly expressed their hostility to the taste of their audiences; today one hears not a whisper of that.

Despite the historical/cultural shift and cultural packaging, free jazz today does keep that vital past in memory, perhaps better than any other classicized music. Because of the emotionality conveyed by the music, new players can come forward who might lack the skill of the originals or of today's headliners, but still represent strong feeling. One of the sources for the Black Avant-garde was the sanctified church, where no sinners could be refused if they cried out for salvation, a trace of which can be felt also among the sixties originators of German free jazz.[97] Having something to say in Free Jazz was more interior to the musicians' consciousness than the patterned expression of a musical personality that had been commercially successful in earlier jazz musicians. "Hard" playing, with faces sweating and bodies signifying ecstasy, today might be stylized but still, as it did fifty years ago, must confront a powerful resistance in the tradition of Western art, always on guard against interlopers who are accused of spontaneous bodily engagement and feeling more than they think. The relation of feeling to thinking has been the bull in the china shop, both of which claim to live under the same roof of art and share neighboring music world institutions.

Both Free Jazz and free jazz relate back to the "action painting" of postwar abstract expressionism, itself a reaction of the Americans not only to their cooler European surrealist predecessors but to the horrors of Auschwitz and the Bomb.[98] At the 1983 Wuppertal Festival (West Germany) I attended, saxophonist Peter Brotzmann, originally an art student himself, played clarinet while hovering over a collaborator making an equally excited abstract painting. This kind of mutual engagement contrasts with the visual scores of the John Cage legacy, where the player is expected to relate to what is already finished as a visual object. The symbolic union of visual construction and free jazz sound-making was re-enacted at the Guelph Colloquium in 2011 (Canada), although there it was a museum-piece reconstruction. In 1983 Germany free jazz appealed to those "68'ers," who had not long before supported the disruption of the political establishment. Thirty years later in North America the demonstration represented left-cultural sixties nostalgia surfacing in academia.

A more significant link with the past is that free jazz has maintained much of the independence of the musician collectivity found in the sixties, continued in the seventies through today. When jazz musicians had some control over their collectivity they policed the level of expertise to some extent, requiring that one know how to play the instrument conventionally and improvise over the chord changes. Private mentoring functioned well for this; however the mentor was unpaid and not hired by a school to mentor anyone who paid their tuition. He would mentor the ambitious, but only those he found interesting and had the right spirit, a subjective judgment. The collectivity held the highest place of honor for those who went past their training and showed creative ingenuity and promise to take jazz further down the road of art, the investigation of new territory. Popular success—concert audience, record sales, and bookings—may have governed the pay scale at the top of the hierarchy, but was kept separate and could not override the collectivity. For instance the top name musicians respected Eric Dolphy highly but most audience did not. This disparity, which was not the first, showed that the musician collectivity held its own court. That court often had split decisions on the issue of whether to exceed the rules, yet it had a subjectivity all its own.

As academic institutions gained control of jazz it became an expert music, a matter of getting it right--the notes, tone, details of style. Following the book is what they do best. They effectively *mirror* creative work according to an existing scale of approval. The advice on graduation to "strike out on your own" resonates with a dull thud. Classic Jazz provided the book they use to train and judge musicians, having no ground for judging outside what has already been done.

Revivalist free jazz has resisted institutions' leadership and has not become their product. Its musicians have retained their previous self-judging collectivity, which operates with a subjectivity that is not determined by expertise. That collectivity includes name musicians and many who are unknown, some highly trained and some not. It is not on the lookout for the next Eric Dolphy, but it has kept its independence from both the dead hand of institutions and the popularity game. When its musicians speak of the need for the spirit of jazz to survive, this must be taken into account. When improvisers today move far beyond the parameters of free jazz but find their bodies and spontaneous feelings are doing much of the heavy lifting, they are obliged to both Free Jazz and free jazz for their spirit.

Turning briefly to the German free jazz musicians, they were in tune with the second wave of NY Free Jazz despite few appearances of the Americans in Germany at the time. From the mid-sixties and for a long time thereafter the Germans performed and worked together as a strong collectivity built around Freie Musik Produktion (FMP), much like the Chicago AACM but without the community-based organization. The best known of the German ensembles, Schlippenbach's Globe Unity Orchestra, 1967, with seventeen members, was perhaps modeled after Coltrane's *Ascension*.[99] Commissioned and paid to perform at the home of the Berlin Philharmonic Orchestra, Globe Unity had steady cultural support from, the state. NY Free Jazz would have had a different history given the resources, legitimation, and the less ambivalent art audience that backed the Germans. The effective path available to the NY black avant-garde, as we have seen, was that of commercial jazz, to operate as star soloist artists contracted on the basis of projected sales. While the

German group continued, with many of the same players over the years, the various *Ascension* re-makes in the US have lacked the kind of core group that Globe Unity found financial support for over a long period.

As the sixties-era excitement passed and finances for large ventures diminished, careers of Germans followed the course of commodification; they too came to be featured as soloists and even stars with reputations of differential value. The audience then attended shows to see the best-known representatives of a by-gone era. The configuration of festival sets, however, would often follow the past, each one different rather than an established grouping, unlike the standard jazz festival. This maintained the original idea of European free jazz, that there was something of an overt collective commitment to pursuing this specific kind of music. Like the New York free jazz revival, the Germans picked up the Ayler spirit rather than the Coleman playfulness and harmonic interest. They abandoned more of the jazz essentials than the early Free Jazz players, yet retained its classic form.[100] When they began to join up regularly with American players later in the states (especially in Chicago) they contributed to turning a defeated Free Jazz into the free jazz that continues today.

The Europeans played with a vigor that Ayleresque Free Jazz may have incited, but their commitment was no subservience to American culture. They consciously sought to break with the European tendency to follow American jazz no matter what turn it took, which had begun in the twenties and continued after the war. Postwar America was no longer distant and idealized but the ever-present military and political victor with troops on their soil, a strong influence on national politics, and the aggressor in an unpopular war in Vietnam. The sixties free jazz Germans paralleled the youthful left rebellion, which accused the fifties economic reconstruction (the "German miracle") of quietly allowing many ex-Nazis to continue running things, with the tacit approval of the American occupiers. The resistant generation opposed Cold War politics, which kept the American military a presence long after the Occupation was officially over, and a government subservient to the US. As an antidote free jazz players asserted European citizenship as well as German unity by collaborating regularly with players from (anti-Nazi) Communist East Germany.

Their music was a political statement as well as musical and cultural. In the early 70s they named their musical collaboration as a movement, *Die Emanzipation*, echoing Lincoln's proclamation and implying the end of European, or at least German enslavement to American culture. NY Free Jazz itself might have been a new turn for the history of jazz but its players did not judge it as being emancipated *from* jazz.[101] Peter Brotzmann's album "Machine Gun" seemed a direct political statement, recorded as it was in May 1968, the international height of the political sixties and only a few months after the stunning Tet Offensive by the Vietnamese. Politics put an edge on their playing that attracted audience far more than was the case in NY, where the culture radicals could get behind was rather emerging rock music.

Musicians can be expected to say "labels don't matter," but titles reflect real conflicts and choices often later forgotten; they are not just imposed by the music world. Perhaps partly to emphasize their freedom from an American-originated music, the Germans tended to call what they did simply "improvised music," "free music," and not "free jazz." ("Improvised music" is what Marsalis disassociated from jazz.) Due to its musicological similarity to mid-sixties Free Jazz this yielded a confusion of terms that has persisted. Jazz is of course improvised, but most German free players did not come into their music via their current jazz community, as did the Americans, and so they felt free to exclude German jazz from what they supported. Another reason for calling it "improvised music" was that in this period of unified European self-assertion the title also covered less jazz-inspired improvisation. It masked differences of approach internal to Europe that remained latent, yielding a sense of unity. In particular, parallel to German improvisation there developed different British versions, the most accessible to Continental taste being guitarist Derek Bailey's, which didn't follow the American Free Jazz spirit. After the disintegration of Eastern European Communist states in 1989 the Cold War political motivation for "Emancipation" collapsed, and latent distinctions of musical approach and form could become more apparent, as was happening in the states as well.

The first large festival of improvised music was more "anti-jazz" than anything that could be found in North America. It was called the Anti-Festival (the Gegen-Festival) of 1968 in West Berlin, and was intended to protest the straight-ahead and popular Berlin Jazz Days. It was later the Total Music Meeting, a title of some significance for classical German music culture since it recalls Wagner's Gesamtkunstwerk or "total music work," yet as a meeting it illustrated their fully contemporary collaborative improvisation. The largest contingent of participants at that first festival was actually British. By 1972 and thereafter almost all musicians were German, and free jazz was clearly the musical direction and not what most Brits were doing.[102] The major parallel festival in Britain, Company Week, began in 1977 and rarely included Germans. What was initially asserted in the "improvised music" title was both musical and European unity; meanwhile national communities, the sites of most playing and collaborating, which varied in ways that illustrated less noticed musicological differences.

Of all the continental nationalities, musically unified East and West German free jazz was the most prominent. It benefited from an unbroken continuity, integrating a second generation with the first, although the door was in process of closing, since the audience was not expanding sufficiently, and to get financial support was always an effort. Players could greet their older-generation audience and partners as former comrades who had been with them from the beginning. An atmosphere of nostalgia created a strong impetus for players to duplicate their original form, a reluctance to take the adventure further.[103]

The Europeans were virtually unknown in the US until the mid-70s, and even then most were available only through rare and expensive imported recordings. In the US in the early 80s they would typically play a New York show and one in Allentown PA, where for some reason the state Arts Council funded a venue for the music. Then they went home. There were few grand tours until the 90s, when free jazz was in revival mode and their names got around. Before the 2008 recession began cutting subsidies, European professional improvisers came to the states frequently, especially from countries that fund improvised music--primarily Germany and Austria, occasionally the Netherlands and Norway, never the UK, whose musicians had to earn their money commercially. Since there is no funding for Americans to do the same in Europe the tour there is possible only for jazz-identified musicians invited to festivals, which depends on the residual belief that the US is the authentic home of jazz.

Let me conclude this chapter by returning to the key figure of Free Jazz, John Coltrane. It has often been said that the turn in his music around 1965 was a move towards the modernist avant-garde.[104] If so he would have narrowed the gap between jazz and postwar Euro-American experimental music, a tradition that was wholly secular and had no major dispute with scientific rationality. Modernism related to the European (19th century) tradition as a rebellious, dialectical opponent and competitor. That parent was stubbornly allied with the humanities, which still drew upon the Enlightenment compromise of "natural religion," which harbored sentiment intolerable to the spirit of the hard sciences. For artistic freedom to be considered progressive, music would have to follow an objective, random procedure that would counteract the composer's lagging personal feelings, with results that would disrupt an audience's usually unreflective reception, as do some scientific discoveries. That was at least the position of John Cage, who was and still is considered the master of experimentalism.

Coltrane could not have been farther from that, especially after his turn; his motivation was incompatible with the concept and method of scientific investigation and the reduction to zero emotionality. When he used live performance for his explorations it was in the tradition of black preachers. Rather than follow a written sermon they extemporized and were driven by inspiration they felt was outside themselves. The congregation would receive it as the word of God directed at each one personally and would honor the preachers for their charisma. His voice was not that of a persona but a prophet, as Henry Miller said of Rimbaud and all true poets, who bore a message to the entire world of whom art lovers were a small fraction. This contradicted everything the experimental composers believed was progressive; their revealed truth was of a different nature.

Not all, but most whites who heard Coltrane were thoroughly secularized, distanced from any such transcendence. They listened as modern intellectuals, analyzing jazz as advancing upon each earlier form. Even if they did liken his performance to a sermon, they would be accustomed to discuss and debate its meaning rather than receive it with bowed head. A black audience, never far from religious roots, would prefer following his playing as if they were getting the spiritual message. However, a preacher's content has familiar, coded meaning, and when Coltrane's explorations left that behind most black audience left. They had no way to honor difficulty as their own limitation, as did the audience of the experimentalists, who could receive it as an ear-opening experience.

Coltrane merged the preacher with the seeker of new truth ("new sounds and new feelings") he himself needed, so rare a combination that interpreters have wanted to split him in two.[105] Those few Coltrane *was* able to move, as many are still today, would not have reduced music to the experimentalists' "organization of sound." They would experience his passion as somehow coming from beyond him and themselves. For some it was a direct-to-the-heart message of personal redemption that binds them in a shared charisma and even determines their lives. That was my experience hearing *Love Supreme*, and I've heard the same from others. It is music that destroys the frame for receiving it.

In his research into non-Western musics and practice of constructed (rather than culturally accepted) scales he put in the hard work of the intellectual and scientist. But while a seeker of scientific truth looks to material reality for confirmation, what is visible to others, a seeker of emancipatory revelation goes where the spirit takes him, trusting in what is invisible. Or, in the words of the Soviet writer Platonov, you "go where the eyes go," without the romantic notion that the material speaks for itself. A strong secularist prejudice awaits any such music, for the spiritual is associated with conventional peace and harmony. One listen to the later Coltrane would correct that.

Especially for saxophonists (due to Coltrane's example), that mode extended into free jazz. Whether as a soloist within a group or alone in front of an audience, the role was not what the British free improvisers had in mind. Now that religious expression in our culture is far from progressive, that preacher-soloist might be credible for a jazz audience, but would be an image from the past and not a bearer of the redemptive word *for now*. Like all others, that musician is one of many soloists, all needing media appeal and steady audience to back up their truth. And should the playing lack key reminders of jazz, they will be heard as experimentalists, expected to play something merely different from what the audience has heard before. In an age when truth-seekers are at best holy relics, "music is the truth and I am its prophet," fresh and pure and a gift to the world, will not be taken seriously.

5. The Situation for Jazz-based Music

Maybe today everyone has an artist within them, but as everyone knows, *that* artist is treated differently from those for whom art is a dedicated career. The two are not competitors and don't need to pay attention to each other. Serious art is the exclusive achievement of artists serious about their career, their apparent distinction. Yet the universalization of "artist" has created a tension, since in the actual experience of art and art-making, what is not authentic art? This threatens to undermine the career artist. It is the social order that comes to the rescue, forcing career artists into its arms to verify the distinction. They are taught that they inherit a long tradition, but there has been a sea change in their relation to the social order. The post-sixties readjustment of that order has been to claim art as *its* achievement. It does so via its institutions and ideology, by abstracting from the artist their work and awarding it a separate historical existence and truth value, adding it to the formally respected register and hierarchy of Art. It is that order which gets to confer credentials, honor, attention and privilege on the artist and their work via its institutions and machinery. Artists then aspire to what they believe the social order alone has the power to confer.

Before this intervention, people commonly limited the designation of art to whatever serious artists valued as such. Artists presumed to make this determination strictly among themselves. The first contemporary models were fifteenth century Italian visual artists and their successors, whom Europeans high in the social hierarchy came to value. They were seen to transcend their lower caste as craftspeople and acquire wealth and fame through talent, intellect and skill. They were the first Europeans to be called geniuses, who by creating miracles were equivalent to secular saints. They embodied the full potential of the creative human, an antidote to Christian taboos.

Four centuries later, the American social order had no use for such art or artists, though they were right under their feet. Americans were busy achieving the most advanced industrial civilization and were ashamed at its crassness and inhumanity, but you had to go to Europe for art. Suddenly, with American postwar world hegemony, a social order that hoped to be the model for the world needed its own real artists. Abstract expressionism fit the bill; once visual artists did something that was thought to have progressed beyond the Europeans, America could hold up its head. However, unlike the European art public for whom art had long been their heritage, the American middle class wasn't prepared; it had to be taught who was and therefore who wasn't authentic. It took the power of media, intellectuals, state and university institutions to empower the upgrade. Voilà, a marriage in the making, in which a bargain is struck: something gained and something lost.

That was visual art; what about music? Whether jazz was to be art depended on whether the musicians themselves could be treated as authentic artists, and if so, under what concept of authenticity. White composers who scored for symphony orchestras could easily pass, but here was a question of both class and race. Can highly skilled craft workers, those who made the concrete sounds of music, be called artists, *and* can they be blacks, commonly believed to be beneath every white person in personal value, even their legal position in the south? The reason that black Harlem writers in the twenties had to make their claim was a matter of race; writers of literature had long been considered artists and intellectuals. For musicians, blacks of postwar bebop were the first to make this claim, and it stuck only for musical reasons. Their playing had an effect on people and the music world that joined two conceptions of art—difficult and enticing *at the same time*.

With no conscious intent, their act was more than a status upgrade; everyone-an-artist was in the works. Given the social position of blacks and entertainers, the move democratized the full human that was thought to be incarnated in "artist." It directly affected all who were not strictly following a score. Studio musicians who ventured a pertinent suggestion would be considered creative artists, but not orchestra musicians following the score, no matter how skilled. Artists would be understood as anyone, trained or not, with the imagination and initiative to do something better than their assigned task. To lament them for encroaching on professionals would deny people the image of full humanity.

For bebop entertainers to claim, get judged, or even behave like a modernist avant-garde posed a dilemma. That position obliged them to innovate, which is either the utopian promise to make *it* new or to make the new *things* consumer society depends on. When a segment of the public upholds the former, it recognizes the artist as emancipatory, bearing the promise of a positive future, against an intransigent and unchanging social order. When the distinction is elided, the otherness and alienation of art becomes commodified entertainment. It merges with the spectacle, which is then endowed with the higher status of art. To make it new signifies the freedom everyone yearns for; in the commodified form of new things everyone can have it simply by buying them, and value is the price tag.

"Artist" still carries the impress of those who don't bow to the needs of society and are idealized for that, unlike citizens, who are the mere holder of enumerated human rights and do nothing to earn them. Musicians who claim to be artists in this idealized sense are in a dilemma: they're under intense social pressure to demonstrate that ideal, and under economic pressure to be collapsed back into the subservient role of the cultural worker (content provider) manufacturing consumer goods. One way artists met this pressure in the past was to create goods the customer didn't like—those who made it new were then known by the marketplace resistance to their art objects. If and when resistance was overcome and an audience develops, the artist moved on rather than let their fame dictate what they must do, which they treated as an insult.[106] Jazz musicians did this—Miles Davis, prime example.

This is a problem for later jazz musicians. Their efforts to break into the Artist club under their own terms were resisted and still are. Access to funds increasingly available to other artists is blocked; whatever would not bend to the requests of a paying audience had nowhere to go. Yet as a social upgrade, "artist" could not be denied blacks in a society attempting, at least ideologically, to unify itself following its second Civil War (Civil Rights; the third one is now in the making). To call them artists when they are classed by income as entertainers looks like patronizing them. The acceptable black artist would be the defender of an artistic *heritage*, not the self-determined artist ideal. This was akin to the ruling tradition postwar academics had been constructing that would provide standards for steady reproduction. Classic Jazz was not popular music but could substitute itself for a jazz that *had* pushed the edge of its popularity, since both were more or less on the other side of mass consumer taste. This move obscured the difference, as if the most advanced art and its preservation in static form, both threatened by popular taste, were one and the same. It made jazz a conserver of values in a world that was being presented as having leapt past it. Both "make it new" and new-product art consumption had for long valued innovation, and under late capitalism the latter meaning came to exclude and incorporate the former. The spectacle would honor the jazz artist not for resisting a *backward* establishment, as with the modernist avant-garde (and at least early sixties Free Jazz) but for resisting its unstoppable *forward* momentum.

This was a major reversal, and technology figured in it. Jazz linked modern culture and technological progress from the very beginning of its popularity. It was identified with and even developing at the pace of technological breakthroughs in recording and radio. It could still be received as a fully acoustic music, thus holding to the traditional medium of performance, even when guitars began to be amplified. All recorded and broadcast music was heard through speakers and so was effectively *amplified* acoustic, so most listening was electronically mediated. Public live performance began its journey to private listening, and jazz was part of it. Yet there was still a magical felt presence of live music being played in the room, such that people only turned on the radio when there was a program they planned to hear.

Technology aimed to represent that acoustic sound as fully as possible. Yet all the while the technical means improved they were opening avenues for *making* music that would eventually undermine the popular position of jazz. Acoustic music was threatened by the very technological progress it had advanced. This became apparent with the advent of rock in the mid-sixties, which attracted audiences with improved and massive sound, post-production studio techniques, and electronic devices. This reversed the position of jazz on the modernity chart. Discos were built on the assumption that dance music was better from studio-created, not live sound. The inability of jazz to incorporate innovations affected its status with young audiences, making it a music for those who had generationally fallen behind, "resisting change." Increasingly the jazz medium became recording, broadcasting and now the internet, rather than live performance, a trajectory that follows the cheapening cost of music, the rise of its omnipresence, and growth of its profitability. All music has been more dependent on technology than visual art, where the long tradition of the oil painting continues to hold its own, aided by its aura of authenticity. The first playing of music is a performance from which endless copies can be made, and is of little value compared to the original painting. Jazz, stubbornly acoustic, was in a position to be betrayed by technology, its erstwhile godfather. It has been compositional Experimental Music that has welcomed every new electronic technology for sound production, enabling its claim to be contemporary and innovative, and casting jazz as retrograde and sentimental.

Ideologies compete for authenticity, and this involves both hardware and software innovations. Jazz-based musics rest on a claim grounded in a period when all available instruments were acoustic, which was as up to date as modernist culture could do. The limitation of electricity to amplification (and the vibraphone's tremolo) was seen as simple multiplication of volume, whereas the electronic instruments just beginning to appear actually created sound that could not be obtained through the body-skills of the player. As with classical and folk music, jazz skill of the body is paired with acoustic sound; an electronic source came on as a kind of cheating. Acoustic instrumentation referred back to time immemorial; human-powered, they appealed to humanistic sentiments, about which modernist "make it new" was at least ambivalent.

Given this, sound powered by electricity, which has been the direction of our culture, would cut jazz off from its roots and change the nature of its authenticity from a music of "now" culture to resistance. Amplification and mediation of sound through records merely required listeners to imagine the presence of the musicians despite gramophone scratches, similar to reading a realistic novel. The distinction between amplified and pure acoustic sound was obscured, but indicated that jazz was in accord with technological advance. Rock music had the same kind of authenticity of "now" and like jazz could not have arisen apart from the latest technology of its time.[107] The claim of Experimental art music to artistic authenticity, like museum-based Contemporary Art, is in a strong position in today's world of a professional avant-garde, for it does not challenge the authenticity of past art in order to stake its claim but seeks to join it.[108] It exists in the shadow of gods overlooking its growth rather than standing on their shoulders for a greater vision.

As for software, jazz was itself a cultural innovation, as were Experimental Music and rock later on, and part of the burst of modernist change in the twenties. Jazz musicians generated new ideas both as artists normally do and as a marketplace necessity for their livelihood, but with great differences over time in how those ideas functioned. Early jazz was often criticized as blandly repetitive, and no doubt most audience preferred that normality. However, the strongest fans called it the music of surprise, the sign of spontaneity. Musicians had something for both the fans and the mass audience. Recorded solos were considered commodities, and soloists gained favor by refurbishing them with new licks, identifying them as their musical property and what they signified to the world. They came up with ideas that first of all might surprise *themselves,* and would affect their musical choices subsequently; a profound effect of technology ever since, for never again would musicians' spontaneity be free of their own critique from the spectator's seat.[109] Fellow musicians would learn the new version from the record, imitate it and, if they could, modify it further. Jazz was then popular and assimilated by the musicians themselves, which was a novelty. Unlike most other artists, they could expect their new twists to excite enough audience to sustain them. On the whole, jazz had to give *familiar* pleasure in order to entertain, while the star provided the aberrations that pricked convention.

The subjective character of the voice, an extension from the blues, also placed value on the individual. This too was deeply cultural; rooted in religious tradition, it cannot be subsumed under secularist modernity. What was innovative against the background of the wider culture was the soloist blessed (charismatically anointed) with a unique quality that came from their individual soul. One "found" his or her distinct vocal or instrumental voice as if pre-existent, through a quasi-spiritual path rather than operating within a wide-open, depersonalized field, as would free improvisers later. This approach was as personal as one's vocal chords and by nature individually variable. Finding one's voice typically followed a period that combined submission to traditional training with individualization. As in Protestant bible study, one learned the text and then assembled the meaning in one's heart. The courage needed to put oneself forward came from the unity of self and voice, a personal faith or truth, since one can judge this oneself. The moment musicians felt "ready" was when they achieved that unity, an identity that would continue through all later variations. This voice might attract some and challenge others, but in either case it related to an open tradition perceived as unfolding from a living culture, with many voices participating. [110]

The self-discovered unique voice was a feature of jazz through the sixties, apart from musicological innovations, which are more abstract and imitable. Charlie Parker is easily distinguished from his imitators by his consistent recorded sound, despite variable recording situations and frequent changes of horns and mouthpieces.[111] To have called Coleman "anti-jazz" and "abstract" was to say, "I don't recognize that voice as coming from jazz," yet given time and struggle within listeners' feelings the very sound of that voice was recognized as authentic (of course, not to everyone even today). In that period a novice would imitate the sound of his hero or mentor but eventually veer off to a sound uniquely his own. The jazz lineage was something of a genetic, family relationship, which contributed to the idea of jazz as essentially black, a color line drawn by nature that whites could never cross.

Like the preacher who has been called, the unity of voice and soul was the special and convincing "it" that determined who got listened to, mediated by the music industry that selected and gambled on the basis of its insight into consumer attraction. That "it" was the meeting point of the modernity of popular music and an affirmed tradition. But what appealed instantly to most was precisely what modernist composers abjured, viewing it as romantic subjectivity, which holds back progress and thus the horizon of human possibility. They faced the same when the classical music world and audience rejected them for 19th century sentimental favorites, making their own tradition a dead hand holding back the living. The question for jazz musicians was rather what part of the tradition they should consider essential, making it possible for a new generation to call on different parts of the tradition as their witness.

Most of all, jazz was improvisatory, and it came not from an intentional decision but from patterns of black culture. In continuity with ragtime and minstrelsy, it was a matter of taking liberties with whatever was given, whether the score, street or church songs, or others' improvisations. This was known as signifyin', bending what came before in some novel way, which provoked another such move by the next player.[112] An improvisatory solo was a kind of mockery and homage at the same time, with no end to the game in sight. It was progressive and yet affirmed the original at the same time. To go back to an earlier solo would not have been a true improvisation, nor to clean up someone else's (for instance to play a Miles Davis solo without his mistakes). Even if an improvisatory twist was somewhat worked out in advance, it was heard as spontaneous against the backdrop of the familiar song and form. Each successive move in this direction could be described as equally "free," which is how Stan Getz described Charlie Parker, reproducing jazz while it wove elaborate circles around the past way of doing it. Jazz then had an identity of constantly being expanded upon, signifying itself and signifyin' on itself. Thus solos were individualized as well as soloists.

Jazz was an advance for entertainment, and improvised solos also "progressed," one upon the other. It did not have an innovative, avant-garde edge until bebop, progressive in a way that approached modernist composed music. Innovation then would mean an internal challenge to the tradition itself, rather than the earlier challenges of one jazz soloist to another. All innovation implies a background, presumably older, conformist and acceptable, against which the new stands out and gets attention.

One bebop innovation was that the differences between solos became not occasional but essential, evident in Charlie Parker's recorded outtakes. Each one is unique and could not possibly be prepared. The continuous flow of differences was generalized, such that soloists were not expected to repeat themselves—a major step on the road to free improvisation. This gave a new meaning to jazz as a music that is progressive because *it* continually progresses, advancing over itself. This assimilated the entertainment musicians to artists, who are (or were at that time) expected to have a body of work that evolves over time. The idea that the flow of new ideas could be *continuous and immediate* was contemporaneous with the postwar "tradition of the new" of abstract expressionism and the "first thought, best thought" of Jack Kerouac. The media popularized the spontaneity of jazz, making it seem easy, such that musicians had to protest that it took hard work, by-the-book study, and analytic breakdown of jazz chord structures.[113]

The musicians were aware that their ideas contradicted commercially popular jazz, such as how to voice the chords, phrasing, speed of playing, the relation to the tune, and so on. They ended up stretching the fundamental parameters of jazz but not out of a grand-scale ambition to do so, as might those with the European concept of "Music." They needed to please a paying audience, who might resist and not be surprised in a pleasant way. Given the cultural bifurcation possible after the relatively unified 30s, popular market rejection (such as AM radio and the Hit Parade) would even validate bebop as a hip artist phenomenon. The beboppers had an impact on the wider society that called them "crazy," the word they threw back in mocking defiance (from whom the poets like Allen Ginsberg picked it up). Take away a wider world that feared its own suppressed craziness and the dialectic disappears, and with it the impact of this avant-garde.[114]

"Avant-garde" was borrowed from European Modernism, and for bebop musicians it implied not a general form of art but a specific grouping or school, artists who learned from and depended on each other, turning away those outside that commitment. Critic-writers would use "avant-garde" or "modern" to tag individuals for evaluation and consumption, as if they were a competitive hierarchy, but players acted more like a collectivity, not isolated geniuses needing no one else. They met primarily at the 52nd st. gigs, where they would leave during intermission and sit in with similar others, besides playing after-hours sessions. Sitting in could also function as an audition, and was understood as such by the players.[115] The collectivity of musicians was relatively closed, with entry via strong judgment and tough initiation. One's market value was a more universal equalizer, graphically evident and out of the hands of the players, yet it did not determine one's admission to the club.

Whatever innovation meant on the consumer market, for players and original fans it meant to take music outside the known. For piano players to "play outside" has been normalized to mean extending beyond the given chord structure and later returning to it, reaffirming the core of the song and its cyclical nature. For fans at the time "outside" was a place few were will-ing to go; if the trickle became a deluge it might be time to move on — authenticity had legs. A music recognized as outside wasn't just low in the numbers game or different, it involved a tension between a perceived inside and outside, difficult to locate in today's musics. The metaphorical outside implies a psychodynamic gap between adventurers on the high seas seeking the blank spaces on the cultural map and those preferring the security of ter-ra firma. The most committed followers were pioneers who might well be outcasts and inner exiles on the home turf, but who conquered the wilder-ness and eventually brought "out music" within the expanding circle of globalized culture. This process is now near-complete, the earlier interstices swallowed up in the spectacle and the present ones invisible to it.

The fifties-sixties jazz avant-garde innovated over what bebop had done and was "far out" by comparison. It abandoned some conventions but also broke with modernist practice by re-introducing parts of the more popular and traditional parts of black culture, blues and gospel. Frank Kofsky wrote of the dynamic in standard avant-garde terms but adapted it to the collective experience of jazz musicians. He said there are innovators, historically signif-icant names, who "define the basic contours that the music will follow there-after..." and assimilators: "it is the rank and file that, collectively, exerts what amounts to a veto power over the innovators" and "both are neces-sary"; the assimilators must approve the innovators for the dynamic to work.[116] This assumes a body of players who are listening to each other, top to bottom of the commercial ranking system, debating each other's merits, and deciding which way to go. All are making some contribution, not just the commercially-determined top players. The New York Experimental Avant-garde composers were also interactive, only their tradition was the absolute--"Music"--above all traditions such as jazz and other entertainment, which were dependent on a specific culture. They could stigmatize classical music fans who didn't fall in line as unadventurous; "Music" had moved on. Jazz musicians loyal to "the music" had no interest in that divorce from their cultural base. For free jazz to sail away from the mother ship would put them in jeopardy — that was the threat over their heads.

Free Jazz was born at a time when "free" and "avant-garde" were not subgenre distinctions that imply levels of market appropriation, but brought real disruption to their home turf and its inhabitants. Or rather, what was threat to some was promise to others, feeding the minor culture war begun with bebop that continued through the fifties, long after bebop was declared dead. The incongruity that irked the mainstream, which was on top of the commercial numbers game, was that avant-gardes were more visible than it was. Those who didn't play the game got the attention, an injustice according to capitalist logic. Normative consumers expect what they already know to be extended, yet here the future was thought to be in the hands of the few.

The more avid fans would grab the latest record to see if and how it had advanced over last month's, and advertise it loudly to anyone who would listen, looking for converts. The world they inhabited through music was not the one they had to face daily but was an other, just waiting for their assent and action. By buying that record they participated in the unknown future and rejected the way things were as if the present was already behind the times. Just as musicians sought to transcend last night's solos, buyers shared in that desire when they hoped to see their own residual conformity shattered. Conformity was the hidden sin of the fifties; here was a way out. Each flimsy record could build a wall of resistance against falling back; it was like holding onto the truth as it kept changing, the answer blowing in the wind. In the existentialist categories that were in the air, they were the Sartrean for-itself, the realized "human" that took action and decided their fate, the becoming rather than the conformist in-itself that was satisfied with practico-inert being.

"Art is the truth" was not said with a cynical smile. Key to the conception of avant-gardes was that its innovators were making a contribution to something in movement larger than themselves, despite its slight visibility. To re-imagine an avant-garde that represented utopian hope, one might compare it with our present quiescent cultural period. To expect a shared, transcendent revelation would not motivate purchases today; "experimental music" does not yield such excitement. Rather, consumers stockpile records of their taste that are serially different but additive, without thinking the future could be anything that would relieve their present state. Who would scan the cultural plenitude and declare it a wasteland? Without a future fantasized as relief from an oppressive, dominant culture, and some kind of participatory collectivity to bring it into being, can people even know their alienation? The avant-garde vocabulary of the outside ("thinking outside the box") is now conventional. Global conquest of culture made the sea-faring explorers and their avant-garde vessels obsolete.

Through the sixties the social and critic's valuation of jazz was divided but ultimately rested on two criteria in tension--skill and new ideas. Skill was the first base all needed to get to for a career, training in the standard code of traditional technique, as in classical music. A career was open to all those who could master that, plus the dress code and proper social behavior that went with it. One had to willingly conform to a collective through personal sacrifice, the basis of any disciplinary social order. New ideas on the other hand meant individuation, for one advanced upon what was learned and therefore put oneself in a dialectical relation to skill and even professional validation, as we saw in sixties Free Jazz.

These unique individuals were the most valued, whom Kofsky called the innovators. They introduced musical ideas and forms that trumped skill, even if they utilized skill to get there. They validated new skills that other artists, the assimilators, felt compelled to follow if they hoped to compete in the same arena. However when subsequent musicians were seen to have skipped past the old skills they risked their professional status. This posed a conflict situation, sharply faced by Free Jazz musicians (though not by the Brits). The old guard, disciplined in the collective jazz code, was threatened by the new one which, more than any earlier movement in music history, was based on the musicians' immediate enjoyment and decision. That conflict exposed non-controversial music as blocking the door to emotions and players that such music could not channel, control, and profit from.

In practical terms, standard jazz, which maintained the same jazz feeling from the fifties onward and into today, had the advantage. Record sales may not have profited most musicians much, but they were essential for exposure to audiences and reviews, and thus the achievement of a significant name, which meant better-paying club gigs. Musicians and consumers desire was relatively free-floating, and the record companies couldn't predict what kind of music to produce that wouldn't leave a pile of unsold albums on their hands. Musicians blamed the companies, but didn't want them to go broke.

Jazz musicians coming up today are individualized not by innovation but by skill level, with soloists rewarded for expressive interpretation of the texts. Once jazz has become the simulation of an abstracted model, to rock the boat is not suggested as a possibility. Given the current traditionalist belief system, even those jazz-trained who aren't making money—the vast majority of graduates--don't venture far. Even in avant-jazz, a body of assimilators, to advertise a musician as "innovative" is misleading and anachronistic. The code binding super-skilled players encourages only the most negligible stylistic differences from one another, which the music world can manage easily. Such difference is privately owned skill and is not available to others, like the unique voice of jazz musicians only more pragmatic than soul-driven. As entrepreneurs they must demonstrate it but not create against what they have already achieved. Their relative prominence as performers confirms the lurking sadness audiences feel despite applause, that jazz-based music is never going to be *that* exciting again. That memory is what the music world institutions happily propagate, even as they tout the latest in circular fashion.

Distinct here from avant-jazz, free jazz musicians are assimilator's who follow the radical innovations of fifty years previous; anything more recent is invisible. Those considered the most creative hold quasi-tenured positions, dependent on a mediatized ranking system. All hierarchy follows a fictionalized narrative; this one is effective only because consumers trust in it. Not only the cognoscenti; ignorant outsiders also will inquire, "Well, who are the best?" The names of the avant-garde are first of all the icons of the sixties and their epigones, all considered family, its front to the world common to show biz. Even if they quit playing they will hold that position for life. Any anthropologist can describe the lengths to which the most gentle-appearing soul will go, beaming grace and respect for all, to maintain his honored seat of prestige in the noble caste, but only if threatened. Their oeuvre extends in a seamless narrative out from the groundwork of what they have previously done. This would follow the banking model of education (specifically, Paulo Freire's term in *The Pedagogy of the Oppressed*), in which learned material goes into the vault as one's valued property. More subjectively, if they feel good about their stylistic difference or likeness to the iconic greats, and need others to like it, they would reasonably be motivated to do more of the same. Then the continuity of their playing from one gig or recording to the next is not just a matter of recalcitrant habit but an integral part of the entertainer role and their own deep psychic attachments.

Since innovation against the model is inconceivable, the most celebrated musicians are those who once created the innovations that all others have now assimilated. Their self-created style resonated first in the music world and those few still living are duty-bound to repeat it, their contract with the media and with the family of assimilators. As with rock legends, they must play their past and leave invention to the pop field, where it is persona and not musical style that competes and changes. The recognizable solo style accommodates the myth of the achieved self projected onto the musician. It defends the embattled artist ego against the pluralistic, open playing field the ideology of art celebrates, with no felt contradiction.[117]

The traditionally unique jazz soloist's voice has changed for free jazz differently than avant jazz. It is far more likely to find mature players imitating the "Coltrane sound," for instance, or having no real distinction. That's a sign they are following a ruling tradition rather than the open one, where one found the specific voice and identity of their soul. Many mime the Coltrane, Ayler, Elvin Jones, Cecil Taylor identity knowing that fans and other musicians will honor it as authentic. Given the impregnable position of jazz education and the general favor for spectatorship, it is not just fans but *musician's* devotion to the greats that counts.

Today "avant-garde" and similar references unite as a continuum the artistic avant-gardists of the past and all those promoted as the leading edge of the most advanced society and culture of the world. This conjuncture symbolizes innovation and enlightenment for the world's betterment, so it includes the technology that goes amnesiac when reminded of its collateral damage. In the arts wing of this mansion, Contemporary Art leads this high-class party, and individuals of the other arts do their best to get invited. The various establishments honor their former oppositions by burying them in archival tombs, making their obsolescence indisputable. That earlier avant-gardes directly challenged the accepted art and culture of their day is no model for today's, but rather inoculates our social order, which has developed a way to prevent that from happening again. Like Civil War re-enactors, the promoted avant-garde is decked out in weaponry but not allowed to shoot bullets at their erstwhile enemy, for it is now on the same side. The "cutting edge" avant-garde has nothing to cut that its liberal guides haven't provided for it. As for adventure, all lands seem to have been systematically mapped, and nothing surprising is discovered; "it's all been done."

What gets titled "experimental music" has the best claim to being included. It tends towards the positivist aim (which began in the late 19th century) to reduce subjectivity to the limit of bold ingenuity. It goes to work on a nature, in this case sound, conceived as inert, interesting, and available to consciousness. This is the alternative to the vast history of cultures, which have seen nature as threatening darkness glimpsed by emotion and entered by sympathetic magical engagement. For some artists, including those of our culture, this is the true meaning of their activity.

To explore and create a range of varieties, experimental music relies on ever-new electronic technology, producing sound previously considered unmusical and displacing earlier conventions. Its claim to be innovative relies on this. It distances itself from the humanities, considered antiquated for their link to the pre-20th century past, like physicists still basing their work on Newton's theories. (A parallel path is the rise of the STEM side of the educational aisle—science, technology, engineering, math—and the view of the humanities as retrograde and deserving to be defunded.) Unlike the history of capitalism itself, the linear progression of new sound material and approaches is narrated as absolutely beneficent and endless growth; critics would be those whose ears are clogged with irrational attachments. Barred is any hint from the past that the experiment is missing something vital. Those who pattern their careers after this optimistic direction depend on institutional backing for recognition as artists, relying for legitimation on a bureaucracy rather than audience enthusiasm. Given that, it is meritocratic; one applies for inclusion relatively anonymously on the basis of academic and other credentials, like scientists who have been quietly working in their labs.

Nothing associated with jazz can compete as an innovative art form. Jazz continues to be commercial music, all of which must build an audience. The competition is for subjectivities to walk in the door expecting emotive fulfillment; merit is far from objectively determined. For the avant NY Downtown Scene begun in the late 70s it was possible to mock the aura of jazz authenticity, whose subjectivity is seriousness. That is precisely what jazz must have, for undiluted jazz seriousness, the weight of history, is essential for its commercial success. The only way to maintain jazz is to provide a hierarchy of names to represent it. Anonymity won't do here. Without recognizable names no one can be picked out of the heap for audience promotion, and the enterprise fails. Its musicians are not a socially-necessary innovative elite but are of relative value in upholding jazz and free jazz authenticity.

What free jazz can say to experimental music is: neither of us break the rules, but you claim to. From Free Jazz it has inherited a position outside the commercial mainstream, the "further out" of the modernist Age of Discovery. Its musicians today occupy a turf where most still refuse to go. That doesn't tempt others to follow, however, because "outside" has become a frozen category of its own, not expected to eventually catch on among those of mainstream taste. At least the name musicians constitute today's "permanent avant-garde,"[118] marginal but recognized and immune to decay and displacement. The media and scholars are pledged to respect them as examples of cultural resistance. The music does resist a present that ignores and marginalizes a valued (sixties) *past* but has no power to enable a promising *future*. Given the postmodern transformation, experimental music gets assigned to the avant-garde future orientation, and jazz-based, blues, and folk-

101

derived music is put in the bin of traditions every civilization is obligated to preserve as its treasure. *All* jazz-based music indeed goes "against the grain"; like the humanities, it resists a present that perceives it as an anachronism.

Earlier, popular culture was so present-oriented that to repeat the music of fifty years earlier would have been laughable. That jazz-based music has survived without change for about that length of time would be impossible without the power of the simulacrum in postmodern culture. Right around the time Classic Jazz was being formulated the French cultural theorist Jean Baudrillard began to argue that we had entered a phase in which the "real" of events, art movements, ordinary life and cultural experience was being eclipsed by simulations, copies of the original that not only symbolize what exists but remove any apparent imperfections. Just as real production in the West has declined in favor of information technology, entertainment, and the media, so virtualization of the past has replaced originality. Called hyperreal, this is what seems more pure, accessible, and enjoyable than reality itself.[119]

This fits the situation for jazz and free jazz since the 80s. Just as theme parks and period-based dramas (such as *Mad Men*) provide a cleaned-up past more easily comprehended than it was at the time, so jazz and (less perfectible) do free jazz simulations provide a past that could not possibly have existed. All past can be mythically symbolized, but myth can be variously interpreted. In an age where myth is denied validity, the simulacrum convinces beyond any further interpretation. And so unlike myth, it can have no effect on the present.

What was *immediate* for the survivalist impulse in free jazz has been the struggle against racism: just as racism has continued unabated from the sixties, so has the fight against it.[120] Music was thought to symbolize this, such that survivalism would replace the originals with symbolic representations, a spectacle performed and reproducible ad infinitum. The distance between the copies and the abstracted models from a half-century ago has collapsed. From the consumer side this is not nostalgia, a longing for the past to return knowing it won't, but a sense that the past is not truly other. The fight continues without any action being taken or frustrated.

An icon is by definition a simulation, it can only fascinate as such, and to gaze on the image replaces any original experience listeners might have had of the musician. It is understandable that fans would feel grateful to the symbolizing authority (the music world) for making these figures reliable, consistent, and widely worshipped. To perceive one's chosen tradition as a "golden age," as Amiri Baraka called it, means we can only inhabit a silver age in decline. The periodization is meant to honor the dead but frames them to fit present needs, including that of the social order, which doesn't want anything like that era to resurrect.[121]

Jazz gets its seriousness today from the image of its solidity and weight rather than from an experience of having musical expectations undermined. For the latter the "it" of jazz is fragile and in doubt, because its formulation can be belied by the musicians. Its weight today comes from being in the hands of interpreters. They, like academics generally, dislike a moving target, which is a rebuke to their power. The shift in power from artist to cultural authorities is deep in implications for all the arts. Who would be looking for change, and criticizing others for repeating themselves from one decade to the next? Both free and avant-jazz deny the meaning of tradition held when "jazz as we know it" confronted "the shape of jazz to come," another emblematic title of an early Coleman album.[122] The expectation then was change, which at the time could only signify a positive future with artists and humanists in the lead, and stood out against a backdrop of resistance to change on so many fronts. In fact it was their swan song. The "change" that is in the air now is climate change, with the image of major cities inundated and life in retreat, not people dancing in the street. (Added to that recently is the prospect of the dismantling of democratic institutions under Trump.) The favored option has been to construct a cultural bulwark against a future now universally conceived as misfortune. Resistance then comes from a left culture dependent on visibility and celebrity rather than an artist collectivity.[123]

Like all commercial musics, free jazz depends on a music world, and the one favorable to it requires its musicology to be locked in place. No one today would think to compare themselves to those who established that musicology, the original Free Jazz musicians. Possible are epigones who honor the fathers but are not in a position to challenge the authority they've invested them with. For jazz this is no problem, for it is a teachable skill to achieve standards of excellence. Free jazz can only do that to a limited extent, for a careful line would have to be erected between standards and "free." Free is linked to an egalitarian assumption that disavows the measurement all hierarchies require. The egalitarianism of free jazz depends on *everyone* being unequal to the giants of yore. These have been passing away one by one and leaving no vacancies, not even standards the epigones could hope to match and surpass. This has set up a dilemma, for the long view would see free jazz in progressive decline with no prospect of recovering from irreparable losses.

In a meritocratic system such as schooled jazz students enter, musicians are presumed to be graded and appropriately rewarded according to a scale (of course not only playing is judged but level of ambition, discipline, entrepreneurship, etc.). One might be mediocre at playing jazz but that would be more difficult to assess for free jazz, for it would imply precise standards. In free jazz, authenticity of *spirit* ranks above precision, in the tradition of the "it" of jazz, and it's hard to evaluate spirit in any objective way. The difficulty of using a yardstick on free jazz helps to explain its lower audience figure, for most jazz followers and the jazz music world require musicians to first meet objective criteria (how fast, how clean, how precise the intonation, relative ability to follow chord changes, etc.). For the musicians, measurement is intensified by the university takeover of jazz, where musicians' normal future is to return sooner or later as teachers, depending on the market for what they can do.[124]

Mediocrity is one's location on a yardstick, a C grade for those who don't meet standards. For instance, I would qualify as a poor and not even mediocre player of jazz, but I could move up if I worked at it. To be mediocre (in jazz or classical music) has a negative connotation but commonly applies to many "good musicians" who follow the score or jazz improvisation patterns. These form the mass of orchestra, chorus, and lounge jazz, performing for an audience that comes to hear familiar compositions and idioms, at least (for restaurant gigs) in the background. They can function well enough without soloists whose names draw attention. Not so free jazz, which lacks the exacting standards ordinary jazz and orchestral musicians must adhere to. To draw a sizable audience free jazz requires advertised names, as does jazz, but free jazz cannot function as background music; the audience even for no-name musicians is attentive and usually enthusiastic.

As the basis for a real free jazz or avant jazz career, to be an anonymous good musician forever backing the soloists is not enough. Any ambitious jazz-based musician will be judged on their soloing and not on how well they support or interact with others, for the ethic of individuality cannot distinguish what is of mixed origin. Though jazz began as a fully interplaying group music, like blues it succeeded as a mediatized music, requiring the selection and highlighting of certain players. Sixties Free Jazz was a collectivity of players but as musical product it too was commodified, and to that extent it followed the soloist pattern, as has revivalist free jazz. Today the ambitious might get media attention for groups they organize but the most honored recognition would be for their playing.

In contrast to musics that depend on an audience, those who go under the banner of contemporary experimental music are excused from the duality of excellence and mediocre playing ability. The claim ascribed to them is to be innovative, which means they are in a permanent state of (presumably) breaking with convention, the known and accepted. If you're the first at what you do, there's no way to distinguish the better from the worse. They are protected against landing in the middle; they have a kind of teflon resistance to criticism along those lines. This is not an aesthetic valuation but an important distinction that helps explain the different lines of development for jazz-based and experimental music. The two form a mutually dependent binary, balanced against each other like bookends facing opposite directions and positioned to ignore each other's existence.

The musician community of free and avant jazz has a different door open to newcomers than their jazz parent. In the postwar period the jazz mentoring tradition was at its height--show up "on the scene" (in NY, that is), go to shows, meet and ask to play with those who impress you, and hope to be included. The alternative was to enter from outside the scene, like Coleman and later Ayler, by making a dramatic impression through their playing, with help from the music world critics. Coleman even had a huge mark against him for being sponsored by white critics, and would never have been accepted into the scene if his music had not impressed other musicians. Unlike popular and classical music, one could not advance *oneself*, get a record contract and be marketed as a serious musician, without getting the assent of at least some of the key players in the scene. There was a built-in antagonism between the power of the musician scene to make its decisions and the music world of entrepreneurs, whose concern was what would sell; case in point, Eric Dolphy, as noted earlier.

Mentoring exists today, but the reproduction of jazz musicians functions without that or approval from performing musicians. Nor is it desirable to shake up the audience or other musicians in order to get a hearing. There is a scene and the ambitious must show up, but it is possible to enter it simply by networking, schooling contacts, self-financing of records, and self-promotion. It is often remarked that you have to be rich to be an artist today. Indeed, music is not the rags to riches career option it once was; rather, it's disproportionately the graduates of the higher-tuition schools who predominate (at least in New York). Whites born into the middle class are unlikely to clash with music world handlers of similar backgrounds. It's no leap to become entrepreneurs who participate in the promotion of their music and, like others in business, make judicious decisions of whom to befriend. Despite their mild leftism they adopt the bootstrap idea that the market is fully capable of discovering and promoting all those of genuine value *if* they work at it. Surely an Albert Ayler would get on stage today, but to go further he would have a conscious or unconscious strategy and would not risk offending those ahead of him in the hierarchy.

Today's musicians trying to advance their names into the charmed circle are not to blame; what else are they to do?[125] Caught in a web, resistance and divergence from the norm marks one as an outsider to the game. The choice to make a career out of playing, even to get paid more than handouts, requires them to abide by what they have no control over, such as how their music is to function in society and even what to call it. Effective promotion will shape claims around gaining a specific audience, the bulk of which, like news-source consumers, have come to think of themselves in terms of differentiated interest groups. Avant-jazz musicians appeal to the straight-ahead side of the aisle; those more comfortable with resisting will favor free jazz. Of course there are blends of the two, but eventually, when private resources run out, all must develop an image and associations appealing to those who filter institutional funds to select venues, the main source of guarantees and a more secure income than the passed hat. Ambition is decisive, considered a marker of individual freedom and not a constriction to whatever will achieve success. For the resisters the sign of ambition is playing that is forceful, fast, extroverted, audience-directed. There are many start-ups; depending on the market a small number will end up with an income.

Career musicians, including the rebellious-sounding, must appeal to the major agencies that fund the few paying venues. Musicians are treated as providers of cultural content, functioning members of the economy and specifically the "creative sector." For these bureaucracies art is simply what people do who want to be recognized as artists rather than make something accessible for the commercial market. The height of creativity in the economy is thought to be current innovation, but for free jazz playing innovation is a legacy and to violate that earlier sound image would be a negative move.

Free jazz might be getting rebranded for a wider audience as "experimental jazz," implying that innovative work is being presented.[126] The term links it to technology and science, as if what the middle class wants to hear is culturally equivalent to a TED talk, something that might help save the planet. The appeal to innovation however rings false when applied to those who can't point to any. Only new listeners of free jazz might say "I've never heard anything like that before," a naïve consumer comment not to be heard from the hard-core fan base. Remove the anticipation that a free jazz concert today will offer music that breaks new ground, and one can enjoy it as an experience of many aspects of the jazz tradition and commitment. In this tradition tension has been resolved into a unity of solid ground. To break new ground would entail consequences no one wants to envision.

When free jazz raises the flag of survival it means to honor the political commitment of the earlier avant-garde, one of the few movements from the sixties to which such commitment has been sustained. To admit that it was transformed into something quite different would be to recognize its defeat, and deprive the music of a large part of its purpose. Only a handful of free jazz musicians make a living from playing; most have day gigs, but their hearts are deeply invested in their playing. They can take part credit that recordings of the originators are today far more available than they were in their own time. Record companies that once hesitated to release those recordings and did so without much publicity release new box sets regularly. More students than ever are familiar with them, and many see the free jazz style as *the* creative option to standard jazz. Knowledge of the historical context of their icons' boldness might lead them to widened parameters. We won't get, and don't need, the older concept of an innovative avant-garde of professionals in order to have a music that once again is alive and kicking. An interactive collectivity that doesn't shun less ambitious players, strongly affecting each other, and free to step outside standard free jazz—that would be *new*.

There are those indebted to jazz and free jazz today who wade into more self-critical, exploratory waters. These are the more hard-to-locate mavericks, who do not form a self-conscious avant-garde and don't wish to relate to other musicians through entrepreneurial competition. They affirm the traditional close relation to the instrument found in classical music and jazz, requiring discipline and practice, but pass over many other aspects of the tradition, treating it as flexible and not needing to be defended. Their playing may have a marketable identity, yet they reach beyond it. If accused of lack of jazz feeling and commitment they would say, fine, we're not trying to put ourselves in that or any other catalogue.

In this more adventurous wing of professional musicians I would include the late reed player and composer Joe Maneri and the guitarist Joe Morris, both having taught at the New England Conservatory in Boston. They are the most widely known and influential of those who have pushed their sound and concept beyond coded jazz expressiveness yet remain in tension with it. Maneri was the godfather of the American version of reductionism in the late 90s, an option to the jazz basis of free improvisation, as well as the promoter of non-diatonic tonality and microtonality, as we shall see. The liner notes from a Joe Maneri CD have the boldness of a manifesto: "All too often, freedom in improvised music isn't a paring down of style or an escape from it, but a rigorous, heavily mannered style in itself. Plenty of it still exists: free jazz based on the idea that volume, extended shouts, triads, and constant, single strokes of the snare drum are the keys to the universe, making it necessary to holler rather than to express oneself with sensitivity. Freedom sounds wonderful, but misapplied it can mold a musician into just a guy with good taste."[127] (Note that "rigorous," "freedom," and "good taste" are here turned against their usually positive connotations.)

For Joe Morris, "jazz has been institutionalized and codified to a point where it now has a de facto center of administrative oversight...it is no longer possible for musicians to attempt to extend the meaning of jazz beyond what it already is. Therefore it is necessary to replace it with a more suitable umbrella term that allows for the inclusion of music that does not adhere to those strict expectations."[128] That term for Morris is "free music," which for him includes the free improvisation of Derek Bailey's direction as well as free jazz. This eclecticism attempts to bridge the gap between improvisation rooted in the jazz tradition, such as his own harmonically-intricate playing, and that which is not, a move I would support. However to this I would argue we must first honor the distinction between them made in practical circumstances by most of the affected musicians today.

Let me conclude this section with a step back to view the dimension of psyche that has evolved in relation to the social order.[129] There is no singular psyche of a culture but conflicts between different psychic arrangements, which help explain the more obvious factors. As a widespread phenomenon, jazz was born in the aftermath of the most brutal war yet experienced. A death drive was unleashed and continued its work by laying waste to much of Victorian culture and mores; the new was almost the reverse side of those values. Yet for Americans, untouched on their own soil, the sunny faith in progress was retained. Now it held that the individual could heroically construct a normality flexible enough to accommodate the one crumbling.

Freud had framed the struggle of the individual as a tension between the pleasure and the reality principles. Although he revised this with the death drive after witnessing the war, that tension is what came in play, with "reality" as the social order seeking to right itself, and pleasure the lure and promise to do so. The regions of high industrialization and uprooted tradition experienced a massive disturbance of certainties; how was the individual to stay down on the farm (order and morality maintained) after they've seen gay Paree (eros unleashed from the grasp of death)?

The fate of jazz was bound up with the project of creating a self that could assimilate what volatile modernity threw at it and be transformed in the process. Jazz as the popular entertainment music was a major vehicle for that, spilling out suddenly through records and radio to virtually all ears. For the dominant white culture, the miscegenation of libidinous sensuality--the assumption whites had of black culture--and form straight out of the European book brought Dionysian release and Apollonian order into each other's arms as never experienced before. Sex and fun were in the air; jazz was the release of both from the horror of the war, which seemed to be bound by association with Victorian rigidities and solemn purpose.

Black jazz musicians discovering their public voice provided, as proxies for the white audience, a merger of deeper self and persona, the mask exposed to the world. Unlike all previous musics, the musician as soloist developed and then represented a self with something to say unique to that person. Such originality was closer to the subject than what was permitted in high art composition, distanced from the composer's physiology and emotions. Soloists were like motivated believers, urged from within to get their message across. This was a soul for a modern, secular society, trailing religious expression, one which can be present, up to date, and not too bothered by the official morality. To listen and dance to this music, especially for the young, was to identify with it as one's own spirit and put on its mask.

Not all personae get on the media stage, only those that capture the ear and win an audience that wants to be mirrored in that embodied soul. By drawing in and communicating with those responding to it, that voice grows incrementally, feeding on what the audience needs and gives back. To be effective in a modern culture it must attract not only for the moment, as fashion does, but be substantial and counted on year after year, providing a continuity of new material. The musician will not stray too far from home, will not change except to expand and deepen, buoyed by a success merged with art. Those considered most authentic were the voices best able to negotiate between the cruel uprooting that modernity brings and a self that yearns for a stability that can ride the waves. It is this dynamic that motivated the commodity exchange; all popular musicians since this innovation are in its debt.

In the early sixties the key figures committed to Free Jazz fit the pattern of such voices. By now they had become artist-intellectuals, articulating and arguing their position, and seeking to build an audience. They were paired with a mostly white educated audience that still expected jazz musicians to have something to say via an individualized musical persona. They also had the intelligence and jazz knowledge to understand it, like all those who wanted to have a psyche adequate to modernity. Musicians of the first wave fulfilled this secular version. They stayed within the parameters of jazz as a commercial music that was demanding the freedom, respect, and excitement expected of art. The avant-garde artist was ahead of the audience and coaxing it to take another step, to expand what they already accepted. The internecine clash with what still dominated the charts was fully within the understanding of modernity and selves capable of adjusting to the new. If society had continued to evolve along the lines of adjustment and reform it probably would have succeeded, for its level of disturbance was accepted as normal for art and for those whose drive for pleasure could only be satisfied by it.

The second wave was impelled beyond these relationships of art, artist, and audience. Its leading musician, John Coltrane, was spiritually obligated to speak, but did not ask for appreciation and understanding. It tells you what *is*, and what you must know and feel to move forward. Put the two together and it tells you what you must *do*. This "outside music" requires a psyche outside that built for sophisticated adaptation, outside of consumer behavior and the contract with culture suppliers. The message came out as glossolalia untranslatable as art, just when protest politics, the traditional appeal to power, was being repudiated as moderate and ineffectual.[130]

This radicalism cut through the playful surface to the root of psyche, giving a new meaning to the "surprise" of jazz. Ayler's and Coltrane's cry was still a persona, but a voice that made those of other jazz seem to be on the side of the bourgeois order, the Establishment. It was unlike bebop voices, for "crazy" was not a joke when the social order seemed to be disintegrating into violence. The audience that had been following it as an unfolding progress was faced with unassimilable experience and not new material for the repertoire. Instead of providing stepping stones the music flowed out like lava from the deep, a threat to art that reached a dimension of suffering that could not be rationalized, though latent in even the highest art. The second wave abducted the Persephone of jazz deeper into the psyche, and the old formulas could not recover. It did not kill jazz but exposed its weakness, its now obsolete solution to the psyche's accommodation to modernity.

More than the earlier jazz wars, the reaction to it one can be seen in crude psychological terms of reasonableness vs. rebellious desire, chaos, and hot emotion. Progress that confirmed the ego faced the death drive, which a few alternately viewed as the full bloom of eros. The next step forward of jazz did not tame the wild beast but egged it on, threatening to tip the shaky psychic balance—what violence did to much of the New Left in 1968. The absorptive, flexible self was faced with artists who reflected back to them an urgent upsurge of desire, contributing to the breakdown of the modernist faith. For a buttoned-down postwar world where Victorian censorship and segregation were still strong and enforced, the lid of repression and the boiling pot are an apt metaphor. The contract of admired jazz artist and receptive audience was violated and the modernist was adrift. As in party politics, it provoked a rallying cry of law 'n order—itself far beyond calm reason--to try to end the whole business.

On the other side of the street, what aroused no such reaction was the Experimental Music of Cage & Co., supported by writings defending it as poetic license (John Cage, *Silence*, 1961, etc.). Here was an art that claimed to stand outside the psychic battle, as its 19th Century European forebears did not. It was carefully positioned as distant from both ego control (the traditionally deterministic composer) and the demanding id of the populace, and so did not evoke their clash. It would take its place later within a fulfilled enjoyment society, where individualized selection would make it avoidable.

In the postmodern arrangement liberalism is sanctioned as intensified consumer capitalism that supplies the new delinked from any vision of a transformed future. With the passing of the Age of Anxiety, sexual repression, and censorship, the individual is freed from the need to put together a self that can sustain itself in the midst of change. This now seems merely transitional to one that is itself a moving image: a protean, polymorphous identity achieved by each individual, the ultimate self-promoter and self-satisfier. Those holding to professional identities that protected them from external pressures were undermined until they are now a thing of the past.[131] Jazz soloists coming up later would not mythical giants mediating between order and chaos, ego and id. They would be expected merely to recall the antediluvian past, and to strategically negotiate minor differences to make themselves noticed. The audience would receive them as performers ambitious to please them, bearing no psychic-cultural import.

Twenty years after the turmoil the context was radically altered; the embattled culture had cooled off, and accommodations seemed in place. The growth of an alternative culture, the end of legal censorship, the professionalization of warfare, and the expansion of civil rights and welfare promised a kind of peaceful coexistence. A postmodern celebratory, consumer culture of surfaces was the next new thing, as if chaos/rationality struggling over hearts and minds was a mere image most never knew. Punk struggled valiantly for honest self-expression but was quarantined by its need to be by and for only adolescents. It was given a place in the culture to make all the trouble it wanted, with a space reserved for complaining retirees. Its sound and fury was not beamed out over New York streets, as Jefferson Airplane had been; the cops would be called only for neighbors' complaints. It is then that the binary of jazz/free jazz was constructed as a permanent resolution, an agreement to disagree, and an institutionalized monument to what the psyche had once gone through and hoped never to face again.

That transformation of Free into free jazz can be viewed as a tragedy of defeat or as holding the space for a visionary viewpoint and commitment. That would require a different psychic arrangement, which has not appeared on the horizon. Art requires a space of ambiguity and a moment of confusion and reflection for both artists and audience, an ability to stand on shaky ground and not the certainty of cultural verities. A psyche receptive to it would have to squeeze its way between the binary of the moralist part of the problem/part of the solution and the unity of personal/political, which complement each other and dominate the liberal and left-cultural mind. Art has been sidelined, sectioned off from psyche as entertainment that echoes what its audience wants to hear. Vision is a consoling memory, lest a darker militancy erupt again—which recently it has, not surprisingly on the flip side of liberalism. Similarly, innovation has shifted to its more reasonable and consistent home--consumer products, military and intelligence hardware, and problem solving, devoid of any radical awakening to reality. Instead of the rebel, Classic Jazz evokes the voice of the complacent mature male, occupying or accommodated to power and looking back on the vibrant period with selective awe and restraint, to be relived at the first bars of a Monk tune.

Revived free jazz is a long-term commitment opposed to the displacements of postmodernity, but its effort is that of commodities--marginal versus mainstream. Its tension is frozen in place like the tragic-expressive Hellenistic Laocoön statue, without possible issue or death, which would enable something new to be born. It is emblematic of this stage of a culture that has encased the past as the only way to prevent art from bleeding through the cracks in the system. For those convinced that this situation is a permanent condition the cracks have been filled, and whatever suffering that art exposes to the world is merely information. To see this situation historically is to perceive it as deadlocked, and no blockage has ever been permanent.

Part II. Free Improvisation and Free Playing

6. British Free Improvisation

In its usage in North America, "free improvisation" covers a lot of territory and is too vague to pin down. For one scholar it is "frequently the name for music of an eclectic group of artists with diverse backgrounds in modern jazz and classical music [who] have pioneered an approach to improvisation that borrows freely from a panoply of musical styles and traditions and at times seems unencumbered by any overt idiomatic constraints."[132] If this is its meaning "frequently" and not even most of the time we are adrift with no land in sight. It is at least "an approach to improvisation," but if it is so eclectic and diverse and borrows so freely, it is nothing more than a loose reference. Any claim to what it is would be equal to anyone else's opinion.

When we look at it as a title used by specific people over the past five decades who have said "this is *our* approach" and especially "this is *all* we do," then we're on more solid ground. Where it was first considered an approach to improvisation and was debated as such was in the UK. When ten years later some Americans who were doing much the same thing got in touch with the Brits they borrowed the name, as well as the British spelling, improvis*or*, evidence of the direct linkage and priority. Its meaning there is still limited to a body of committed practitioners and a historical genre, and that will be our starting point.

In the mid-sixties professionally-oriented British musicians initiated an approach to playing outside the framework of the jazz and entertainment scene in London. Before it was given a title as a musical option it was an informal activity, which its practitioners called "just improvising." Still today the modest, even apologetic "just" indicates its status below what one normally presents to audiences as music. It was a musician's way of saying that different standards of judgment are at work--don't bother us. They knew of Free Jazz, which helped open a musical space for their adventure, but were not significantly influenced by it, or by the German version of it.[133] Its earliest advocates were musicians trained and experienced in jazz and 20th century classical and experimental music. Chief among them, for my purpose here, was guitarist Derek Bailey, who came from the declining world of musicians who provided live music for dancing, or at least a background for social gatherings and conversation.[134]

There were many others besides Bailey and the circle of partners he played with around the same time who later figured prominently in the history of free improvisation, most notably the Scratch Orchestra, Cornelius Cardew, and the group AMM. I have focused on Bailey because he is by far the major influence on American free improv. The others shared in much of his direction, compared to Free Jazz, but unlike his, their projects often had intentional social and political meaning, an orientation, and/or groupings of more or less defined membership and aesthetic. Of these AMM is the best known, partly because it has continued into the present. It headed more in the direction of a specific aesthetic, which Americans who identify themselves specifically as free improvisers have avoided.

Modern classical music played a significant part in Bailey's own development. One of his two earliest partners was bassist Gavin Bryars, strongly attracted to an avant-garde/experimental direction, and even after Bryars quit improvising, he and Bailey continued to dialogue on the relation of composer and improviser. The first freeform British improvising group of these two plus jazz drummer Tony Oxley was the Joseph Holbrooke Trio (1963-1966), named after an obscure composer as a joke. This group engaged in private exploratory sessions off to the side of their work life as entertainers, and began with improvising on tunes as jazz musicians do. Bailey was listening to compositions of Anton Webern (1883-1945) steadily during the period, which surely affected his specific way of playing. However he and his partners weren't thinking to contribute to a European avant-garde, or to add a new twist to what was known as "British jazz."

It is often a professional responsibility of entertainers to come up with something new to attract audience from time to time, but their bosses didn't care what they did on their off hours so long as they showed up and did their job. Their improvising was for themselves, on the leisure side of work, from which they felt a large degree of alienation and boredom. Private time with their instruments was exploratory rather than practicing for gigs, which was not necessary. What genuinely new approach doesn't begin in the negative—frustration with what's out there in the culture, alienation from the job one's paid to do, disgust with one's own repetitive patterns?

In letting their musical imagination expand they were developing instrumental skills and knowledge of pitch and rhythmic possibilities beyond what was needed for the job. In terms of the analysis of musical details they were much like the bebop explorers in the mid-40s. They had no concept of what they should be doing other than to construct a language different from the music around them and suitable to them personally. This would not have been possible without the accomplishments of jazz and modernist atonal composition, nor at a time when both jazz and high art were being publicly challenged, which will shake any music on a pedestal and open the door to invention.

The British improvisers gradually opened their sessions to audience, retaining that exploratory character on stage. They thought their music might be of interest to someone, and didn't wring their hands that it was only a few who showed up, sometimes none. In the meantime they kept their regular jobs. For a long period they apparently had no problem with keeping their explorations in one pocket and their professional careers in another, unlike American avant-garde jazz musicians, who could not imagine keeping the two separate. The New Yorkers were positioned at the point where the "it" of jazz originated and changed; they had a responsibility and commitment to jazz these three lacked. They could not treat it as optional and leave it behind, could not float freely among various approaches. Jazz for them could not be "a" music but rather music itself. This was the source of difference between the British free improv and the Free Jazz movements, as it did later for American free improvisers. The Brits did not *have* to be jazz musicians. As whites playing for white audiences there was no racial politics implied, no accusations against them as rebels and firebrands. They were committed to their way of playing but without the stigmatized identity at variance with and defending itself against the world of their main audience.

In the audience were curious musicians and some who wanted to become musicians once they heard the music. The lack of grandiose purpose for this adventure, the fact that the players were not well known or seemingly headed for fame, and the ambient sixties hunger for new experience untouched by the music world encouraged ordinary players to pick up this mode of playing without heed to the ladders of professional, structured musics. Some of these became professionals through this musical experience and well-known only through their identity with this music and each other. It was not the road to a career through music school (in this way similar to early American free improv) but through aesthetic decision.

To view this in the light of other musics at the time is to see its radicality. Briefly for now, the direction Bailey and his partners invented was a moment-to-moment music, and moments can stretch out indefinitely in time. This was not because these individuals had anything "to say," as with American jazz soloists, but due to its open-ended form, even though in performance players obeyed normal limits. It conflicted with "the work," a Western—even Germanic—high art musical concept of the 19th century. The ontological status of the work was assured by the score, and so it was of determinant performance length. When the baton descended for the last time the work was finished, and the audience could sum up its judgment. For a music that in performance seems determined merely by the formal ritual of set length, and in sessions is interrupted only by eating, fatigue, or a bathroom break, is there ever an appropriate moment for analysis? Free improvisation was also distinct from the classical narrative tradition of developmental and integrated form, which influenced all other forms of music, including jazz and Free Jazz. It was a player's version of what Theodore Adorno discerned in 1961 as a new possibility for composition, *musique informelle*, music that is relatively freeform and subjective compared to fifties serialism, which worked from an external model.[135]

Unique form was what Bailey's and his partners' playing had as its potential field, where there would be no pre-structures, no self-contained and duplicable pieces, no stable meaning in the conventional sense.[136] Consequently there was no easy transformation into commodities, which are normally grouped by patterns of resemblance for replication. A work is expected to have a conscious and deliberate structure of beginning and end, which accords well with the record industry. In the case of serious art the portable, material commodity is a perfected realization of the original score, the authentic and mysterious thing-in-itself. The recording even surpasses the score in the direction of greater composer control; for instance, towards the end of his life Igor Stravinsky himself conducted recordings of his early works, chiseling in stone his concept of how they should be played. As often noted, with the development of greater technique and technology, the perfected recording can challenge and even supplant the variable performance in authenticity, while the performance merely confirms that the stars who made the music actually exist.[137] Both Free Jazz and free improvisation produced recordings; the most iconic were those that had a compositional frame, such as Free Jazz, qualifying them more easily as artworks. Those of free improv retained in its concept an uneasy relation to the commodity, since one can be quickly reminded that the musical object had been open to all possibilities at the moment of playing and not just what resulted.

Despite this it is a misconception to say that the music of early British free improvisers is unstructured or formless. Rather, they dispensed with planning and the model, where conscious intent is realized before the actual playing, and with the Platonic notion of form which subsumes the particular under the general. Earlier, even when composers played their own compositions, structure had been the task of the composer separate from the one who made the sounds. In free improvisation the musicians developed structure in real time, eliminating the division of labor between roles. The player is not literally a composer, which would imply a continued division of creative work from its realization, such that it can be well or poorly realized. Rather the creation of structure is *displaced* from the composer directly to the player, thereby changing the meaning of structure. There is no way an improvised structure can be established apart from the playing, yet it does not for that reason disappear. For the improviser the form of each musical event could be unique, theoretically in the minutest detail, and thus potentially shocking to anyone who has normative expectations of an artistic event. It was highly indeterminate, since what one played depended heavily on what others did and the array of options players developed privately. These dependencies structured the event yet they were mobile, as one's explorations expanded.

If we think of the musicians as the workers and the composers as owners who hire workers to carry out their plan, then these improvisers would be like workers taking over the factory, only to create what they themselves want, collectively determined as part of their working activity. They work according to an intelligence that is not reflection split off from physical engagement, as is the specialized composer-intellectual. Despite apparent chaos there is an order to what they do, one they can at least subjectively, retrospectively, and collectively perceive. The workers would have no interest in creating commodities for the market, and abandon that effort. Since "work" is ordinarily defined as yielding goods of a certain measurable quality, this would more properly be called play, a coordination of mind and body without any end product or monetary reward.[138] If the split consciousness returns, bringing the boss and management back in charge, it is either because the workers have no other way to pay for rent and food or because the division of labor is too firmly rooted in the social reward structure, which turns out to be of greater significance for them. The bulk of consumers — and musicians--prefer music that more or less predictably follows from a conception, a form already in the minds of the makers, a kind of vault of invested principle of which each performance is the fluctuating interest. That is not all they hear but what they listen for; without *conceived* pieces there is for most people no music of aesthetic interest. On the other hand, as soon as musicians start to abandon prepared structures they gain confidence in that, a very different playing experience. At that point they can see the division of labor, together with the predictability of production, as unnecessary and not the most interesting frustration to deal with.

It is British musicians who have given us the most written reflections on free improvisation, such as composer Cornelius Cardew, percussionist Eddie Prévost, and Bailey, including music philosophy and reflections on its social/political import. Several British players of the sixties generation did not hesitate to put their politics into music. The group AMM in particular, of which Prévost has been a consistent member, broke up for a time over doctrinal political differences; such "splitting" was common with modernist avant-gardes, such as Surrealism and Situationism. While the British economy was floundering the left politics of improvisers tended to be working-class socialist as well as communitarian and anarchist in their critique of hierarchy. Implicit and explicit left political opinion helped sustain European improvisation. A British magazine like *Musics* saw musical and political commitment as going hand in hand, a common understanding among the sixties generation of improvisers. In Germany, on the other hand, advocacy of socialism would have indicated a more difficult open support of the socialist states, one of which geographically surrounded the Berlin musicians.

This close association of music and left politics loosened once the British Left had to face its long-developing crisis after the rise of neoliberalism (especially Thatcher's defeat of the miner's strike in the mid-80s). After the collapse of the "really existing" socialism of the Eastern bloc, the German improvisers no longer needed to declare their emancipation from American culture. The practice of American commercial culture, to draw audience on the basis of "name" promotion, became their mainstay as well. The music could then expand to a more apolitical audience of consumers aiming to hear noted performers, and as a musical genre would have to develop a competitive position in the marketplace.

Shortly after the beginning of musical exploration, the British were apparently calling what they were doing "free improvisation," an act of consolidation without which there can be no genre. Given a specific name the playing was likely to attract new partners and audience both. Bailey declined to present himself as playing any version of jazz and denied his very real ability to do it in his years as an entertainer; perhaps he meant to say that he couldn't play it with originality and commitment. At that time British Jazz was in full swing and for Bailey it was a kind of rival, *the* other from which he wanted to distinguish his approach in order not to be subordinated to it. A newcomer in process of establishing its identity competes with that music it most closely resembles, as if it could be completely separate, while a more distanced view would see them in tension.

In the spirit of deflating musical seriousness, which is a British and Dutch option (not always taken!) distinguishing them in general terms from the Germans, Bailey's guitar playing was sometimes referred to as the "plinky-plonky" school of improvisation. The phrase derived from an earlier curse against the twelve-tone music of Arnold Schoenberg and Anton Webern, and is not far off course, except for the jazz-like density of Bailey and most of the players close to him. They could play very driving music at times but then would pull back into realms of soft, quirky sounds, breaks in continuity, and pointillistic restraint, in which making a statement politically or emotively with cathartic effect, which second wave Free Jazz had, was not at all the point. Even Evan Parker, whose solos often came close in drive and density to his German counterpart, Peter Brotzmann's, described them as a technical solution and not emotive expression. In approval a *Village Voice* writer called Parker's solo "depersonalized" in an early 80s NY concert review.[139]

What was innovative about free improvisation compared to American Free Jazz (and closer to the Art Ensemble of Chicago) was that all instruments could play equally in a group rather than as functional roles. Abandoned was the obligatory rhythm section behind a front line of soloists, including the solo spot and the musical personality usually found in Free Jazz performance; in its place was an integrated group without parts assigned to members. Not Bailey himself but others even mocked the formidable musician-to-instrument bond of conservatory training. At one concert all musicians had to play an instrument they *didn't* know how to play—British humor, yes, but a point to it. The ad hoc grouping programmed by Bailey, rather than prepared and experienced groups, was the principle of his festival, Company Week, which brought together a wide range of players. Ad hoc reflected Bailey's own willingness to play with practically anyone who knocked on his door. Unlike conventional postwar jazz festivals and the near-universal practice today, Company Week didn't aim at drawing an audience to witness stars in action, but often relatively unknown players working imaginatively with whatever came up. Some were from classical and rock backgrounds, not even very familiar with free playing but with a strong interest in submitting themselves to it. An audience of the curious was drawn to a situation where the resultant music was in question—it could easily fail to convince. All were put in a difficult position and had to make the most of it, a potential for failure that the traditional musician, contracted to please the audience, would avoid like the plague. It took a shift in a large enough audience at a particular time in history for this to establish free improvisation as a music genre.

7. Free Improvisation in North America in the 1980s

Let me renew the caveat that this is an interpretation and not a comprehensive history or description of American free improv, which has yet to be written. I have not researched its origins in detail, nor are any studies available, although I do draw on my own engagement which began in 1979, and that of a few players active at that time.[140] My focus is on New York City, which does no justice to other concentrations of this music, especially in the Bay Area, as would any reasonable history of the music.

That being said, New York was the magnetic center of sixties Free Jazz, and similarly for free improvisation it was where most musicians of the East Coast, the smaller cities of the Midwest, and some from the Northwest came together in order to play as improvisers. Most had come to know Free Jazz, creating at least a geographical link of inheritance between the two musics. New York had the most interplay and tension between the two, which is crucial for understanding their musicological dialectic. Also the East Coast artistic culture, including free improvisation (in New York and later Boston), is tied historically and geographically to Europe, just as the West Coast received relatively more Asian influence. Commercially available Free Jazz could spread west and become a non-native borrowing, such that Bay Area free improv was less likely to fall under its shadow than in the East. Since there has never been funding or sufficient audience support for touring it has not been widely known in the East.

In North America professionally-oriented musicians, audience, cognoscenti, and institutions have always taken free improvisation less seriously than in Europe. Here free playing is catalogued with jazz, which has the strength of a native music, as it does not in Europe. What is not jazz-based here has been primarily a DIY music of players who don't expect to build a career on it. It did not develop through direct inspiration from the British, yet a common Anglo-American culture contributed to a relation of like minds.

Even if NY quickly became its major home, what came to be known as free improvisation in the mid-70s was, unlike Free Jazz, spontaneously generated by individuals from different parts of North America. Those most influential for its later development were from Alabama--guitarist Davey Williams and violinist Ladonna Smith. Davey was a country blues guitarist who had been mentored by Johnny Shines. He was drawn into free playing in the early 70s through a loose grouping of non-professionals oriented to Surrealism and Dada, "sessions where all manner of creativity would go on." When he heard records of British improvisers Derek Bailey and Evan Parker "doing much the same thing" he connected with them immediately.[141] Only one of the earliest American players, John Zorn, was a native New Yorker, if the first release of albums is any indication. These were by Henry Kaiser from the Bay Area (1977), Davey Williams and Ladonna Smith from Tuscaloosa and then Birmingham AL (Transmuseq-1978), John Oswald, saxophonist from Toronto (1978), and three on the Parachute label: Eugene Chadbourne, who started out in Calgary Canada (1977), and in NY Toshinoro Kondo and John Zorn (1978), who founded the label. In 1975 Milo Fine of Minneapolis exhibited the free-jazz side of free improv but more free of structure than the sixties music.[142]

Musical activity of course preceded albums, and this was also scattered, with players not necessarily knowing about each other. In 1979 I myself began playing freely in Philadelphia and I had no reason to think anyone else in the states was doing it or that it even had a name.[143] Some of those inspired by Free Jazz put free playing within composed structures. John Grundfest, for instance, had participated in NY Free Jazz sessions and after moving to the Bay Area organized a performance of a forty-horn ensemble, the Free Music Festival Orchestra, playing his pieces in a festival.[144] Others were similarly inspired and open to playing with no pre-structures. In the early 80s free playing appeared in the Denver-Boulder area of Colorado, and in Seattle and LA even earlier. Some who came into it had no orientation to jazz but rather to classical, No Wave, or electronic music.

At least on the East Coast the earliest players called what they were doing simply "free playing," "free music," or "free improvising."[145] Only later was the phrase for an activity replaced by a noun, which could then also refer to the kind of music and product of that playing, as in Europe. Free improvisation could then be an object that was thought to refer back to the playing, the necessary price for making it publicly available as a musical option. Generally we called themselves improvisers (by 1980 I would include myself), meaning *free* improv musicians. Jazz was of course also improvised, but musicians playing it identified themselves with that specific idiom and name.

The strongest relation to the world outside North America had always been to the Brits, although improv oriented to free jazz was also influenced by the Germans. While "free improvisation" was at some point borrowed from the British, the playing did not follow an imported model, the long and earlier tradition of American high art. The American initiators spurred interest for some, but they were not musical personalities to be followed. The playing was too various to be put in a single box and marked as an extension of jazz or any tradition, and this was part of its attraction. Without a tradition there was no mentoring to create and maintain a hierarchy. Some caught the spirit of Free Jazz, but by avoiding any kind of tune intro or pulse, and often playing in ad hoc groupings, they were still making a significant distinction in calling themselves improvisers. The idea was anarchistic--just start playing and go 'til we're done, or in performance to observe the limits of the set.

American improvisers were farther from being approved artist-musicians than the Brits, who in turn lacked the status of Continental Europeans, something of a continuum. Though Continental artists haven't gotten the kind of income of American pop celebrities, they have the status of professionals respected for their service to the national and local culture and ultimately to humanity. Art there is not a luxury but a cultural necessity, an elevated spiritual realm supported by the middle class and all levels of government, despite recent austerity budget cuts. It is part of the essence of European heritage that even the nationalist right can call upon and defend. In those highly secularized societies art is a substitute for religious observance, compared to America, where religious belief and institutions are still strong. There Modernism was something of a serial Protestant Reformation, purifying rather than destroying the humanism of art, and sustaining the idea of artists as a respected elite. There, "everyone an artist" is not very convincing.

When postwar New York became the world art capital it imported Modernism but not the concept of art and artist honored by the larger culture. Authenticity here was to be in the hands of the marketplace and the burgeoning mass media, not the self-declared artist and artist collectivities, as in European avant-gardes. The result of this is that still today improvisers unknown to the media who perform on the Continent suddenly discover what it means to be "treated as an artist," as many say on returning, apart from any mediating judgment of what they do or their popularity.

The caution exercised here with regard to art music would legitimize only those who produce compositions or improvise within a protected tradition, namely jazz. To create music outside conventional forms would be acceptable so long as it retains at least the hint of a composition stamped with ownership, the keyword for an increasingly consumerized culture. Artistic activity deemed worthy presumed conversion into objects that could be most easily mediated and assigned an owner. What could occasionally escape the hard-copy artwork in Europe could not do so here, where only owners and sellers of commodities can be considered serious artists. The mediating music world would be in charge of their status and not the artists. That would include the serious-art avant-garde, which was to be recognized only if it could acquire institutional credentialing. There exists an audience for European artist-musicians and for Americans who can cloak their performances in a reverential aura, but not enough to be supported as performers. To succeed here requires playing to a larger, hip-culture demography and drawing a sizable paying audience. Otherwise one is sorted into the bag of "everyone is an artist." For the few of that big bag to make the leap to visibility, "everyone a potential celebrity" has served as the transitional slogan, provided by the first one of his contemporary type, Andy Warhol.

Blocked from recognition, free improv had something generically American about it--pioneering into open country and underground rebellion. To be disrespected and ignored engendered players' loyalty to their community, rather than hope for a *Village Voice* pick of the week. The expectation of finding compatible others drew many to NY, where this was most likely at the time, and a community of relatively new enthusiasts emerged. Part of the attraction was the presence of John Zorn, known for literally taking the clarinet apart and playing its pieces, and using duck calls for a mouthpiece. By the early to mid-80s he and Eugene Chadbourne in particular would develop careers outside free improv.[146] Zorn was instrumental in supplementing the existing Downtown Scene with a "popular" avant-garde, whose individually crafted playing styles, projects, and personas represented for many *the* hip edge of culture.[147]

The 80s grouping of improvisers was not an adjunct or farm league for the popular avant-garde but was shaped by those who continued to be strongly committed to free improv, were unknown to the press and communally oriented. Among these were Davey Williams and Ladonna Smith, who visited NY frequently, and others such as Polly Bradfield, violin, and Leslie Dalaba, trumpet, who were crucial in defining the small scene.[148] Almost all were white; blacks, whose options for success were primarily limited to music and sports, had largely turned to other musical forms. The exceptions were drummer Dennis Charles and bassist William Parker, both of whom had been involved with Cecil Taylor and had strong roots in Free Jazz.

What was possible in NY for improvisers to perform was below the media radar: spaces anyone could enter but known to and attended almost exclusively by the performers and friends, plus those who could imagine themselves as such. There were few if any followers. A music that lacked a known title, commercial availability, and an audience of non-players was not a true scene or subculture. It was unselfconsciously open to anything "out," all sorts of sound, ranging from jazz-based and loud electric free playing to invented instruments and often quiet, cheap electronics, out of the box or trash or rewired. One could easily pick up on what others were doing. With no rewards to speak of, they weren't competing with each other, so there was no danger of treading on another's reputation. Some hoped to increase their audience, but this was not the right thing to do for that. It was the music of last resort, gathering together those who need to play and would be homeless without this community of players. That, and not a genre boundary or even a taboo on genre identity, was the determining factor.

Speaking as a participant myself, it was an open question what this music was and who it was for other than ourselves; some of our records were reviewed, so maybe someday it would be marketable. It didn't inherently defy commodification, though that was a common assumption that functioned to protect our activity. If a record company A & R man had dropped in by accident he would have felt he was intruding on something quite private and resistant. Such was the feeling of self-protection and self-determinacy in that era, with hardcore punk and No Wave bands the more visible representatives. We could keep the music to ourselves, and we weren't trying to market ourselves in the terms understood today. The means were not available and the entrepreneurial spirit was only beginning to find roots in the soil of "out" music. Some had music degrees, but it was not the union card it was supposed to be (and has become today); rather the matter of pride was how far they had gone off the track from what their teachers would have approved. A trumpet player told me, "My teacher would shit his pants if he heard me now!"[149] That might be oedipal rebellion, yet lots of such taunting was around that could expect to get daddy's approval in the long run. Bolstered by a strong sentiment that we were accredited by no one but ourselves, the music was first of all *for us*.

Contributing to our partly-chosen isolation was the extraordinary expense for an individual to take the career path. It required not so much a degree but a manufactured product, a vinyl record, with no expectation of sales to recover the investment.[150] Besides close association with others similarly career-oriented, that foot-in-the-door would have to be followed up on a regular basis. This created a huge gap between those who were able to get into the hip culture market and actually sell stuff and those who couldn't, and music that lacked some kind of compositional framework did not qualify for sales. The only DIY technology for producing and distributing our music was cassettes copied in real time, few of which made it to stores but were passed hand to hand. For those such as myself who had professional aspirations in the direction of touring, it was understood that only one record was required to accredit oneself as serious; the music would have to do the rest. That put the emphasis on what we actually did, rather than spending our effort on image-building.[151] In the era of print publications devoted exclusively to jazz, there were two that included free improv, *Coda Magazine* out of Toronto and *Cadence* in NY State. The reviews legitimated the musician enough to find willing organizers, usually other musicians. To find a media-recognized venue around the country was more difficult. Who would book someone who said, we don't know what we'll play until we do it?[152]

This music was a form of cultural politics that, lacking a mediatized, public existence could not arouse conflict, as had Free Jazz. It was in part a musical extension of the sixties rebellion, cultural anarchism, and anti-authoritarianism. The Reagan presidency and the inauguration of the neoliberal era aimed at overturning that heritage provoked widespread resistance, and free improv was part of it. It is safe to say that all considered themselves in some way on the left side of the spectrum, at a time when political views and musical art were integrated in the NY community where improvisers gathered. Located in the Lower East Side (the East Village), it had inherited the cheap lodgings and cafés of the hippy, poetry, and Free Jazz scene of the 60s-70s. It was also witnessing the undermining of that culture through gentrification and commercial development, and its replacement by an upward-mobile consumer lifestyle culture that presented itself as a cleaned-up version, later to be called "bourgeois bohemianism."

By the end of the 80s improvisers were moving out of Manhattan, with the majority going to Brooklyn, which continues to be the major home for improvisers and their venues. To be a cultural mover and shaker, such as the popular avant-garde, one must be as closely associated as possible with Manhattan. At least since the late 80s the Manhattan/Brooklyn divide, in terms of musicians' residence and the status of small venues, has been a significant marker for music considered worthy of media attention. The forced migration of improvisers from the lower east side to Brooklyn was a step down for those expecting to become full-time career musicians. It was also something of a diaspora, for there was no other concentration of cheap rent apartments where musicians could live within walking distance.

All this reflected broader cultural developments. Late sixties advertising and corporate strategy had opened the way for individual rebellion to become a personal lifestyle. This path fit the wish of many to escape the negativity and conflict that protest politics implied. By the late 70s theorists were lauding popular culture as a valid form of resistance, and by the 80s, for musicians to indicate they were on the avant edge of the popular, with an ironic, mocking relation to it, would help find an audience and legitimacy. No Wave and punk radicalism prompted the media and recording industry to create room for an amorphous genre more suitable for commodification, New Wave. It was based on composed structures, with the term "improvised" sometimes bolted on as a tantalizing selling point indicating spontaneity, but not taken too literally.

When the Downtown popular avant-garde targeted the post-sixties demographic it was perceived as breaking the wall separating art from ordinary life. This was a trope of art avant-gardes from the Russian and Italian futurists through the Situationist International, which had deeply affected political events of May 1968 in France. However, contrary to them the popular avant-garde aimed at full commercialization, which was indeed ordinary to the lives of consumers.[153] With this strategy they could free themselves of association with "difficult" or "intellectual" modernist music and a stuffy Establishment. On the other hand, the popular avant-garde needed to distinguish itself from its other on the opposite side, those *not* seeking public approval, and unable to reach an audience in a period of social and political retreat.[154] All in all, improvisers were caught between submission to the new political and cultural order and exclusion from it.

As long as cheap rentals were still available, improvisers formed a relatively self-sustaining community, strongest in the East Village. There was a regular Sunday afternoon dance/music improv at PS 122 on First Avenue and a few blocks away an evening performance in the 6th St. basement space of an anarchist group. This was Amica, the name formed from the letters of the sign "Alchemical Theatre" that remained after the others had fallen off.[155] The series itself was often called "the Bunker," fitting for how people felt in relation to the rest of society. These were open but not truly public performances, since they were unadvertised and unlisted, attended almost exclusively by the community of players, and discovered by word of mouth. Most thought of themselves as musicians and practiced regularly (to the best of my knowledge), to this extent not following the anti-disciplinary direction of the sixties, yet also welcome were the untrained, as well as experimental instrument builders.[156] There was no formal principle of exclusion; if a group of people playing in a living room for their own amusement heard of the series and wanted to perform they were invited. The venue was available for music that continued the private free playing of earlier decades, now assumed to have little chance of popular acceptance. These performances were not competing with others for audience the same night but were more in the category of communal gatherings. Accordingly, listeners received almost everything at least sympathetically; more than likely they would soon be performing there themselves. Witnesses not only discovered partners there but participated virtually in each other's playing.

The beginnings of free improv in New York and especially Amica were facilitated by an active organization. This was the Improvisors Network, founded probably in 1979 by trumpet player Leslie Dalaba and coordinated by her and guitarist Chris Cochrane. It was the kind of membership organization to be found before internet networking, in which the applicant had to cross a line by answering a detailed form, thereby gaining a sense of being evaluated (though I doubt any were rejected!), belonging and commitment. It was open not just to New Yorkers but to any improviser, at a time when people were moving to New York from all over the country to play music. To my knowledge it was the only free improv organization in the country that had a mailed newsletter, a list of everyone's address and phone number, and concert listings. It differed from similar sixties Free Jazz efforts, for it was not intended to provide gigs and publicity for professional musicians to perform and earn a living but to realize a community of like-minded players with direct access to each other.

The Bunker itself was a concentrated version of what was going on sporadically in a few other cities. For instance in Philadelphia, drummer Jim Meneses and I created a performance space called The Wet Spot that lasted one year, 1982, until we were evicted (the building had long been slated for demolition for the business makeover of Center City). It held weekly concerts of "improvised and experimental music," combining a set of locals and one of traveling improvisers. It was a true underground; *The Philadelphia Inquirer* refused to list its events, then hypocritically lamented its demise. We created it as a counter to the funded and media-supported venue for "outside" art music, The Painted Bride, which would not schedule free improv events.[157]

In Chicago one could play in the back of The Occult Bookstore on North Clark St. run by cellist Russell Thorne, a once-active Free Jazz bassist who had bowed out of the career life. Around 1985 things began to open up for performance in Chicago with a series at Links Hall further up the street, created by dancer Bob Eisen and percussionist Michael Zerang. In search of partners I had traveled to the Bay Area in 1982 and found the earlier lively scene extinct. Around 1985 enthusiasts such as Tom Djll, who had attended the Creative Music Workshop in Woodstock, Hillary Fielding, and others picked up the organizing effort where 70s improvisers had left off. They created a scene and a small publication, *Freeway*, and generated an interest that has not let up. Elsewhere practically no venues were prepared for this kind of music, and of course no internet to locate the occasional show. Yet to come were the local organizers and player/listener scenes that have grown up in recent years for music considered experimental; until then one played wherever one could get away with it.

I was the only one touring widely with this music in the 80s, and so I will refer to my files here (soon Davey Williams would call me "the Johnny Appleseed of free improvisation"). By the end of the decade I found people open to free improvisation in all the big cities as well as non-urban university towns (not students, however). Besides my own desire to play and find partners, how did this happen? The conventional bio that boasts one's rank with other known players meant nothing in Lincoln or Wichita or Boulder, where the name I could list were unknown. A music no one had heard of and a musician with no credentials to speak of meant that the small audience came out of pure local curiosity, with some perhaps thinking I represented current urban culture. Notices in free entertainment weeklies in the Midwest were easy to come by, unlike today's internet age, when the general audience will not be exposed to even the existence of such music. It attracted musicians who had never imagined playing without a song structure; the closest thing they knew was The Grateful Dead. If they wanted to hear it, and maybe join or play on the bill, they would have to organize a show and invite their friends. Of course many were just generous, and happy to see someone come through on a shoestring tour and help out. I don't think the quality of my playing or my occasional partners' had as much to do with it as our adventurous spirit and the strangeness of the music.[158]

Free improv was included in the 80s underground "cassette culture," which paralleled mail art as a largely non-urban development across North America. Cassette culture was an extension of alternative culture, at least that which found American commercial existence and "making it" irrelevant to life. Cassette zines were modeled on the early *Whole Earth Catalogue* and mostly from the West Coast, the major home of alternative culture, with tapes traded at shows and by mail.[159] Cassette culture partisans formed a network of usually self-expressive, non-virtuosic players, not music-schooled or aiming to establish themselves, whose audience was a local and distant musicians with similar intent. They could be found almost anywhere, a preview of the internet today, but then it required more initiative and determination to find each other. It was popular in the sense that anyone, regardless of expertise, was welcome to self-produce music independent of the music business. Four-track cassette recorders facilitated elaborate overdubs. Cassette culture blurred the sharp distinction between professionals and amateurs, as did garage bands earlier. The music of many did not stray far from commercial music, but the network was self-enclosed and not looking for wider distribution.[160]

Free improv shared the DIY features of cassette culture with punk and hardcore, the most obvious parallel in the more visible underground scene.[161] It was 70s punk and No Wave that first associated "scene" with antagonism to major-label music and mainstream culture, but hardcore musicians took this to the limit by rejecting as collaboration with the enemy any signs of acceptability to the corporate music establishment and conformist taste. Yet it desperately needed to be popular with an audience, a contradiction it resolved by making absolute the distinction between its following and the larger world. Hardcore was pointedly expressive and messaged, often faster and shorter than 70s punk, like little balls it threw at the audience in quick succession: "I want to say what's *exactly* on my mind, and in 32 seconds."[162] Band members aimed at the pleasure of harshness (a useful adjective later, as in "harsh noise") that sometimes extended into violence. It would have come off as hostile to the audience except that injuries were apparently experienced as a communal bond, separating insiders from outsiders. Hippies running on peace and innocence would not have imagined this as their thing, a sign of breaking with the earlier ethos they emphasized. Violence was partly a surrogate for politics; since Reagan and restored middle class conventions were the prime fun-killers, there was a considerable political and generational edge to the music and provocative flyers. The press didn't miss this and wasn't meant to; it deplored hardcore in vicious terms equal to the attack. The earlier generation of milder rebels, as represented by rock critics, felt they had turned the mainstream in their own direction, and further radicalization would only be counter-productive.

For hardcore there could hardly be an end to negation; straight-edge asceticism was even an internal self-negation. It denied tradition, including sixties blues-based music, and so it was as anti-revivalist as any avant-garde art could be. An absolute us vs. them movement, it raised the flag against appropriation of their style and hardcore groups that seemed interested in success beyond the core audience. Unlike Free Jazz, it aimed to be *dis*qualified as art, which meant adult culture. That extended to instrumentation, making it minimal and conservative. "'Inclusion of instruments besides guitar, bass and drums is still considered somewhat experimental' (one reviewer remarks on a band's use of 'exotic' instruments: flute and saxophone!)"[163] Art was thought to be distanced from rage, yet with hardcore, rage began its career as the fashionable art of the rant, a recuperation they could not have imagined. Hardcore rage had its solid audience, politically powerless, with its adolescent border simply policed. By contrast, the earlier jazz audience had projected black rage *onto* Free Jazz, creating a break; stylized free jazz would recuperate that image of rage for a very different audience.

Lacking lyrics, the music of free improvisation could not provide any radical meaning even if the players wanted to, and they had no interest in enforcing ideological unity. There was no jealous protection against appropriation; it was even laughable that other musicians would apply "freely improvised" to music that was so obviously structured.[164] "Free" implied that the result of one's playing was up to the individual; despite interactive playing it was too heterogeneous to be summed up as a singular product. Improv was the greater *musical* challenge, for it lacked any of the conventional hooks into the audience such as hardcore's song structure and beat. Having an edge was something the two shared, yet in being so explicitly anti-musician and anti-career hardcore lacked the ambivalent, potential ties to art and anti-art of improv. Those ties included the concert decorum of chamber music; no one playing in improv shows was about to stage-dive into the audience. Had the press critiqued free improv they would have accused it of nihilism, but unlike hardcore and punk it aroused no fear of social disruption.[165]

Hardcore had a short prime period, late 70s-1985, after which the prominent bands thought it finished, whereas improv continued with an apparently built-in cycle of hibernation and re-awakening, with no later accusations of betrayal by the originators. Since it was not encased in a public historical memory as was hardcore and Free Jazz, it could not be an object of survival efforts, resistance, and nostalgia, restored and re-enacted. The resurgent Right led by Reagan wore down the context for both improv and hardcore, at least blunting their élan and commitment. Both held some unacknowledged

131

utopian belief that they could have an impact, and so the second Reagan election in 1984 was hard to swallow—get ready for an endless winter. Hardcore was strongest in cities outside NY and came from the generation younger than the 80s free improv players, who had a more positive relation to the 60s. Free improvisation was a kind of no man's land, influenced by the militancy of the time but fed more by Jimmy Hendrix and Free Jazz, as well as by late 70s avant-rock, which led some from the UK (Chris Cutler and Fred Frith of Art Bears) to become active improvisers. Players held a space few could imagine inhabiting, rather than trying to get their voices heard by feeding an underground scene. Unlike London improv of the late-80s, there were no musicians that a public looked up to as the real deal of a real music.

At the core of both hardcore and improv was DIY, taken as a positive means of making things happen rather than a regrettable necessity for the musician who can't find an agent. As Brian Baker of the hardcore band Minor Threat said, "If there's something you want to create that does not exist, do it yourself." That kind of attitude got me driving across America playing free music in the Reagan 80s, and has become the basis on which most improv gigs happen today.

Unlike every known form of music no writers or publications outside the improv community supported the music critically and considered its distinct approach.[166] A music without a music world (public media, critics, venues, funding organizations, etc.) will have too few audience and no careers. Music worlds mediate the musician-to-audience contact, providing what they imagine audiences want, so they can at least buy *something* valued by others. To read a review *in print* (more than today's online blogs) presumes other readers who accept the opinion. The music world also mediates the contract without which there would be no careers—public respect and financial support. Careers integrate musicians into the economy, and those showing the strongest ambition are most willing to accept the music world's terms. The career turns playing into a job, a transformation all art must pass through if it is to be labeled art. If free improvisers had been unequivocally ambitious for a career, and clearly distinct from those who weren't, improv *might* have acquired music world support. What drew people to playing freely, those career-oriented and those not, prevented that from happening. To say the music failed to acquire an audience because people didn't like it tells only half the story; market success can never come to a music whose door is open to walk-in players. A profession implies expertise, standards, and selectivity.

One can caution endlessly about the difficulties of free playing, but if you tell someone, all you have to do is make some sounds and I'll play with you, then you'll have trouble convincing any potential music world that you are a serious musician.

Music worlds deal in genres, usually defined by common positive characteristics; for instance, the blues audience exceeds those who patronize the famous names. How can there be an audience (or music world) for a music with no characteristics other than being defiantly *not* like other musics? Some played similarly to the Bailey direction, but there was no search for a new, shared musical language. Rather, especially ad hoc playing aimed to see what would happen when someone else's music did not necessarily conform to one's own. Most played fast and vigorously, but that was accidental, there was no principle or desire to exclude those who played otherwise.

The explicit theoretical base was minimal and not binding. Davey and Ladonna (as improvisers have always called them) thought of free improv as a musical version of Surrealism, at least its artistic side.[167] Improv denied the structure of music, presumed to be reasonable, and seemed to conform to the unsystematic practice of automatic writing.[168] If the irrational is grounded in the unconscious then to play out of spontaneity is a universal human possibility and not subject to learning a code. In the sixties the meaning of "surreal" as incongruous and spontaneous spread beyond artists to parts of the urban middle class. Likewise, free improv could not be limited to people traditionally called musicians. Given this, it could be extended beyond its earlier known form as a fan- and legitimacy-oriented venture specific to NY career musicians.

For an art music to abandon the usual jumping-through-hoops of professional advancement was a radical innovation that went beyond amateurism. Literally anyone was welcome to do meaningful, exploratory playing, onstage or in sessions, since presenting an attractive public music and image was not absolutely necessary. Moreover, an event could go literally any direction, not only sound but nonsensical speech and movement.[169] In fact free playing found wider participation and organization in movement than in music, though minimally structured. This began in the late 70s when dancers began popularizing Contact Improvisation, which spread beyond professional dancers to take root throughout North America and other parts of the world.[170]

Davey and Ladonna began publishing *The Improvisor*[171] in 1980 and annually through the decade, soliciting articles from anyone interested in free improv and reviewing every improv recording sent to them. Everyone could say what they thought free improv meant without fear of being contradicted. It was broad in its definition of improv, yet was more a trade or in-house publication than one aiming to supply fans with consumer advice. The concept of an open community of players, even international, whose reach was not limited by marketplace appeal, brought them in line with cassette culture and the counterculture in general. The open form of this kind of playing and the magazine gave it the appearance of a movement, with its social philosophy in range of Derek Bailey's approach to other musicians, though his partners tended to be trained professionals.[172] *The Improvisor* didn't present improv as breaking the mold, or any other appeal for art-public attention, but they did project a sense that this collective approach to playing and its community were going somewhere and would be joined by others.

Jacques Attali's *Noise, the Political Economy of Music* circulated among a few of us. Written in the mid-70s, it shows the mark of the sixties spirit, only appearing in English translation in 1985. Early chapters critically analyze the history of Western music from its Greek origin as a series of economic-anthropological stages, something no other book had done and still a model of its kind. In the final chapter Attali promises a utopian future for free-form playing over structured music that gave it a radical cultural import and added to his claim that music is the harbinger of political and social transformation.[173] His enthusiasm exceeded his knowledge and the clarity of his concept--he knew American Free Jazz of the later 60s only through French sources and nothing of European free improvisation. He lumped together John Cage and Free Jazz, and he strangely called the coming phase "Composition." However, since those interested in Attali located themselves somewhere in that mix, his high expectations for the future bolstered their own. I don't know anyone who looked at Attali critically back then, since we were happy merely to find an island of theoretical defense in a sea of ignorance and silence.

In retrospect of course it's easy—too easy—to see why that situation of the 80s was not fulfilled. America improvisers were not even producers struggling for a place in the world of consumption. They had no tradition to validate them, nor pressure to grow beyond their present capabilities. A few were invited to the UK in the late 80s, and had they become ex-pats more experienced players would have challenged them and taught them new things. Rooted in the states, and with funds for the music in Europe sparse enough, few moved there. Free improv here would have a separate history.

Given the nature of the music, the music world, and players uninterested to do what is needed for credentials, it was not their fault that few outside the player community appreciated or even publicly dissed the music. Without public discourse and reaction from the world, self-satisfaction and stagnation can easily settle in; jazz, for instance had grown from the controversy it provoked. The supportive, egalitarian acceptance that was the strength of the community closed it to self-evaluation, as if any critique would be harmful. As in anything with traces of oedipal revolt and collective unity, self-understanding was defensive, and never had to be made explicit.

Free improvisers celebrated not having the standard of judgment over their heads that conventional musicians had. What they did share was that they were performers. Even though they performed mostly for each other, the role does not entail self- or other-critique from an artistic perspective. Most (including myself) repeated themselves without imagining they could be playing entirely differently. The weakness of spontaneity, of saying "don't think, just do it," is that choice never enters the picture. The freedom to do whatever does not include overturning that "whatever." This relates to the anti-art strain that prevailed, continuous with the sixties anti-disciplinary spirit that was part of improvisers' camaraderie. Writers and visual artists have infinite time to explore their assumptions; the painter Agnes Martin's had twenty years of dissatisfaction with her work until she found a suitable path for herself. Improvisers have to make the time for reflection, which is easily skipped. Most had studied and continued to practice, yet the content of that (scales etc.) probably carried over from training, maintaining chops rather than disturbing the structures they took for granted. To imaginatively construct one's own practice, to get disgusted at clichés and limitations, to compare notes with others, to generalize what one is doing and reflect on it, to wonder about process in relation to the other arts—these things may have happened occasionally but weren't central to anyone's agenda I knew of.[174]

The lack of self-critique was related to the politics of a community that viewed itself as a self-contained alternative, similar to youth culture two decades before. Art alternatives last until they are either absorbed into an institutional framework, such as academia and funded venues, or become acceptable enough for significant consumption. By the end of the decade questions earlier suppressed surfaced, like: "I thought I was going to be a real musician; where am I now?" The community weakens when it looks like some were going to make it and others not. For good reason players so thoroughly ignored build walls and trenches, or as I said at that time, operate as a ghetto, as if this were forced on them and not also partly their preference.

New York *means* hipness, a standard for the wider culture, such that its musicians are judged whether they qualify. That makes rejection a more potent factor for their motivation there than in the non-urban, only locally-competitive town.[175]

Urban-oriented improvisers were alternative-culture, while a career is a conventional adaptation *to* the culture, obviously necessary if one is to earn a living. Those who choose that can also change that culture, and the popular avant-garde did that. It was aligned with the growing entrepreneurial spirit of the age and bolstered by the culture war, a rerun of the sixties' artists vs. the Establishment, whose substitutes were now the neo-conservatives. Those out to establish themselves could not compete inside the jazz music world, where the playing was matched against an internal standard. Playing free improv would not do this; like jazz, little could be said of significance apart from hearing it.

What could generate discourse and build a musician's oeuvre and reputation was structured improvisation, such as John Zorn's game pieces (Hockey, Pool, Archery, in the late 70s, and Cobra, 1984). These were comprehensible as compositions; a leader-composer determined who would play, controlled the outcome, and it was his name that was tagged. The improvisation it involved was the icing of spontaneity on the cake of structure that is the real meaning of the event. The very inventive novelty of the game structure made the content a result of the structure, consequential and less necessary, like all conceptual pieces. As for Zorn himself, first his playing was highly original, then he shifted to structures that were; his playing became representations of his oeuvre and the structures repeatable. Paralleling free jazz, his career was built around recalling its origins, except that those origins were individually his and did not recall a collectivity working out its music together.

Around the same time, critically recognized visual art was being reorganized between two poles. On one end was high art, to be acquired as cultural capital through education in the continuum of Art History; on the other was entertainment for an audience that felt *it* was part of the provocation, the radical other of the popular avant-garde. High art observer and popular avant-garde participant could be separate persons or collapsed into one, blurring the previous line of sharper distinction. The postmodern devaluing of "difficult" art elites and the favoring of popular celebrities helped to bring this about. Modernist artists who had been scorned were converted into remote icons, which made them more compatible with the accessible pop-avant-garde celebrities of the 80s. Art ceased to be an exclusive category whose borders needed defending against interlopers.

According to this schema free improv was the free choice of a few non-popular, eccentric musicians playing relatively privately for themselves. A wide-open tolerant society let them do their thing. It could be both a commitment for those narrow-minded enough to do it exclusively *and* something professionals could occasionally play alongside other skills and interests, but not a music in its own right.

8. What Good is Free—An Excursion

The musics discussed here have "free" as their master term, yet any unified definition of the word would make it a battleground for priority. It is an amorphous, plastic word that has been ideologically useful so long as its precise meaning can be picked out of a hat.[176] Psychologically, it is the respectable word for desire that hasn't quite escaped a sexual implication. It points to a deep longing potentially so radical and penetrating that power cannot leave it alone. It can cut both ways, as part of an ideology meant to protect Americans from inclusion in the rest of the world, or as recognition that the world is none other than ourselves, our consciousness and experience freed of mediations and pressures, however momentarily, and that's too disturbing to be righteous about. Freedom is the rose in our grasp or it's a thorn in our side, opening us to our situation in ways that can be excruciating. To cover this up it must be gilded and honored as the achievement of progress.

This contested word joins together jazz, free jazz and free improvisation musics. It is no coincidence that "free" distinguishes them as "live" rather than composed and reproducible replicas of what is now inert. "Live" is so attractive that it is commonly shorn of its literal meaning, such as the contradictory "recorded live," as if the dead were just as capable of making music. It still implies something *alive*, as in the here and now unstable human reality—who knows what you and I might do this very moment? Live music points to the contingent, the unpredictable, and the troubling. Lenny Bruce disturbed and excited the American consciousness with comedy that was so live that the state felt it must shut him up. Those playing live have the chance to step out of any box the social order has prepared for them. The question is why they don't, when they so often claim that they do. Art gives us all that option.

"Live" would be a useless designation before the technology for replicating sound appeared. The technological novelty swiftly became the other to ephemeral performance in Janus-faced modernity, which is both the anxious desire for movement and the effort to contain and deepen where movement has landed. The free musics are historically grounded in Western culture,

138

from where they join—or rejoin—the improvisation found in all the world's musics. As ethnomusicologists scurry 'round the world to record the last scraps of them—Progress aiming to recover from its own effects—the built-in ephemerality of music continues to face its obsolescence.

Free of what and for what is the root question. As a legacy of the Platonic tradition carried forward into Christianity, "free" is complicated. The philosopher Alfred North Whitehead said "All of philosophy is but a footnote to Plato," and that includes spiritualized high art Music. For that tradition what is overcome is the body, the primary image of corruption, decay, and contingency. This is the dream of leaving behind the finite material world, the imperfect, and what is destined to die. Free then means transcendence (in Christian terms, the Resurrection and, yes, the Ascension) over immanence, or History-Spirit-Geist over daily material existence, otherwise known as reality, in which psyche has its roots.

A quite material social process is at the origin of art's spirituality today. A corps of specialist-critics selects what is to be endowed with a holy aura and their god-like creators. As for music, audiences have no means of demanding artworks be put on the list that aren't already there. Here is the stage machinery no one wants to see, covered up by the blanket of faith in the spirit. It has put the score of selected works beyond full earthly realization, and awards the composer pride of place in our culture. It still does, according to the funding sources of serious art; even John Cage and his silent composition 4'33" would qualify as among the acts of the highest spirit.

Jazz improvisation that began to be perceived as an art was the first frontal assault on disembodied spirituality to be popularly welcomed and successful. It celebrated the ephemeral body here and now, the tangible and sensual even linked to illicit sexuality. Free jazz reasserted this and formed the next major challenge to sound split off from the body from which it comes. Here "free" was even more down to earth, when it poured from the emotive and skilled bodies of players, freed of most of the compositional inheritance of earlier jazz.

For the body to simply declare itself is not enough; culture can spiritualize freedom above present possibility. In the dialectic of mobile life and inert death the earthly imperfection of Free Jazz came to be embodied in works and figures considered perfect and holy. The decline of music's spontaneous relation to the body can occur before inertia becomes the bodies permanent state; it is ever faced with that threat. Many artists fear that the mind's intellect can kill the body's impulses, but the mind can also become aware of how the body is prematurely dead, and through the shock of that awareness can kick it alive in new ways.

"Free" implies "made only this very moment," maybe because what one is freed from is a past condition. This indicates that current both free jazz and free improvisation are under pressure to avoid pre-arrangement. When "free" was appended to playing it was intended as a wall against intrusion from any nailed-down code or habit from the past. The word also has implicated the two musics in a specific social and political direction that is the very hinge of modernity and its ambivalence. "Free" means for the music itself to be emancipated, but also to emancipate others. The two musics are elevated (or burdened) with the universalist, utopian promise of modernity beyond its containment within a recalcitrant social order. This was one public aim of the Enlightenment; for instance Immanuel Kant's "maturity" meant progress beyond the blinkered childhood of mankind, a progress which has turned out to be cyclical.

This was subsequently essential to the concept of modernist avant-gardes, serially advancing on each other, discovering the limitations of earlier emancipations. They typically perceived the dominant culture and/or social order (originally feudal and ecclesiastic) as the negative from which to liberate themselves and lead the way. Just as the Enlightenment depended on its nemesis of myth and religion, so have art avant-gardes promised to liberate its bourgeois (middle class) public from the grip of whatever limits its awareness. As the advanced part that leads the whole, avant-gardes prided themselves as leading humanity—that was their arrogant assumption.

For the European tradition of musical avant-gardes, including those of the sixties, the act of making something free *from* and free *for* have worked in tandem and in tension. Freedom-from is music emancipated from its past, as noted by musicology; freedom-for is *emancipatory* for listeners and musicians, music that progressively moves the world beyond its present conditions, and so is effective in the sweep of history. By the 20th century the spiritual freedom expected of music was encased in 19th century classics, which would be violated by continuing the original dynamic of advancing on one another. Those considered cultured wanted their taste flattered; there was "good music" and "difficult music," which few would listen to.[177] What the avant-garde was free from was what most people needed music to do for them, so it was experienced as the failure of composers to deliver. What was emancipatory for audience continued to be a private, Platonic elevation above the crudities of existence and did not plunge one into contemporary modernity.

Eventually (post-WWII) some American composers who counted themselves as the authentic avant-garde (not without contestation from the Europeans) were able to persuade the state and universities to grant a modicum of support. At the time, these institutions needed to demonstrate their allegiance to contemporary artistic modernity, spurred more by competition with the Eastern (Communist) Block than by the taste of politicians and boards of trustees. The very strangeness of the music signaled freedom, that is, Free World superiority over Soviet artistic controls. Social democracy (French and German at first in the fifties, the Americans the next decade) was willing to create a space for noise-making artists. Given the reigning technological euphoria, universities were especially attracted to high-tech and costly computer music. The "free *for*," the "why do this at all" emancipatory question was obscured by the radical impact of "freedom *from*" attachment to the past. Modernist music in its postwar context was framed as tough-minded progress versus a tender-minded populace, and never the twain were expected to meet.

This is not the situation today. Post-Cold War, the state doesn't need art to symbolize emancipatory freedom as it once did; now value follows the market, a freedom that needs no support. The most successful artist-musicians are part of the intellectual class that is perpetually overturning "received truth." Academia and the media claim for them the inheritance of the earlier adversarial, progressive role. Their art "stretches our boundaries," which is all for the good, as NPR often announces. Artworks that get promoted are the fulfillment of Art, and the institutions that provide it is the gift horse whose mouth one does not inspect. This interpretation of emancipation favors cultural production within a stable framework rather than the earlier one of exposure and conflict when, despite its normally quietist artists, art ran on a track parallel to political radicalism.

For a history that elides the difference between the historic and the current avant-garde, it has been easier to note "free from" victories notched on the belt, as if the next were waiting around the corner, rather than examine why one should care in the first place. "Free for what?" Is there an ongoing aim other than the mound of overturned assumptions about music? The answer to this fundamental question might be: maybe we end up with just another kind of slavery. Maybe art music of the guidebook and lesson plan, intended to expand the taste limits of the audience, inoculates us against music that explores outside that project.

First a little prelude. In 1917 Marcel Duchamp submitted a urinal he entitled "Fountain" to a major New York art exhibition; its rejection fulfilled the expectations for avant-garde art, to which few had been exposed. It was later interpreted as having liberated art from stuffy, sublimated Art by expanding it to include the ordinary, the manufactured, and the body. The urinal is the often smelly and filthy mirror to the flaccid male sex organ--could any object provide a more striking foil to the overt sexuality of blues and jazz, just about to arise? This art-audience-shocking event eventually brought the low butt of crude jokes, and with it Freud's hidden unconscious, into the space of High Art.[178] Resurrected in the sixties, Duchamp's move was almost democratic and people-friendly, a triumph of the expanding museum.

The chief art of the 19th century was Music, placed above visual representation; progressively new forms grew out of older ones. As visual artists added new shocking achievements, so did composers, yet they needed the financial backing for orchestras and halls and a sizable audience, whereas a painter could survive on a few wealthy patrons and critics. The composers' equivalent of urinals and prostitutes with heads painted as African masks (Picasso's "Demoiselles") never overcame the costs and a resistant bourgeois audience. Their music was free from a musical code that itself had progressively emerged, such that Brahms had often been criticized as not taking full advantage of what Wagner had accomplished. Emancipation seemed to have reached the stopping point of its effectiveness, but it was more likely that the bourgeoisie that had funded it was changing. Instead of getting a room in the musical museum the new music was buried in the storeroom of artifacts.

The original concept of free music and its title belong not to improvisation but to concept and composition. Announced over a century ago, it referred to visionary music.[179] Thus the Russian philosopher, painter, and futurist Nikolai Kulbin in a 1910 article, "Free Music," referred to the sounds of nature as a "cosmic concert" not made by human hands. This romantic reaction (as earlier, Friedrich Schiller's "naïve" poetry) is the compensatory flip side of careful, deliberate composition. Kulbin prefigures composer Olivier Messaien's use of bird calls but had no impact on composers. What did affect them and the artistic culture was their efforts to free composition from its formulas and cultural elite for the sake of widening the horizon of musical ideas. While Igor Stravinsky brought in exotic elements external to the European tradition, Arnold Schoenberg, coming out of the central tradition (in particular, Viennese), was its internal critic. He introduced tonal relations that were considered non-musical, though he used standard pitches, orchestral instruments, technique, and timbre. He shifted from expressive use of tonality to free-form atonality, then created a substitute system in the early 20s, replacing the hierarchy of pitches in tonal music with an egalitarian arrangement, the tone row. He did not refer to his compositions as free, but he was driven to free music for greater expressiveness. His innovations furthered the affective range modernity was capable of, from his late-romantic to his last major work, which was a response to Auschwitz. The deepening of affect rather than divorce from it was his unifying feature, the *why* and *what for* behind his work. Writing for small ensembles and arranging concerts at his house, he was able to afford presenting them and hearing them, bypassing the major music institutions which were too conservative for his work.

Schoenberg's motivation preserved the lineage associated with tradition by denying the limiting concept of a ruling tradition. He knew precisely who his predecessors were; not a diversity of immediate competitors but only those with the tallest shoulders for him to stand on. Collective opinion reinforced this notion and the specific hierarchy; otherwise it would have appeared arbitrary. Each composer knew music as a matter of History, which didn't mean official recognition, commissions, or public response. For instance the narrative of irrevocable historical advance treats Gustav Mahler as transitional, a midwife to Schoenberg's advances and not a competitor.

Earlier, composer Ferrucio Busoni extended the 19th century concept of "absolute" music (meaning its form alone minus literary and other imported humanist content) to question why music should not be free of all prescriptions. Later, the Italian futurist Luigi Russolo's "Art of Noises" took this vision beyond the long Germanic tradition of serious music. He proposed that not Kulbin's Nature but the very human-created industrial machinery overwhelming it in volume and urban presence would free mankind from traditional music, part of the inevitable working of Progress.[180] Music was to be set free from what even Schoenberg took for granted, the sound and training of conventional instruments, so Russolo's was an emancipation of huge proportions.

Edgar Varese (like Russolo, very close to the Dada movement in early 20s) took the hint, emphasizing sounds of percussion and electronics which, incidentally, have become the strongest presence in current free improvisation. These blurred the key element of serious music--pitch and harmony; electronics has increasingly been replacing acoustic instruments, for reasons similar to automation. Electronics ultimately weakened the domination of the factory known as the orchestra and its training regimen, requiring mentalities drawn from science for its execution and a different kind of specialists. One of Busoni's students, the Australian Percy Grainger, embraced the breaking of so-called laws of tonality and harmony, and experimented with sound material. Grainger, who moved to the US, entitled a 1938 article "Free Music," for the realization of which he made instruments out of vacuum cleaners and electric drills, predating contemporary invented instruments by several decades.[181] While newly created sound might fit the European classical model (new techniques for string players), many of its successors, such as field recordings, sound installation, and much of computer composition, are not called "modern classical" but have retained the aura of art music.

Music seems to get ranked as art if it attracts a somewhat hesitant, judicious audience, too few to sustain the creator's living, thus justifying institutional support. Secondly it must be pre-conceived, or at least appear to result from intellectual work in advance. Neither requirement is sufficient; both are necessary. Its rank is questionable to the extent it is semi-composed or if the audience is too thoroughly and automatically enthusiastic.

Some Europeans (Stravinsky and Ravel) called on American composers to take their native jazz seriously as art music. However, with the exception of George Gershwin, they and critics accepted the tenets of their segregated society and worked to keep art music as white as possible. One of the chief representatives of the Euro-centered Americans, Charles Ives, was as rejected as any modernist could be. Rather than take the Europeans' advice he publicly denounced the popularity of jazz in the 30s. He privately ventured to improvise, so like John Cage later he was perhaps more seduced than he would let on. Though improvisation continued as a musician experience (for instance the cadenza of the violin soloist), it was forgotten among European composers, including its modernist sector, which continued to elevate the composer to the highest position of artist and above the practitioner. What some got from jazz was not improvisation but occasional codified, idiomatic memes for orchestras to be inserted, read and executed as any score.

A duality of artist-composer as ruler and practicing musician as obedient subject has been presumed in Eurological music.[182] After WWI this social contradiction was threatened from the Afrological direction. "Free" began to take the form of impulse in the moment of creation and not just new musical material and forms, discovered and then worked up for presentations that would presumably be the same each time. *Every* improvisation is a world premiere. Spontaneity later became a challenging idea within all the arts, from the high art of abstract expressionism to a major popular entertainment, jazz, in its small-group bebop form. Along with the perpetual tension between popular and art music, the artist-composer/performing musician gap began to be threatened and bridged. Spontaneity has traditionally had a place in creating art, yet as a human possibility apart from the expertise of professionals it isn't the exclusive property of anyone.

Jazz, an Afrological and improvisational music with adapted Eurological material, had been *the* popular music and was as segregated from art as its players were from both white and black polite society. Bebop musicians' bid to avant-garde status implicitly challenged Eurological musicians in their claim that advanced art was their exclusive turf. Bebop also included composers, but they didn't want total control of what players did with their scores; rather they opened the door of improvisation wider than ever. It is significant that musicians made their money playing for primarily white audiences, for whom many had a generalized contempt. The lack of black audience embarrassed some later defenders of jazz as a black cultural heritage, but this distance freed the musicians from identifying with the entertainer's instinct to please—an overlooked meaning of freedom. They were creating white hipsters without trying or wanting to, as blues and free jazz musicians inspired so many whites of a later generation. Fans heaped praise but weren't expected to give up their privileged position. With some exaggeration, the musicians were playing for each other and making a living doing it—a rare treat, as it has turned out.

A different situation faced the white American avant-garde, the New York School, whose independence from the audience was not based on dissociation from a racial other but on rejection coming from their own social kin. Whatever contempt they had was for those they expected eventually to persuade, and not those they saw as oppressors.

This avant-garde developed a high-culture and more theory-based version of spontaneity, called indeterminacy. Musicologically the freedom of both avant-gardes was rooted in the independence of musicians from the pre-established score. Bebop did this openly, burying the melody lines of its given core of tunes and chord progressions, which turned them into parodies. On the other hand, the New York School and John Cage in particular were at pains to establish that indeterminacy is not improvisation. Not only was improvisation associated with the black entertainer underclass but it would have to be performed by classically trained musicians whose job it was *not* to think for themselves, as improvisation required. John Cage's public rejection of improvisation was both musicological and reflected a middle-class scorn for working musicians who stepped out of their place. He viewed as the mythical mass-man driven by habit and incapable of truly creative work, a (Eurological) argument later implied against free improvisation.[183]

As a brief aside, it should be recalled that the fifties was the height of union membership. Even as unions had declined in militancy, any paid performing musician had to be a dues-paying member of the American Federation of Musicians. The NY City chapter (Local 802) was integrated, but not the orchestras; it was black and white jazz musicians playing as peers who broke the color barrier. Musicians often complained that the union didn't do enough for them, but at a time when the minimum wage for all workers was $.75/hour (in 1950, which was my own starting wage in 1958) musicians relied on the union to set a higher floor for their wages, and clubs had to agree to it or face picketing and boycott. Composers were not performers but on the other side of the line, and like music world managers and conductors were barred from union membership.

Today the weakness of unions in general vis a vis management goes hand in hand with the creation of the entrepreneurial musician, completely unprotected in the workplace and without pension, benefits or backup in case a promised fee is not provided. Equally important, there is no material basis for solidarity with other musicians against management, or even to gripe about their conditions. The flip side of musicians performing strictly out of musical interest is that they are treated as librarians before their unionization. People characterized as loving their work have the least success in complaining about low pay, since spontaneous love and the job are in opposite corners. To provide signs that they have invested labor in their achievement, and view playing as a form of work, is what enables the career musician to claim a place in line at the pay window. At the window looking out to the audience they must tell a different story—all just part of the contract.

In the mid-forties bebop period a regimented, war-directed and segregated society became synchronized with the culture industry and churned out comforting musical product. If to be free within the dominant society and culture means to contradict them in practice, then bebop, born in hiding, had a fundamental and contradictory relation to "freedom," the professed and motivational value of FDR's war program. Its players broke with many of the musicological norms of commercial music without attempting to take its place (as a new dance music, for instance). In the media its musicians came to be imagined and envied as bohemians living free of the mores of the surrounding "straight" society--the very world the white avant-garde wanted a response from. Later, in the private jam sessions of fifties' jazz musicians, "free" referred to the creative side of playing compared to what they did on gigs for their livelihood. "Jazz" became the recognized label under which they appeared; "free" was what they did in private, free from the club bosses and audience calls for standard tunes, and free for their pleasure and experimentation.[184] When musicians made a bid for artist status they were challenging the fundamental concept of art established by the Eurological tradition and not asking for admission or permission under the same terms.

Jazz could never be avant-garde in the way understood by the white modernists, and is still not.[185] The originators of Afrological music had former slaves for family; "free" had a historical meaning for them that could never be strictly musicological. Collective and solo improvisation was emancipatory; musicians knew implicitly what it was free for, which gave the entire history of jazz an urgency and collective bond. Europeans had enslaved others and were proud of never being enslaved themselves ("Rule Brittania...never, never, never will be slaves"). Freedom for American blacks and whites has always had this ineradicable difference—emancipation vs. pride of not needing emancipation. For the Eurological avant-garde, freedom was from their own older musical forms, and its relation to audience held a different meaning of "progressive." Since jazz musicians could relate personally to their historical, physical emancipation their music could remind the world that they were still not treated as free--even when they were not ostensibly breaking any conventions.

When it finally came around, Free Jazz did involve a self-conscious breaking of conventions. This it shared with the Eurological tradition and so to a greater extent shared the modernist meaning of "avant-garde" and called itself by that name. Dismissal of the non-comprehending audience was at times similar. Yet its practitioners reasserted how jazz history might be described from its very beginnings, a music that was always already progressive--self-replacing and self-critical rather than discarding the past as a defeated older generation. Jazz development can be seen in the microhistory of a player's nightly solo, inventions that became stabilized conventions for periods of time, then were bypassed or at least twisted as new ideas came along (either one's own or borrowed). As I stressed earlier, the jazz tradition needs to be understood as neither a constructed neo-traditional canon to be preserved nor as hide-bound, with shackles waiting to be broken, the positive/negative binary commonly used to interpret the European Enlightenment inheritance. Rather, on the macro- and micro-level it consisted in irreversible advances on the materials of earlier inventions, with improvisation (signifyin') as the tool. Today's reversible jazz is something different.

Much of the sixties criticism of Free Jazz and the Black Avant-garde was that it denied the authentic jazz tradition, a view that would approach the NY School's relation to its past, only a reverse valuation. Amiri Baraka's ambivalence about it in 1966 was that to be an avant-garde would draw it closer to his bête noire, the European-leaning black middle class, with whom he felt it would be associated--incorrectly, as it turned out. What its critics perceived was the discontinuity rather than the continuity, a negative turn for what they saw at stake.[186] Critics ignored that Free Jazz musicians maintained the initial composed line and very often played runs that only jazz musicians would have done. It didn't matter to their critics that they followed the old saw, "you've got to know the rules in order to break them," which frequently operated as a brake on musicians, legitimizing them only if they could be called back to traditional conventions. By following the rules they could hope to counter the frequent charge that "you just don't know how to play the instrument," but it didn't help those of Free Jazz who were obvious masters of instrumental technique (for instance, Coltrane and Eric Dolphy). Even in the second wave it wasn't that they couldn't play by the rules, rather, they chose not to.

Even in playing that sounds very spontaneous, and therefore considered free, what came through was attachment to strong personal feeling, gospel and blues. All of this could have legitimated this music, but only for a wider conception of jazz as Black Music, not as musicologically emancipated. It could be argued that critics rejected it because it wasn't modern in commercial *or* European-modernist terms. Unlike urbane cool jazz that enabled Playboy seduction scenes, it recalled the early blues and collective improvisation of twenties jazz as well as the physical and emotive church spirit of poor blacks, which was a large part of Baraka's attraction in his *Blues People*. The paradox of rejection is that this occurred in the very period when white urban audiences were beginning to turn to new, previously incomprehensible experience, of which Free Jazz could be seen as taking the lead. Alien experience from the *past*, such as blues, filled the bill for them better than the emerging present. What's coming is more threatening because *it has not finished arriving*. It is going somewhere else; the past is going nowhere else. That audience had money and was eager to spend it, but it could not identify Free Jazz as the experience they craved. This would not happen in significant numbers until the mid-70s, at first among college youth.[187]

In contrast, the parallel radicals of the New York School won at least consideration as a proper avant-garde and so did not have to compete as entertainers on the basis of audience attendance or club owners' taste, only among their own kind. *Their* version of free playing--indeterminism and other inventions--shocked the audience in a way that engaged them even as they walked out. Rejection of what is *beneath* one's imagined class taste (the few, hesitant and judicious)—the emotionality of second-wave Free Jazz—shares no ground with rejection of what is too far *above*. In the latter case an audience can retain its sense of cultural capital by rejection. The music is "ahead of its time" and I'm catching up. The avant-garde difficulty then requires straining the ears to reach into the future. The mystery of music is no threat of disorder to one's being. Rejection can at least claim to know what's "out," in both positive and negative senses—available for the cognoscenti *and* beyond the pale of current convention. To the cultural authorities this avant-garde, and not blacks unleashed from commercial constraints, was what audiences preferred to experience.

When applied to art music, "free" referred to music with norms and believable forms from which musicians seek to free themselves. Conventions are retained in the background as the validation of innovation, reminders of what the social order subtly informs us is taboo. This is a dynamic that spurs musical progress as a child is spurred to do what is forbidden. Even as the parent form is being dismissed as inadequate to expression or musical truth, it will be the context that looms in the background and provides the argument on behalf of emancipation. Always a choice must be made: listeners and artists line up as either progressive or retrograde. All this is standard pedagogical and even therapeutic logic for the function of the avant-garde: Emancipate art and therefore the mind from its attachment to the past. The outlook is progressive and so it is your future, like it or not. [188] As a corollary, it was believed that this avant-garde must also in some vague way lead to a better world politically and socially, with the audience following the lead. In the later sixties one would not find among avant-garde artists support for legal segregation or for the American war against Vietnam. (Still today artists and audience are a bastion of liberalism.) Even holding one's ears at an avant-garde concert was a punishment that might alleviate some of the middle class guilt. Presumably the rest of the world would catch up, and it did, at least in theory. That theory validates what goes for "avant-garde" today, when it is unable to reproduce the earlier dynamic or the attraction to it.

The experimental avant-garde, a broadened title sometimes including the Classical Avant-garde, today carries the same connotation of doing good. The social order, via its media and institutions, has provided different targets—the current list of world problems, in the back of every liberal's mind.

Context as brake and avant-garde as dialectical protagonist has broken down along with the urgency and possibility of a better human existence. The perception of the past as a rearguard and resistant culture to be overcome disappeared decades ago in the postmodern shift. History is no longer bunk, implacably there and needing to be transcended, but precious memory of the heights that need continual endorsement. What is buried are the negative affects of conflict and disturbance, the trauma the past represents, which when recalled only add to present trauma. The permanent avant-garde stands alone on the field of battle, its armor and boldness only for show, but the show's the thing and must go on. This frees "vanguard" and "cutting edge" to be as commercially useful as "revolutionary" once was, retaining the vague belief in the human goodness of advanced art.[189] For this to have a touch of American Optimism, whatever political, economic, and social mess lies outside of art is put in a separate bin. Or rather, if the world is set on its course and can't be turned from its fate, then the faith in art saves us from total despair, as redemptive as ever. (Nietzsche: "We have art in order not to die of the truth.") What that art concretely is or does is of less importance.

Emancipation has taken the form of personal growth, largely dependent on consumption, enabled by the image of a progressive social order and postmodern globalization. In this image the final solution is presumed to be the market, which is too big to fail. Respected art goes along for the ride, offering enlightening, mild transgressions that are routinized as entertainment, a parallel to technological innovations. This requires belief that we are now liberated from the past; that is the very form of our existence. Meanwhile the summing up of all this emancipatory growth—what exactly has been the point of all this?--is thrown on the heap with old religious questions.

It is this neat formula that is now seriously threatened by the rightward turn in US and world politics. The trust in market forces has buoyed the vision of tolerant neo-liberalism, comfortable with art. That trust is now championed by the antagonist of that vision. What happens to the permanent avant-garde of capitalist society when capitalism itself is split right down the middle? It's not like we haven't been here before...

The unspoken rule of the modernist avant-garde model was that breaking conventions must yield a consolidated music. A result-orientation yields an accomplished fact that will replace the threat of challenge. Conformity, to which we are all socialized, will follow the oedipal model of rebellion, stimulating yet another rebellion. Thus the tradition being overthrown in the fifties was not the classical one of 19th century romanticism but serialism, which had triumphed over the one earlier, at least in the ivory tower of progressive music. The resulting music was then added to the storehouse of culture, available to be claimed as one more achievement of freedom.

The free musics would seem to claim the avant-garde as their home and heritage today, but "made only in this moment" rebuffs those historical stepping-stones and throws a monkey wrench in that machinery. As British free improvisation emerged in the sixties it showed signs of a different approach. It didn't seem to stir deep conflict of a social nature, like Free Jazz, and so was not blocked from carving out a separate space for itself, where it was merely strange to man-in-the-street taste. Nor did it lend itself to later incorporation in a popular avant-garde of showy transgression. Players used "free" in a new way, which avoided reducing their search to the convention-breaking of a specific musical tradition. Their focus rather was on whatever they found interesting to do with their tools and imagination, a very mundane act. Their playing could not be attacked as needing further emancipation, since with music individualized, each is responsible for their own musical dis/satisfaction. And no one has to converse with Music to do this.

Granted, some argued for improvisation's superiority over composition in an avant-garde-progressive relationship (I myself, to some extent, in the later 80s).[190] But that was not essential, for improvisers implicitly raised the question whether music needs any norms at all, such as the avant-garde scenario, as a background against which to pick out keys on the piano or bow a piece of styrofoam. The improviser might ask, "What sound or silence would we make *if no music existed*, nothing even highly trained players know how to do?" This approach is what I call free playing, as we shall see. It does not depend on audience, critic, or posterity (avant-garde progress) and is not mediated by score, genre, code, one's secure habits, or the music world. Rather it is the players' decision or even momentary whim, based on commitment to the love of playing. When what they've done gets solidified as culture they still have something quite liquid in their hands. That is the discipline, not an applied theory but right at the moment of loving what one is doing. The space for that love resonates best when the current knowledge of how to communicate with others or with the god of Music is not in the room.

9. Derek Bailey's Concept
of Free Improvisation

In the mid-70s guitarist Derek Bailey began writing a book on the broad topic of musical improvisation, based on his experience and inquiries, a book he added to in 1992 for a second edition.[191] His position throughout was that of a player making some musicological points without accepting the usual musicologists' perspective. His comments on recordings, the material they normally consider, are sparse and his appreciation of them slight; he even somewhat scorns recordings of his own music. The section on free improvisation opens with a chapter simply entitled "Free," and is less than half the book. For those in the states Bailey is the most prominent representative of that music title, and musicians and listeners have used his book as their common basis for understanding and agreement. He is an authority for anti-authoritarians. The challenges to him do not touch the nerve of what the title "free improvisation" evokes for practitioners in the states. What I have to offer is my interpretation and critique of Bailey's view and its extension to some topics he did not discuss.

Bailey presents free improvisation in the context of all musical improvisation in the world, though he did not intend to be comprehensive. Free improvisation continues a strong tradition of the world's music, and thus is not allied with the specifically Western avant-garde, whose breaks with aspects of its past did not take other cultures into account. Bailey's method is mostly to interview prominent individuals of their respective approaches—Indian, flamenco, Baroque, contemporary organ, rock, and jazz. He throws in comments as a curious and respectful peer rather than a journalist, anthropologist or critic, instead asking, "How do *you* do it."

Writing in the 70s, Bailey did not consider how traditional forms were artifacts beginning to be tracked down by ethnomusicologists like endangered species, captured and replicated industrially for westerners. On their home turf they have been largely extinguished in favor of western models of studio-finished perfection. Their improvisation is the work of skilled players, which would include some village musicians and not just urban profession-als. It continues in small private pockets but much of it is protected by state and cultural authority as those cultures' high art, not just for its own sake but as part of the identity each culture claims to be. When for this reason flamen-co *must* sound like flamenco then like jazz it is frozen in place, a simulation. Free improvisation can affirm an approach to playing being crushed by the juggernaut of globalization (international fame) and simulated theme-park "culture." In western society it is cast as part of the avant-garde but its role elsewhere has been one of cultural resistance.

Improvisation shares its live quality with all tradition. The score and re-cording technology originating in Euro-American culture both tend toward greater exactitude and elevation than live music, while the world's music has traditionally depended on the conjuncture of immediacy and memory. Play-ing that recalls a tune or musical idea provides the space for improvisation rather than attempted replication, and that space is occupied by the player. Self-conscious improvisation has a long history of being accepted as high art in India but has been virtually eliminated in western classical music. It is the strictly followed score of modern western culture that is the anomaly, and that culture has considered its exceptionalism as the argument for the great-ness and superiority of its musical achievement. A cultural order that honors scientific predictability also favors the exact following of a code, score, or recording. It must distinguish between acceptable imperfection, elaboration of a remembered song, and improvisation free of the song form. Any live music is to some extent unpredictable, which puts it at a disadvantage.

Performers trained to reproduce classical (Eurological) music are judged first on their note-perfectionism, the orientation most antithetical to freely improvising. What's not in the score is taboo, as if the dead or absent com-posers are masters whose intentions must still be observed. The claim linking authenticity and tradition is everywhere threatened in our era of competitive halos, and this puts additional pressure on classical musicians serving the composers and their own musical persona. A mistake would indicate the player's incompetence, but if she goes beyond that she might be considered willful, as if her need for self-expression has gotten in the way. She would have been improvising, preferring individual choice over prohibitive author-ity, a contest of opposed authenticities both valued in our culture. This has posed a dilemma in the formally egalitarian world of today. It is resolved for some by merging the two, turning composers into performers of their own work. If the performer improvises, the piece is still safely presented as an author's composition, for there is no effective difference. Self-expression is then justified, a compromise that straddles the score that prohibits and the player's enjoyment that allows.

The jazz version of this merged the two differently--you've got to know the rules before you may break them. Classic Jazz transformed this by prohibiting the breaking of rules, which Bailey sharply criticized.[192] Traditional craft training is uppermost, with educators (now the paying vocation for jazz musicians) authorized as judges. Outside of jazz training and located rather in the academic branches most touched by postmodern theories, improvisation has been making its way as a category that, contrary to the Classic Jazz canon, often includes Free Jazz and its current followers. Like most academic discoveries of the marginalized, free jazz is not subjected to any internal critique. They are considered victims, close examination of which would add insult to injury and not enlightenment. Given that focus, the revisionists have ignored improvisation that wanders outside of free jazz. The lack of an audience for this helps to invalidate it among scholars. The possibility of improvisation outside jazz is "under erasure," as the post-structuralist would say. It is suppressed from the text of valued music but, since it represents the full latitude of free playing, it is still there potentially undermining the acceptable version.

That erasure shares the fate of broad swatches of the Euro-American imagination. The North American colonies emerging out of no-nonsense Protestantism adopted late 17th century Lockean empiricism, which banished "fancy" on the way to establishing the predominant pragmatic-scientific episteme. Music became serious and respectable only as romanticism was seen to conform to the eternal laws of nature. It counterbalanced the mentality of materialist science and was no threat to it, though it prompted our first internal culture war (Emerson, et al.). Romantic pleasure was the core of late 19th century bourgeois art, which followed Europe in showing signs of dissidence. Serious American music was conceived as classical, straight from the (European) horse's mouth. Beauty followed tonal and harmonic legality, and functioned to drown out capitalist rapacity and social upheaval. An orchestra modelled on the factory turned out copies of the Original dropped down from on high via the sainted composers, whose moments of imaginative freedom, or improvisation, were hidden away in the published text. They had apparently followed the natural law spontaneously and made art comformable with practical reason.

Improvised playing had been the practice of which composer-performers from Bach through the Romantics had been the masters, as part of their paid job and not just their leisure. In order to entertain patrons and the middle class such play was subordinated to The Work discussed earlier, a score with increasingly detailed instructions. Theodor Adorno, speaking here of the fate of philosophy in its submission to results-oriented science, said that speculation (which could be the free-floating imagination of an improviser) has been relegated to "the non-committal chatter of a private Weltanschauung."[193] That chatter could easily be derided as what the improviser had for breakfast that day, the familiar rebuke that caused musicians such as Ornette Coleman to counter that freedom doesn't mean arbitrariness.[194]

In the 60s to 70s, avant-garde and experimental musics were considered distinct titles for compositional music. Avant-garde referred to European and uptown NY music—Stockhausen, Pierre Boulez, Milton Babbitt, etc.—and experimental was the American, downtown NY direction—Cage and the NY School.[195] Beginning in the 80s the two were more often merged as "New Music," and more recently the 2009 documentary "In the Ocean" promotes its examples as the "Classical Avant-garde." Bailey, on the other hand, wanted free improvisation to be clearly distinguished from both of these.[196] For him "new" does not apply to free improvisation. Despite its relatively recent appearance as a movement he does not claim it as an innovation that will conquer the field of music, since it's been around virtually forever.[197] Bailey's book discusses compositions that call for improvisation, with especial concern for how classically trained musicians have faced the prospect of improvising. In his 1992 revision he saw 80s New Music as a decline from the more adventurous earlier period, widening the gap between composition and improvisation. He pointed to a major shift towards greater audience accessibility, which would conform to the anti-elitism claimed by the academic postmodern sensibility.[198] A small number of free improvisers were holding their own within the larger field of unconventional musics, and were neither superior-elitist nor embattled survivors. Obscurity was not a curse word to be overcome but an open space for music, yet he must have wanted his book to make a dent in that obscurity.

The Joseph Holbrooke Trio discussed earlier was the meeting point of popular, idiomatic improvisational music (jazz) and the compositional avant-garde, yet the trio aimed to escape the limitations of each. The jazz improviser was pushing away from commercial moorings and the composer was abandoning the strict model of the score and the exclusion of player initiative. Engaged in both was Bailey, somewhat in the middle of the two others. He took the of contemporary composers' license to create without any pre-given form and put it in the hands of the practicing improviser of jazz. In

NY, given the socio-cultural distance between jazz and classical, this had not worked out, but in the UK it produced the first wave of musicians specifically dedicated to free improvisation.

As a player rather than musicologist, Bailey's strong distinction is between the *act* of composing and improvising, a focus on approach and method rather than finished product. Most improvisation includes some pre-structures, and briefly in the sixties some composers included improvisational sections. Some classically-trained Europeans were drawn to improvisation, such as New Phonic Art and the Italian sextet Gruppe Nuova Consonanza. What predominated was the cultural favor given to pre-structure and thus to composers—as it still does--over the relatively free flow of improvisation, which is in the players' hands. This has to do with Christian culture's preference for *conception*, whereby the thinker and artist repeats the work of divinity by creating out of nothing (creatio ex nihilo), rather than out of existent formless material, or chaos, as is common to other cultures. The latter is more consistent with improvisation that has no conception (aesthetic or structure) at its origin which then shapes the result.

Bailey sought to comprehend the distinction of free improvisation from other musics and provide as consistent an identity for the term as possible. His writing assumes that music must have something that takes on a symbolized form and is not just his private practice with analogous other musicians lost in space. He intended to legitimate what he did in his playing in part by providing a model, which he did at the expense of some confusion and controversy. He said "only an academic would have the temerity to mount a theory of improvisation." Then he took a stab at it himself. He coined "non-idiomatic improvisation" as a musicological, explanatory term for what he normally referred to as free improvisation and free playing.[199] In other words, the only positive thing to say about it analytically is what it is not; the rest is merely what individual players do.

To call it non-idiomatic implies that it is not a form but something of an anti-form. It also means there's no essence that can be symbolized.[200] "Free improvisation" is a construct. The name is only a handle, or a general pointer that can't determine what is and is not genuine. However there are boundaries that operate fully as if we had apples and oranges. "The characteristics of freely improvised music are established only by the sonic-musical identity of the person or persons playing it." This is circular, for who are those persons, any who say that free improvisation is what they're doing? Moreover, forms are boundaries, prohibitions that exclude each other, but Bailey won't go so far as to draw a strict line between idiomatic and non-idiomatic: "Many of the characteristic features of idiomatic improvisation are to be found in free improvisation." (*Improvisation*, p. 123). Musicologists wanting clear definitions would tear out their hair at this. Often forgotten is that Bailey only used his term once, in the introduction, and there he does not exactly equate it with free improvisation: "'Non-idiomatic' improvisation…is most usually found in so-called 'free' improvisation."[201] Here he is dealing with the lack of clarity of what has been *called* free improvisation, yet he adds to the confusion by saying "most usually," and "so-called," implying that there are other kinds of free improvisation, whose boundaries he does not explore. He further modifies the term by admitting that it could still be individualized as a style: "while [non-idiomatic improvisation] can be highly stylised, it is not usually tied to representing an idiomatic identity." (*Improvisation*, p. xii) But if non-idiomatic is defined against idiomatic then "usually" would mean in practice it doesn't necessarily follow the supposed distinction.

There is room to question the meaning of idiom, such as George Lewis' comment: "it may be difficult to see how free improvisation avoids becoming an idiom like all the others out there."[202] Earlier Lewis equated idiom and genre, so if we substitute the latter here he is correct for the time Lewis was writing, when free improvisation *had* become a genre, "like all the others," a defined marketplace category. However, there was still no recognizable code for free improvisation, and non-idiomatic did not function as one. More pointedly, other British improvisers took Bailey to task for his concept, at the Association of Improvised Music (AIM) Forum of academics and improvisers in 1984. In a commentary on it Eddie Prévost argued that one's own way of playing, or stylization, can be considered an idiom; "habits and therefore conventions attend each and every performance—even of 'free' improvisation—and habit becomes idiom…"[203] This is close to John Cage's critique of all trained-musician improvisation, yet Prévost's realism here does not stand in the way of affirming improvised music. Prévost was here representing improvisers who were operating under the wide banner of free improvisation but did not characterize what they did as non-idiomatic.

To respond, Bailey's usage of "idiom" is limited and conventional. It refers to socially recognized patterns, a code abstracted from a large number of players over time, and widely enough known that a non-player could categorize an unknown piece of music. Of course there are idioms within idioms, but that merely requires a more specialized knowledge; they still refer to groups of players and not a diversity of individual styles. Listeners might detect idiomatic conventions in a non-idiomatic piece, but if they expect them to unify it they will be confused and possibly disappointed. One might hear the normative tone of a tenor saxophone, which strongly signifies "jazz," but the jazz *idiom* depends on the player's intention and ability to reproduce a roughly consistent version of that historical direction throughout.

An idiom is a code foundational to the intent of playing and meant to identify it, at least roughly. Habits might be common to the idiom but are still those of the individual. The bassist Steve Swallow, discussed earlier, implied that habits were personal attachments which "hadn't been transcended." To put it this way might lead to discovery and awareness: what in my playing indicates the performer persona I trot out there every time I perform? Do I truly need it? A musician-entertainer depends on it to draw an audience and earn a living, what one's name symbolizes to the other and to the music world. It can also be what one commits to and defends in the face of rejection; to "transcend" it is then to back down. Taken together, it's a complicated position to be in.

To at least provide some shorthand explanation of what one is doing makes practical sense when an audience asks "What do you call this music?" It must be some *thing*, symbolized as a meaning. Without detailing a specific approach to playing, "free improvisation" is just a floating signifier up for grabs. The playing might be heard as a contemporary composition, especially if the players work with close precision and stop cleanly together. This error is not due to the obscurity of an explicit aesthetic, for the more improvisers one hears the harder it would be to identify any common traits beyond what was lacking. With Bailey's formulation, in trying to predict what players will do tomorrow all bets are off. To say the music I choose to play is free improvisation would indicate commitment but is not a very objective standard. This subjectivity has allowed the title to spread to music that is quite obviously idiomatic and pre-structured. When that is the case the question should be, what does "free" add other than ideology and advertising? The only way to deny it for a specific performance would be to discern a particular idiom as an overall effect, still a very arguable determination.

What spectators demand in today's entertainment market is *genre* identity rather than the nuances of idiom. The substitute for free improv would be a generalization of affirmed qualities, which is most possible for individuals, and specifically those relatively consistent through their years of playing. What any experienced player tends to develop is an *idiolect*, patterns repeated enough to identify an individualized way of playing, which says, "Here's what you'll be getting." It is precisely what a trained orchestral player seeks to avoid and no improviser can avoid developing. Beyond the moment of experimenting it's what one finds oneself doing and so qualifies as an attachment, whether called a habit or not. It shows up in all improvisers when they are comfortable with their playing. What varies for the player is one's relationship to it. One might cultivate it as one's soloist persona ("my music"), just ignore it, or be disgusted with it as knee-jerk and boring. The idiolect would certainly be relevant to the choosing of partners, but is not necessarily or initially common to others. One might prefer playing with those whose idiolect is at a far remove from one's own.

In choosing "non-idiomatic" Bailey is not seeking to avoid confusion with the classical cadenza or Indian improvisation but specifically with jazz; he is opening a space for non-jazz-based improvisation. That sounds like ignoring the elephant in the room (jazz), as did John Cage and the Eurological composer tradition, as argued by Lewis, but it's not the case. It is one thing to deny the obvious debt to jazz; it's another for players to move away from their closest environmental influences. Bailey was creating a path independent of jazz during its period of great strength, when jazz and free jazz were the inescapable context. "In the late '60s there was a lot of confusion between free improvisation and free jazz. To a lesser extent it still exists. In fact free improvisation is very often confused in its identity or in its attempt to find an identity."[204]

Bailey's relation to jazz changed over time, only scornful of Classic Jazz and later free jazz.[205] His early partner Tony Oxley developed experimentally away from familiar jazz structures at roughly the same time NY jazz drummer Sunny Murray was breaking through to freer playing. Oxley's reasoning was akin to Murray and Free Jazz: "the exclusion of the jazz vocabulary was an emotional act of feeling...When you're wearing chains you don't become aware of them through intellectual processes. You can feel them."[206] What many analysts miss is that musicians can push against what initially seduced them into playing, grappling with it intimately to the point of feeling its limitations as chains, a dialectical process. In a blind test the Bailey-Oxley playing in both 1967 and 1996 recordings could easily be called idiosyncratic, borderline free jazz, a judgment that would be musicologically correct, but ignores important distinctions in the musicians' orientation and associations.

If "non-idiomatic" signifies merely the relative turn away from jazz it refers to the Brits, not the continental Europeans who were prone to the free jazz direction. Neither were friendly to the Americans politically, but did not identify the New York movement with the American colossus. Both would have said they appreciated it, though the problem of similarity only affected the continentals. As Lewis points out, German pan-Europeanism was not that different from the cultural unity posited by black cultural nationalism, though the former was applauded rather than criticized.[207] The title "improvised music" was employed as a rather soft term in which the specific difference of the most prominent British improv, and not just Bailey's activities, could be overlooked. On the practical level of partners and festival invitees, however, "improvised music" was not a happy family but divided sharply between the Brits and the others.[208]

That time was long past when Bailey revised *Improvisation* in 1992, for he was highly critical of how jazz and free jazz had evolved since 1975. His sense of estrangement would indicate his appreciation for those musics during the sixties, as if "non-idiomatic" was an earlier fraternal distinction from a jazz that had since parted ways with its past. In his interviews with Steve Lacy and Max Roach for his revised chapter on jazz they are all obviously talking about a common idea of free (though idiomatic) playing, but these were the champions of the former approach to jazz, a still-living old guard that had little control over where things had been going.[209]

George Lewis associates "non-idiomatic" with modernism, as if Bailey were arguing for an aesthetic historically superior to jazz and Free Jazz: "The most historically consistent answer to [Bailey's attempt to posit a non-idiomatic music] would frame it as drawing primary sustenance from modernism's negative aesthetic."[210] He assimilates Bailey to the view of Anne Le Baron, who sees free improvisation as a progressive step beyond jazz.[211] Indeed, formalist critics made arguments about progressive advance, most boldly about abstract expressionism. But neither Free Jazz musicians nor Bailey and friends were thinking of negating the authentic tradition of jazz. They were doing something more mundane, positive, and immediate, merely ignoring parts of the tradition that were of no use to them and retaining others.

Bailey wanted his playing to be distinct from others'; as he said in 1997, referring back to the mid-60s, "the very thing I was trying to get away from...was imitating somebody else."[212] This was like many professional musicians, who need to think in terms of their uniqueness. Yet to find the sounds of his particular interest against the background of his environment did not require grandiose formalism. He wanted as full enjoyment possible for himself alone mediated strictly by his instrument, and what "out" music performers are expected to have is a personal style (an idiolect) and not a collective idiom. Others might then imitate *him*, and maybe later develop their own, which was neither his hope nor responsibility. To achieve an idiolect involves a certain naïve assumption, however, for exploration will not necessarily solidify into a style but keep on going.

Bailey's and his partners' playing has traits common to popular musics that are also within the jazz idiom. It is relatively dense with all players steadily playing; the volume is a relatively constant medium-loud. In the spectrum of British improvised music this puts Bailey in the middle between jazz/free jazz and some contemporary improvisation, which is often sparse, quiet, and leaves gaps of silence, as we shall see. Moreover, Bailey is similar to jazz in the relatively parallel nature of his playing with partners, where a duo can often sound like separate tracks have been laid down. This is what Eddie Prévost is getting at when he criticizes his "preference for musical co-existence rather than conscious processive interactivity."[213] This will become crucial for the future, when "the New London Silence" appears around 2000, and the Bailey approach is cast as the old guard.

Lewis' criticism has the advantage of raising another issue. While analysis of an idiom commonly says where a particular music can be expected to go, "non-idiomatic" tells us nothing concrete and guides us to no shore. It is ineffective as a musicological tool, for by only telling us only what *not* to see in it declines any terms of judgment based on the definition. This frustrates many exposed to it and especially the traditional critic, who would like to go beyond description and like/dislike opinion. Bailey brings together two different things that do not necessarily equate. In abstracting, Bailey takes the position of one seeking to distinguish free improv in terms of its form; his accounts of himself and his partners presume they are the prime examples of that form, but the form offered is empty. Thus "non-idiomatic" leaves us with an image of players swerving to avoid the potholes of idioms, which doesn't fit the reality of the players' or audience's experience. Instead we get a catalogue of players and partners choosing to call each other free improvisers, as if whatever they do determines the meaning of their musical category.

As every performer must, Bailey had to deal with the needs of the music world; otherwise he wouldn't have been in tension with it. The allowance of style is helpful, but the resistance of his musical enterprise to formal definition makes it difficult. It is primarily the mediating music world that needs this, first sorting music and musicians into the popular or art bins. For players to go with the category of art requires artfulness and caution in showing signs of the popular, whereas some in the popular bin want to display artistic taste and others rely on willful artlessness. Since the idiom of jazz is in the commercial and popular bin, to be strictly non-idiomatic would drive free improv away from the popular and into the arms of an avant-garde, defined by its distance ahead of, or at least distinct from the popular. Even though Bailey had been bored playing popular music he refused the division for himself as musician; he eschewed the upgrade of "avant-garde." He imagined himself in some way straddling the two—at least refusing both.

That is an understandable but difficult position to hold. Aspects of free improv common to idiomatic improvisation would get it classed as a popular music rather than an art music genre. It is the most professional performers who have wanted to be perceived as art musicians, their most reasonable path, given failure to attract the kind of audience sustaining popular musics. According to the rules of the most acceptable art music, playing should approach the artwork and so shouldn't change from one night to the next. Nor should it validate personal feeling, specifically "feeling free." Each of these appear in idiomatic improvisation, on the popular side of the divide. The reputation of the Grateful Dead, rock improvisers, has been based on "the expectation of change" from one concert to another (*Improvisation*, p. 42). For Flamenco guitarist Paco Pena change is the basis of "free": "you feel so free because today you are going to play differently from yesterday," and he relates this improvisation to "improving" the composition, which is both endless and motivating. (*Improvisation*, p. 16). Free does not relate to an absolute condition here but to a momentary and subjective feeling. For jazz improvisation it is needless to elaborate on how much feeling, change, and "free" have been central.

What we find in the writings and interviews of those representing free improvisation in the marketplace today is that their expressed aesthetic, like their idiolect, is a permanent fixture, putting them on the art side of the ledger. Change is minor and de-emphasized, and fluid personal feeling is irrelevant. Any hint that playing is personally emancipatory, a freeing act as in later Free Jazz, is absent. They might discover new techniques, or start partnering with electronics that modifies their sound, but radical change that seems irreversible, like the turn of a Coltrane or Ayler, does not apply to them. It seems that "free" is just a word in their music's title.

This is then a central dilemma. An attachment to idiom comes with built-in affect, a home base one can leave knowing it is always there, embodied in a tune the player "jazzes" or an expansive spirit, without which there is no jazz. Non-idiomatic, as a binary distinction *could* lead to merger with the experimental art music tradition, which reduces affect to an externality. Moreover, how can players think of each day making something fresh when there is no standard from which to deviate or a sense of their trajectory from which they launch forth? What slips in to take its place is a comfortable and familiar style of playing from which one merely deviates, an unacknowledged, individual (non-divisible) home that is always there and personally owned. In that context any fundamental change would have the effect of unwanted self-alienation. This is not part of the persona of art music performers, nor the genre as it comes down to us today. We will return to the implications of this dilemma later.

If Bailey meant non-idiomatic to be applied as a descriptive test then it fails as a practical distinction. How long must one listen before deciding that the player is following an idiom? Is it jazz when two chords are played in succession that have merely been used in jazz? Some of Bailey's playing can be described as improvisations on Webern, so did he himself violate his musicology? Moreover, non-idiomatic stands in for a host of specific negations, such as diatonic tonality and precise equal temperament pitch. How many notes are needed to decide that the music is "tonal," when any relation of pitches can be plucked out and given a relationship of continuity as meaningful as diatonic tonality once did? In practice, lack of melody is frequently called a sign of free improvisation, but what could be lacking melody or harmony when these depend on one's range of listening experience? What about melodic ideas or fragments, which could be almost any succession of pitches? Melody can't rely for its meaning on its repeatability, since anything at all can be repeated. A sequence of pitches that a listener has difficulty remembering could still be classified as non-melodic. A steady beat or pulse is also problematic, since they can become so disguised (as Tony Oxley did) as to disappear to the non-expert listener. In short, as a test, non-idiomatic is more hair-splitting than the disputed borderline of jazz, where a subjective jazz feeling usually bridges the gaps.

In its favor, the definition does not close off the future or determine who qualifies. Besides, although a theoretical determination of what is non-idiomatic is impossible, one that is functional for the music world and consumers is easy to make. The exception would be modern compositions, which are also in principle non-idiomatic (the freedom of the composer to do whatever). They could easily be confused with free improvisation in a consumer blind test, but since compositions are directions to the musician they cannot be any kind of improvisation.[214] Apart from that, anyone who can feel a steady pulse in music will tell you when it is missing. Since there is very little music that lacks a pulse one is on the right track of identifying what Bailey is talking about. Given other absences noted above, there is no need for a formal determination. "Music" for our culture provides the security of pulse, etc., which all idioms must provide to some degree. From a perspective that sees music as a cultural construct, however, free improvisation must find its security elsewhere, if at all.

Bailey intended non-idiomatic to specify what a spectator could expect from music labeled free improvisation to be free *from*, as if "free" was a technical term limited in meaning. Presenting it as a description of actual playing, he qualified this freedom as relative, just as a wheel said to be spinning freely is never without friction that slows it down. However, in common usage "free" has the strong positive connotation of being emancipated and even emancipating, which "non-idiomatic" does not address. This meaning made improvisation that was called "free" attractive in the sixties and later, when the title evoked an exuberant promise, free *for*, a distinction discussed earlier. This suggests a wider cultural and political scope, as did Free Jazz, later linked back in time to the sixties spirit. Anyone hoping for audience would want to relate to this, even if they privately put "free" in scare quotes.

Bailey's approach describing what improvisers do muted his claim about its form, while the implication that he spoke for the scene of free improvisers imposed the form on others. To both speak of form, as non-idiomatic does, and describe actual playing would then require delimiting free improvisation to a more coherent group that roughly agreed with him. Since he was motivated to do the analysis as a player this would be his immediate circle, while also interviewing people with whom he disagreed, including Prévost, and accepting them fully as improvisers even though they might bristle at his formulation. He claimed to set forth the "central tenets" of free improvisation, and in the revision he said that while musical fashions come and go the nature of improvisation is so "fundamental" as to resist change.

To propose the identity of free improvisation and non-idiomatic was not innocent musicology, for what Bailey was describing was specifically the playing and intentions of himself and his circle of partners. To characterize that grouping may have generalized their intent, but it also presumed a unity. To publish it gives that unity a public presence and prestige, from which those not wanting to be huddled under Bailey's umbrella will exclude themselves and seek another formulation. If the non-idiomatic concept is thought to speak for the whole scene then it is not descriptive but prescriptive. It was bound to run into opposition, which he later acknowledged. In 1992 he saw his writing as continuous play, and could see himself as "some fool writing a book about improvisation. You know that nobody's going to agree with it, and by the time the thing comes out, the music's gonna be different. If it stays alive."[215] Apparently by that time he had doubts that it would; we can imagine that "alive" meant more to him than the existence of the name. But what is "alive"?

Referring here briefly to the Americans, it has been detrimental for players and academics to accept Bailey's formulation as unquestionable and to be ignorant of the opposition, discussion, and critique it has provoked in Britain. This oversight has allowed for the easy merger of free improvisation with all improvisation as a unity of expansive positivity. It has contributed to the lack of impact of the first real break-away challenge to free improv, reductionist or lower-case improvisation of the later 90s (to be discussed in Part III). Why commit fully to a music whose title is so generously inclusive that it evokes no controversy? Music known to be capable of controversy that touches the nature of how musicians play requires a different participation than what does not.

Improvisers who were not in Bailey's circle *also* discarded much of conventional musical language. The most articulated criticism came from Eddie Prévost, whose major interest has been to realize a specific, collectively-shaped aesthetic and method, that of AMM.[216] He is concerned for the results of improvisation, and not only aesthetic; he projects social and political meaning into it. Coming from an originally Maoist political direction at the end of the sixties, Prévost sees the ensemble of players as a communitarian model of how players are to interact that rejects capitalism and competitive behavior. It has the aim of exploring sound, not unlike what others like Bailey have done without it being an explicit aim. Any method has parameters that also function as prohibitions for the player-adherents, much as a culturally known idiom does. Given that, Prévost is able to give a concrete assessment of whether a performance is good or bad, what has been adhered to or violated. While the non-idiomatic viewpoint is classically "free from," Prévost's is not free from an aesthetic aim the players seek to realize, but it is "free for" a certain kind of player community and successful performance. These are two different understandings of freedom, each with their own problems.

Bailey was aware of results but did not aim for them consciously and programmatically. His view projects no desired effect, so it implicitly criticizes the developed musical and extra-musical concept, which is then a kind of taboo, as Paul Helliwell criticizes.[217] Instead, Bailey and those of his view who became prominent--the actual representatives on the descriptive side of his analysis--quite intentionally delved more deeply into their specialized idiolects. In this way they became soloists, the usual road to musical prominence, which Prévost does not seem to have taken. Musical meaning for them was the soloist's development, influenced by others but not by an overall model. Even if an aesthetic is more loosely defined as a summary of their playing tendencies after the fact, the result looks exactly like an identity natural and comfortable for them, and they are bound to follow it. They held to individual styles that impressed and built an audience; they did not branch out and persist in a direction people rejected. To say they were geniuses who just naturally made the best music is naïve. Those daring to hold to a way of playing people don't like and ignoring their preference is very like pursuing a model of player interaction with no assured audience: both risk failure. The latter Prévost has done and so has achieved a different kind of success. At the same time, those who set up the model are presumably in advance of those learning it, which establishes a teacher-student hierarchy different from that of competing soloists.

Prévost's argument that improvisers play out of habit was true to the extent that idiolects did not change much over the years. Those "habits" were the consequence of a conscious act of freeing-from that took place in the sixties. In neither case was there indication that fundamental change would or should occur thereafter, once their careers and reputations were launched. Both positions accord with the concept of a cultural divide found in the shift from Free Jazz to free jazz. The sixties comes across as an era of unsurpassable creative movement against the backdrop of earlier artistic stagnation; at the same time it has blocked any further change that would challenge that accomplishment.

Prévost could make the charge and not feel self-accused because the discipline to attain a concept can override habit. To an extent, an aesthetic (and social) effect is where the artist already stands, looking backwards towards the means, which are then of less significance. Bailey's emphasis was on developing whatever pleased him immediately, and so at least in the moment he could ignore the effect. This put Prévost more on the side of compositional music, making it awkward to defend his view as at the core of specifically *free* improvisation. The model might be emancipatory, but the concept creator knows in advance what that emancipation must be and feel like.

Prévost sees AMM as progressive and cannot be thrown back into idiomatic music, which they discarded (that is, jazz-based music) as did Bailey.

Despite the respect of both for jazz it must have felt like an emancipation (as Oxley expressed) at that time of their move away from convention. Prévost's concept is a projection of emancipation for others; his own is past. Yet "free improvisation" suggests it is emancipatory for those playing *now*, which would include the initiators. Is it possible to be playing freely when what it means for music to be free is already known? This is the problem for a genre and title represented by its initiators. They all saw themselves within the title and collectivity of the scene, and for the sake of careers and bonds with other musicians they needed to be included in "free improvisation" despite differences, which contributed to rivalry around the title.[218]

Linking this back to the dilemma mentioned earlier, what does it mean to ask "What is free improvisation?" Is it a musicological form such that anyone playing according to its tenets is an improviser? Or does the playing of those most prominent in the scene determine it? What's in a name? A genre can usually be discussed in general terms, a code of what can and cannot be played. It transcends any number of musicians said to define it; with patience and skill theoretically anyone can learn it. Yet if one leaves out Louis Armstrong, Duke Ellington, Charlie Parker, then one has not grasped the meaning of jazz. A genre then is both a learnable code and is represented by specific figures. Since free improvisation defies the definable characteristics of a code it is unlike other genres. For it to have a positive meaning it will coincide with whatever its representatives do, and this would be true even if they don't follow what Bailey called the tenets of their music. That's because those tenets do not describe musical results, as would a code; it's only the *approach* to playing that is available to anyone. It can then be asked, who follows the approach, rather than who has come to represent it publicly. A potential gap opens between the representatives and the approach, two realities that might contradict each other despite being covered by a single title.

This introduces a kind of debate difficult for music theory, for it gets to the motivations and aims of the players, and not just what they say publicly. That free improvisation is a music played each time for the first time is implied in the approach and at the core of the appeal it has had. The dream of escaping "the same" relates back to the artistic value of spontaneity and has been more fundamental to the use of that title than the non-idiomatic distinction. Just as "jazz" means both the code and the hierarchy of career musicians, those presented as representing free improvisation would be the ones expected to illustrate the approach, even if they never say it explicitly. For a professional improviser to say, "My music is not created in the moment" would be a radical rejection of the claim of spontaneity and thus of free improvisation. Even at a more realistic minimum the title presumes that players choose to face the widest range of options their imagination can come up with each time they perform.

This conflicts with observable reality. For the representatives the media advances to play in the moment would imply a continual flow of new musical ideas, which is not in evidence. Nor does it seem that they are trying to follow that approach and failing; rather that it's something they have privately dismissed or never held beyond their early years.[219] A comparison of recordings will find that they play solos as loose compositions night after night, at best variations on a theme. Some who would categorize their music as free improvisation prepare a specific new solo for a tour, which is not improvising afresh. Groupings over decades are reunions, which also play very similarly night after night, and develop patterns of response to each other that make performances close to identical. Art audiences prefer a well-honed performance, music they can follow given previous iterations, requiring from performers a consistency that quirky moves do not provide. It can be defended as simply a buildup of knowledge through experience of one's choices over time and of one another. To call it "playing in real time" then does not distinguish it very much from improvising on a jazz composition, such that a tour will be very close to that of any idiomatic music, where a set list is followed. The gap between free improv and idiomatic improvisation, indeed any concert music, is then minimal. This is not a criticism of the results, only a question of the unacknowledged disjuncture between the musicological understanding of free improvisation and the results of its representatives.

A career as performer presumes that improvisers have developed what John Zorn called a "personal language" on the instrument. "What you play is totally up to you," Zorn says, yet a personal language comes into being long before the immediate situation.[220] It is this detailed identity that includes personalized sound, phrasing, and the bag of tricks specific to that player that becomes a consistent and unified way of playing. Serious aberrations will confuse listeners and anger one's partners. One can not escape anonymity without a musical persona, which every professional artist must achieve and maintain. Bailey's "highly stylized" playing, or idiolect, will become familiar to an audience and a comfortable home for the player, for whom it gains a market value as a commodity. That persona might even be enhanced by comments of opposition to the commodification of music.

For those who want to "live the dream" of getting paid to do what they most want to do in their life there is good reason to go with this flow and not dismantle what they have come to hold as owner. They might have a secure position financially, yet any deep self-questioning will weaken their position. In today's shrunken performance market such independence is discouraged in professionals. Only those working within a consistent personal style and mining the same vein discovered early on can expect to be considered among the permanent avant-garde.

Bailey is ambivalent here. He sees that it can be more marketable to do this than to seek the change of new experience. He says he prefers the latter but he comes out more in the middle, divided. The solo is essential yet problematic, with this stark statement: "the easier it becomes to play solo the harder it becomes to improvise solo." The distinction between the two is crucial; the truly improvised solo stands as a critique of one which is merely played—presumably a repeated style. His solution is a compromise: to build a vocabulary that is "usable in a playing situation," an idiolect with new material consciously added. The new would be change for the sake of change, which eloquently captures his early sessions and private work in retreat from groups. An exploratory, self-developed style in a steady group or with ad hoc partners, he says, can work as a balance against the pressures to create a group sound.[221] In the end Bailey's playing has been characterized to the point that someone can be called a "Bailey school" guitarist, an incremental growth over time that had a huge influence over others.

Are musicians building an attractive and useful identity or maintaining free improv as a distinct approach? Here the musicians' attitude to their patterned performance enters the picture. Like most truth about them it is hidden from the audience but musicians themselves know if they feel satisfied with playing the same way each night. If free improvisation is taken as a possibility of opening new ground--throughout their lifetime of playing and in the very moment of performance--then it would threaten to destabilize their ordinary playing. They will be occasionally self-critical and disappointed, a difficult emotion to handle for those presented as masters. They will open themselves to moves they had previously not considered, overcoming the gap between playing a free improv gig and playing freely, denying the title its function as accomplished fact. On the other hand if they feel that a tour of repeated performances accomplishes what they set out to do and satisfies the audience, then the title of "free improviser" is defined by what they do and not by a demanding concept. Due to strong pressures on professionals to validate their music in public, their statements on this cannot be any kind of test. However, I have not heard them or others claim that they open their music to radical change. The broadest, most ill-defined meaning of "free improvisation" is the perfect solution.

If free improv does not begin with a list of those operating under its title but is a concept of what it promises, then anyone who says they intend to play according to it can be equally included. To put it more radically, one has no good reason to refuse to play with any other such person.[222] This was the basis of ad hoc grouping, Bailey's practice, though on reflection and further experience he also approved "semi-ad hoc," allowing for both the continuity of regular playing partners and any who would seek him out.[223] Ad hoc implies that all have gathered out of equal interest in improvising together, with no instructions of what to do and the same rewards available to each. In performance, no one is paid extra according to their name, which is normal for festivals. One is faced with moves from others that are *in principle* unexpected and can be disruptive. It can bring out the most inventive twists, since players can be stumped to the point of silence guessing what to do in a situation not encountered before. This is rarely the case, but ambivalence of what to do is implicit in the approach. All this benefits people with no previous experience playing together. Workshops, on the other hand are master class situations, like Prévost's, led by a respected professional who as a teacher gives instructions to relative beginners. Their relations to each other are then mediated by the instructions, reducing the surprise and difficulty of ad hoc.

The ad hoc invitation may have been the original attraction for new players, eager in the later sixties to overcome the performer/spectator gap, which discourages entry into music. The set arrangement of Bailey's Company Week festival (1977-94) was ad hoc meetings, a contingent situation where invitees had no control over who they would play with. However, it was not the practice of all improvisers, for it goes against the grain of the professional musician role and all that entails. Those who avoided one-off situations performed almost exclusively with those they were used to playing with; at least Evan Parker felt the musical experience was richer with close intimates.[224] Ad hoc implies an inconsistency of results and so conflicts with the idealized and marketable conception of art as "the best," always a scarce commodity. The best are tried and true, not contingent but follow conscious development over time with a minimal risk of loss.

Bailey had some frequent partners but was not keen on playing in established groups, except for the two early ones that were for private exploration rather than performance. The one that followed Joseph Holbroke was the Music Improvisation Company (1968-71), also "a nameless, audience-free situation," (*Improvisation*, p. 133). It included partners whose closeness over time encouraged willful responses that were playfully disruptive. When musicians know each other well enough to anticipate each other's moves they can purposely create problems for each other, which Bailey called "mutual subversion." This fly in the ointment is a playful violation that runs counter to the ethic that avoids stepping on others' toes. This caution is commonly found in all improvised music, where there is no composition to keep individuals safe from each other. To be faced with unpredictable mutual subversion can be a stimulus; it risks tension, even hostility if put on stage, where one is urged to "make the other musicians look good," as Steve Lacy put it. Bailey may have considered disruption one of the central tenets of free improv, at least what he'd *like* others to do, but he did not explicitly say so.

To understand Bailey's position and contradictions the changing situation over time must be taken into account. His ideas were formed when his music and that of his partners were unknown outside their small circle and a handful of audience. Given very little public and funding, for a long time none were able to support themselves through performing. By comparison NY Free Jazz players had a brief promise of commercial growth that gave them an expectation for income by doing precisely what they wanted. Not until the mid-70s did Bailey himself earn a living exclusively from playing improvised music. Increasingly however "improvised music" became more widely publicized, attracting attention in Europe and acclaim for individuals. A music world providing criticism, publicity, venues, recordings, and festivals was taking shape that would accommodate and facilitate the best known professional musicians. This meant more touring abroad and funding, all of which increased the appearance that, like other art musics, the serious audience for this music would follow those musicians above others.

Art musics are supported by critics, publications and institutions that recommend and fund them. They attract audiences that trust the art music world, perhaps because quality art is thought to come from above. Those on the receiving end are unofficially tenured, just as programs once established tend to receive continued funding. Commercial musics have a different arrangement. They depend on crowd attention and celebrities who must compete with newcomers entering the market. Celebrities can be selected and shaped by the media, but they are still more affected by audience opinion than those funded by institutions. By the 80s free improv was no longer a movement but a stabilized art music genre, and the media was not chasing after the next musician with bold new ideas. Whether Bailey liked it or not, he came to be viewed as one, if not *the* representative for free improvisation.

His book surely contributed to his stature and to the influence of his concepts on audience and new players, as Prévost pointed out. Bailey, his partners, his festival, and his book, more than any other factor, turned what was practically a musician's private music into something widely known and competitive (though barely) with other performance genres.

Each generation of audience, media, and musicians raises and lowers the values of these representative figures. As they either die off (Bailey himself, in 2005) or are seen to repeat themselves endlessly, the music category which sustained them comes to be seen as "that sixties thing," automatically out of date no matter how it is played. It becomes "classic," yet with no cover songs for a new generation to revive interest.

The music world mediates all this, and like all performers Bailey depended on it for funding and income, yet criticized it as heavily as the sixties black avant-garde.[225] The music world must be distinguished from the musician struggling privately with questions of what to play, which is not necessarily reducible to external demands. Critics might be more articulate and at times more perceptive than the musicians, old and new, but will see them strictly as performers to be judged by output. Writers function as Virgils guiding the innocent through the unknown hell of alien music. They may not explicitly present individuals as representing "free improv" anymore, maybe just the best experimental musicians. However there is no "best" without a taste category they represent and compete in, while what they do *not* do is silent in the background.

As with jazz-based music, spectators and critics writing for improvisers pick out the individual voice and tend to ignore the subtleties of momentary interaction.[226] Their focus, evident in attendance at concerts, is on the musical results of performers considered prominent, the targeted subject of the critic's sentence and essay, which becomes the basis for consumers' understanding of the music. The player is a singular entity with a unified career trajectory that has risen in quantifiable fame (as measured, for example, by the standard fee each professional musician gauges and sets), and is recapitulated with each recording. Venue directors, funding sources, labels, publicists, all follow the same pattern. In a society whose bedrock since the 17th century has been possessive individualism and the defensive function of the ego, the solo is owned as a property, and would reasonably be valued over collective experience, so difficult to symbolize.

To sum up on Bailey, he hardly qualifies as a theorist by academic standards and was not trying to be one. He qualifies practically every theoretical statement he makes. He draws a line between composition and improvisation yet until 1974 Bailey occasionally played compositions of his partners, some on labels that reached a wider audience, and so at times he agreed to the composer's parameters. His sixties partner Gavin Bryars had turned to composition and later returned to improvising, and in *Improvisation* Bailey gives him an extended opportunity to present opposing arguments. He also pulls back from advocacy to say improvisation is just what he has come to himself, and repeatedly locates himself within the wider community of all musicians, not just improvisers. He thinks an improvisation can be good or bad but unlike Prévost he doesn't characterize the difference via a generalized standard, or suggest an ideal audience response.

By the early 70s Bailey probably thought he and his peers would eventually be able to earn enough to perform their music as their fulltime professional occupation for the rest of their lives. Of all those he played with, few gained sufficient music world attention to attain this, limited mostly by the potential audience for the genre. Their choice, and that of the larger community of non-professionals, required them to maintain free improvisation as a distinct art form and to prevent it from being diluted. Yet lacking a professional standard to back them up, as other art musics depended on, it was always a precarious venture.

10. Free Playing

In the following I abandon the past tense to introduce a term that lacks the historical and cultural conditions of a genre: free playing. These two words both point to universal human actualities, possibilities, and problematic interpretations. Free playing could be intentionally walking awkwardly down the street, acting willfully in a serious setting, or thinking and articulating something contrary to common sense. It is outside the ordinariness of a functioning life and stands apart from the context it disturbs. I will delimit the term here to freeform sound-making activity for the benefit of those playing, apart from any interest to advance themselves or what they do in the world. Anything such players do to enter the competitive gig economy or even to achieve acceptance by others can be distinguished from their playful interactions. The desire to play freely is rarely found completely separate from the desire to play for others, but the two are not identical. I will be using "free playing" as a specialized term but do not intend to monopolize it or criticize its variable usage among musicians.

When asked, those who do this in pubic call it free improvisation, but as a title used to draw an audience, others can be substituted without much complaint. What we call ourselves and the names we give our activities in public—always a messy business. Free playing is my term for the activity of a collectivity of players with a particular self-understanding and is not the approach of all those who might use the genre title. One can play a free improv gig and with no sense of contradiction admit disappointment that one wasn't playing very freely. An audience might be in awe to hear strange sounds and gestures, while the musicians feel like bored entertainers. They are internally pressured to break out of whatever paralysis they are in, but not to live up to "free improvisation." Like free jazz, that title includes its performed-music history, its recognized representatives, festivals, and classic recordings, its occasional discourse, its packaging, and a functional relation to society, to the market, and to the livelihood of musicians. To block that off as extraneous to the activity and collectivity of players provides an opening for something else.

"Free playing" is not a new phrase. It was meaningful for the Brits of the early period discussed above, just as "freeform" was for Free Jazz. The early American players called what they were doing "playing free," and Derek Bailey spoke of free improvisation but interchanged the term with free playing, which he also used in reference to some jazz.[227] A genre can be described as an actuality, with a place in the world that can be pinpointed. I will be discussing what free playing opens as a direction and a possibility, and the possible motivation for doing it. I will lay the ground for understanding its distinction from free improvisation, and in the next chapter I will elaborate more specifically on the relation of the two in practical terms.

Free playing is the pursuit of pleasure through making sound that is as truly of one's own making in that moment as possible. This makes it distinct from audience interest and from structures culturally known or self-prepared. It would seem to fit one side of the common understanding of art, namely, what artists make in their own interest without conforming to any external demand. This is what they should do if they are to represent the idealized autonomous subject, but that "should" is irrelevant to their consciousness. Contradictory to this is the view that art provides something of positive value for the non-artist other, by mirroring, attracting, and/or challenging society, or at least the more humanistic, educated members thereof. On that side of the aisle, musicians are said to need an audience in order to make art of any value; all we can know of art is then what they bring to the world, is judged and disseminated as part of the culture.[228] This means that for musicians to be respected as artists they must be performers with an act to present on a public stage.

In the first case the artist is an isolated visionary and possibly a socially dysfunctional genius; in the second, sociological view, the artist is functional to society in providing its non-material needs. The apparent contradiction is removed by the assumption that both are rewarded by recognition, some sooner than others. Besides, since our institutions select and reward all the authentic contemporary artists *now*, eliminating surprise discoveries later, the present arrangement is more efficient than the past. Furthermore, artistic autonomy is like the right of free speech, and "this is just what our society needs and gets from artists." There's also the caveat of realism, that there is no true autonomy since "we're all slaves to conditioning." Those whose names provide an example of "artist" receive recognition at the hands of the mechanisms of the social order. This complex of assumptions is central to the ideology of art today.

Whatever legitimacy the ideal of artistic autonomy might confer on free playing is withdrawn by its failure to accord with the second view, the social role of art production. The private concern of players is disqualified as serious art if they don't aim towards the art*work*, namely performance. Free playing is not the activity of marginalized artists seeking legitimacy and attention, since what is done strictly for oneself needs no audience. Nor do players even think of themselves as artists except as an afterthought, if at all. In today's society of enjoyment, people want as direct access to enjoyment as possible, and performers are expected to provide that. [229] Organizing oneself and partners to construct one's own pleasure out of the raw material of sound is something else. The word "art" is used for all creative work, and that applies here, but not its narrower meaning of work aimed at audience consumption, which is a necessary component of "serious" art. This creates the paradox of being serious about art without creating serious art.

Free playing is distinct from jamming, with which it is often confused. As the word is used today, a jam is built around a known and unquestioned code such that it can usually be typed as blues, jazz, or rock. Some British free jazz musicians in the early 70s invited a fellow musician to jam, telling him to play whatever he wanted. He proceeded to improvise on a tune the whole time, which irritated the free jazzers. He did what they asked, and was indeed playing free, that is, free of involvement in what the others did, while a proper free jazz jam would require following the code of that music. A jam is free from the operative judgment in the rehearsal but lacks the exploration of ideas outside its code. There's nothing difficult to deal with, nor is anything expected to stick in the mind as eventful. It is love separated from work, common to most life.

The story about the British free jazz musicians illustrates a common misunderstanding around "free." Jamming is the assumption for many musicians, a passing moment that has no lasting effect on the players; one can exit as if nothing much happened, a boys' night out. A free playing session usually goes beyond "great session." Players often discuss and assess a session or performance, processing it in words that might affect future meetings. Making recordings can show how much change has occurred over time in a regular grouping, as people have changed individually from private work and playing with different partners. Occasionally some weight seems to shift and they can sense a new horizon opening. A free playing invitation is to join others as a collectivity, even of two, to do what they would not do if they were disconnected individuals playing their chops. There is usually tacit agreement, which at times must be made explicit to newcomers, in some cases stopping the playing and talking about any misunderstanding. This aspect brings the session close to the workshop, where players are prepared to judge their own playing and discuss how they are affected by each other.

Full engagement in a free session means players will not be thinking how to make the best music. It's "let's play" not "let's play music." It seems simple but it is a radical difference. Music implies following a code known to the others, who then judge what they're doing accordingly. In part this comes from the expectation that they will perform. An art music performance presumes an audience that expects the musicians to have their own code and follow it. Without that a sense of unreality or chaos will prevail, a situation musicians prepare for in their sessions. They will unconsciously imagine the presence of the audience and seek to prevent that from happening.

To be thrown into a free playing situation can undermine one's usual behavior. For most people, including musicians, the prospect of that would be highly unpleasant and a waste of time, which is one reason few partake. Those who do this anyway likely find it difficult to follow the course they would in other situations. Passing familiar landmarks as they run the same patterns with slight variations becomes uncomfortable; the feeling is that it isn't working. Satisfaction with your playing is fine until you've *been* satisfied and comfortable a while, then it's boring and frustrating. To be uncomfortable is then strangely exciting. For the performance-oriented musician there's a danger here: what if free playing gets me interested in musical ideas the audience doesn't like? Will they still be interested? That question hits home like nothing else.

Escape from one's usual inclinations doesn't always happen, but if it *never* happened the motivation for free playing would collapse. Since players don't know what their partners will do, especially in ad hoc meetings, they might be forced into areas they have even wanted to avoid. To be tempted out of one's patterns provokes inner resistance. Without meaning to, players put pressure on each other to abandon what they know how to do and to invent new twists and elaborations, as if to say, "Excite me!" In the atmosphere of full interplay they don't even notice they're learning new stuff until later, and thinking anything is changed is not even necessary.

If "free" is misleading, it can be called "open-field playing," where the fences one runs into are one's assumptions about what can be done. It can be a kind of acrobatics, with players finding themselves leaping and contorting as they deal with their inhibitions and others' freedom not to follow their lead. A good session might be when they make each other more playful.

Free playing is rooted in the session because the only external stimulation and reinforcement is from others similarly engaged. Players commonly say it is "just" a session, as if to say, "What we do here doesn't matter," meaning, to the world outside. The alternative is the rehearsal, which is consciously aimed at realizing a musical preconception. "Rehearsal" can be used loosely, yet it usually implies a projected event, such that musicians merge their private judgment with that anticipated from others.[230] The fantasy of perfecting an object predominates, a goal-oriented work under the sign of efficiency and progress. It is a supposedly adult concern compared to the jam or free session, which has aspects of child's play—totally absorbed but pointless as to achievement. While theatre rehearsals can use improvisatory techniques to loosen up actors and get them into their roles, music rehearsals are more like learning one's lines, including the details of expression. A free playing session rather has the aim, motivation, and engagement of difficulty minus the goal of external reward. It is free of the performer-role contract with the world, the pressure to make a fruitful exchange with an audience and thus integrate themselves into the economy. It functions to dispel the ghosts that haunt anyone self-identified as "musician." These include any parental, superego figure to be pleased or appeased, such as one's music teacher, "Music" (the ghost of classical musicians), "jazz," the imagined audience, and the critic who demands to be aroused.

Playing of all kinds engages desire, and from a social point of view desire is infectious and mimetic.[231] Imitation plays a major part in the professionally-oriented arts scenes and normally involves competitive rivalry and individual success. Without it there would be no code to collectively adhere to. In jazz history these factors once encouraged musical growth and change. Currently that is not the case: witness what goes under the name of "avant-jazz." This is the embarrassment jazz enthusiasts refuse to acknowledge and explain.

The free playing session stands outside rivalry and blockage—at the expense, of course, of the obscurity of its participants and any effect on a scene. The closest it comes to a scene is the specific gathering of players, each one lasting a few hours and often differently composed. Players are engaged in the same collective project, but since there are no favored or unacceptable moves there is nothing to determine a winner. Whatever sounds like rivalry is playful and not meant to stick, as in one-upmanship competition. Imitation normally results in "creative difference," a hierarchy of one player's musical persona over another. When this is dissolved in free playing, following and leading disappears into interplaying. In this version of imitation *I'm playing what you're playing, only in my own way*, even though to an outside listener this will be hard to discern, especially in a group larger than two. Even if they want to playfully contradict what others are doing they must listen closely in order to do that.

Players who disengage from others and carve out a little solo space are not invited back. That's the brutal truth. The social code of jazz requires each soloist to withdraw to make room for the other, a kind of natural right. In the code implicit in free playing, the very assertion of that is the infringement.

Without an audience and music world to take notice there is no socialized innovation, not even in the sense of Free Jazz, where that collectivity of musicians advanced upon what others did. Rather, whatever feels new and fresh is shared amongst players present at the session, without any reward of prestige. And it would make no sense for players to imitate the music of any scene, since whoever is not present in the session is ignored. Shards of different idioms might slip in but don't get honored or used to validate what they do. In organizing a session concepts of good instrumentation for a band are frequently overruled by the sheer desire to play with whoever is available. There is also no reason to distinguish oneself from the others in ways that will be publicly recognized, the strategy of minor differences for consumer goods. This creates the antithesis of the scene—a pool of players who are open to any possible grouping or newcomer, with selection based strictly on whether they can anticipate excitement in playing together.

Free playing legitimates a player's musical ideas to him or herself, and partners return this legitimacy in kind, a conspiracy of equals. This mutuality depends on sharing a physical space. In performance mutuality might extend to those other players who normally form the bulk of the audience, but less likely by non-players, even less for the physically distanced listener of recordings. Given the ritual distinction between performers and audience, free playing in front of other improvisers might not qualify as a genuine performance, where one is expected to produce a particular, positive effect on a spectating other. There, role difference is essential to motivate performance, whereas the other of most free playing performances is not very "other."

To indicate that lack of role I often refer to those performing as players, an aspect of the universal subject, rather than musicians, a word implying obligations, expertise, and rewards. "Musician," like "artist," has lost much of its connotation of career orientation over the past thirty years but to be distinguished by the title is upheld—much depends on it. One reason that few who think of themselves as musicians commit themselves to free playing is that it doesn't require musicianship. "Musician" is for many still a calling, not as respectable as "serious artist" but nonetheless an appeal for recognition that one has a valid place in the social order. It is a first step towards achieving respect and legitimacy, and implies that one has signed the contract to provide music behind one's back. To bring free playing within that contract is perhaps the greatest personal temptation the player has to face. For those of us who have invested ourselves in being musicians (and I am one of these), free playing only begins to open up when we drop the need to be respected for what we do. That's a tall order, but we're constantly reminded of the negative consequences of that need.

Sessions do not stand in the way of performance but provide a space where musicians can gather strength and momentum, experiencing a flow of musical ideas that stand a chance against the pressure to please an audience. When they sense an audience is egging them on, however, they can even go farther into unknown territory: "Yes, go, we want it." This is most likely in DIY spaces such as certain house shows, the most welcome space for free playing. In more formal and recognized venues or recording studios, internalized pressures often come to life and threaten the adventure.

One presumed blessing of an advance plan is that it gives the performers a task, something to follow resolutely in the face of a potentially unresponsive audience, or more likely the unconscious fear of such. Compositions can go into some hell-broken-loose spaces, as in those of Iannis Xenakis, but only thanks to those black dots and musicians who turn them faithfully into sound. Those who have abandoned pre-structures in performance are most equipped to escape the fear-based projection by turning to each other as they have done in their private space. All that matters then is the collectivity, obliterating thoughts of audience response.

The free-playing solo is so vulnerable and precarious because one is starkly alone in front of those who will be judging the player alone, with no one to help carry the burden. It is a terror for the socialized being we all are, a setup for the fragile ego. But to imagine all guns drawn around you, with only some squeaks of sound to defend yourself, *can* be flipped over to a motivating excitement. When death feels most certain you come to life—"What do I have to lose?" Putting oneself fully into the hands of the audience, the player can feel completely present to them and not dutifully performing a rewarding task. Imagination of disaster shifts to a mingling of desires. To make the solo a virtual composition is the more common improviser option; after all "solo" usually means just that. It can be trusted to be effective because it was worked out in private, out of all one's experience of what works well. Maybe that's what the audience thinks it wants, but there's a chance it might be stirred by something new in the moment rather than a demonstration.[232]

"Risky" is the key word to draw the more media-dependent of the avant-garde audience. The idea promoted is that the musicians will go so far out the audience might not be able to "take it," and that the musicians themselves are risking success. This drama is a weak version of the macho-aggressive excitement of stock market trading, danger sports, and other gambling. Since avant-garde musicians know what they'll do in advance, they minimize any risk that the audience won't be won over. In free playing that doesn't come into play, but they do risk themselves, at least their comfort and self-satisfaction. They do risk failing, but for them that means conforming to the performance contract, pulling them back from whatever adventure they reached privately.

Live art attracts to the role of performers many who have strong needs for immediate and long-term career success. Psychologically this is the need for approval, easily confused with love and obedience to authority. The ego tries to manage the exchange with the other to get approval, and to hide the desperation and trauma of loss behind it. Normalization of this as "just the way things are" is how it all gets swept under the rug. For performers, approval that is not structural (one's position of relative prestige) comes in the form of applause and the biggest audience possible, with the well-funded festival at one extreme and at the bottom the pass-the-hat gig. Any time musicians' fear of a lack-luster response surfaces they will be tempted to depend on what they think will satisfy their specific audience, perhaps displaying an impressive technique, or playing more aggressively than they would otherwise.[233] Those who perform regularly, including myself of course, are like actors who know the tricks of how to put a smile on the other's face and evoke hearty, rather than perfunctory clapping. We call it derogatorily "playing our bag of tricks." We are tempted to normalize our familiar moves, thinking of the audience as consumers who were (as convention would have it) thrilled with yesterday's playing and so want more of the same. In the free session players are better prepared for that situation. If they become aware they are bored with their playing they will wake up from their trance and refocus. Whatever they do will mean playing against the grain of their all-too-human inclination to obey the social code—give what you think the other wants and they will return the favor. That's a powerful command even for those who imagine themselves quite free. Free playing sessions guarantee little when it comes to performing, but they *can* reinforce an alternative.[234]

Seasoned performers who think their music is truly "theirs" will do well to ask why their music is consistent over time. Is consistency a natural development and possession that finally becomes an inert commodity? Is there a subtle exchange going on? Playing that derives from one's position as performer requires an unconscious effort to close the distance between what the musician can do and what the audience wants. It will evoke a sense of duty to provide it over time as the artist's persona and identity. The effective audience (not all listeners) sustains a reciprocal pretense: to the extent that performers are socially legitimated, listeners feel they *should* accept what happens on stage as the real deal of art, silence any voice in them that rejects it, an perhaps try to censor dissenters through shame. However, neither audience nor performer can know *for sure* what the other wants. Nor is there a law that says players must be consistent. Career musicians rely on prior music world recognition and credentials to get on a significant stage and to get a positive response, but is the audience really connecting with the music? The audience is trained in how to respond, but do they know what they really want, not in general but *right now*? The need to hide and ignore their dissatisfaction, or uncertainty of satisfaction, keeps everything locked in place.

The music world prefers musicians and audience bound through consistency and pretense, but they are both missing out on being directly confronted with raw experience. They must break out of that dynamic if live music is ever to be a living and emancipatory, which can only be for audience and players simultaneously. In free playing if the leap to enjoyment is made it is a surprise to both. That leap might well be overt dissatisfaction and confusion on both sides, a situation in which pleasant entertainment is shattered, and enjoyment revealed as a rough ride.

As for the free session, the substitute for security of the musical code is the collapse of distance between player and sound/silence, the stand-in for what used to be called nature. At each moment one is on the solid ground of sensuous reality, without the intervening judgment of what is the right thing to do. Players might feel uncertain or disengaged but still they *are* the sound/silence they are making. It is when immediacy is not in doubt that its status as music is irrelevant. What make it work are the minute interconnections of play without any gap for making the right choices, which is where one's personal code intervenes. What blocks conventional choices is not the self-conscious avoidance of codes but the assurance that whatever move a player makes will be not only accepted but grist for the mill, something for the others to work with even if they appear to ignore it. At the same time, there is no assurance players will accept their *own* decisions just because they are free to do whatever. Freedom is the question, not the answer.

If "Free to do *what?*" motivates the playing, then over time one becomes adept at locating those who know best how to pose it. In the open field every move can be a direction somewhere, maybe nowhere interesting. Desire does not only flow forward. Impulse can deceive; one might easily leave a session or performance disgusted with one's playing. What went wrong? Nothing. It is as reasonable to repeat what one did last time as to be bored with it now.

The above is how experienced and committed players might think of a free session. For the uninitiated the basic introduction to playing freely is usually simple to get across. I might just ask, "Do you want to do a free session?" For those unaware of this kind of experience I would add that they can be free of everything they expect of "real music" beyond the very basics—sound and silence. "I'd love to but I don't know how" is easily countered; you can come to a session and not make a sound, or something inaudible, which might provoke discussion but not judgment. Today the dogma of music professionalism has broken down such that "everyone is an artist" is in the air. Many are willing to give it a try, and not just music. Imagination is ready to take over, which is a cultural change since I was growing up in the postwar period, when the imagination was distrusted in those didn't hang out shingles as poets and artists. For starters, any literate person can be an artist by simply reading every third word—pretty soon they start throwing their own words in there and making things up. Anyone who moves can move freely, that is, erratically. Nothing prevents them beyond the limits of their body, and the claim to know those limits ends once they start moving.[235]

For the reader who hasn't ever engaged music actively, the best way to grasp this is to put yourself into the situation of actually playing. Just make a sound, then another, without singing. Do this in private, with no one in earshot to judge you. You might be surprised how difficult it is, a kind of embarrassment, an attack on your self-image as a mature adult. Or get your hands on a physical instrument. Maybe a cello and bow, those aura-endowed objects only a priestly caste is supposed to handle. The thought of it can be frightening—what could I possibly do? Why am I doing this? Draw the bow across the strings and say to yourself, "This is the sound I'm making," a simple statement of fact. You are in the existential situation of being free from any external judgment and face to face with your full capacity to humiliate yourself. The superego voice rebukes you as foolish; it defeats you or you go ahead—your choice. Each sound you make will fly in the face of that voice, and you will be slashing it to the ground with every untutored stroke of the bow—with no one but yourself to hear it. You will not approximate a "real" cellist, but in listening you will discover a new relation of your ear and your sound-making body. You will be drawing energy away from the straw man that has been mediating your relation to music, and gaining power for yourself you never knew possible. Since you are not aiming to become a musician, this power will have no roots in identity. Moreover you will be within the circle of those who play freely in performance, and will immediately get what they are doing. When you ask to play a session with us we will do it.

There is no pedagogy for free playing, at best perhaps a broad discussion of what it means to play music, or to play at all. "Do you know how to play the saxophone, or jazz?" asks whether one can conform to an acknowledged technique designed to produce a particular music and is usually answered yes or no. Quite different is "Do you know how to play freely?" This can only be answered yes *and* no; "yes" to the extent that free playing is a universal human possibility, and "no" because "how to" implies judgment, and where free playing might go is indeterminate. Anyone who claims to know how to roam the open field without coming to a fence has a false understanding of the concept. The point is to go up to the fences and then deal with them *at that moment*. The preparation for doing it is to open a space of curiosity about all the things one might do, possibly stimulated by others. Cognitive and critical faculties are involved in taking any path, but here there is no prerequisite "how to." In the end "I *won't* do this" is possible, not "I *can't*."

The ontological status of free playing, like freedom itself, is necessarily in question, a substantive that is already undermined. It is performative: it doesn't exist until you reach your hand towards the door. Finding and taking the path are one and the same. Getting lost, losing the thread of connection is ever possible, and then discovered to be merely an extension of the path. The epigraph of the event is "Let's see what happens."

"Free" can be applied critically to all of today's music genres. Free playing clashes with the identity of being a musician, a status above non-musicians, for it signifies that all are free to enter, as a human and not musician-bounded act.[236] This is functional for those committed to it, open to engaging as many new players as possible as a means to discover and break down the fences blocking their own horizon. When new players are welcomed the correct relation is immediate and conscious *trust*,[237] rather than loyalty to the musician caste. This is not the trust given to the social order or the consumer's trust in the music world. It is the social foundation to playing with whatever the other does, responding only with sound, silence, movement, and speech released from prosaic effectiveness. Ultimately it is trust that the other will "get it," will hear and be drawn into the connection possible to the others' playing, not despite but because it is given the widest range possible. This yields the apparent paradox of the greatest musical intimacy possible and the greatest latitude of musical material.

Given this trust that freedom of movement will not tear us apart, a rarity in any society, the content of free playing is formally indeterminate. However, often players and listeners will sense an absolute determinacy of whatever is happening, as if the piece were scored. In those moments everything is known to be unaccounted for yet experienced as precisely correct. If music is expected to elicit a response of inexplicable mystery, this would be it. Observers cannot achieve this through analytic work. For instance, to the extent free playing is realized, listening to x number of samples will not yield generalizations capable of predicting what the next moment will yield. Player and any concept of that player will not match up, just as free playing as a concept cannot predict content.

The implication of this is huge: no players can be selected who represent this approach better than others. There are people whose music can be understood as coming from the intent to roam freely, but there are no "free players" as an identity like jazz musicians. Moreover, to claim something as "my music" would merely be whatever I am playing this moment, not very satisfying to the needs of music world discourse.

Some will close off other options and perform in this mode exclusively. But given the lack of identity, their concentrated focus is not generally known or considered by spectators and the music world. Concert-goers can barely assimilate that players have chosen to expand beyond their current knowledge in the midst of performing, even less when hearing a recording.[238] It conflicts with what is universally expected of art entertainers: give us only your best, most scrupulously prepared music. Free playing may be the originary base of current free jazz and free improvisation, but under the unwritten agreement with art consumers and the music world professionals are pressured to work under the yoke of conformity to what is expected from identified artists. Musicians say "We're free to play what we want," but they must fulfill that contract. In free playing they might also say that, but they won't know what they want until they play it—too late for adjustment.

Players might say, "what we just did was very free," indicating that they broke through a wall they may not have known existed, with no assurance it could happen again. It is about as far removed from the concept of creating an artwork as one can go. Free playing is not an avant-garde music; it is an innovative, radical approach when taken as an end in itself, with no additional aim to be innovative. Players might arrive at material that listeners would experience as unique ("I never heard a saxophone sound like that"), yet to prepare that for presentation would require a mental operation at odds with their playing. To break out of conventions and genre boundaries, which Paul Hegarty claims was Derek Bailey's aim, might help legitimate free improvisation but is of no concern for free playing.[239] It might seem constructive, but then the result is too easily compared musicologically with what already exists, as if the intransitive, "playing," could be reduced to the transitive—the *what* of music.

Free playing lacks the continuity of progressive development, as one can say of a genre like jazz in its heyday, when players seeking to outdistance rivals ended up altering the code for others. It is on the cusp between possibility--it *can* move in any direction—and singular actualities, which would include Coltrane's long solos, free sessions today, and much in between. The urge to play freely has brought different players together at different historical junctures with no causal links between them, such as learning from the masters, nor influence from peers.[240] It is then fortunate that North America has no recognized masters for free playing to follow; only a music world can churn them out and at present its radar does not notice anything of such small value. In the dynamic known as the "anxiety of influence," Harold Bloom's thesis, the artist (in his case poets) seeks to build on established predecessors by borrowing from them to impress others, while seeking to appear unique. What joins moments and individuals playing freely is rather the collective space where this contradiction does not apply.

This creative freedom is cognitive, musical ideas potentially multiplying by intermixing and creating mutants no one recognizes, including oneself. The instrument does not dictate inherent rules for making music but is a mere vehicle for sound. A cheap, even broken instrument can even hold an advantage over one acclaimed as exemplary for the correct sound. One might say the love of the instrument is transformed from veneration for its access to tradition, like a sacred relic, to appreciation for whatever about that specific instrument enables endless mutation. The results vary with time and artistic culture. In the sixties, "free" in Britain took place in a culture where Webern's dispersed tonality, the materials of Free Jazz, and John Cage's indeterminism were unavoidable, emancipatory paths that were there to be being taken. Today the background is more likely sound in all its varieties, unleashed by Cage and fed into the general musical culture as a potential aesthetic through electronic manipulation and synthesis.

A free session today can still involve only real notes. The players' common orientation to sound is not an in-principle aesthetic for free playing. What is usually understood as artists' aesthetic is something specific they have intended and are expected to follow, such that results will accord with it. They might change it over the years through deliberation, for which they provide an interpretation for the public, located in the artist statement or indicated in the shorthand of genre titles. This discourse is the basis for internal critique, judgments of how well artists meet their own criteria. Artists can then meet rejection with the argument, "you just have a different aesthetic, you don't get it." For most improvisatory or experimental musicians an aesthetic would be a tacit or explicit binding agreement that precedes the playing, a program shared by partners and within which they are free to roam, thus providing a meaning backed by discourse and legitimately closed to those who are unappreciative.

Those playing freely must admit their vulnerability here: there is no way to defend what they do on these grounds. All the elements of playing they employ (vocabulary, phrasing, dynamics, etc.) might be absent the next time around. Any such specific, symbolized aesthetic that can be articulated will miss the point, for it can only be post-hoc, a generalized summary of what was played, noting features left out. It will be the result of analyzing from the spectator position, projected on players as if they intended it. All playing can be analyzed and reviewed, yielding a summary of results roughly predictive, as the empirical sciences might provide. Yet in each free playing situation the result is unintentional, which enables the playing to be as open as possible.[241] Only *free listening* of the engaged subject will correspond to free playing, unencumbered by expectations and the will to contain their experience in aesthetic concepts they have pre-approved.

The effort of free playing and free listening is to keep the play going, what James P. Carse calls the infinite game, the metaphorical opposite of the finite game of winning and losing.[242] It is not free of rules; there's at least this one: to keep the playing so interesting, so capable of ambivalence, that its end cannot be imagined. Rules are exclusionary, so as I said earlier, those who seem to prefer the finite game will not be asked back. This gets complicated however when the game is played before an audience. The moves and strategies to create interest in what players do, essential to getting most gigs, constitute the finite game, as does the effort to fulfill a life pattern players have set for themselves. Both games are motivated and have their thrilling moments. This is obviously going on everywhere we look; it defines the generalized activity of humans, including myself. For those who elect to engage the infinite game as sound-makers at least some problematic will creep in to the extent they engage the win-lose game of competing for gigs. The two kinds of games are mutually exclusive but the turf of the psyche and its needs are not. The infinite game can feel like an impractical ascetic move requiring a pledge, yielding a real internal as well as external division. From one point of view people who go towards the empty hole of their desire are living in a dream world, perhaps admirable but lacking in the realism essential for existence. From another perspective, what is essential for one's existence is to follow desire down the rabbit hole and see where it gets you.

For trained musicians the attraction to free playing involves the realization that the finite game of a career is lacking something essential. On the side of realism, why would musicians who have paid for their training and value it be attracted to free playing? Yet this does happen; some recognize that training may ground a career but does not add up to their musical pleasure. The question then is the nature of that pleasure, whether the self of the musician includes the desire to create something of their own origin, without shifting to the composer role. Classical musicians, trained to strictly follow the score, often openly express fear at the prospect of a blank tablet: "What am I supposed to do?" They haven't been expected to intuit what to do out of their own feeling and exploration but to place themselves within the frame of the composition.

To lure them out of that, first of all the blank tablet is a useful metaphor, not a truth. No one starts from scratch; in free playing each sound players make is in the background for what they do next, either to repeat or extend it or to do something different. And of course it's always possible to simply go along with whatever others are doing as the easiest path. Secondly, anticipation *can* be an enticement found within fear, exciting a desire to move from the passenger to the driver seat. In a world bent on security the risk of free playing can appeal. The strongest argument for doing any art might be that, unlike truly asocial behavior, we can do anything at all without risking our material existence. Risk only appears when we base our existence on getting approval for it.

Classical musicians are far distant from the approach of free playing, yet if they knew about it they might even be more eager than jazz-based (including many free jazz) musicians. Jazz musicians treat free playing as only a bit more open than jazz improvisation, and they already have the tools to do that, so in playing freely they don't stray far from home.[243] For classical players, the understanding that the music can go on perfectly well while they are silent—the concept of the rest, and of exiting and entering differently for each composition—is built into following the score. Modern compositions are even highly erratic in that regard; moreover they require a wide range of techniques, which is why the actual sound can be so similar to free playing. To ease a classical player into it they might simply pretend to be following a score. This would bring them closer than for jazz musicians pretending to be playing jazz, for the jazz code is more in the results than in strict following of classical compositions that can literally go anywhere.

The standard way for improvisers to acquire new musical ideas is consistent with normal learning; ideas and techniques that appear relevant and attractive will be added to one's bag of tricks. To be included it will have to pass an unconscious screening to determine if it fits what the player already does. In free playing it is possible to ignore the musician's bag. One plays anything evoked in the situation and not necessarily what has gone through the filter of judgment. The greater one's range of experience and ideas, the more is available in the moment of playing. Some ideas come as the result of experiences of boredom or in the heat of excitement, when one doesn't know what the hell is happening. Something goofy or amateurish might then show up, at which the Serious Musician in one's head wakes up: "Do I want to be the kind of player who does this?"

Perhaps the most powerful social demand on young artists hoping to be admitted to the guild is to reduce their application to something that can be described. That establishes a boundary, a code in their very handwriting that then tells them what they may validly do—as if their desire could be precisely aimed--while tacitly forbidding what is taboo. The attraction of the taboo, where desire is hidden, is what the social order needs to frustrate (civilization and its discontents). For all their advertised radicality, "Here's what I can do" is the resume, the record filed with the guardians of the social order. Make that promise and I've ceded my desire; I call it "my music" but it's no longer mine.

It's easily forgotten that genres indicate what players will *not* do; shock and surprise there may be but kept within bounds. This follows the linguistic theory (Ferdinand de Saussure's), that a word, in this case signifying a code such as jazz, is defined not by an essence but by difference from other meanings. For all it includes, what and whom it excludes is fully present in the background. There are different forms of exclusion however. To present oneself as marginalized is to pluck the string of pity—"I've been put in the background." It establishes a claim to be included as a variant within a code. This sacrifices the right to set one's boundaries anew each minute of playing, which makes each period of activity concrete and unique. Free playing makes no application for admission and claims no such inclusion. To affirm it as *already* music would be the argument for inclusion. Then the burden of proof is on its players to define themselves according to a constitutive aesthetic and examples of what aiming at.

I have touched on motivation above but need to delve further into it if I am to explain an apparent conundrum. If players can't expect to get a financial reward for doing this, nor a sense of accomplishment by following a structure, nor a socially respected identity, then why do it? There is even more on the negative side of the ledger. Free playing opens Jean-Paul Sartre's "vertigo of possibility," an experience of terror in the face of too many options, exponentially increased in today's situation of the protean, destabilized self.[244] "Anything goes" has been on the banner waved for sexual freedom and was once an accusation against players of music entitled "free," as if the dangers of going too far in sex and music are joined at the hip. That's an interesting parallel, since of all the arts it is music that is most often related to sexual life and dreams of fulfillment.

That charge presumes that players take a devilish delight in being free of all constraints. On the contrary, the Pandora's box of anything goes is what players and critics both have reason to fear. If everything is an option then nothing stands out as more valued, such that the "everything" is not a plenitude but an emptiness, an endless desert with no direction home, or alternately endless foreplay. Frustrated would be the hope of musicians to finally get somewhere, to achieve meaningful results. To achieve something that can't be taken away would end the anxiety of the accused before the judge's bench, and we're all the accused. To take on the absolute freedom of choice makes vulnerable whatever the players decide to do. It is strictly their private decision and indefensible according to any recognized code—there's no "other" to turn to for support and final judgment.

The fear is universal; players are not exempt, and can only engage this vertigo in circumscribed situations. Perhaps their engagement will have them barging into other realms of art, such as poetry or visual art, or behaving oddly, all of which used to be assumed of artists. "Why not do this instead of that?" This question raised to the infinite degree in music can be extended to the questioning of *all* codes, conventions taken as reasonable and agreed upon. "Anything goes" would seem to get people opening up creatively, but something is hidden, namely, that only what is sanctioned within certain vague boundaries will be valued as truly creative. Over that border is the plunge into unleashed desire and an audience response that's not necessarily what one wants.

The response of a social order to existential vertigo and the contagion of dissolution, for which the word "anarchy" is popularly used, is to back a system of codes, including latitudes of behavior. Most of these are minute patterns learned through imitation and transgressions forbidden without any rule ever pronounced. As for artists, finite results can be obtained, sorted through, evaluated, and kept roughly predictable once their path is chosen. For results to be presented and judged significant, the period of play must aim at coming to an end, releasing from the anxiety of judgment those the social order has determined to be serious artists. In democratic fashion, all this is considered the will of the people, at least of those who care about art.

Free playing is an alternative to this, perhaps even contrary to it. In the first place, it is not accurate to say it is fueled by anything-goes in the long run. It is more like "use anything"--make everything available, look under rocks and into cubby holes, and make something out of it. As for fear, instead of causing a retreat and defensive reaction fear can energize. Maybe the intentional absence of a plan or an enabling code--the imagined blank tablet, with unlimited tools and materials--will arouse agency, the excitement and anticipation to engage the real situation of ambiguity and doubt. To be parachuted into Dante's dark woods is indeed frightening; to intentionally walk into it is a different story. Humans are known to have done this; for one reason or another they disregard cultural codes and wander into the wilderness, finding it livable, even the basis for moments of sublime experience.

To help explain why the avoidance of free playing is so automatic, the fearsome dark woods is the trauma most hope they'll never visit or revisit.[245] Freud advanced the idea that every human must deal with trauma, from birth, through childhood, continuing through the repetition-compulsion of neurosis and breakdowns of the will, and often right at the moment of death. One reason Freudian insights have been exorcised from contemporary therapy, and Freud himself demoted from hero of emancipation to Fraud, is that to unearth one's personal history of trauma—or a nation's--is harder to stomach than liberation from sexual constraints.[246] For Freud, civilization— roughly what I've been calling the social order--functions to repress this memory and turn it into benign, enlightening culture, in hopes of making trauma and its consequences bearable.

Predictable, soothing music—for that matter, rock or jazz transformed into a pacified, desiccated memory—is one way to escape hard, humbling realizations, a parallel to this heavily drug-dependent society. Not surprisingly it has increasingly meshed with the gears of consumer capitalism. It must be consumed endlessly as the background of the individual's and culture's life in order to maintain the avoidance of all that is disturbing. This is not *listening* to music but *hearing* it as pleasant background, like the screen saver of favorite photos stripped of the power to evoke feeling. "You're already too tense, don't let anything put you over the edge" is the message to a society that, beginning with the anxiety and guilt of unleashing nuclear death seventy years ago, now sees itself assaulted on all sides. Music, the most ubiquitous and popular of all the arts, has the greatest potential to waken the demons, which is why it's called on to put them to sleep.

Flipped on its back, fear of freedom is "I've got nothing to lose," which sounds like fun but it's mostly living-on-the-street poverty, something to fear in the current economy. If free playing is the art form of the beginner's mind, able to scrap one's knowledge and reputation, then one's arms are never filled with very much in the way of sustainable life. The situation of Ivan Ilyich, the Tolstoy character who found his hands empty of meaning at the end of a satisfying life of achievement, can be experienced in the fullness of life and welcomed.[247] It is possible to go right towards that fear as the heart of darkness, glued to the moment, excited (in the psychological paradigm above) to meet trauma head on and unlock the secret of Pandora's box, ignoring the result and judgment day. When excitement is deprived of some component of fear, "adventurous music" is just advertising.

When energizing excitement is missing what settles in is boredom and scattered attention. Players work to get past that and restore the focus on the "nothing" they're aimed at. "Fear signifies proximity to something of value" and our concentration focuses on the white screen, blank page, or silence that both blocks us and is the elusive, troublesome "it." It's the search for the unmediated experience, and the only one we have ahead of us is death, which we'd like to mediate as best we can but ultimately cannot. This is the region of trauma: "For Sartre, fear is the shock of the new; for Freud it is the shock of the old," the uncanny, which the (Freudian) Surrealists pursued. [248] Fear of the new and the old work together; the new is also the disguised old that haunts us. When Modernist art promised emancipation from the cage of tradition, it was ghosts it was exorcising. That relation to tradition is now a crossed threshold for the approach of free playing, though not for recognized art music. In the endless, open field results don't add up to a heroic narrative. The attraction of finding a "new paradigm" (which entered the lexicon in the early sixties) has been left in the lurch. No future generation will channel the story of this era's greatness—the word is even an embarrassment.

Young musicians schooled or unschooled, committed or half-committed to the musician role, to rewards and conventions that indicate their significance to others and promise a more meaningful life, might feel something's missing and express it in an offhand moment. Whatever stumbling and doubt they experienced while developing the musician ego is presumably behind them. However they were bound up with a vitality that was once their motive force, an eros, boldness, and love of playing that, as they advance in confidence has grown cold. What is missing is the excess of desire that doesn't know where to turn. That is where free playing comes from. It's why no conditions can be given for its achievement, no idiomatic or aesthetic code can fulfill it, why it is the infinite game and the open field and cannot inform the world where it is going.

For trained musicians and those who have achieved some recognition, free playing is a test case as human beings and not just musically. The palpable absence of desire in playing provokes an anxiety reminding them of what they've already lost and have adjusted to. Fearing the great power of desire, like everyone, does not brace us for adventure. It tells us that unless we're tied down we might fly off in any direction, play anything at all, lose the confidence we've worked to acquire. We let down our guard at the risk of our stability. Given our freedom we might just pack up and go home, abandon any thought of what we've achieved as musicians with a will to play. This fear stands between us and knowing all that we disown, decisions once made that have proved valid and effective for us externally but block the "self-knowledge that tells you your future selves are unknowable; they cannot be predicted."[249]

To see that the content of free playing depends on the relation to an "other," a player or one's own patterns, we will find the psychology behind that equally complicated. Who are you *really* playing for? is no simple question. Musicians that follow genre rules aim to satisfy an *audience* "other" as well as to qualify in their genre, which is a *cultural* Other (capitalized because it and not the audience is treated as a god) whose allowances and prohibitions are clear enough.[250] In free playing such others are ineffective guides. To operate in terms of the immediate situation means to play strictly in relation to the other players and one's own developed range of possibility, which grows in the impact with the others. Aided by experience or whatever moves their partners make, one teases their desire and negotiates a kind of merger with it.[251] However, this is no easy matter. Free playing properly begins with facing what one does not know about one's own desire and turning to the other, who's in the same predicament. One asks oneself "Why not this?" and immediately answers, "Go ahead," not knowing for sure if what one imagines is truly the desire of the other player(s), but trusting that it can be evoked. In listening, which goes in and out of direct attention, players imagine what is latent in the imagination of the other. One plays what the other is playing in one's own way.

A long partnership involves a high degree of experimentation and negotiation to find points of bonding, such that at each meeting a consolidated music re-forms and elaborates itself. Since this form represents a mutual desire it is hard to escape; to disrupt it threatens to be almost cruel. Free playing gives license to do just that, in effect boldly imagining there might be a gap in the apparent satisfaction of the other as in one's own. It's as if the partnership had been annulled and the other's desire is a complete enigma — back to square one. In doing this the player is suggesting he or she knows what is hidden from the partner--"I know what you want better than you do yourself." In any normal situation this would be an insult, so this kind of playing escapes the normal social rule. If that move is sufficiently trusted the other is led on to counter-"violations," a fully playful situation. However, this is tricky business. To assert a solo style as one's violation is a destructive act, which is why it is taboo. It is what the soloist has created out of imagining what the Other or audience desires and has validated outside the session. It is not playful but aggressive, for it promotes the priority of one's exclusive desire and is not intended to evoke interplay. When the soloist stands up, musically speaking, the others remain sitting and, as in jazz, shut up.

Imagination that plays with what's right in front of them is what children do without coaxing, and we don't deny the meaningfulness of their play because of their paucity of experience. It is often non-idiomatic; they can turn a game full of rules into a more playful situation, and they'll do so compulsively. Children's play that yields art objects is lauded as the essential spirit of art, yet when they get recognition for it (such as the child beauty queen JonBenét Ramsey, whose parents made her into a desired art object) they are no longer effectively children but objects serving others' need. Similarly, the musician-entrepreneurs' wish to make themselves into an art object erodes their playful focus and defines artistic success as a game of sales and respect. The *actuality* of music is predetermined, which enables the effort to repro-duce it. To step back to *potential* music would mean entering an uncertain space, where sounds lack cultural identity and may never attain it.

The source of what came to be called free improvisation was located in this kind of imagination and was not the avant-garde melodrama of competi-tors aiming to redefine Music.[252] Media victors of avant-garde status in the sixties were recognized for rejecting whatever was publicly considered most advanced, as if those joining them would not be judged backward, like the rest of mainstream culture.[253] Clear distinctions functioned to advance one's claims to superiority. Today the presumed avant-garde can be broken down into various groupings, each of which provides guidelines for what the mu-sicians of each one are to do and what to avoid. If free improvisation is listed among them and is non-idiomatic, it would appear to be avoiding every path leading to music. The free-playing improviser however will more likely do the reverse, avoiding nothing at all that comes up in the imagination.[254] Mak-ing immediate choices at every moment, they come too fast to be called an act of choosing. If the playing avoids settling into an idiom it is not from con-scious avoidance but because the imagination does not find a resting place. Players don't swing wide of potholes but plow into them, opening them wider--not a smooth ride for those who don't know the road. What keeps them from slipping into a groove or a familiar idiolect is the imagination craving a wider space. This field full of fences and potholes is the players' experience and not retrospective results. Results, of course, but they're back there in the tread marks.

For professional improvisers of the avant-garde (a title avoided among artists but implied in promotion), there are four "others" requiring negotia-tion: the many who constitute the field of competitors, the audience other, the music world, and the music-culture superego. This last is the law-giving Other who, following school authority direct into career, substitutes for the parents and exposes the musician to fear. Superego authority has a voice: "Cradle to the grave, you belong to me." It has power over us to the extent we need the kind of love that keeps us in line and rewards obedience. Think of the adult's cruel game with kids, hiding candy in one hand and asking the kid to guess. Even if the guess is wrong the kid gets the candy, but the point has been made. To play freely exposes the game, finds it boring and laughs in its face. Sneaking behind the curtain we find what's missing, what Music hides from us.

There is no legitimated context for the players other than what is happening, and those capable of entering and sticking with it are not under the thumb of internalized parents, at least not in this area of their lives. Free playing explores a space where recognized contexts are "others" not to be negotiated with or extricated from but are simply irrelevant. Conventions, habits, and bits of tunes and sounds will inevitably be included, but do not stabilize the identity of the music or musician. Identity is a matter of survival or advancement, something that depends on social others' recognition of it. It is how one is identified, for better or worse. For artists it is the reward for those who play the game and have reached a level of satisfaction that feels assured. To know who you are in the world through your internal search and determination is something else.

To bring this down to earth I'll briefly switch to the first person. I'm not what "free playing" would seem to result in, since I myself generally fail to escape the way I usually play—my stuff.[255] I must have some "way" of playing but it's fairly broad, thanks in part to the differences between my partners. The most radical change was from the time I was playing what would be called free jazz, which was more consistent from one partner to another. Still, when I listen back I can identify my way, like clothes that fit, shaped around a self whose contours I'd have difficulty describing. A reviewer once described another saxophonist as having gone to "the Jack Wright School of Screech," though now some other image would typify my playing. If my way is problematic for analysis, so much the better, but to purposely contradict the analyst is the transgressor's game. Asked about "my" music I'd have to say, you mean right now? and then for the answer play something. If the analyst can abstract from it something I always do, I will benefit, for I will aim for that pothole and smash into it, possibly mocking and exaggerating it. As improviser I sit right on the hot seat of the contradiction between what I am confident to play and the vast field of possibility. That's the briar patch I'm thrown into, and like Br'er Rabbit that's my home, inaccessible to most. From a distance I can respect the bears of the world who can't imagine my pleasure, but given their power, I enjoy fooling them ("Whatever you do to me, please don't throw me into that briar patch).[256]

The free playing orientation holds out the promise that I might play what the audience doesn't know it wants to hear. That goes right to present experience and escapes any identity they might project on me. It's hard not to be the advertised "Jack Wright, saxophonist," even "legendary," and, perhaps because I'm obviously old, people reflect back to me the image of an accomplished, interesting musician. This humiliates me when I realize how I like being rewarded and how it locks me in. I'm free to bypass what I think others want, including appropriate artist behavior, but apparently that hasn't happened!

For some, free playing is emancipatory, with disruptive moments that break the inner tethers holding them. The modernist avant-garde saw those tethers as external (the tradition of "rules" that validated 19th century classical music). They saw their work as permanently and irreversibly freeing art from taboos, giving them the role of emancipator, though recognized mainly by each other. This idealization continues today but it's fraudulent in an era when those few who defend taboos are not taken seriously. The tethers that have gone undetected are internal, and for artists to break them they must first of all quit their job as musician and find out what it means to play for themselves. It is humbling to discover and get past forms that have pleased an audience or might do so. I ask myself and others, "Can you play something meaningful to you that you're pretty certain will disappoint the audience, if you can also do something you know they'll like?" And "If I have given myself license to play anything, then why is my range so narrow?" If there is a test of artistic discipline, that might be it. I'm not too proud of my score, but having the question in front of me opens the field wider than anything else.

To play spontaneously from the imagination, the most basic ground of free playing is not the path to art. This opens up the area of limitations, where it becomes clear that free playing is not the be-all and end-all. For instance, first thought-best thought is implied but that's a slippery slope. It's what Jack Kerouac promoted but didn't follow himself, so there is some ambivalence here. Psychology might laud first thoughts as the unconscious breaking through but only prosaic analysis cuts to the quick. Socrates' conversational partners gave their spontaneous opinions and he facilely demolished them. Without a second, correcting thought we tend to compulsively repeat the first as a belief we're invested in and will defend, narcissistically delighted in our expressive selves. When our opinions complement each other we acquire an identity as a kind of gift to which we owe loyalty; we must not betray it by coming up with something contradictory. (That might be the psychology behind the faith in reason, essentially the law of non-contradiction...)To reflect on our opinions from a distance, a bunch of facts about oneself, is to experience them as if they're someone else's, allowing us to investigate the identity we've become.

Given its immediacy, free playing is closer to the Surrealist's automatic writing, mostly kept private, than to poetry that writers have scrutinized and aimed at an audience. It's like a come as you are party, a private joke. It seems unable to defend itself, exposing its theoretical failing. This is the heart of the suspicion surrounding any spontaneous activity, and justifies rewards for the edited final product. The romantic defense of spontaneity will not suffice. There is at least this: Freedom to do absolutely whatever, if taken seriously, can collapse the fear of doing what we didn't quite mean to do. Naiveté that makes us feel ashamed operates as a kind of virus protection; giving license to first thoughts temporarily disables it and we get infected. It is momentary and possibly an accident, like a Freudian slip, but ineradicable as a fact. It links impulse with the adventitious (and unintentionally erotic) quality of all improvisational music. However, like an opinion, spontaneity never starts from nothing, and if the starting point never changes, what was once spontaneous is no more. It comes to function as our *best*, which implies we've fully experienced and processed it, when instead we've just become attached to it. It passes for an authentic self, and that implies our investment in it; meanwhile that expression is sealed off and can't go any further. Our playing is then akin to a reified belief system, a performance machine we own which operates passively, our consistent musical persona. Active creating is over, at least for a while; it may take a sense of crisis to wake us up.[257]

This is a lot to expect. Players may be relatively free from external judgment and the internalized judgment of a musician ego, but not from their way of playing. The most reasonable thing to do is what they already know how to do. They might fully doubt their first thought, yet in the midst of playing the space for doubt easily disappears.[258] A music teacher asked Debussy what rule he followed and he said, "My pleasure," but he must have known that pleasure is fickle, unreliable, and temporary. "Use everything" is an open door but the horizon of "everything" can become just what is in immediate sight.

External factors discourage exploration. Socrates and his conversational partners had leisure time for doubting, a necessity for any reflection. To explore the open field takes time spent alone with the instrument and together with others and it doesn't pay the rent or lead to it. To locate those most stimulating to play with takes time and often travel, as does organizing gigs and publicity. With today's excessive work requirements time is hard to come by; an efficient life rules out excess.

There are also internal limitations. In the session or private study it's fully possible to avoid going against the grain, even most of the time, so for players to recognize their stuck position and to loosen the bonds of attachments requires a timely willingness to be negative. It is difficult is to express disappointment with a group's playing that by definition and commitment is their own authentic choice. One is more pressured to approve than to be critical. That pressure is built in to the presumed absence of standards—on what grounds would one bring up any negativity? An approach that boldly claims "the moment can never be improved upon" is hard pressed to find anything specific to change. Free playing champions the desire of players to find satisfaction in what they do with as little mediation as possible from the external rules of society. If the ruling power of *internal* conventions is denied, it will lead to self-satisfaction, the familiar union of freedom and ignorance. Career-directed or not, they will show no dissatisfaction with their work.[259]

By itself, free playing does not directly require practice and study, which when self-constructed provides the seedbed for exploration and change. Practice is associated with what most of us remember from study: repetition aimed at perfection, essential for a music where one will be punished for mistakes. For many, free playing is a release from that disciplinary system. The career orientation encourages practice to keep one's chops and bag of tricks competitive. As free improv has increasingly attracted only non-career players, private work on the instrument is not on the agenda. Lacking the incentive of potential recognition, why should they spend hours on it, when whatever they do will be accepted? Moreover, the increased time required for income work affects everyone. Few have the option to spend time studying and practicing that earlier generations had. To create in the moment easily becomes what people do when they have only the moment of performing available.

Even if players had the time they would still need the motivation to break out of the idiom-based practice routine they learned, such as diatonic scales. To fashion one that would open them to everything the instrument can possibly do would take will, applied imagination, and the conviction that self-reward comes first. This is reached as a conclusion of rational thinking, that by shaping private practice one's range of choice in playing will be affected. In order to expand my understanding of what makes harmonic sense I focus my practice of intervals on those outside fourths and fifths; when I am playing freely I can tell the difference. That is an if-then argument, not something that just pops up in free playing.

The Free Musics

Following the pattern of most musical interest these days, free playing attracts those aiming to perform. Work on the instrument and sessions easily become mere warm-ups or are avoided altogether. In the large expensive cities, where improvisers tend to locate themselves and expect to perform, living space is cramped and a decent room for sessions is rare, or must be rented. "Just a session" will then mean that it's nowhere close to the value of performing. And even non-career players tend to think they are serious musicians and are insulted by rejections. This can yield, however slightly, "What do we have to play in order to get the gig?" How consistently can they approach their work as if they were at the ground zero of the beginner? How can anyone live in the real world without wanting respect, and who reaches the point of having enough? It is virtually impossible to be a human, functioning even grudgingly, and not be at least tempted towards respect and achievement. A vision that goes deep enough to divorce one from the all-too-human is something no one can do consistently.

Free playing is a paradoxical situation: it's disinhibiting, since one is permitted to do anything at all; at the same time players exclude soloist playing and those they find boring. In spotlighting serial solos, small-group jazz and free jazz prompts ambition, which *can* encourage strong, interesting musical ideas. Those playing freely, however, can easily hide behind the collectivity and never feel pressured to judge their individual playing and be self-challenged. Ambition for the group does this only indirectly, and without being held to some common aesthetic groups easily dissolve. To play with others whose range of ideas and techniques never grows can inhibit those who do. The selection of partners compensates for this weakness, yet there is no inherent reason that free playing alone will increase the pool of players bursting with fresh ideas.

A monkey wrench has to be thrown in to make free playing worth doing over a continuous period. That begins with "This is boring." The slightest intimation that something vital is missing prompts the search for ever more partners, tools, and materials. It's still free playing, but has escaped the stagnation that infects the music of our culture.

11. Free Playing and the Real World

"We have no position in the world--absolutely no position except that we just insist upon being around." Willem De Kooning, 1950

Most available discourses that speak of free improvisation distort what its most dedicated practitioners do. The title has three categories of meaning and discourse, one of which is ideal and universal, one is practical, based on the music genre and musicians, and a third tends to combine the two but is unknown beyond a few, mostly first generation American improvisers.

The first presents all improvisation as a broad humanistic or spiritual philosophy of creativity with implications that it is something of a life choice, though its primary instance is music.[260] "Free" indicates a spontaneity that can be tapped by all, though epitomized by a wide range of recognized artists. The outlook is socially and personally positive, and is sometimes associated with communitarian, left-liberal social-reformism. As an American-optimistic philosophy of creativity it would have to include brain-storming for innovative ideas, a decent TED talk topic. This discourse continues sixties themes, ranging from new age spiritualism to the artistic critique that became management language in the 90s. Aimed at a general audience, this view is often held by musicians who, when they improvise, identify what they do as pure creativity. Discourse by and for academics specializing in the inter-disciplinary field of improvisation is similar. Entitled "critical improvisation studies" by its foremost North American advocates, it too celebrates the humanistic benefit, extending it as the keyword for creativity and sometimes even social justice. Given its focus and message, it elides any distinction that "free" would add to "improvisation," treating well-known free improvisers as instances of the larger category.[261]

The second category of discourse takes free improvisation to be a genre, the musicological choice of specific musicians, which is usual the meaning employed in this book. Today it is found mainly in publications directed to music consumers, and is the meaning most widely known to musicians. Since it shares the same name as the first discourse, promotion of those most publicly known to be identified with it leans for support on the philosophy of creative freedom as its core and its musicians' motivation. It would seem to bridge the gap between the wide number of committed players and those representing the genre, as does "jazz." However, the relation of these two discourses is one of distinct lodgings under the same nominal roof, for the playing most widely known to represent the genre is more grounded in the realistic demands of the music world than an idealized philosophy of personal freedom and communality.

There is a third category of discourse, which is upbeat and supportive of free improvisation yet is the voice of those specifically committed to free improvisation and not of a music world that reaches consumers. Through the early 90s these advocates included professionals as well as those who weren't, and reflects the era before professionalization drove a wedge between them. The earlier-mentioned *Improvisor Magazine* is the major example, a clearinghouse for recording reviews, information, and published writings of all those self-identified as free improvisers. Offering wide-ranging articles in non-conventional music, it was a vehicle internal to the community of players and not useful for musician recognition, career, and consumer attention. The last print publication was in 1996, just as a new generation was arising, which had little knowledge of or interest in that community. As a community-dependent source of discussion, similar to others grounded in sixties alternative culture, it came to suffer from the easy access of the internet, where no effort or commitment is needed to have full access. Identity as a specifically *free* improviser declined as an option even as more people were checking out free improv, as we shall see in the next chapter. The later, more individualist generation had no such vehicle as *The Improvisor* to present free improvisation as their serious interest and no body of work that could be said to represent them.[262]

When free improvisation was perceived as a specific approach in the 80s it ran into criticism. To claim to play a music that has no specific form is either fallacious or self-indulgent, playing only what communicates with oneself. Musicians have an obligation to provide music to a public. Communication is impossible without a form known to the public; musicians who make up their own arbitrary forms on the spot are narcissists unworthy of attention. Many players as well as critics treated the music as a radical offshoot of liberalism, such that Rousseau is ultimately its guide and musicians are born free and breaking their imposed social chains. It is then caught between the romantic "We play free from restraints" and the cautionary "You go too far."

This was the dynamic faced in the sixties of rebel adolescent vs. the paternal society, extended to free improv in the 80s and similarly criticized.

Critique of any kind is rarely heard today. First of all, the guardians of music's purity gave up the fight long ago and been replaced by those who recognize that music has been pluralized. A proud Music has disappeared into the laissez-faire marketplace ("it's all a matter of taste"). Secondly, "freely improvised," once loosely slapped on album blurbs of music obviously structured, is no longer popular advertising. No music that is fully inventive in the moment is advocated in the public media today, nor is anyone bemoaning its absence. And finally, in North America free improv has been promotionally merged with other, more compositional musics, such that criticism or defense of it as a special approach is beside the point.

The European professionals who exclusively play non-idiomatic improvisation are recognized by state agencies (mostly on the Continent) and have a loyal and experienced audience, though probably not growing in numbers. They are serious, full-time performers, serving a public in the normal way, and no more self-indulgent than other musicians, in fact they seem self-sacrificing by comparison. When it does appear, "free improvisation" refers not to an activity but a positivity of results sorted and labeled. The ontological status of free improvisation is de facto settled and legitimate in Europe, and not on any public or even academic agenda in North America.

Between the approach of free playing and the historical genre of free improvisation there is a disjuncture, with no inherent reason why they should coincide. If the approach is at the origins of the genre, then what has evolved is not its simple consequence. Something happened along the way that was necessary if some musicians were to be able to earn a living, and that is external to the playing itself.

Free playing would roughly name the sixties approach of what Bailey later called non-idiomatic and what the Americans would pick up on, to the point of taking his book as the description of what they do. Bailey and his early groups did their work in private sessions, discussed what they did, and gradually evolved a music of their own uniqueness. The great advantage of their situation over the NY Free Jazz players was that they were not obliged to justify their approach according to a parent music that was in the throes of becoming standardized. Moreover no racial issue existed for the Brits in this regard. They could build a space for themselves in the cultural landscape that would appear sui generis, and soon would qualify as an art music genre.

The Joseph Holbrooke trio sessions could be called collective workshops (clearly distinct from master classes). These did not aim at releasing recordings, performing, creating a genre for others to follow, or creating a historic imprint on music. They did their work in Sheffield, isolated from London and the music world of the London scene, and they only recorded a few of the sessions, finally released in 2006 (*The Moat Recordings*). What they did was not stabilized as music until they arrived at a point where they could say, this is (apparently) our direction. Here was not only an intellectual quest but "more an emotional, or instinctive, search to find something that was logical and right, or at least appropriate, to replace the inherited things which we found stilted, moribund and formal." (Bailey, *Improvisation*, p.87). Bailey's next group, the Spontaneous Music Ensemble (SME), was similar. His valuing this experience extended to his general conception of free improvisation and amounts to a renunciation of music world functioning in favor of musician-created events.[263]

They brought their individual, private work to the sessions but while searching together they were free-playing and not-knowing where they were going, as if the search could go on forever. This was an avenue for confident professional musicians, who would reasonably think they would land somewhere publicly as the result of their private search. Any dynamic based on professionals providing music and getting rewarded has a potential audience and supportive music world waiting outside the door of the private session. To mess with the title of Eddie Prévost's book, *No Sound is Innocent* would mean that no professional can prevent their music from becoming a commodity nor themselves from becoming mini-celebrities, no matter what they intend or say politically.

Free playing today that utilizes its potential for exploration is comparable to that of those early groups Bailey was in. Sessions are workshops that encourage learning and choosing over time, with discussion, at times conflict between players, and occasionally irreversible advances within close partnerships. Players might well find their previous playing "stilted, moribund, and formal." However, the cultural and historical differences are crucial. Especially in London and in that era, relatively unknown musicians could gather an audience for a performance of exclusively music made up on the spot, which stood out against other approaches. The draw of their names depended on that audience experience; the names were mediatized only subsequently. The musicians might have thought and increasingly assumed that free playing would become a substantive thing of monetary value, but that was not their immediate motivation.

Today that situation would be a stretch for the imagination. The advancement of specific musicians from listener experience of them to mediatization no longer operates. And performance as the locus for on-the-spot exploration has disappeared in Europe and has never been the understanding of what Americans do on stage. No market has ever arisen for those at ease with their anonymity. The free-playing bunch of sounds, lacking a consistent and packagable aesthetic (their "sound"), resists what every present demographic would purchase as music. Rather, with neither a place to take it nor the will to make a name for themselves, the search itself becomes for some their *continuous* activity. Whatever plateau they come to in the course of playing would be just as vulnerable to modification as what originally bored or disturbed them.

As for Bailey's "non-idiomatic" designation, though it says nothing about how free playing actually proceeds it does aid somewhat to insert that title into a world that knows only the idioms and organizes its knowledge of music accordingly. It hints at what territory listeners might expect to be traveling in; then in the midst of experience any name for it can be handily forgotten. If non-idiomatic improvisation is one very small country on the continent of art (at least in Europe), free playing is the country of no-country. It is definitely a somewhere; a few live there and thrive, but as a musicological territory it is not even a fiction. Even as an intention it is usually presumed rather than explicitly asserted. Empirical societies, cultures, and art movements can be analyzed, historicized, compared with one another, and assigned a place at the table. Free playing cannot. It is purposely ignorant of history and cannot be reduced to the usable narrative required of genres and names competing with each other.

Among such real world factors, musicological analysis is also irrelevant. There is no a priori form of free playing to which content can be held responsible. It is whatever happens given a prior agreement of *not* knowing what is coming next and not attempting to disguise that ignorance. After the fact one could conceivably learn and repeat a recorded improvisation sound for sound. The content would be identical but it would have acquired the form of a composition repeated as exactly what is expected. The act would be similar to creating the simulacrum of jazz and free jazz, copies according to a model, attempts at faithfulness and authenticity. Free playing cannot be repeated *or improved*; as such it is the epitome of live music. To improve it would require a consensual standard of beauty, perfection or goodness that every musical idiom has, a yardstick by which each instance can be measured. When discussed in terms of a player's characteristic moves abstracted from all she has done, discourse violates the real-time playing, treating as regular what the player experiences as unique. Sonically, a recording of a performance could easily be superior to what some audience have heard, yet the difference and the implications for drawing conclusions is crucial. Strictly speaking free playing is inaccessible apart from hearing it at the same moment the players experience it.

Despite internal challenges, musicologists still speak of artworks as the only form in which art exists, and that puts art into their hands.[264] Musicologists, teachers, and the avant-garde commonly call artworks "organized sound," Edgar Varese's formulation from almost a century ago. This is an advance that gets around the necessity of a material score but would still exclude any performance of sounds that lacks intentional organizing effort, such as improvisation. It implies that music is a branch of scientific investigation, which also denigrates the feeling, intuitive player. To avoid "artwork" and present free playing as process, a work-in-progress, also distorts it. Players are in a dilemma, not in relation to themselves here but to consumers and the music world, which has no reason to contradict musicological opinion here. To assert that their activity is indeed art would mean defining art apart from the artwork and its potential repetition. Spontaneous improvising is often acknowledged as essential to the making of art, but as the messiness preceding the perfected product. Something ephemeral is in principle outside art as a category within culture. Free playing fits neither of the two major meanings of culture, either what people habitually do and can be generalized, anthropology's lower-case use of the term, or that which is specialized, hierarchically valued, and the result of professional activity (Culture).

The non-idiomatic designation posed a conundrum at a time when idioms were more like fixed categories and musicians had to secure themselves within one or another and maintain the borders. There were stars of course but audiences were also loyal to specific *kinds* of music. This was already being undermined. Dylan and Miles Davis violated their respective genres and scandalized people loyal to them, but those moves were immediately successful, which validated violation for the future. Today that path to success is quite worn and does not attract the attention of scandal. The borders have also weakened under the pressure of whatever audiences are most likely to buy--top names more than genres. Musicians must adjust by aiming at a demographic rather than defending their professional, specialized knowledge, which would hold them to a musicological boundary. Genre is still there but a matter of signals that its intended audience will be sure to get based on their assumptions. Genre is now a tradition that is signaled; for instance, it still holds that if the music has a saxophone it must be jazz. Loyalty flares up here and there, as a violation of tradition, such as the jazz police and older punks who resent those who have built off their earlier initiative. But that doesn't seem to hurt the contemporary poachers on their turf. As for the stars of the free musics, they are more names in their own right than representatives of their genres, partly because audience wants to hear not the genre itself but "the best" of a category, the hierarchy more than the genre, which theoretically anyone could represent.

Free playing is an anomaly in the world of music. For the sake of performance and promotion it must be located in some category, which has become that of experimental music. The category goes beyond original free improv in its resistance to any signals that it is jazz. When experimental music is presented and funded as art music, all the rest of the category relies on the discreet artwork with an intended aesthetic. Each piece has its own boundaries, such as dynamics (volume), timbre, and instrumentation, more or less prepared in advance and adhered to. As art, the category is a collection of subgenres and hybridized styles meant to attract the polite art audience and not the boisterous enthusiasts of punk and noise. When free improv is grouped together with formal art, the approach of playing freely is obscured. The musicians might actually play something not unlike a composed new music piece but there's no guarantee of that. Guarantees are essential for paid gigs for art audiences, who have precise taste expectations. For this reason free improv is justifiably denied contract-based funding. Gigs are however occasionally funded via curators who, out of personal taste, a perverse desire to upset some of the audience, or ignorance of the potential incongruity, don't follow the pattern.

The lack of fans, stars, and funding for free playing is mostly structural rather than for reasons of unpopularity. Popularity is a scale that implies that audiences have actually experienced it and reject it, and people have not been exposed to it enough for that. Or rather, when an art audience is exposed to it they often respond positively but don't know what to do with it. Where it belongs can be extremely important. It is made more comprehensible for such listeners if they can refer it back to a known tradition but then the point of the approach is missed.

An audience accustomed to good music might experience free playing as an act of cruelty and violence, which is what Antonin Artaud believed to be the truth of art ("The Theatre of Cruelty"). It doesn't feel like that to the players themselves, who are walking through a phantom wall without noticing it. Not resisting authority, but failing to acknowledge its existence, free playing does not transgress. That is the pose of the constituted avant-garde performer, who gets honored as the hero slaying the authority-dragon. Since the late seventies or so the left culture audience, perhaps feeling it has lost the cultural power of its sixties origins, has identified with proxy transgressors, and patronizes art that puts them on the right side of heroic action. Free playing is not heroic and has found no audience there. It treats authority as nothing scarier than an inflated Halloween lawn decoration, and gains no support from those who want to shoot holes in it. The popular avant-garde can expect to be permanent so long as people feel that need. This is the *perpetuum mobile* of the social order, which relies as much on those who affirm it by pretending to fight it as on those who trust in it.

What makes free playing irrelevant to the world of art music on the subjective level involves the musicians' relation to pleasure and satisfaction. They might be pleased with the results of a session but then return to the work of pushing against and altering what has just pleased them. One can imagine the Holbrook Trio following that pattern until they reached a plateau of satisfaction, which then became a different pleasure, that of solidifying and extending what they have come to, giving it the shape of music that qualifies as art. Only then could they reasonably expect to be rewarded, however meagerly, through public recognition. There's also this: to have introduced something new and self-created during the turbulent sixties probably provided the excitement of participating in the apparent paradox prevalent then, of a flow that goes upstream against the gravity of normality.

Today every claim to the radicality of going against the grain must be examined carefully; the choir preached to and nodding its head *is* contemporary art culture. What is rewarded proves to be well within normative bounds and raises only the imagined eyebrows of those outside the door. On the bright side, for free playing to reach and consolidate an achieved level, where it could be valued in the media as troubling, is not externally or internally reinforced. The pleasure of self-surprise may well be followed by the pleasure of achievement, but it's then vulnerable to subversion, with no encouragement to formulate it as the new radicalism. What is ignored in the common lauding of "playing in the moment" is that all moments of that pleasure are short-lived, and the futility of trying to reconstruct them is depressing. Consumers act as if they could repeat a pleasure by pushing the repeat button, but it becomes wallpaper unequal to the original burst of enjoyment. When it's the players pushing that button only a sense of mild defeat follows, urging them to a different experience next time, coming up with an original continuously. For them the potential of pleasure to collapse is ever present; the unsustainability of pleasure may be fuel for the cynic but it's the player's next moment. What those outside this activity perceive is not the musician's sigh at the end of a show, "we played the same shit we always do." When that happens applause is an embarrassment, and the performers who show their gratification are just acting their role. They did their job but not what they could have hoped for. Clicking on a different track or making a different purchase next time doesn't get them out of "the same old shit."

All musical language the musician learns—not just the idioms but the details of training, the scales, good tone, all the entry-level requirements for social recognition—is socially constructed. Trained musicians are free *within the limit of these choices*. Part of learning is the knowledge of how far to go in playing with that language, mocking it, tearing it apart, up to the point of walking out the door and making just any old sound. The further removed the playing is from the socially known language, however, the more risk that audiences will depend on an art performance frame firmly in place and a venue socially validated for the predetermined audience. Otherwise they will either exit quickly or go, "What is that? What happened?" Some might have seen through the thinness of what is presented as a pleasurable musical experience. Those will be inadvertently linked with the pleasure of the players; *both* are anticipating what they cannot quite imagine. Such alert individuals do not however constitute a public, such as the British improvisers found in the sixties. That public had some awareness of itself as a collective body searching for an "other" that would even grate on them a bit.

That avant-garde music today is understood to be experimental deconstruction *off*stage has increased the reliance on credentialed music education, which aims at just such preparation, like any trade school. As with any consumer object, it is imagined that the dirty work of making it is rewarded only on completion—don't give me a bunch of parts that might not even fit together. The sites of deconstructing and moments of seeing-through for free playing are self-determined, which is not what "training" means or prepares one for. In live performance players actively experience the pleasure/pain of acting on what they assemble and discover with the doors open. They prepare for this only in the most general way, discovering in private what may not get used for years, when suddenly they are evoked or provoked in the situation, each player's boldness encouraging the others to go further.

If Bailey's idea can be glimpsed as grounded in free playing, it would imply that, just as players do not replicate a cultural idiom, they would also avoid turning their performed music into an individualized, marketable style. My alternative term, open-field playing, indicates that the map covers the full potential of what can be done with an instrument, beyond what Bailey thought appropriate for performance. This contradicts the tendency to level off at a plateau of duplicable form that is found in all musics that attain visibility and media attention. Stylization stabilizes one's playing at a certain point of exploration, most probably where it gains a significant increase of audience and fellow musician acceptance. This is how the avant-garde is constituted as a collective noun covering all who do this. What the art audience notices is usually some impressive technical finesse or invention, for others simply a consistency and predictability. Stylization gives fans the feeling that the musician is almost a family friend, a bond they can count on.

Fans trust the music world without knowing they do so. They don't know that buzz and discourse have guided them to this musician, or that she must in turn create herself as a person *for the other*. Moreover, known musicians are a package deal; the mainstay audience of a musician will be loath to dispute the status of others at the same level. Out of an undifferentiated number of improvisers the music world has selected individuals as if all along they had been just waiting for that release from anonymity. The for-others musical persona is represented by the soloist. Whether she plays many solos or not is irrelevant; what's heard in a group is a collection of individuals whose styles are fixed and so can be expected to fit alongside each other rather than be interdependent. The same rule applies in all media-presented musics-- only as soloists have musicians' trajectories been useful to the music world for discourse and judgment.

As with a distinctive pattern of writing, a style implies a set of parameters that are only exceeded by occasional exceptions that maintain the rule. I am not here judging any particular style but analyzing what it is and how it functions. It is the ground of the supposed two-way street known as communication that distinguishes the roles of performer and listener. The boundaries of a style form a completed, discursive whole, with the limit or horizon of each player assessed as the meaning evoked by that player's name. Without that one's birth name will never be handed back to the artist as a stage name. Albert Ayler was just a saxophone player before he became

"Albert Ayler."[265] When he turned away from his mid-sixties playing, followers and critics reacted as if he'd abandoned the name they'd given him, similar to genre betrayal, only it didn't work. Actually, at least in that moment he'd thrown out that musical persona and taken his name back.

To act against being alienated by one's own playing is the work of conscious defamiliarization, for what is familiar is its cause. It would be more difficult for players than composers to do this, for composers have a valued time away from the audience in which to construct something that violates their familiar pattern. Randomness was the method John Cage hoped would separate the composer from his attachments, yet that method was still distinctive of his particular self and interest. Since one can only defamiliarize what has become familiar, just finding out who is family and who isn't is a deep and possibly painful exploration—is there some self I *have* to be? This question was relevant to the postwar period of Cage but uncommon for today's dissolved personality and self-constructed identity. It is especially the player who might raise it, for familiar habits disappear into the body and its enjoyment in the normal process of learning any technique. It can be upsetting to realize the distance between one's intent to play freely and the stability of one's normal playing. It can lie like a heavy weight on those who feel that the question of selfhood is at all relevant. Randomness is a good practice routine to overcome the familiar, but to apply it directly in performance is a mechanical solution. Given a passage in a Cage composition marked for randomness, the musician turns into a machine creating what *sounds* random. To be an active agent of defamiliarization is a very different experience. The reader of the score will miss the *self*-distancing, which in an insightful moment could even be called self-transformative: "I am more than this self."

To experience self-distancing on stage even for an instant threatens the relation of performer to the listening other, especially in the standard art music situation. Not knowing what to do next, the player is no longer the functioning, expert performer but an experiencing subject, in a context that resists that move. Performers are supposed to be good boys and girls, after all, with audience hovering just like their parents did, hoping they will do good and impress others. An awkward moment can be confusing for the improviser as well, for it sets up an inner division between reflective self and role. He has not come to that state of confusion by conscious decision, so he must accept it as almost an interruption. He must either *play* the confusion or fall back on his role. This kind of alienation glimpses a world that off-stage work has not prepared him for. If he chooses to go with the flow of interruption and trusts the confusion the music opens up. The opening is evoked especially if the others are moving together similarly, which unifies them actively. While solidarity normally shuts the doors in its defense, this bond opens them.

What I've described above is my understanding of an authentic creative situation. If we remove "creative" from the plastic- or fluff-word glossary, we'd more precisely call it a mere possibility, an accident that, being welcome is partly prepared for. That is the closest playing can come to being innovative in some sense of the word. The musicians ignore the cultural pressure and are driven from within to do what they haven't done before. This happens only in the moment of playing, mainly affecting their partners. There is no public or discourse to validate it as innovative, not only because the artists are relatively anonymous but because the structure of the arts has changed since innovation might have applied to them.

A normal situation of not-knowing prepares them for a situation where creativity is forced on them. That's a curious concept, for it doesn't make them sound like artists, who are thought to be creative as their nature and inclination. Free playing is more like the ordinary life situation of improvising. If I don't have the part to fix a running toilet and don't have time or inclination to run to the plumbing store I will improvise with a bit of wire and string. It might not hold up too long but it is more interesting and ingenious, an expansion of knowledge that denies the professional or commodified solution. Improvisation is nothing sure or permanent, just works for the time being. On the other hand, "creative artists" are presented as *continually* creating—each performance offering their creative results, automatically fulfilling their stage name no matter what they do. Formalist art critics used to mimic science by speaking of visual artists "solving problems." Once found the solution was irreversible, applied to the entire field of artists and labeled an innovation. Today, a distinctive style might be called "innovative" but it need not be; for the general public that is implicit in the word "avant-garde." Few will ask, "What exactly did the guy innovate?"

What generally impresses audiences for acoustic music is technical mastery, which for jazz and classical mostly boils down to socially conventional tone and expressiveness, speed, and accuracy. What else could mastery be but convention? For audiences of specifically unconventional musics it is sounds and occasional lack of demonstrative skill that will likely please them; it is at least neutral and sometimes negative towards what is culturally acceptable. That makes this music the most individualistic but also the most dependent for audience approval on the *uniqueness* of players' technique, however slight is their difference. Normative skill is presumed in the player's background, such that reputation depends on violating the dominant jazz/classical music. It cannot violate itself; only a timeless style can be commodified. Once won to a style, consumers don't want to see their taste betrayed. Whatever the technique, it must be appear to have taken work to create it. Art without the work ethic cannot be culturally validated; like any commodity the price tag presumes prior sacrificial labor.[266]

For free playing, unheard-of technique that might get noticed is subordinate to the flow of playing. Some are highly capable of conventional technique and others not. For a trained violinist to play a beginner's tone and hold the bow strangely would not be interpreted negatively, since a performing adult is assumed to know how to do it correctly (such as comedian Jack Benny). A beginner might be able to fool an audience. Free Jazz musicians of the early period (Coleman and Cherry especially) had to be hugely self-convinced to withstand the judgment that they didn't know how to play their instruments. To play aberrantly is still out there in the open field and available. Part of the attraction of playing with those who've never had an instrument in their hands is to recover the sound difficult for a trained player to recreate. Free playing does not eradicate built-up memory but aims to make all of it available, including what comes from one's youthful love of playing, and not just one's acquisitions as an experienced musician.

In Western and especially Anglo-American culture, objectification reduces experienced reality to information, as in the common-sense "let the facts speak for themselves." A fact is material, and its materiality can be pointed to and described; it exists to the extent it can be mediated by discourse. Reality is then beyond subjective determination, with no choice but to trust the stage machinery of mediation. This is apparent from the get-go in the word "music," whose only factual evidence is a score or a recording that operates as one.[267] The perfection of music is the masterpiece, originally the work of the apprentice qualifying to be a master, who has full knowledge of how to make the perfect object. That became the *bel ouvrage* and the artist's lifetime oeuvre, a documented summation and legacy of the genius. *Ars longa* is the antidote to *vita brevis*, but only to the extent it can be documented, an act by definition external to art-making. Music may be a text physically concrete, but it only achieves value if available for and subject to the mediating operations of abstraction, selection, and evaluation. This makes the document and evaluation more real than the sounds made and the experience of listening. For instance, it's not music if it can't be analyzed into its elements--melody, harmony, and rhythm (as Charlie Parker himself put it).[268]

Recordings, including those called free-improvised, are solid objects abstracted from the act of playing and subjective listening. This converts what is real in the experience of both, which is ephemeral and contingent, into the appearance of reliable permanence. The height reached by such objects is the venerated icon, the inheritor of "genius." However, history has intervened — always intervenes! For a contemporary work or artist to go beyond permanence to iconicity is inconceivable, despite artists going through the motions. True iconicity is awarded individuals, acts, and periods that were disruptive in the name of a fulfilled human future. If to be human shifts from the answer to the problem, as it has today (the environmentalist assumption), artistic disruption would only *de*humanize. The present is then the wall art must maintain *against* the future, which few imagine will improve the lot of mankind. The only trace of the icon possible in this situation is the celebrity, whose stature by definition is disposable and has only superficial effect.[269]

To the extent one is caught up in the experience of playing or listening to any music, the duality of note-taking observer and musical object vanishes and the subject has little to report back. (Students experience a similar disjuncture if they try to take notes summarizing a lecture and simultaneously get directly engaged in thinking the material.) The best accounts are poetic, an extension of the music that joins it and keeps it going, but are worthless in a prosaic culture that consistently rejects poetic insight as its guide.[270] Music seems to require the abstracting maneuver of distinguishing, comparing, lopping of what doesn't fit, and assimilating it to otherwise disparate material? An object with recognizable features is presumed, indeed forced, to form a unity with similar others, a grid laid over the whole of artistic activity ("that's jazz, that's heavy metal, that's electro-acoustic improvisation"). And since it's ultimately not the specific musical event but the musician-as-innate-genius that's up for sale, his entire oeuvre must be seamless and sanctified.

Symbolized unity guarantees the stability of what is categorized, which is what the ambitious and the tenured hope for. It is the sine qua non for the musician's public fortune, the very possibility for sound to become a more direct experience. Reduced in this manner, an improviser's style can be learned and ranked according to taste held to its standards, noticing rare flights into aberrant directions as hints that the authentic artist is still alive and present. It is a socially generated and useful identity, with a symbolic code legible to its followers. To be understood as producing music of that category, musicians must provide evidence that they *want* to conform to it musically and believe it possible to meet that demand.

Commodity fetishism begins with the work of discourse, classification, and identity on the one hand, and musicians making their music conform to the needs of entertainment. In the early days of jazz this was unconscious, simply accepted as the terms of employment. When bebop musicians began thinking themselves artists they had the temerity to complain that what they were doing was hypostatized as "jazz," but their pleas were sidelined. They were corralled back into the genre and its (symbolized) narrative, of which recordings formed the skeletal structure. The shift to the musician-entrepreneur has made conformity a conscious act. It is entertainment when one *must* present oneself as a self-defining artist. It doesn't have to fetch buyers on the funding or commercial market for this exchange to take place; presentation is everything. A describable object will take on a commodity form more easily than a music that appears to be nothing but illegible aberrations--of what, no one knows. All such non-sense and their creators go into the same massive discard pile, as if some real person had scrutinized them and found them wanting. This is the fantasy the faithful believe; at the same time and paradoxically, they will acknowledge that no actual process of decision-making takes in all the music out there.[271] Those most easily commodified are partitioned in a section of a record store, publication, and consumers' mental storehouse, all of it reflexively known to be shared information. The social order is criticized heavily as failing to do its job, but if that were true we'd see much more daylight through the cracks, especially coming from the avant-garde, promoted as the most enlightening art.

While a commodity tagged as popular is offered to the entire populace, one specified as art is promised to be *in*accessible to some—those who presumably don't care about it. Established art cannot survive without snob appeal. Fine-art musicians are directed to the bastion of liberalism, the state and institutions, which are "up there" with the rest of sanctioned authority. The prerequisite for presenting art to authority in the states is to be packaged as a saleable object, as if the musician had done her best to sell it but the populace just doesn't get it. While individuals make choices by calculating their personal satisfaction, art music institutions think in terms of satisfying the image of a social order that provides for higher needs. How else can it appear to be bringing balance and harmony to this messy world? It may be a vain attempt, but validating art and artists disdained by the populace at least shows that it tries. To be selected, artists must give clear signs they want to receive the imprimatur of authority on those grounds, and that's hard to fake.

Although anything can be commodified, free playing runs into problems here. First of all, as an activity aimed at their most personal musical satisfaction, players can hardly present themselves as solving world problems, a spin most helpful for any commodity these days. Secondly, its inability to be formalized as a code means that no promises can be made, and without that a commodity is a hard sell to *any* customer, individual or institutional. Players experimenting on stage are not standing behind their product; to defend it would take actions and discourse that contradicts its meaning for them. The advantageous position for a commodity is for its future to be mortgaged to the past or otherwise guaranteed, such that buyers can reasonably predict and purchase their satisfaction. Given this roadblock, free improvisation in Europe has commodified only the names associated with it. This leaves most of the activity uncommodified and lacking authority, though a receptive art audience and organizers for it can be found. To be commodified in the states to the extent of free jazz, players would have to discover demand outside the music world's selection. Unlike the days of the jazz aficionado, however, consumers have no squeaky-wheel voice to do that, no vehicle to say *"This* is the music we need!" It's not consumer taste that influences the market but management, which hides its operations. Commodification of American free improv today would only be built on the basis of individuals singled out for their marketable appearance, given an identity they may not betray, and split off from their approach and the open field of partners.

Names may be more in vogue than genres now but the latter are still essential in marketing. The taxonomy of genres begins in the distinction of vertebrate art and invertebrate entertainment, discussed earlier in terms of the psychology of desire. This division has shifted and needs to be examined historically. Serious music was once defended as a staple essential to full human existence and even advancing it, while entertainment was an inessential luxury. This followed the Christian legacy of a spiritual/material split, whereby secular art displaced religion and inherited its sanctity (Matthew Arnold's tought). Through public museums, concerts, and libraries, the rich attempted to validate their wealth by buying up art treasures and making them available to the masses, aiming to uplift or divert them from their material need. In the sixties the social-democratic state was taxing the rich heavily and could largely take over this function.

If the state was to represent human good it must then support art music, while entertainment would continue as a market-dependent contingency. In a society that still honored the Victorian value of moral goodness, cerebral restraint took precedence over bodily pleasure, which was up to the individual to choose and pay for. At least through the eighties the expanded state was authorized to take its democratic-humanitarian task seriously. As planned in the sixties, state arts councils supported orchestras at a substantial level, and unconventional projects at a token level (even a free improvisation festival).[272]

Neoliberal ideology, increased class division, and the privatization of public goods uprooted this arrangement.[273] The shift from the rich absolving themselves of class guilt to the state doing it for them had brought an increase of state power that was later easy for them to resent. The public fate of art is once again in the hands of private wealth-based institutions and the intellectual and upper middle class art audience which identifies with them. The most comfortable class has their art back; however, this time it is guilt-free. Meanwhile the number of art musicians has grown enormously, which presumably the state would be somewhat obliged to respond to. Here the always potential split between serious visual art and music has played a part: *image* is for serious intellectual reflection, *sound* is for pleasure. For the comfortable rich, serious visual art (traditional and Contemporary Art) has long been their mark of superiority. Even if they don't like it, it is their cultural capital and association with intellectual life. As for art music, they favor the traditional (classical and jazz) over what is not instantly recognized as enjoyable. As they feel fully entitled, they are not obliged to support art music outside their comfort zone. Music that follows the New York Experimental tradition begs and receives some state money. The bulk must come from corporations, to the extent they want to advertise themselves as culture-friendly. Musicians must take steps to boost their audience, as any other marketed product, without allowing it to be re-classed with entertainment.[274]

In the enjoyment society art musicians are to boost attendance by making music that is non-abrasive and easily interpreted. This pushes art that might initially disturb people into the underground, where the middle class art audience would fear to go, if they even knew of its existence. The arrangement has radically altered the previous structure for musicians aiming to become professionals. Performance of "difficult" art music is still expected to have official support and legitimation, an anachronism common to higher arts education. But the realistic professional track today envisions not life-long performance but teaching and affiliation with institutions, while creative work is done for in-house projects or on the side.

Below the attendance levels for big names, musical product is still sorted into categories that apply to those musicians said to play within that category's parameters. Whether a genre title is slapped on or not, it need not be mentioned; hints are more effective. Genres that depend on sales but not mass popularity, such as free jazz and acoustic blues, might attract audience and some non-professional players simply on the basis of their genre identity. If it is unclear from hints and context, the first thing asked of a musician is "What kind of music do you play?" Media discourse requires terms that are presumed fixed if it is to shape audience anticipation and purchase. Musicians' will to build attendance leads them to adapt themselves to this. "I am a jazz musician" means "I am one of the subjects of all that history and public narrative," which substitutes for their lack of name recognition.

Some classically-trained musicians are comfortable breaking with their genre and widening their audience base, a quite American ambition. "Old-school" musicians and audience, however, resist the novel hybrid forms of commercial musics and the drive to popular acceptance. Their purity indicates austere commitment, as in, "Don't think I'll do anything to bring in the crowd and the almighty dollar!" These include many new music composers, who compete for meagre funding partly on the ground that their music has no possible popular acceptance. The allegiance here is to the more European idea of the artist.

As the title is used, "free improvisation" is a catchall, and scholars contribute to this. David Borgo, the American musician-scholar quoted earlier, does this in such a way that it would have to include much commercial music, such as rock guitar solos and standard jazz, but his focus is narrower than his definition.[275] Excluded, or minimized would be classical music and most new, experimental music, whose composers surely want their work faithfully executed according to plan, most often achieved when they do so themselves. Such definitions substitute for discredited "grand theories" but have a similarly grandiose sweep. For many publicists (critics) and musicians clear distinctions favor specialized, closed-minded commitments that limit the potential audience.

If a title indicates what the musicians are actually doing, the meaning of those two words must be avoided. "Improvisation" might even contradict "free," since one typically improvises *on* material the playing elaborates, something culturally stable and not free of it. Bach improvised in the context of tonality and known harmonic patterns, jazz took Tin Pan Alley songs and "jazzed" them, and free jazz goes out from an inside it refers back to. And "Free" often means immediate release from something felt oppressive, a concept that has appealed to the civilized bourgeois at least since Rousseau. As we've seen, that isn't what sustains the playing. One might be emancipated but is not playing the emancipation. Recently a player looking forward to his first session anticipated "letting loose," but that will get complicated if he keeps at it. Cast-offs must discover how to go outside what they have imbibed, beyond the improviser Robinson Crusoe, who rebuilt his familiar culture out of new materials with the sturdy ethic he never left behind.

In Europe free improvisation qualifies as a minor art genre with cultural authorities, some of the art public, the '68 generation, and its younger admirers. Since for US audiences it has no notable heroes, it has no true representatives here, and audiences are unlikely to be specifically attracted to it.[276] Nonetheless it is the correct title, and they commonly use it to inform the curious where to locate them in the spectrum. Offered without further explanation people assume it's a version of jazz, maybe leading them to think jazz is more widely defined than its defenders would ever allow. For that welcoming audience the group's playing would become the empirical meaning of free improvisation, perhaps confused when they hear someone else. In Canada it has a somewhat greater and more knowledgeable audience, is more established among players, has an institutional presence, and is occasionally presented as a distinct form in academic discourse.[277] There too, however, it is most commonly understood as a relative of the jazz family.

The strongest reason to carve out a distinct space for free playing is that an activity apparently artistic yet not aimed at perfectible performance, audience expansion, or official recognition, is unique. It is an anomaly for a music to lack prescriptions, and difficult to discuss, since value cannot be assigned without knowing where players intend to go. One cannot even come close to representing a specific event of free playing through discourse, as a score or recording can be. Graphic scores whose symbols have no determined sonic meaning may seem to do this but can only disguise the activity that takes place and upgrade it—at least the musicians are presumably following *something* beyond their noses.

Anomalies such as free playing are just what the media claim to be seeking out and finding, the exceptions to the rule, but there are disabling conditions. Music critics seeking legitimation in the cultural field equate significance with market visibility, which of course they seek for themselves. Discourse flounders without a mention of where the subject ranks within a category. Visibility *means* "among the best"; any perceived gap in the spectacle will be closed by expanding the spectacle to include it, if the market is thought able to bear new inclusions. Moreover, to be practical, writers prefer names that people are already acquainted with, and for a name to stick in the readers' awareness the numbers in the pool must not be legion. And there's no point in promoting names of those who don't seek attention for themselves; that would disrupt the notion that diverse interests are harmonious, united and not competitive in their desire for inclusion.

The *activity* of free playing is a primary drawback. Imagine those who push it so far that their playing varies significantly depending on the others involved and the situation. Even the instrumentation and their physical distance from each other are not standardized. They are under no pressure to make a unified and consistent impression. Given the absence of soloing, such players could be treated like sidemen in jazz groups, commercial session musicians, or chorus members, who hopefully don't bring in their own musical ideas. What listeners experience sensually might astound them, but what they hear and take away is a collection of musicians, perhaps skilled, talented, and perfectly blended, but not something easily characterized. To feel I *must* explain and defend my experience is the pressure imposed on all witnesses to art events. Perception rarely advances beyond what can be said.

What is best understood and conveyed is voices that can be reduced to the continuum of a style. The mystery of music is reduced to the discursive hierarchy: the voice distinguishable from the other is assigned a place. Only those voices perceived as responding to this need of discourse for individual identities will matter. Their music can be assimilated to a concept of disciplined work in ascetic isolation much like composers, and their personas can be picked out of ensembles and framed with their name on it. The musicological term for what gets heard is the solo, the more repeatable the better, and its function is to abstract players from the group and from their own aberrations. The musicians might have no intent to go along with this, but it makes sense if they want music to be their sole profession and their life prospects to be better than bussing tables. Or the players have invested themselves in constructing their solo voice over time as their real intent and have a personal need be noticed.[278] Either way, only by this means can a significant audience be attracted to concerts over the long haul, record buyers provided a narrowed-down, manageable list of names, and funders made confident they're dealing with serious musicians. In front of them will be an aural and discursive image of each individual with whom they might contract to satisfy their managerial or consumer needs.

If free playing is to stand on its own, the players themselves must keep the approach distinct from media discourse. Fogged-up glasses that see free improvisation as a blur miss distinctions that are crucial to their musical choices. For practical reasons they themselves need clear lenses, for they must continually choose those they will spend time playing with and exclude others. Career musicians will avoid anyone whose playing does not refer back to their particular field and peers. Improvisers dedicated to free playing don't want to waste their time, either. They play ad hoc meetings but are mainly on the lookout for those most interesting to play, record and tour with, not as a musical evaluation, just compatibility, which might mean those who will push them to some new place.

Unfortunately a division between career and non-career players has evolved with resistance to collaborate on both sides. In the early period of British and American free improv a middle ground existed where the two could meet and learn from each other, but that has mostly disappeared.

For free playing, a chart of lines could be drawn up showing who's playing with whom at any particular time. There is no stable order but a shifting and empirical one for each player. You hear someone who attracts you at a show; if both are willing to check it out and it is promising, a new partnership is born. A group together for years gets bored and the group dissolves; lacking a brand name or significant audience there is no pressure to continue. A few years later it's possible they are each in a new place and the partnership re-forms.

As for finding partners, it is abnormal for people calling themselves musicians to commit to a music that promises so little materially. Those who do so are probably odd in some way, have failed the test of full socialization. The idea of fulfilling a vocation is standard and has been ever since the bourgeois subject was formed. The vocation, or calling, is a way of thinking about a lifetime of work that is not oppressive, like that of the worker. For those who can discern a vocation, mostly from the middle class, the American Dream means to rise above alienating labor. One such idealized vocation is the artist. The contract to provide musical satisfaction is slipped in so quietly people don't notice that they are merely glorified workers providing a product. Free playing is that unalienated work, in a society proud to say we are all free here. No fuss need be made over this, no promise of emancipation. It is simply the choice of those who for whatever reason don't need to disguise work as vocation, whose day gig is not regretted but is merely what they give to Caesar.

The imagination invoked in free playing can be similar to that of composers except that its time is real time.[279] Players may find it joyful (not always, to be sure) but at least one kind of joy is indeed emancipatory—to escape being responsible to the musician-entertainer contract. To freely choose what to be responsible for and what to ignore is the Enlightenment (that is, Kant's) version of mature adulthood. One is free also of ego-dependence on applause, so easily manipulated, and childish dreams of being engulfed in others' love. This kind of freedom seems to be far removed from the well-travelled corridor connecting the dots of need with fulfillment, the struggle of which the world is made. It doesn't attract many musicians for long, and not just because their music doesn't sell.

It would be good for players to reflect on how few people actually walk in the door because they need to hear this strange music, or who feel uniquely gripped by it. There's no way of knowing, but this playing might be torture for the vast majority of people, who would find it even an injustice to the real musicians.[280] It is rare and startling when someone comes out with "What is this thing you're doing?" My usual response is to ask, "Do you want to play?" When listeners *are* pleasured by free playing it's likely by not knowing how to read and categorize their experience, then letting their mind wander. After the playing, some have recounted dreams the playing reminded them of or other references from daily life; they are then poets continuing the play by other means.

Free playing transforms musical time from the length of a score, recording, or set to interminable. Called free, play has no time limit, and correspondingly no psychic limit. No one has the power to call a halt in any direction. If it can go on forever without reaching a climax and release it is not a drama, nor can it be confined to the stage, record, or size of a hard drive. It doesn't look to the future, in the linear schema of the avant-garde, but into the infinity of the present moment. The materiality of sound captured in technology is released, we might say volatilized into the ether, once known as spirit. At the same time music is returned to tradition before it was written down. Why did it ever have to be repeated, and be called music only if it could be? This can be answered historically but then we need to ask it for the present, when music is just so much information and there is no longer a need for memory to hold onto things. Free playing is the anomaly that makes perfect sense in our situation.

It undermines specialization, in this case professionalized music, on which the hierarchy of musicians rests. Free improvisation has attracted many who also devote themselves to poetry and visual art, polymaths who don't change from one identity to another, like the protean personality, but merely follow their overflowing imagination. This brings free playing in line with one definition of everyday life--whatever is left over when specialized activities have been eliminated.[281] Music is entertainment for everyday life; free playing is that life. It is direct to the senses and cannot be boiled down to a clear meaning of this object compared to that one. Like everyday life it is vernacular as against the official, which here is sacramental art, the impressive statues it mocks from below and eats away at or merely finds irrelevant.

Earlier I suggested that to begin to grasp the nature of free playing you have to get your feet wet by simply playing, with no thought of how to do it. You're a child walking towards the ocean for the first time, excited by a vastness you can't possible know is dangerous. Your parents are simply in the way, forgotten though they cling to you. You have a taste of the sublime before you can imagine how complicated it will get.

Culture claims to be knowledge, implicitly cautionary; without it we are told we will drown.[282] We have all bitten the apple of musical culture and are not that child running on pure feeling towards the water. Very early on, do-re-mi diatonic scales, intervals, and regulated pulse are osmotically fed to us and become so engrained that we seem to be hard-wired with them. Nothing else we do with sound can be music. Yet escape is right within our physical grasp. We are humans, we've walked away from our culture before and found beauty. We've made beauty something culture doesn't know. We'll do it again.

Part III. The New Old Things

12. Resurgence of Free Improvisation and the Present Situation

Beginning around 1996, and cooling off ten years later, a fresh and unexpected interest in free playing sprang up in North America that had its own distinct character. It was soon noticed by the press, at least in Baltimore, whose *City Paper* in 1998 spoke of "the current tidal wave of improvisers sweeping the music underground."[283] Especially young people had become computer literate and were communicating through the internet, and listservs (electronic mailing lists) focusing on improvisation began to appear in urban areas. The virtual community of players and would-be players had specific nodes in the Bay Area, Seattle, Chicago, Boston, Philadelphia, and Baltimore (the listserv of the last two were conjoined as "Phiba"). Although the listservs were initiated mainly by players active in the eighties, response came from a generation discontinuous with the cultural politics and dreams of the post-sixties. A few were schooled and career-oriented; most were not.

Though it was a general phenomenon on the continent, the new growth was strongest on the East Coast.[284] Assorted young players were looking for a music they could make that was more interesting than what was commercially available. They were not entranced by musical heroes or aimed at music schools, which still excluded improv from the range of "teachable" musics.[285] With no music world promoting it, and no interest from career musicians, free improv was invisible and had no known past. The old guard, such as myself and a handful of others, represented nothing of particular significance, even increasingly so, such that the new players weren't obligated to pay us attention as models to be imitated or displaced. Those few who were career-oriented wouldn't need to find a place for themselves within an established hierarchy of musicians, as in Europe. Those in Philadelphia and Baltimore were not in rebellion, as was punk in its relation to rock, but were mostly just curious about what could be done with sound, as if they were starting from scratch, in the position of free playing. In the listservs they asked: what is this kind of music, how far can you go, who wants to play, what about structures? It was a period of discussion, learning, inquiry that might be called philosophical (educated but not academic). John Cage's writings and the New York School tradition were available and influential for their inventiveness and use of electronics, but they were not yet framed in eulogy; anyway, they were composers, and these new folk were players.

To launch something without being concerned for historical precedent, as was revived free jazz, focused strictly on what their impulses and experience would dictate. The relative vacuum gave the new players an aesthetic freedom to create a direction completely suitable to them. A kind of tipping point had been reached, a new way that society, culture, technology, and economy would relate, generating a new optimism. An open door was created and they found it. Of great significance to them were laptop-based electronics and reconfigured analogue components, which enabled some to become sound-makers almost upon purchase. Unlike free jazz musicians, they could bypass the mastery of conventional instruments, whose training requirements and aura of reverence were a formidable obstacle. At times they may have been reinventing the wheel, but so what? Their enthusiasm, plus the desire to perform and the new individualism that filled the air in the booming 90s were the origin of the grass-roots expansion of outside music still continuing today.

As free jazz was getting closer to its jazz roots, this generation tended to see anything coming from jazz as old and used up. They embodied the hyper-present postmodern, unattached to any tradition that had shut its doors. Moreover, to them the free improv Europeans were remote professionals, not models for these more ordinary players. As in the New York School tradition, acoustic and electronics players could easily work together. Curiosity went in the direction of sound--electronics, invented hybrid instruments, prepared, table-top guitar and objects, and extended techniques on acoustic instruments. This was a more tech-oriented generation than earlier, more self-taught than trained, and so putting oneself on stage was an assertion of the unschooled. As the late Dennis Palmer of Chattanooga told me, "no one can tell me how to play the synthesizer."

Undergirding the resurgence was the massive increase in people generally who wanted to play music in public yet were not interested in going the career route. The stage in North America, far more than in Europe, became open to all. When blocked by "adult" professionals they could enact Mickey Rooney's line, "Hey, kids, let's put on our own show." The democratic and can-do ethos, the American Dream principle of popular music, and the attention-getting society all joined to create "everyone can perform" — and today everyone signed up with social media is on stage.

To be inclined to perform without professional status had its origins in the sixties. Similar to popular poetry-writing, anyone who felt the spirit of folk music strongly enough bought a guitar, could pick out a tune and maybe play for friends. To go further then still required a shift of identity to becoming a professional and operate as one, a leap up. DIY punk and free improv was the transition; the 90s completed it. Playing on stage was twice-rewarded, as fun and as attention-getting in the new youth culture. In a couple decades technological advances that cheapened the cost of making and duplicating recordings brought more to original music-making. Then the internet proliferation of private stages led to non-career players outnumbering the pro musicians by a huge margin. They had no the worry that file-sharing was eating away at their incomes, which depended on day gigs.

Musicologists and other academics have not found a place for this sociological fact in their understanding of current culture, even as the universities have benefited from the general upsurge of interest in performance arts. The democratization of free improv that Davey and LaDonna introduced in the early 80s exemplifies the trend. Through the resurgence of free improv the career-oriented and those who had no such aspirations were merged; they both lacked the music world superstructure to hoist them up. Some performance ritual remained, but it was common that the performers could not be greatly distinguished from those who came to hear them. Even when specific interest in free playing began to wane in the mid-00s, the informality and mixing did not entirely disappear.

The only career-oriented and school-trained grouping of musicians that fits the concept of an improv resurgence was a circle of primarily acoustic Boston improvisers. Free improv appeared there in the midst of, and somewhat competitive with, an existing free jazz scene.[286] This soon changed, especially as it included electronicists as full partners in what was called electro-acoustic improvisation, or "eai." The leader of this circle was Bhob Rainey, who early on had a promising career as a soprano saxophonist skilled in conventional bebop. He became disenchanted with this and in the mid-90s went back to school, Boston's New England Conservatory (NEC), which for long had been the East Coast institution that led the field of avant-garde music. There Rainey learned the technique of quarter-tone playing from saxophonist Joe Maneri, who had himself been a straight-ahead New York jazz musician in the sixties and later was a microtonalist player and composer.[287] Although Rainey has since moved away from exclusive focus on the saxophone to become a composer and electronicist, his saxophone playing today maintains his orientation of the late 90s. The microtonal component of the 90s generation is still evident in Maneri's son Mat, a violist and violinist, though that edge was subsequently softened in playing with tonal jazz-oriented musicians in New York. Other Boston improvisers, such as the violinist Katt Hernandez, also imbibed Maneri's teaching, but in general the distinctiveness of microtonalism—off-pitch but with a precision and self-consciousness lacking in blues-influenced Free Jazz—is today rarely performed (unfortunately, in my view). It was a direction of trained professionals, who cannot continue long without institutional support (Maneri died in 2009) or a loyal art audience and music world.

The duo of Rainey and Boston trumpet player Greg Kelley, called Nmperign, at the turn of the millennium, was radically different from everything else. They were improvising, yet they consistently followed a specific aesthetic. The duo worked well with some Berlin improvisers and toured coast to coast more extensively than improvisers had done since the 80s. To my ears, Rainey was the most original sax player on the planet; he turned my head around the first time I heard him in 1998. A saxophone signals jazz, but that is not his sound or method, and his improvisational timing and eccentricity would not be found among classical saxophonists either.

Those in the Rainey circle generally held to an approach called frequently "lower-case" rather than the European term, "reductionist." (Lower case alludes to uncapitalized letters, an absolute distinction from "upper case" music such as classical or jazz.) It was distinguished from all musics that filled the musical space with sound and familiar emotive expression, most immediately found in free jazz. It countered the saying-too-much of free jazz with saying little. Newcomers admitted to the circle would have to adapt to it rather than changing that concept. Holding to the quiet and sparse side of the earlier New York School, especially the work of Morton Feldman, their music was reflective and calm rather than overtly disturbing or passionate. John Cage's music had a radical, disruptive effect because it was aimed a general art music public, as he intended; the Boston lower case was rather aimed at a specialized scene and had a admiring audience. This circle's unity of form meant improvising within specific parameters, chosen for aesthetic reasons in order to achieve a specific musical result and effect. Later the Boston circle was formalized as the BSC (in some ways paralleling the British AMM, a similar aesthetic and acronym with no specific reference), and played together as a band. It often went beyond the parameter of low volume and sparseness, yet it seemed aimed at a unified, convincing performance.

The players' musicianship was obvious and very high, something the Boston audience would easily identify and support as a sign of their seriousness. This was a good fit for a city proud of its musical taste and well known for its famous music schools and high-culture proclivities. Their very aesthetic aimed at precision and conciseness, and required the kind of work on the instrument found in compositional art music. This Boston group thus implicitly stood apart from the tendency of earlier American free improvisation, which accepted good and poor technique alike. Their approach differs from what I've been calling free or open-field playing, yet remains within the broad field of improvisation.

The music went against the grain of many other improvisers, most of whom received it with attitudes ranging from indifference to resentment.[288] By highlighting form the lower-case aesthetic implicitly challenged free improvisers' usual disdain for form as contradicting "doing whatever you feel." However it impressed a small audience, partly because consistent and bold musical ideas confidently presented will always *seem* composed, the hallmark of art music. The tours of Nmperign and the Berliners were received well, but there was no music world or substantial scene to accommodate something so startlingly new and unique. They received some response in New York, but without any crossover interest from the older NY Downtown avant-garde or the free jazz community. Greater exposure came with the Erstquake Festival, 2004-2006, and various shows produced by Jon Abbey ("Amplify").[289] Its links were to European reductionism, which had made a far greater impact there and could expect state funding. If it had been composed it might have joined the small, funded New Music composer groups that dotted the American landscape. However these mostly acquired a funding track record before deregulation; lower-case improvisation would have faced a double obstruction, despite its resemblance to composition.

The Boston circle would not have achieved what it did without being something of an exclusive club, far more careful of those they would play with than other improvisers. For free playing the problem with a predisposed aesthetic is that, like a belief system, it will block any collaboration that would challenge it, without putting that to the test. It made things difficult for other Boston improvisers, who could only thrive in a more open situation. They were frustrated and in some cases resented audience attraction to those who appeared culturally advanced and presented a united front. Gradually members of the circle moved away from Boston, mostly for further schooling and academic careers. Geographical accessibility of players is always a plus for the strength of a musical direction, and by at least 2010 lower-case playing ceased to be frequent and dominant. As with any music that is limited to specific players and cannot be extended by a successor generation, the improv scene changed considerably when they left.

New York area improvisers, many jazz-oriented who had migrated there, were so enthusiastic about free improv in the 00s that they ignored its lack of prospects for income and audience. As often before, digging in the same trenches of the cultural capitol created the camaraderie of a dedicated, active musician scene. Though most now lived in Brooklyn, the strongest effort was to find gigs in obscure Manhattan spaces, since for most musicians and audience that's where authentic art happens, regardless of audience size. Amica (from the 80s) had found an acoustically challenging space in the Knitting Factory until 2003 or so. Meanwhile in 1998 reed player Blaise Siwula began a similar series at ABC No Rio in lower Manhattan, which he called Coma. It was, and still is, even more open and known than Amica had been; anyone could show up and play with the featured performers, often visitors from outside NY. One tireless organizer, Ty Cumbie, could always find a place few had heard of before, with an audience of sometimes just a couple other musicians.[290] In 2003 James Ilgenfritz, bassist, began a series in his sister's smoothie bar in Tribeca once a week, called "Sound Infusion," lasting until 2006; percussionist Lukas Ligeti was also involved and continued the organizing. Bruce Gallagher's Downtown Music Gallery held two free shows every Sunday, with room for at most twenty, in a store on Bowery, an area of other alternative culture such as CBGBs and the Bowery Poetry Club (founded in 2002). (It has moved since then but continues the Sunday concerts.) These gigs were in the spirit of 80s free improv--booking almost anyone and promising little reward. The point is, despite being unadvertised in the press, improv was performed in public if people were looking for it.

Squeezed out of Manhattan, improvisation started appearing in gentrifying Williamsburg, Brooklyn. The Lucky Cat, Eat Records, Café Grumpy, The Red and Black, BPM studio, and The Cave (improv music and Butoh dance) are the ones I knew and played 2003-2006. Percussionist Jeff Arnal organized the Improvised and Otherwise Festival in Brooklyn around that time. The enthusiasm of musician-organizers led to small venues and series popping up. Owners waited to see if audience would come and spend some money; that didn't happen. Rent increases became a problem for small audience gigs in Brooklyn as in Manhattan, and there was a gradual shutting-down of easy access to public venues. Added to that was natural waning of organizers' energy when free improv doesn't draw audience. The 2008 financial disaster had a discouraging effect, and enthusiasm for free improv declined.

Through the 20th century Manhattan was where real careers doing the most free-wheeling art were possible. The rest of the country was the boondocks, which fed the center and honored it. A long-term process has been eroding the conditions for that center-periphery model. Not only are non-conventional artists no longer so drawn by that magnet, but there is no other locus that actually functions to create such careers. Its reputation lingers, aiding artists with a NY address, but outrageous art has found homes elsewhere. Some are tiny pockets where it gets fueled by being an in-your-face alternative to the surrounding normal culture, something unlikely to happen in New York.

Baltimore is no tiny pocket, but it has long harbored nose-thumbing, adventurous artist-types (an indistinct merger of artists and audience) that have been the alternative other to more career-oriented New York. An anarchist collective in Baltimore set up a performance space devoted specifically to free improvisation in 1996. Called the Red Room, it was located in the group's used bookstore (with the ironic name of "Normals") that had a generous landlord. The space has housed regular open sessions called "The Volunteers Collective," introducing newcomers to improv through structured situations very similar to those of Eddie Prévost's in London.[291]

The collective mixed anarchism and situationism, leaning to cultural rather than political activism. They wanted to see what a self-organized group would do musically if it didn't follow the normal rules for music. It did not shun the strong direction of John Berndt, then in his mid-thirties and closely identified philosophically with the sixties experimentalist Fluxus and later Neoist movements. Unlike so many musicians who use their organizational efforts to promote their careers, Berndt always made it clear that he did not want to control the series or to perform more than others, and withdrew to allow others to become decision-makers. The collective was not interested in defending free improv as a scarcity art of the experts, but took the direction initiated by earlier free improvisation, that anyone can play this music. As the enthusiasm for free playing has waned in favor of more prepared art-work, the Red Room series presents a more varied field: "experimental, im-provised, and harder-to-describe music (not to mention vital film, language and performance)."[292]

A measure of the growing popularity of free improv and the best public marker of the resurgence was the High Zero Festival, which the collective initiated in 1999. Today, as originally, it is composed of roughly a third to a half of local players and the others from the rest of the continent. For finan-cial reasons, all but a few are from the East Coast, plus a few Europeans (of-ten able to get funding from their governments for festival invitations). It brings together several categories of players: men and women in increasingly equal numbers; those oriented to careers and those who are not; some unfa-miliar with free playing as well as a sprinkling of "name" players, although not exploited to draw audiences, the standard festival practice. The festival has been collective in format; at least in the early years no one was featured with a solo. Invitees are joined in often improbable ad hoc groupings deter-mined by the collective. Sets are ad hoc meetings, as exemplified by the long history of London's Company Week. It has occasionally tested the limits of cooperation by mixing a jazz-based musician with others playing electronics and invented instruments.[293]

Unlike other festivals there was no guarantee that a particular set of di-verse players would work; the audience was often in doubt as well as the musicians. One set of the 2003 Festival illustrated this: five musicians went on for a bit until they realized they were not connecting. In the spirit set by the festival, the group was honest about this and simply stopped playing. This is uncommon for musicians, for "the show must go on"--they are ex-pected to continue playing and ignore any reservations they might have. Af-ter a tense few monents they began again, ending half an hour later in com-plete triumph. They had created an empty space where they could reflect, cast off the weight of failure, regroup, and begin again—from scratch.

In contrast to both New York and Baltimore, Philadelphia has been cursed and blessed with close access to NY and a traditionalist-culture persona and protective elite. It is a conservative bastion established in the twenties by The Philadelphia Orchestra and the Curtis Institute of Music. What is not com-posed classical-tradition has always had a rough time getting valued as art; for the others New York is more welcoming and a short hike. The NY popular avant-garde had occasional entrée, but only because institutions here habitually defer to the cultural capitol, marking the city with an inferiority complex worthy of a small town.[294] Almost all avant-garde jazz was imported until Sun Ra moved his Arkestra here in 1968.[295] Philadelphia musicians whose musical uniqueness might have contributed to the city's cultural reputation have found the doors of publicized, funded venues locked. They would not benefit from the aura of home-grown origin available to most other urban musicians, each city identified with the authenticity of a specific genre. Equivalents of NY or Europe improvisers would have to move to NY or be confined to an unpublicized, semi-private underground.

It wasn't until Dec. 2004 that free improv musicians in Philadelphia began to multiply and perform on a similar scale as Baltimore. They were activated by two organizers. Percussionist Eugene Lew found venues open to improv and electronics and arranged concerts roughly monthly, with the number doubling in spring 2005. After that it was mainly Dustin Hurt, a composer suddenly turned on to free improvisation, who in Feb. 2006 broke through Philly musicians' ingrained sense of hopelessness. He had the social skills and chutzpah that musicians lacked, and the drive to book spaces virtually anywhere. Audiences were receptive; at least no one seemed discouraged by their small size. He named his operation Bowerbird and was known to set up shows for practically anyone who wanted to improvise. The mix of locals and touring musicians from every level of credentials and reputation included no stars to draw audiences, and so shows were close to today's open mic nights. He scheduled as many as nine shows in a month, with sometimes five short sets a night, in a large variety of neighborhood and entertainment district venues.[296] This was a bold decentralizing strategy that drew audience from their neighborhood, though mostly in West Philadelphia, which had a tradition of community and political radicalism.

Sporadic opportunities for this in the past had never caught on as the word "scene" implies. The zeitgeist timing for these shows was just right; people came out for them, partly to see and be with their friends. Before the social media kicked in and turned the underground into a relatively private affair, these shows were public events. The word-of-mouth feature endowed them with a radicality that media-sponsored entertainment lacked and social-media advertising would never acquire. The series fit with the political atmosphere--the wave of anti-globalization and alienation from the intense and repressive wave of patriotism after 9/11, just as 80s countercultural improv had flourished in part as a reaction to Reaganism. Not incidentally, its duration paralleled Bush II's second term and ended around 2008, just as the left lost its oppositional edge with the election of Obama.

After this period Hurt lost his enthusiasm for free improv, phasing out local improvisers. He became an art music curator, which typically selects conventionally credentialed artists. He would feature mostly out of town player-composers with individualized aesthetics and styles, and a wider variety of art forms. Bowerbird became a funded operation of contemporary, avant-garde art music with himself as director and fund-raiser, receiving grants of $30-60k from the Pew Charitable Trust. Hurt now says that his former passion, free improvisation, is something audience and funders perceive as "conservative or old-fashioned" and not avant-garde.[297] Indeed, considered as an historical genre like any other and given the laws of fashion, free improvisation can be accused of being passé. However the approach of free playing, which has never depended on audience approval and success, has never been fashionable. The very resurgence that Hurt's improv period thrived on exemplified its resilience and potential future of serial disappearances and resurrections. Though players may create things whose strangeness attracts people, this is incidental, since free playing is not seeking to impress people with skill, novelty, or augmentation with other art forms more attractive to audience. Hurt's charge represents the same mentality that dominates technology and consumerism, which merges fashion with progress. Playing founded on immediate, present experience is neither driven by the will to progress *beyond* it, bypassing it for a fantasized future, nor is it held to the fortunes of the genre to which it is assigned.

Implications of the Resurgence

In the background of the free improv resurgence is the changed social-cultural situation for musicians beginning around the mid-90s. Jazz musicians had been more able than those of any other genre to control access to their ranks and thereby determine their music. This control they were losing, as they were absorbed into formal education, with academic credentialing taking the place of musicians determining their own music. At the same time, the decline of performance by professionals in proportion to non-professionals was evident in punk, noise, and singer-songwriting, soon to be boosted by the internet. Henceforth not only vetted professionals would have access to a paying audience, a major challenge to art music. This was countered by music world consolidation for the benefit of professionals: institutions, media image, and commercial concerns came to legitimate and stabilize all music careers. The pro musician had to *learn* how to appeal to audience—as student or as entrepreneur--rather than merely play for them.

This helps explain the widening of the always potential gap between jazz-based and non-jazz improv musicians. The career-oriented affiliated exclusively with jazz, and free improv'ers were more solidly divorced from career than before. The idiom that "non-idiomatic" had denied would refer to *marketable* categories, those with music world backing, historical validation, publicity, and career expectations, not just the *musicological* categories.

The marketable music closest to improv was and still is anything jazz-related. That relation, always in the historical background, is stronger than its ties to experimentalism partly for financial reasons: like almost all jazz musicians, free improvisers cannot expect institutional funding. Even though few musicians make any real money from performing jazz, there is the plus of cultural legitimacy that improv lacks, the sense that they are linked to an authentic, valued music. Free improvisation is considered music only in an ethnomusicological sense, a remote, incomprehensible tribe better left alone.[298] The exclusion is mutual; when free players self-advertise as "experimental improv" it usually marks their variance from jazz and thus from entertainment, yet is too underground to be promoted as art. The more anxious musicians are about their career the more they tend to avoid playing with non-career musicians, a steady shift from the 80s to today. Why should curators favoring legitimated professionals muddy the bill with anonymous musicians who might not even be grateful to be included? Granted, the usual audience response to professionals makes it unlikely anyone else could steal the show, but since listeners can potentially make autonomous judgments, the threat is there.

In the sixties, the urban audience of the curious, like those crowding into happenings, gave some vague assurance to Free Jazz musicians and others that they had a future. Attendees were few, but given modernist assumptions they were expected to be merely the first wave. That audience was comfortable when they were assaulted by something a bit disturbing, or threatened to go farther into taboo country than others had gone before. This could even be the definition of radical listening, where you feel bumped out of your seat and get the urge to leave. The attraction of challenged naiveté is to cognitive dissonance, which some craved and others feared. That audience suspected the weakness of their culturally provided knowledge of music, art, sexuality, drugs, and politics. They were ready for an outside stimulus to push them towards whatever could overturn the given, sometimes violently.

In today's enjoyment society that audience is invisible; it's not fun to be faced with a music from outside one's comfort zone. This includes that portion of the DIY scene whose taste increasingly faces a barrier of political morality, a sheltered family where musicians are censured for PC-incorrectness on the grounds that some of the audience feel "uncomfortable" and "unsafe."[299] Today's audience more likely considers itself *already* radicalized, a point presumably reached by their predecessors, beyond which there is no unknown. "Weird" advertises a pleasant simulacrum, not a jolt of psychic radicalization. Its etymology looks back to prehistoric times, when there was a tension between a secure home and a threatening forest outside, which is now fenced and filled with protected species. Weirdness must be manufactured, distinguished from what might hit people from out of the blue.

Besides the burst of new musician-enthusiasts in the resurgent period, the split of career and non-career players, and that of free jazz and free improv, there was a related musicological trend. Boston musicians formulated their aesthetic as lower-case but as a more general trend it was more widely practiced. The new generation often sought a space free of the cultural pressure towards volume and density, the continuous flow of sound, and the display of their musical personae and mastery, a specific need of professionals. Low-to-moderate volume and density levels would disappoint any audience that expected to be kept at the continuous energy level of most commercial musics and cathartic free jazz.

The new improvisers' attraction to electronics signaled both popular culture (no schooling necessary) and art (advanced technology is innovative), with the art direction predominant. Electronics played a large part in the new aesthetic direction, for it can achieve low volume at the turn of a knob. No need for the special training that acoustic instruments require to do so or the sacrifice of sounds only reached at high volume. On the other hand, for an audience that wants to tune in with the musicians' bodies, electronics operations offer none of the physiological-emotive release of witnessing and identifying with hard-playing acoustic musicians.

This release is part of the cathartic, joyful, and personally expressive effect essential to all jazz, the root of its popular acceptance *and* its distinction from high art. When Free Jazz musicians fought for acceptance as artists they could not escape such expressiveness (opera once faced a similar dismissal of its claim as high art). Emotional display implies that the music is personal to the musician, an attachment that denies the distance of experimentation and forbids the conscious, intentional aesthetic expected of art. That puts the expression of freedom at odds with the free choice of one's aesthetic. The latter is exemplified by the Berlin reductionists, who carved out a space for themselves in a city where free jazz and its old guard dominated.[300] The lowercase Americans also treated jazz self-expression as the other to their aesthetic. They reacted against the broad, noisy, egalitarian aspect of earlier American free improv while retaining improvisation. Their parameters roughly determined the next iteration, while allowing much freedom in the details.

Lower case raised the question of whether art requires an aesthetic from which artworks and performances result as instances, or can be an activity in itself apart from results. If all art and artists must represent an aesthetic of specific parameters, chosen or not—and better chosen than not—then free improv is not art. Lower case was not a known idiom yet it had the form of one; its analogue in Europe could be called a movement. It was unadaptable to ad hoc, free playing situations of musicians who had no taboo on volume and density. A new phenomenon, it was consciously aesthetic and validated by the Experimental Music tradition, yet improvised. It introduced structure, providing a relative consistency that could be expected. To assert it as *free* improvisation would deny the tension since the early days of British improv between ad hoc free playing, even Bailey's "semi-ad-hoc," and music of an elective aesthetic orientation. As the latter, it helped open the door for the genre of contemporary experimental music and performance, within which free improv performance is often included.

It would be helpful here to see this situation in the light of certain terms used in rhetoric. *Syntaxis* refers to the socialized rules of grammar governing the construction of sentences, such as word order, which ensures the communication of meaning. Very different is *parataxis*--short, simple sentences relatively independent of each other, such that the next sentence is unpredictable. Paratactic transitions are more implied than stated and can be received as nonsensical, as in much Dada poetry, and so can produce both confusion and surprise. It's up to the individual reader or listener to create the flow from one to the other and so is participatory, on the terms of the creator.

Syntactic playing could even define music internally, beyond the simple external performance frame placed around human-made sound. Almost every composed piece seems to follow a specific syntactic structure in order to produce a more or less unified result. Soloists do the same when they improvise within a specific set of musical ideas. Their skill is in constructing meaning according to syntactic rules that are consistent and unique to that musician, which reduces the strain on the listener of comprehending it as meaningful. On this is based the musician's meaning and significance, the critic's ability to sum up the work, and audiences' ability to receive it positively. It applies as well to a music that follows parameters such as lower case, where what is to come flows more or less evenly from what has just happened.

Although for the uninitiated the difficulty of comprehending the soloist or a collective aesthetic can be intense, some minds will be attracted to absorbing it. After a time of struggle the unexpected will become expected; the groove has been laid down. The mind is released from frustration, yielding a touch of pride in accomplishment. The listener joins the already initiated in a celebration, which gets directed towards the performers.

Free playing is more likely paratactic, which provides no guarantee of even flow. Each "sentence" is internally consistent but no one knows, including the player, how long it will last and what will come next. The effect is a kind of *self-renewing* difficulty for the listener, and so complicates the work of the critic and listener and limits their numbers. Few will be stimulated by continual cognitive dissonance. Jumping around freely might be called a consistent style, as Samuel Beckett's later writing might be identified. However, that doesn't make it easier to comprehend the meaning, which the listener must continually work to construct or chase after, without closure, and music promises closure more than literature or visual art.

Lower case playing as an aesthetic held by a specific group of improvisers had a brief life but showed the way for musicians of individualized aesthetics to create more syntactically meaningful music than could ever be achieved by free playing. It also introduced a kind of reverent spirituality, a message to slow down, stop compulsive noise-making, and be receptive. One quiet sound can be enough, and it doesn't have to be novel, it's the details of how it is done and the timing that attracts. It may have fallen in with high art but it disabled some common East Coast virtues: intellectuality (dense, complicated, difficult new classical compositions), recognizable training (classical and jazz), speed, volume, and easily communicated emotion (free jazz). The response of "I don't get it" is because it does not engage the emotionality expected of almost all music.

By comparison, free playing might qualify at times, but the door is open to slip right into that noisiness. It could be said to have a different spiritual path, one of non-attachment to any particular aesthetic or vocabulary. It is rather playing for its own sake, like meditation where no goal is aimed at. This keeps it at the door of fulfillment and outside the room. Some might argue that to be perpetually at that door--dealing with frustration, finding new techniques and experience--*is* the desired perfection, rather than entering the room via a specific aesthetic and ending frustration. "A man who is on the Way deviates and does not err."[301] Lower case would treat deviant sounds and movement as an interruption. For free playing there is no such thing as an interruption; everything that comes up is part of the picture and precisely what is needed. Inefficient digression keeps it from getting to the point where meaning can be wrapped up. Free playing is meaningless compared to lower case, whose players aim to get their point across. Both are mysteries, and have lacked audience and musician interest over the long haul.

For new improvisers outside the tight Boston circle, quiet, sparse playing was a break from the past. In the 80s "free improv" included the consistently hard playing of free jazz and other loud, dense musics. Those playing with continuous energy and volume (such as myself at the time) entered an ad hoc sessions with those playing differently, and tended to overwhelm whoever didn't conform. To make the session work, dense/volume musicians would have to surrender the very energy driving their playing, or the quieter ones would have to boost their volume just to be heard. This situation was an unfortunate side effect of the communal bond, whose ethic thrived on ad hoc playing—we can all get along. Those coming later were unpersuaded by that and introduced an aesthetic that required excluding those attached to the density/volume model. This meant dispensing with ad hoc arrangements, for the simple reason that any louder others would easily dominate.

Musicians attached to the earlier model were often tagged "free jazz," which was not just a musicological difference but meant to protect whatever happened at a lower or even variable dynamic and density level. Those who today fail to distinguish between free jazz and free improv are referring to the earlier period of inclusion, and not recognizing the internal split that began twenty years ago and is now fully in place. That split is then not just one of the market for jazz-based music, nor a free aesthetic choice alone, but follows the practicality of what partners will do in playing situations.

The new generation as a whole expanded the early British improvisers' exploration of non-traditional sound, which further distanced free improv from jazz. Electronics led the way and acoustic players joined in, some adding wires and electronics to their instruments, others (like myself) taking a "no-wires" position but learning new techniques for sound-making.[302] Free Jazz had only been open to sound outside the instrumental norm in the spirit of expressive ecstasy, whereas here it was the exploration of sound that attracted, opening the door to abandon all normative sound as a reference for music. This is still a part of free improv today, and continues as a strong mark of distinction from the consistent timbres of all music, with the exception of some new composition.

The discontinuous sound/silence pattern and more careful, less impulsive playing might be judged as the postmodern "waning of affect," often deplored—waning, that is, from modernist expressiveness.[303] Those who approved it were bored only with the bundle of affects culturally most familiar—fierce intensity and personal feeling. Those who resisted the turn argued that those affects are vital to music. (Only in Europe, where free improv was taken as a serious music, was the division sharp and expressed, largely along music-generational lines.) Musicologically it's as if quiet and sparse NY Experimental Music compositions had been resurrected in an improvised form, with the same antipathy to jazz and its predictable effect on the audience. The flat, even hypnotic affect of some improvisers' minimalist drone music might be seen as an extension of Lamonte Young's work in the 60s, now issued directly from players with no music world support. That lower case was closer to composition helped attract its professional-oriented improvisers to academic careers, which favor the self-conscious aesthetic of composition and obviously skillful playing that is attractive to an intellectual class. The wider phenomenon of playing more quietly and sparsely can be ascribed only partly to the influence of the Boston circle (and European reductionism), which as an unmediatized underground music few got to hear. It did not find the level of audience support around the country that would have encouraged careers as performers.[304] Rather, it arose spontaneously among this generation as part of a general reaction against expressiveness that sounded canned and inauthentic by then.

A very significant contribution of the new improvisers was the normalization of a different kind of musical relation of partners, obvious among those allied with the lower-case program but found generally. They tended to listen far more closely to each other and depend on what was specifically happening moment by moment. For instance, in the 80s if someone dropped back radically in volume it would probably be ignored and treated as a withdrawal from participation, licensing others to play over it. In the later period it became more likely for the others to pay heed, sensing a possible change they might also welcome. The smaller the group, the greater the effect of an individual's shift, but this could extend to large groups as well. Everyone might cease playing for a period, yet the music would continue because of clues that the players were still actively engaged. As in a string quartet, the raised bow signals a pause in the score and not the end of the piece. This is a major distinction from the popular music rule, including jazz-based music and most earlier free improv, that sound should be continuous from beginning to end. An improv group now, even ad hoc, might stop and shift on a dime without any external directive to do so. By this means free improvisation has drawn closer to a chamber music—assumed to be high art composition--while retaining the free flow of intuitive movements. "Free" then does not put the individual in a box of private expression, impulses, and habits, but in a situation more fully collective *and* individually self-determined than any known music.

Playing with others came to mean putting the subtle movements of the music ahead of the urge to present whatever dazzling ideas one had developed. The individualism implied in a collection of performer idiolects or a mishmash of voices playing cacophonously alongside each other was countered by a preference to adapt very precisely to each meeting. A single partner disregarding this player-relation will throw off the others. Consequently players will tend to choose partners that are sensitive to others' moves, a criterion that ignores audience-impressive playing and downplays open-invite ad hoc groupings as something more occasional. Such awareness can be a personal trait ingrained or developed but not necessarily; many beginners, anxious for acceptance in an ad hoc session, will be all the more glued to what's happening out of caution. Once they feel more secure either they leave that behind or prefer it that way.

This is perhaps the greatest advance bequeathed by this generation to the present, assumed rather than explicitly communicated and theorized as an innovative leap. It has become an added marker of difference from free jazz, but this need not be a permanent condition.

Along these lines, and following my long-standing attraction to large group organizing, from 2000 to 2005 I assembled nine groupings, each with roughly nine players. Most were weekends of sessions in Philadelphia and included a performance or two; I called them No Net, for the double meaning.[305] They tended towards quiet and sparse playing, but then I had selected those who seemed to me disinclined to let loose, so the sessions were representative of generalized lower-case playing but not of all improvisers. Once, when I suggested we follow the common practice of breaking into smaller groupings, one musician was insistent that we all continue playing together as a group. That would be more challenging and has been my principle since then—however many come to the session, we all play together. This is a player-based approach to large group improvisations, an alternative to relying on a conductor or model for player interaction, such as the structures of

Butch Morris (a cornetist whose more than 200 "conductions" involved large numbers of musicians) and John Zorn. With the right people No Net is a workshop where players learn ways of dealing subtly with each other. Unlike some similar attempts, the groups functioned similarly in performance, which would have been unlikely in the earlier days of free improv.

The situation today

In general, the East Coast enthusiasm for free improvisation began to wane soon after the mid-00s. The realism of "no money, no audience" caught up with many. After a few grant applications stating the music as free improvisation one learns there is no future in it financially. Sessions, the necessity for free playing collaborations, became less attractive for those career-oriented, who added "composer" to their bios and even dropped "improviser." Some turned to more jazz-based music; some towards forms less conducive to mixing with diverse others, such as super-quiet electronics; some went for advanced degrees and institutional affiliation to secure a livelihood. Adding wires to an acoustic instrument helped some avoid the impression that they are out of date jazz musicians. Brooklyn has a large number of improvisers, yet whatever dedicated community there was in the 00s that was able to push its way into public spaces was not sustained. Over that period Baltimore's High Zero and Red Room were the sites of the most continuous community, while in Philadelphia and Boston things quieted down.

In recent years things seem to have sharply turned around. Free improvisation does not have the energy of a movement, as it did in its origins like Free Jazz, but it seems to be in a new phase of growth. Any summary of the present situation and trends will be speculative compared to the past, but apparently now (2016) free improv is gathering new players, organizers, and opportunities to perform. Small audiences can be found at least as far west as Kansas City before one runs into the roadblock of driving distance to the West Coast. That would take flight money, unrecoverable by the door gigs out there. Between DC and the Northeast there are organizers and small venues available, and a proliferation of players who aren't bothered by minimal audiences.

In New York, the only choice for audiences tends to be name musicians (not all, of course), who give classic demonstrations of what they're known for. Patrons willingly pay to hear the greats and respond with predictable enthusiasm. Crowd behavior rules, and it would be gauche not to clap and whistle for those universally acclaimed in the media.

The Free Musics

It is the wide Midwest and the Southeast that have seen the most growth in the last ten years. Audiences in medium-size cities are small but show up in proportionately greater number than cities, though they often must be coaxed to pay. Knowing the musicians are *not* names, listeners are more likely to have an unmediated experience. They are in a position to respond from how they feel about the music, which is the strength of an underground and what stimulates improvisers. Also, the smaller total entertainment audience has less specialized tastes than large cities, such that improv advertised as free jazz will not turn off those who in cities might be disinclined to hear jazz. An improv group can easily be the only non-conventional music in a month, and will be able to do a full set rather than the standard short set in urban settings, to accommodate as many as five groups. Where audiences often feel deprived ("You must play in NY a lot." "No, hardly ever; much more welcome here.") and business rent is less a constraint, avid organizers have little trouble finding a venue and even dig into their pockets (the frequent $20 bills obviously don't come from audience). A single well-funded gig, impossible in the competitive big city without major hustling and pretense, can cover the rest. I would guess touring of improvisers has doubled in the last three years. The advice I published in 1987 for improvisers to get out of the cities and circulate, which fell on deaf ears then, now seems closer to realization.

Unfortunately the split continues between free improv and jazz, which is mainly a club and concert music advertised in the press. Jazz musicians mostly think of themselves as trained professionals expecting to be paid from admission fees or funding. Free improv is mostly house shows, small galleries, and informal, so it's outside professional concert expectations. The private concert advertised through Facebook event pages, donation optional ("gas money for the touring artists" is the ritual plea), has become its major option and path of growth. Noise electronics and other experimentalism, like performance art, can be expected to share the bill. Unfortunately organizers avoid mixes with jazz, folk, blues, classical, or composed new music, which would expose audiences to something different. Please as many as possible is the entertainment rule. While a few free jazz musicians also tour, they are able to build name-recognition through the media and reserve their music mainly for venues that promise guarantees and jazz-size audiences.

In Philadelphia the most hopeful sign in decades has been improvisers moving and settling there, attracted partly by the cheaper housing compared to other cities. It's even possible for a minimally-employed musician to buy a house, as one young percussionist from Columbus did, Ben Bennett. Underground venues available to free improv pop up like rhizomes and disappear with regularity, often from noise complaints. Reliable organizers locate them, such as Steve Tobin, who moved to Philly from the Bay Area in 2006 and began organizing a wide variety of shows the next year, including improv. His "Fire Museum" began on a small scale and grew, filling a much-needed gap. Tobin says he missed the wide offerings of non-conventional music in the Bay Area and wanted to create something similar in his new home town. Regular and irregular music-makers have different needs and expectations, and Tobin was the patron for the latter.[306] The problem as usual is finding venues that are truly public spaces, where those outside the scene might hear of them.

Percussionist Flandrew Fleisenberg moved from Boston to Philly in 2012, and became the most enthusiastic and talented organizer specifically for free improv since Hurt. For the first time in thirty years music advertised as exclusively free improvisation was presented at a festival, the NowHere Festival in Fall 2015 and Pfff! in 2016. Similar to John Berndt's effort in Baltimore earlier, Fleisenberg instigated the Festival's ongoing committee of seven members, the Impermanent Society of Philadelphia. It was previewed in the press, as underground events never are, gaining access to an audience that normally would attend only traditional and compositional music. It included a community outreach program, gained institutional recognition to the extent of a panel discussion at Temple University, and the Impermanent Society is active in presenting year-round events.[307]

Contributing to this has been collaboration with improvising dancers, begun as monthly open sessions in 2011 and expanded when more musicians moved to Philadelphia. The Impermanent Society's festivals are dance/music events, with musicians encouraged to join in the movement and dancers making sound. Collaboration on stage brings improv into the realm of performance. This implies something of visual and often humorous interest to audience, whose focus is easily distracted from the music. In our culture the visual can overcome the rough edges of abrasive sound, as if harmonizing the dissonance for audiences that would otherwise avoid it. It remains to be seen whether enthusiasm for performance will spill over to music that does not have the aid of the visual to grow its audience.

The Northeast began to experience a shift of direction around 2008. As the tight circle of Boston players declined through attrition, those who had been outside it and its aesthetic pushed into the vacuum, led especially by visual artist-electronicist Walter Wright (no relation). The new Northeast musicians have no singular aesthetic focus but are eclectic—loud noise rubs up against acoustic and electronic free improv, occasionally super-quiet. This was possible because the scene has adopted a radically open-door policy and often ad hoc, one-off combinations, in the tradition of the earliest free playing. Unlike the bulk of the British originators and the Boston circle, these players don't appear to have career ambitions, preferring to perform in the DIY scene and expanding it rather than going legit.

Increasingly these musicians have moved out of the (high rent) cultural center of Boston to the Pioneer Valley, a corridor of universities and counterculture in Western Massachusetts. That is the home of XFest, the first five years of which were in Lowell MA; in 2014 it moved to Holyoke, an old industrial town in Pioneer Valley. In numbers of participants it is the largest improvised music festival in the world. In 2015 there were around a hundred: 70 from the state and thirty from outside; in 2016, its eighth year, it was close to the same. Over three days, one-third of performances were groups of performers more or less known to each other, and two-thirds were ad hoc sets determined by the organizers. Each participant played in one fifteen minute set per night and was invited to an afternoon of workshops. All but a few audience were fellow players, making this a series of short sessions of people playing for each other. In contrast with the norm of music festivals, the lack of public has elicited little surprise or disappointment. Perhaps it is a convention rather than a festival, except that it is a free event; should it be adequately publicized it would find a public.[308]

Increasingly the sets have included dance, such that in 2016 almost every set had dancers. Dance brings in women as performers, making all three current East Coast improv festivals (including High Zero, which is now about half women) more gender-balanced. The 2016 XFest aimed for half its invitees to be women, which it came close to realizing. Generally there are more women than men vocalists, but a significant number of women instrumentalists are showing up as well, many now blasting out with electronics and giving the lie to the gender stereotype of women as preferring quiet. As jazz earlier bridged the racial divide of musicians, improv is overcoming the typical gender roles (women fronting as vocalists). No other music can celebrate itself as an open, egalitarian community as does this one.

This is not a move of political correctness. Every gender enjoys bonding, but without fanfare male improvisers have disallowed that for the community of players, since a true community will mirror the gendered world. Men were the first active organizers and so the ones initially opening the door; as women see others enjoying themselves, more come into the scene. Following the same logic, that few blacks and hispanics are involved is not due to exclusion or discouragement by whites; only a few have shown up. Women's attraction to playing this music likely comes from the openness of the musical form and lack of competitiveness. However much this balance might please liberals, it is no strategy to attract them, for by itself it will not persuade anyone to appreciate a music that, given the cultural meaning of music, most find unendurable.

The small town location of XFest is symptomatic of the current situation. Urban venues struggling to make the rent are increasingly charging musicians to perform, which makes most shows private and underground. Even without the centralized urban scene individuals have been discovering this kind of playing through chance encounters and internet threads that expose them to it. So long as niche marketing defines the limit of culture there will be curious others, dropouts and discoverers who go beyond the fringe. "Weird" may be hype but it expresses the desire for something less boring than the music worlds have come up with. There's an elusive excess in the pleasure scheme that makes some search for a place to land.

Even music schools are showing interest where a quarter-century ago teachers scorned free improvisation as harmful to music. It's unpredictable where this will go. Will the University of Alabama students eager to learn about experimental music take up playing? Will the improvisation-studies scholars take notice of what's happening in house shows? At least for now, it is apparent that no amount of formal training can realistically provide a lifetime performing career, so it is in the schools' self-interest to follow the market of growing student interest in something different. Although audiences are too small to merit the music world's attention, this little puddle (compared to the ponds and oceans of other musics) has more young musicians swimming in it than ever. The wide region where XFest is located is the first non-urban scene; others—Ohio maybe?—are waiting to be born.

With the joining of free improv and noise under the same roof, loud electronics has been part of the show, and the decibels are commonly at ear-plug levels. Titling music "noise" implies volume and obliteration of anything unamplified, which gives it the edge of power for the powerless—nothing new there. Noise is not based on free playing sessions and ad hoc group configurations, but like all performance-oriented work aims at creating a positive effect for its audience. Towards that end preparation is necessary, at least a conception of what would be worth doing. The title, chosen by its players and not meant as a curse on it, challenges its inclusion in the family of musics more directly than free improvisation, for the word specifically connotes obstruction to traditional music and not simply sound beyond the limits of unprotected ears.[309] Luigi Russolo's version of noise a century ago was part of a more intentional public artist revolt against the social order until it was brought into the fold as experimental music. Today's noise can avoid mainstream acceptability partly by not claiming to be in advance of it, which would pressure the culture industry to confer its blessing. But perhaps this is the permanent outside, alongside the permanent avant-garde, each within its own space. Noise and free improv musicians do seem to tread common ground. A show billed as noise, DIY almost by definition, can easily include a normal-volume improv set without violating the understanding of noise, while a jazz or new music venue would exclude both on musical grounds.

The collaboration of the two has its problems.[310] The gaps of silence and shifts of direction of free improv would disrupt the intent of noise. And the austere advice I heard in Europe in 1983, that "a saxophone never needs to be amplified," is useless when one must hold one's own against high-amplified electronics. For some, it seems, noise is not just pleasure but for the displeasure of conservative America—a merely symbolic cultural-political act, since their dissent only reaches other dissenters. This is not true of electronics players who accept the spirit of group playing and adjust to the level of acoustic instruments, if necessary down to a whisper. In contrast to the homogeneous aesthetic of most noise, these players are open to uncomfortable combinations.

As for free improv itself, in the earlier, resurgent period strict lower-case and quiet eai were the strong trend, and advanced the full attentiveness of each player. Now improv has opened to a more diverse level of dynamics and density, and close attention can be achieved by bursts of loud, boisterous playing that would have frightened away lower-case players. It can be assumed that what goes up will come down after a reasonable time. It is common for players to suddenly and arbitrarily break off from volume and chaotic density, as if uninterested in what they were doing, instead opening up an entirely new direction, and nobody knows what that is or will become. The arrival of players with an interest in both lower-case playing and close attention was essential for this change, but it has turned out that the parameters are not needed. Free improv performance today is capable of a wider range of options—silly, serious, child-like, and off-the-wall--than ever before.

By all appearances, the split of free jazz and free improv is as strong as ever. In New York, improv that lacks the continuous intensity of free jazz, free to wander into other spaces, is hard to find. Career musicians cannot ignore how audience interest and the music world are structured. Playing that claims or sounds rooted in jazz always has a better chance of drawing audience and media attention. The "real" audience wants *visible* musicians, selects from a night's entertainment offerings, and pays for the show. Unconsciously, musicians want to give some hint of cultural legitimacy, to feel the world observes them and approves their activity. Their ambition is confined to success, they cannot turn their back on it, but their denial of its importance is a hopeful sign. It means they know it is possible to be ambitious for the music and simply don't think "music" can go anywhere.

Those who for whatever reason don't have that relation to success will tend to form a world of their own. They will be out of sight, as implied in "egalitarian community," where no one is special. Free improvisers are among these; some even balk at writing a publicity bio, for it implies self-importance and an objective self. For them the significance of what they do is below the scanning, surveilling eye of the culture. They are comfortable with a DIY audience notified through Facebook announcements for a home event filled with recognizable faces, like an extended family. For many this prevents them from becoming alienated from aspects of their playing, to feel stuck—why should they? Ambition is for something beyond where one is now, and *can* stimulate such self-aware change. This means escape from one's secure place in the family to reach a wider social field, and not just numbers and attention. The something beyond of ambition can be purely musical. As such it might reach career musicians, giving the two a relation they lack. As it is now, both hit a stone wall. Should they become aware of their limitations, the split might not predict the future.

While improv musicians have been losing their earlier relation to jazz, from the mid-2000s on they have increasingly been included in the eclectic category of experimental music, discussed earlier. "Experimental improvisation" sometimes appears; it indicates their distinction from jazz more than "free improv," and to an extent that's needed. It is difficult, for myself and others, to avoid "experimental," now synonymous with all non-conventional music. Given that new music and all other musics that are part of the package are prepared in advance, the audience receives free playing as also a prepared show. That the others do not experiment on stage makes all the difference, but is invisible. To perform at a show that presents itself as *representing* experimental music, such as a festival, pressures improvisers into a formality that suppresses signs that their playing is made up in the moment.

In Britain free improv has a certain autonomy, since it is assumed to be continuous with its origins, but even there more recent offerings of electronics and performance have been challenging its position. To the extent "out" music is under pressure to be the most recent cultural option, free improv there no longer holds that title.[311] It would seem that their period of experimentation is long past. More recent experimenters, who also do not experiment in the moment, at least have no long history to be perceived as trapping them. Professionals who have staked everything on their inheritance of a distinct approach are threatened not with a new generation of improvisers but with cultural obsolescence.

In the states, for improvisers to get under the experimental umbrella is difficult to resist, but they don't fit as well as composers. Experimenting, which implies trial, error, and progress, is something they don't do and never have, and they are not trying to innovate and cut edges, as much new music and electronics is presented. For them experimentation is a lie but is advantageous for getting gigs and audience. It gives the appearance of greater cultural significance than the odd-ball approach of free playing, which apparently takes a few chapters to elucidate. "One size fits all" is the best market strategy, for it collects musics that would have little appeal on their own. The other musicians can more easily collect the benefits of identity as conventional artists, with a composition or aesthetic to show for it.[312]

Despite how little publicity experimental music receives, from the perspective of recognized art it is the revamped avant-garde music of today. Or rather, it bears the reputation of the 20th century avant-gardes but functions quite differently. Those art avant-gardes of self-determining collectivities of visionaries were at odds with the social order and audience, movements that sometimes produced manifestoes as well as artworks.[313] Acting as if they might change the world, they were not underground but put themselves right in the face of the public. A collectivity that moves is historical in the sense that it can dissolve and cease moving. Today we have an avant-garde that is *a*historical. It cannot dissolve, change or die, and is in no one's face. It does not operate as a collectivity headed somewhere under its own steam but is a cultural necessity, a fixture. It offends only abstractly and by association, with few people ever experiencing offense. It is the Newspeak means by which society is protected against artists offending them.

"Experimental" is an occasional adjective with synonyms to advertise it that change as they get worn out. It points to the future, but nothing utopian, which would put the future in question. Its future merely extends the present, like technology, building upon itself ad infinitum. The cutting edge does not come into existence or attract an audience spontaneously; it must be supported. Unable to move on its own it must be provided a vehicle. What once put artists' fate in the hands of a collective vision now depends on an institutional reward structure that promises selection and reward. Movement is then *within* that structure via the competition for favor, however hopeless or miniscule, rather than the self-movement of visionaries, who create their own formal and informal institutions to insure artist control.[314]

Critics, consumers, institutions, and many musicians presume a single, meritocratic hierarchy of all, with the best at the top, awarded the greatest visibility, those who show promise in the middle, and at the bottom those whose music has been tested and is not worthy. In reality the two-tier division mentioned earlier is in place. Those who show career ambition and play the musician game are the only ones taken seriously; there is no reason to notice those who don't care to be. This makes the work of evaluation easier, for it eliminates the majority of musicians. This is not a moral issue, it is not deplorable, in fact it is completely reasonable. The only question is, are the musicians satisfied with it, is this system creating what they want?

The prospect for change depends on some of each category finding common interest in the music itself and inviting the other to collaborate. Career players would first have to disregard their closed circle of associates and judge what these others are doing with their most imaginative musical ear. They would have to feel frustrated with the current situation, and shift their ground away from their scene. To be inspired by those independent of the music world and its acceptable forms is the obvious thing to do. For a session to be fruitful, however, they would have to join the other in the equal collaboration of a free playing session, without bringing their solo and other assumptions into it.

Their non-professional counterparts are likely aware of what career musicians are doing and often have negative judgments about them. Yet those judgments are based on the assumption of separate tiers and don't take into account what the other might play differently together with them. They have sorted themselves into a comfortable category, but their playing is often indistinguishable from what professional-oriented musicians do. Knock on a few doors, find whoever is willing, and see what happens. This is a compromise only in the common recognition that we can influence each other without one being absorbed by or subordinated to the other.

A more open, player-determined music might yield an alliance that would be a horizontal continuum rather than the vertical hierarchy. Instead of tiers of visibility, mere relative difference. My guess is that the interplay of the two will break the current musical stagnancy and submission to the music world's needs. When that happens it is not impossible that listeners will take notice, audiences that are self-empowered and willing to step outside the normalcy of well-publicized offerings. It is up to musicians to initiate this, for career musicians to cross their name off the unwritten contract, and for the free improvisers to drop the safety of playing for an exclusively underground scene. This is the only way to create both a music that is self-determined *and* a public that prefers as direct a communication from the musicians as possible.

13. Conclusion

In some respects I have been playing freely in writing this book. It is not an artwork of finished propositions but an art-*working*, a continuous elaboration of thinking and experiencing that this bound book will not bind. It is reduced to a concrete form only at the moment of handing it to the printer, a moment that could have easily been sooner, later, or never.

This book's incompleteness is not a failure but a warning that thought and the impact of thought does not naturally solidify. To say there's more coming melts the ice of meaning, reveals thought as movement that cannot be dammed up. If it is incomplete then I do not own the thought, its true readers will continue it, and that will not contradict it. It is not mine; as an object on the shelf with my name on it, this book is an illusion. It does not make me a writer any more than making something that comes across as music makes me a musician. Musicians and writers have their respective métiers, and free playing, like the writing in this book, is done sans métier. Or rather, to the extent I have imbibed these métiers, my work has been to relieve myself of them. I emancipate myself; to call that work completed is to abandon my life work. I am not resisting full objectification, for that would imply that objecthood is the natural end, which I must then work against. Rather what I do is nature, and the métier and oeuvre of alienated objects are the distortion. As in playing, we're not giving you something finished for you to deal with, a piece of music like a slice of pie, but the whole thing at once. Music interminable—movement of thought and action interminable.[315]

The book goes beyond attempts to master the situation that I share with other improvisers. Though mostly consistent with my thinking over the last thirty-some years, it has taken me places I could not have imagined when I began it. In my earlier project, *Shaky Ground*, I saw myself painted into a corner and exiting through the window, but that didn't happen, I couldn't bring myself to closure. Now I see past that roadblock. I stand by what I've done here, as well as beneath it, over it, and past it. I am learning how to play and how to write, and that is superior to the pretense of knowing.

Kierkegaard said, "We live forward but understand backwards," yet the two are intertwined. The fence between living and understanding, action and contemplation, turns out to be imaginary as we stumble over our earlier assumptions. What I do now is not always what I've expected to do. Reflection on the implications of free playing, as I read the text staring back at me, has affected my daily playing, reinforcing my motivation to write. And putting into words what I and others do as players pushes me towards reflection and opening up my playing. The mystery of music can lull us to sleep but be re-awakened by the intervention of focused thought. Long ago I fell into a hole where I recalled, as something lost, the joy of playing that first lifted me from despair. I sought the road to recovery, with success never a foregone conclusion. I've learned that despair and doubt, humiliation and fear of loss are not hindrances but at the core of artmaking, which includes writing. This, and not "creativity" is the true spirit of art for the artist.

Some of what I write will seem harsh and disturbing where it concerns free jazz, tenured professionals, career pursuit, and the stagnation of the avant-garde, but it's what many know and hesitate to say in public. In a musical world that appears complete, every niche filled, all that is asked of us is to elaborate with minor variations. The past has been turned into guards against our urgency. My intent is slip past them, to clear the brush that's grown up in the open field, to reimagine the range of the possible, and to join with others who have come to similar conclusions. My direction comes from deep inside, a thread I can trace from my early teens in the mid-fifties to to-day. This book is not that story but a temporary plateau on that journey, where the open field is revealed to me more fully than I have ever known. What it can be for you is not for me to say.

To aim to discover what is authentic to our inmost selves is to enter the shaky ground on which we either learn to dance or we leap away to the safe-ty of our culture and social order. The dance follows the thread of truth that runs through every self. Instead of that, the social order provides the roles of musician, performer, writer, and artist, and it is the role that is taught, achieved, and rewarded for what it--the role, not the artist--has produced. Achieved is the security of a positive response from some demographic or institution. Every role rests on the image of a self that becomes fulfilled only as it provides for the needs of a rewarding other. This model preempts the future; we either know the script already or can learn it.

In the contemporary situation the open door to artist roles is an American Dream directed mainly at the liberal, educated middle class. That open door has been integrated with the constructed tradition of Art and an honored hierarchy the newcomers cannot possibly equal. The notion of social progress would have the deluge of artists-performers-writers overturning that older valuation system, yet the way is barred. The most sanctified art has been framed, interpreted, and promoted as the treasure of our culture. The Contemporary Artist and avant-garde musician were born too late for that. They are selected according to different criteria, and perform on a different stage. Contributors are at best content providers for the art spectacle, and must scramble for the spotlight.

Especially those just coming into the market have imbibed but can barely fake the mystery of Art and Genius. The models for that are the Modernist progenitors, who scorned the assent of all but a few other artists. They were out of sync with the culture providers of their day, until a few bold critics and eccentrics stood with them. The "cursed" poets and painters were then proclaimed progressive and worthy of attention, and a paying audience was eventually brought along. Since this was often post mortem, many artists experienced little social or financial reward. Art would not have become the centerpiece it is today without an audience initially intimidated and humiliated as philistines, only capable of the lower appetites ("mere consumers"). That social history has been converted into the myth of a bygone golden age. Its last, final heroes were artists who cut their teeth in the fifties and sixties. Many of them, far from making grand Pulitzer speeches, were beset by crisis, the dilemma of whether to destroy their art, or themselves, in order to save their artmaking.

The present arrangement purportedly aims to create artists who can define art for themselves, but it celebrates those no one would dare elect to the pantheon of the past. The question is, will art achieve the kind of power it once had to shock and awe people into an experience of not-knowing, and what would be needed for that to happen? Can art only be functional to the culture, blind to the absurdity of our social order?

No resurrection of the past is possible or desirable; the attempts only go to feed the art and music worlds' myth and power. My vision for music calls for a different configuration: 1) An even wider open door—anyone who can imagine playing freely as the entry level, and professionals who long to collaborate with them. This is the social backbone of real change, and not only for artists. 2) An artistic discipline of self-critical focus, and a proud collective spirit that doesn't fall for the blandishments of media and audience attention. Together with the first, musicians would undermine the claims of the present hierarchy to represent the limit possible for music. 3) A handful of players and non-players who fanatically pursue and trust their experience, articulate it, play wherever they can for handouts or big checks, and have the will to move a mountain of complacency. 4) Listeners distrustful of cultural authorities and experienced in their judgment, who perceive themselves as a collectivity despite their market irrelevance. Their ability to discriminate and criticize will encourage greater artistic discipline.

Of these four the first, at least the open door to free playing, is already here. 2) exists embryonically among those of arrogant self-belief. As for 3) my life work and my voice in this book aim to incite and collaborate with like-minded others. Concerning 4), listeners who are experienced, critical, and conscious of each other are few and scattered. At this moment of publication in late 2016, looking at the planned neo-conservative roll-back, what artists and listeners will do is unpredictable, and as you've been reading, that can be a good thing. No matter what, "let's play and see what happens" will not go away. That bold step might be just what musicians at this political conjuncture need to do and people need to hear.

The philosopher Ludwig Wittgenstein discouraged a young academic with "there is no air in Cambridge for you," but that for himself "it doesn't matter...I manufacture my own oxygen."[316] This is our exciting task today.

Notes

For direct links to sources online as well as further writing:
http://www.springgardenmusic.com/the.free.musics.appendix.htm
or References on p. 302

[1] "Music world" will refer to the network of institutions and individuals that select, finance, critique, and present music for audiences. That includes music venues, record companies, funding agencies, critics, academics, and the media machinery that promotes and sustains the recognized names. It does not include musicians except as they take on managerial and curatorial roles.

[2] This would be Tatsuya Nakatani, percussionist with a strong business orientation, who tours almost constantly in the US and lives here. He is a career musician without seeking to be included among competitors for media attention, and does not depend on association with media-familiar names. He has a jazz background but that is not how he chooses to present himself.

[3] This phrase is not to be confused with the "outsider music" of Irwin Chusid in his book *Songs in the Key of Z: The Curious World of Outsider Music* [2000]. (See the bibliography for full citations.) Chusid covers a wide range of individuals somewhat arbitrarily selected, and not musical categories or approaches, which is my concern.

[4] A sample of personal writing from a bit earlier is "You Know the Story" [1989], available online. See References.

[5] Academic interest in improvisation has been steadily growing, but there has been no sign of interest in a social analysis of avant-garde music, in the relation of musicology to the livelihood of the musicians, or in the community of players devoted specifically to free improvisation.

[6] The "spectacle," for this study, refers to the long-term development since the 1920s of both the national media and the everyday consciousness suitable for an economy in which desire is to be satisfied by consumer spectatorship. It is regulated and inspired by institutions of the social order and confirmed currently by the wide demand of individuals for visibility and attention. The Trump candidacy is the most obvious instance of this; reality is how things appear mediated by the spectacle, whether factually true or false. The spectacle was created as the need of capitalism and now is the mechanism that runs it, not greed. The radicals at the 1968 Democratic Convention who chanted "the whole world is watching" appealed to it to get their politics across (for instance the 1969 film *Medium Cool*). Others followed suit, leaving the left in the dust.

On this topic see Guy Debord's The Society of the Spectacle [1967]. Also see the analytic biography by Vincent Kaufmann, *Guy Debord: Revolution in the Service of Poetry* [2006]. Debord was the key member of the Situationist International, highly influential in May '68 in France. He did not foresee that the spectacle would swallow up much performance of the contemporary avant-garde (such as the popular fringe festivals). Nor that it would counter the charge of "passive spectators" with an interactive internet. Marshall McLuhan was Debord's North American more positive analogue, whose term "global village" he later changed to "global theatre." McLuhan is celebrated for his advocacy of the spectacle as democratically progressive, but later he had reservations: "The electric surround of information that has tended to make man a superman at the same time reduces him into a pretty pitiable nobody by merging him with everybody." Interview of 1974 in Benedetti, Paul and Dehart, Nancy, eds., *Forward Through the Rearview Mirror: Reflections on and by Marshall McLuhan*, [1997], p. 85

[7] My study concerns the duality of free jazz and free improvisation as I define them. However significant are the AACM and Art Ensemble of Chicago in the history of improvised music, I will be omitting them, since the usual Chicago focus was the composition. As with the Sun Ra Arkestra they included free playing as solos or sections within a composition. Valerie Wilmer's book-length *As Serious As Your Life: The Story of New Jazz* [1980] has a chapter on the Chicago AACM, otherwise she considers strictly the NY musicians. Her focus is on the broad phenomenon of the Black Avant-Garde as it appeared from the 70s perspective and not specifically sixties Free Jazz. Although AACM members came to New York and gained respect, they did so after the crucial Free Jazz period of the mid-60s and did not affect the generalized model for most free jazz today, nor free improvisation.

As an organization the AACM was inspired partly by the Jazz Composers Guild, which Bill Dixon set up in 1964 in NY, and it continues today, as Dixon's has not. Especially the Art Ensemble, consisting of AACM members, had a separate, sustained trajectory, introducing humor and theatricality in contrast to the emotionality and physicality of much NY Free Jazz. It had an unconventional compositional approach, and at times an interest in sparseness the New Yorkers lacked. Their concern with structure and use of silence even anticipated later reductionism of the 90s, which however turned sharply away from jazz-inflected improvisation, as we shall see. Recordings of the more playful Art Ensemble are often found in the libraries of free improvisers who have little interest in free jazz. The primary textual source for the Chicago avant-garde is trombonist and scholar George Lewis's, *A Power Stronger Than Itself, the AACM and American Experimental Music* [2008], which extends far beyond jazz biography.

[8] The title does not merit even a footnote in surveys of contemporary American music. It is not popular enough to be hated, apparently, for it doesn't appear in Christopher Washburne et al, eds., *Bad Music: The Music We Love to Hate* [2004]. It is recognized in Todd S. Jenkins, *Encyclopedia of Free Jazz and Free Improvisation*, two vols. This is a catalogue of musician biographies, including those focused on free improvisation (including myself) and free jazz, along with many jazz musicians who have had no association with either but have at times merely played outside standard jazz. For a topical encyclopedia, broad inclusion is the norm, which is only possible if the titles are not clearly defined. One sentence in the 68-page introduction suffices for British free improvisers, to which are then added British free jazz musicians as part of the same "movement." (xlviii)

[9] Much of this discussion is based on John Gennari, *Blowin' Hot and Cool, Jazz and its Critics* [2006], the writings of Bernard Gendron (see bibliography), and Paul Lopes, *The Rise of a Jazz Art World* [2002]. Ann Douglas presents the wider cultural context of jazz in *Terrible Honesty, Mongrel Manhattan in the 1920s* [1993]

[10] This is especially true of the sixties, when it is evident from interviews in 1964-65 that jazz musicians thought deeply about music and were engaged in literature and visual art of the time. Garth W. Caylor, Jr., ed., *Nineteen + Conversations* [2014] These interviews, which only appeared in print fifty years after the fact, shed light on the complex situation of musicians at the height of the freeform direction.

[11] Surplus lyricism is "what that which is called the avant-garde desires whether it accepts or rejects the name...Such blackness is only in that it exceeds itself; it bears the groundedness of an uncontainable outside." Fred Moten, *In the Break: The Aesthetics of the Black Radical Tradition* [2003] p. 25-26 Freud called eros the drive "to establish ever greater unities and to preserve

them." Thus understood, eros is what motivated Ellington to create a music "beyond categories," rather than the postmodern blurring of lines.

[12] This was an advertisement blurb for a concert, quoted in Schwartz, *New Black Music: LeRoi Jones, Bill Dixon, and the Making of Free Jazz* [2014], draft edition, p. 19. Schwartz quotes trumpet player Bill Dixon: "'The audience consisted of a certain class of strong music lovers or music *movement* lovers and intellectuals, some who thought they *had* to listen even though, in effect, it is conceivable that they might have even *hated* the music." p. 70 italics in the original.

Chapter 2. Sixties Free Jazz

[13] Valerie Wilmer [1977] documents the jazz avant-garde after its major period of public presence and controversy, and is still the source best known to musicians and fans. Amiri Baraka's *Blues People* [1963] is the first contemporary social-historical understanding of jazz and blues, and *Black Music* [1967] covers Free Jazz in then-current reviews. Philippe Carle and Jean-Louis Comolli's *Free Jazz: Black Power* [1971], based largely on Baraka, is now translated [2015], newly prefaced with an argument for its value as an historical document reflecting the time it was written. Closer to the NY scene is A. B. Spellman, *Four Lives in the Bebop Business* [1966]. John Litweiler's enthusiastic *The Freedom Principle: Jazz after 1958* [1984] appeared when musicians commonly assumed Free Jazz had nowhere new to go. Recent scholarship focuses on individual players rather than the movement and its context. In my opinion the most useful writing on the music and its political and cultural ramifications is that of Jeff Schwartz, whose *Albert Ayler*, is available online: see References. He has graciously made available to me his unpublished dissertation and his most recent writing, the draft of *Free Jazz* cited above. Received too late for my consideration is Richard Koloda's yet unpublished biography of Albert Ayler.

[14] WWII was "an event of homogenization in which presumably outdated territories, identities and social fabrics were obliterated. It was the making, wherever possible, of a tabula rasa that would become the platform for the latest phase in the globalization of capitalism." Jonathan Crary, *24/7: Late Capitalism and the Ends of Sleep* [2013], p. 67. The effect of America's initiation of weapons of mass destruction was more apparent and theorized on visual art (abstract expressionism) than on music. (For a different emphasis see Daniel Belgrade, *The Culture of Spontaneity: Improvisation and the Arts in Postwar America* [1998]). As for cultural alienation, a decade earlier the poet Delmore Schwartz's deep distress about his own survival merged with fear that poetic art could not survive under American conditions. A dark poetry of thinly-veiled personal reference had not been seen previously; in this Schwartz can be seen as the predecessor of the postwar beat poets. See James Atlas, *Delmore Schwartz* [1974]

[15] I would recommend to any saxophonist Andy Hamilton's *Lee Konitz: Conversations on the Improviser's Art* [2007]. An equally inventive tenor player, Warne Marsh, preferred to stay in the background of the scene. Konitz, even working with British improviser Derek Bailey briefly in the sixties, still exhibits a strong free-playing direction. In the mid-70s I heard it was possible for serious non-professionals to come play at Tristano's house sessions. For me it was a missed opportunity; maybe I feared becoming one of the acolytes.

[16] I remember hearing this put-down myself at the time, which helped to dissuade me from a music career (my sound was a clone of Desmond's, whom I heard play live in 1955). The idea that whites cannot play true jazz (or free jazz) is not heard today, when the vast majority of jazz musicians are white.

[17] Online, see Varese in References.

[18] Sam Stephenson, *The Jazz Loft Project* [2009]

[19] James Moody, in a *Downbeat Magazine* "Blindfold Test" interview, quoted in Jeff Schwartz, *Albert Ayler* [1992]. Ayler himself frequently used the term "free form" for his approach. It was also the term my partner in the early 80s, Marv Frank, used to describe what he had been doing in the sixties, and is sometimes used today.

[20] At the time, "avant-garde" was often capitalized as a proper name, in conformity with earlier European modernist groupings that had a unified program and the kind of solidarity of membership-based political parties. What takes the place of "avant-garde" today is often "experimental," an adjective to which musicians do not have such loyalty and commitment as to a specific Avant-Garde. "Experimental" is equivalent to "cutting edge" and is applied casually to technology and business, so it is far from its earlier meaning. I will be using the lower case "avant-garde" in the narrow sense of an art movement, when it was in process of becoming more an adjective than a noun. Even when Amiri Baraka inaugurated the title "Black Avant-garde" it did not refer to a unified movement but rather to individuals, many of whom would probably not have applied the term very seriously to themselves.

[21] According to Willener, *Action-Image*, [1970], whose sources were limited, "new thing" was originally a pejorative term of trumpeter Don Ellis, but since Ellis himself was involved with avant-garde musicians I doubt *he* meant it to be negative.

[22] By accident in 1967 I met the bassist Charlie Haden, who put me on the guest list to hear him play with Coleman's group, and he referred to the music as the "New Thing." I experienced it as anarchy, the chaos that Free Jazz signified for many at the time. Its musicians knew full well that audiences would be challenged and divided, many reacting like myself and feeling burned, or negatively "experienced," as Jimi Hendrix might have put it. For me that brief traumatic encounter worked underground in my consciousness and five years later I came back for more. In that time of upheaval there was a small number like myself that both feared and desired to be uprooted from their musical opinions and, as musicians, from their usual options. Recently bassist Richard Messbauer told me that, in contrast with today, to be challenged in this way is what attracted him to jazz concerts in the 70s, along with many of the audience.

[23] At that time Lacy was not in NY but Argentina. However he encountered it in the person of Don Cherry as early as 1959, when they played sessions together: "he used to tell me, 'Well, let's play.' So I said, 'O.K. What shall we play?' And there it was. The dilemma. The problem. It was a terrible moment. I didn't know what to do. And it took me about five years to work myself out of that. To break through the wall. It took a few years to get to the point where I could just play." Steve Lacy, *Conversations* [2006], p. 50. Lacy ended his experiment with free playing, but it is hugely present in his later playing.

[24] "Sometimes I [Haden] would play what I was hearing instead of what he had written, and he usually accepted it." 2007 interview with Haden, printed in *Downbeat Magazine*, no longer available online but several others are, see Haden in References

[25] "Even when his supporting cast tried to prod him with standard chord changes (as pianist Walter Norris and bassist Don Payne repeatedly attempted to do during these early L.A. sessions), he mostly ignored them...Norris told me in a 1990 interview: 'We rehearsed two or three times a week for about six months leading up to the recording... At every rehearsal Ornette would change what we had done the last time. He would change the structure of the song or where the rubato was. And then when we finally showed up for the record date, *he changed everything again*.'" Ted Gioia,"Where Did Our Revolution Go? Free Jazz Turns Fifty" (italics mine). Online, see Gioia in References. This compares with bassist Charles Mingus around the same

time, who also asserted strong direction against what musicians thought was required of them. He complained about his crew publicly in the liner notes to *Mingus Dynasty,* where he said they "ignored [Mingus's] intentions and instead played bebop clichés." Schwartz, Dissertation p. 12

[26] It took assertive leadership for players to abandon the habit of following the leader. This seeming paradox escapes those who believe that applying the simple rule of levelling should do the job, and that free playing means being free of the initiative and trust in others.

[27] There was also the American black/white cultural divide, soon to be discussed, which did not affect European classical musicians, who were freer to take their technical mastery in new directions. Some enjoyed the improvisatory spirit, such as the Italian sextet *Gruppe Nuova Consonanza* and the group of mixed Europeans who recorded "New Phonic Art" around 1970. This music was sufficiently acceptable as fine art to be produced by Deutsche Grammophone.

[28] Ekkhardt Jost's *Free Jazz* [originally 1974] is the standard book for Free Jazz musicology, presenting transcribed solo scores for analysis and treating them as compositions, as one would do with classical music. For Jost, the category of free jazz covers all the music of the jazz avant-garde, including compositional forms of Sun Ra, the AACM in Chicago and Charles Mingus, which justifies extending traditional, rationalistic musicology to the results of free playing. He obscures the phenomenon of not-knowing where the playing is going, which cannot be comprehended by a rational schema, which was standard for musicology at the time.

[29] In 1957 Shepp asked Coltrane for a lesson and was invited to his house. Coltrane played a bit of "Giant Steps" and asked him if he could play it. Shepp admitted he couldn't, but that didn't seem to matter to Coltrane. The two spent the rest of the day talking about music. Source online, see Shepp Interview 2001 in References.

[30] The full quote continues in a way that captures the spirit of the time: "I want to make music that opens the possibility of real spiritual communion between people. There's a flow coming from every individual, a continuous flow of energy coming from the subconscious level. The idea is to tap that energy through the medium of improvised sound." Note that the "not nice" comment sounds antagonistic but is followed by reference to its transcendent unity, a conjuncture that at that time was consistent: "nice" was commercial but not fulfilling. From an interview by Robert Levin at the time, recounted by him in 2010, "The free jazz revolution of the 60s." Online, see Levin in References.

[31] Interview in *Nineteen + Conversations* [2014], p. 185

[32] Willener [1970] p. 233

[33] The October Revolution is discussed in depth in Bernard Gendron's, "After the October Revolution: The Jazz in New York, 1964-65" in *Sound Commitments* [2009], and in a chapter of Benjamin Piekut's *Experimentalism Otherwise* [2011] Earlier Amiri Baraka (as LeRoi Jones) said in *Blues People* [1963] "The music has changed because the musicians have changed." p. 225.

[34] 1966 Interview in *Coda Magazine,* May-June 1968, p. 6, as quoted in Kofsky, *John Coltrane and the Jazz Revolution of the 1960s* [1998] p. 325. Without citing the source, John Litweiler presented this as a literal figure in *The Freedom Principle; Jazz after 1958* p. 99. But Thiele was probably joking; Coltrane called him frequently recommending musicians, and Thiele could only accommodate a few of them. Research to assess the number and range of musicians playing freely at the time would be helpful here.

[35] The quote is from Downbeat magazine, qtd. by Jeff Schwartz, *New Black Music* [draft copy, 2014] p. 4. *Ascension* still featured solos, yet escaped the usual small group format, rehearsed and disciplined to follow a score. The eleven players merged in the ensemble passages as never heard before, a mass speaking roughly the same melodic lines but lacking European-style synchronized precision, thus giving the feel of individuals voluntarily joined into a collective voice.

36 "All the drummers are now tryin' to be Sunny Murray." *Nineteen+ Conversations* [2014], p. 182. The interview was May 1965. His rage at the others masked his huge and righteous pride.

37 My own first experience of long-form playing was around 1983 with bassist William Parker, who is today the predominant link between Free Jazz and its later incarnation. We joined in sessions of an hour and a half, though our few performances and singular recording were more moderate in length. I felt forced to choose, to cross a line into deeper serious commitment, and I came back for more, a radicalizing experience. (The recording is online, see Jack Wright in References).

38 Players might still defend the concept of playing all they have to play, but its validity depends on being convinced that they really *do* have something meaningful to say and are not simply going on emptily. An audience that doesn't buy it calls it self-indulgence, of which Coltrane and others were amply accused, a judgment denying the artist's selectivity. Very likely many left Coltrane's shows early with that resentment; the few that stayed would find it hard to articulate why they did. The current performance-audience situation does not encourage that, and players can play/speak their truth, trivial or profound, without thinking it might be overtly rejected. Musicians commonly talk of playing a music many reject, but that is in sales and attendance, which has mostly to do with hierarchical rank and not people walking out. Compare that with Coltrane, surely aware that his declining popularity late in his career meant he had forfeited his tenure and authority. Without the possibility of such rejection today what kind of validity adheres to promotional claims?

39 Amiri Baraka, the most insightful writer on Free Jazz in its time, had a more subtle understanding, calling Coleman's music disturbing because it introduces a calm that seems uncalled for (a reference I can't locate). Free Jazz was a step beyond the taste of the Beat poets, who didn't go beyond bebop as their music of rebellion. They had labeled it cool, and thought cool was beyond the comprehension of square culture. Their Americanized Buddhism was likewise a cool disavowal of Cold War passions, for Jack Kerouac a full retreat from the sixties political turbulence (and for the militant Allen Ginsberg a cause for engagement). Free Jazz was rather a hot fire bursting against fifties cool jazz, which by the end of the fifties had become fully commercialized. Baraka was associated with the Beats but shifted to Free Jazz, making a parallel move against his Charles Olsen-inspired poet circle when he moved to Harlem. On this topic take a look at John Leland's *Hip: The History* [2004], journalistic but useful. One who bridged the Beats, politics, and music was the poet Ed Sanders, a founder of the Fugs, a band recorded on the same ESP label that was the major outlet for relatively unknown Free Jazz musicians.

40 In 1974 Baraka publicly renounced the Black Nationalism of his earlier period and declared himself a Marxist, yet this complex individual of many turns continued with much of his earlier cultural politics intact, re-embracing the black avant-garde.

41 In 1963 Rollins chose Paul Bley for his group, who reflected later, "When a Jewish white musician gets to play with an all-black band it's not because there is something for the Jewish white musician to learn, it's because he has some ability that the all-black band wants to acquire from him. Socially it's an impossibility to get hired into a culture to which you don't belong. So I was hired for some information or skills I possessed that Sonny needed…" *Time Will Tell: Conversations with Paul Bley* [2003], p. 72

42 For an account of Ayler's partners, see Schwartz, *Albert Ayler* [1992] Ch. 6

43 My partner of the early 80s, Marv Frank, had been a professional white drummer uninterested in playing straight-ahead jazz. He was crushed and bitter at his exclusion by blacks in the later sixties. He dumped his kit down the cellar steps, unable to play again until I revived his interest.

The contradiction takes a new form today. The obvious question is, what does Baraka's "The song and the people are the same" mean for the majority of those calling themselves jazz and free jazz musicians today, who are white? Is it their song? What is *The Shape of Jazz to Come* (Coleman's 1959 album) when this is the case?

44 For the account of the political activities of musicians prior to the second wave as well as during it I have relied on Schwartz, *New Black Music*

45 Walter A. Davis, *Deracination: Historicity, Hiroshima, and the Tragic Imperative* [2001] The sublime is the experience in which "The surface of ordinary life is fractured by the intrusion of excess and extremity. Habits break down. Perception collapses before images it is unable to process. The continuity of life is rent asunder. The world has become unheimlich [uncanny]. We live in the landscape of the waking dream...[The sublime is] descent into an inferno that is utterly one's own, and that one has created by steadfastly seeking to avoid it." p. 60

46 To combine the two I could use George Lewis' term here, "Eurological," which he coined in his essay "Improvised Music after 1950" [1996]. Much of my argument concerning the relation of the black avant-garde and Cage's circle follows that essay. Instead I often use the shorthand "white" to emphasize the language of that era, and reserve "Eurological" for a later discussion

47 "The Burton Greene Affair" in *Black Music* [1965]

48 This is elaborated by Daniel Robert McClure, in "New Black Music or 'anti-jazz': Free jazz and America's cultural de-colonization in the 1960s" [2005]

49 Gabriel Rockhill criticizes this concelption as a misunderstanding of the relation of art and politics: "a successful artistic object or practice is supposed to be capable of directly provoking changes in the world via an obscure preternatural alchemy." *Radical History and the Politics of Culture* [2014], p.6-7

50 As for many such seekers, his references to the real world were often enigmatic, bringing together the cosmic and the political. On the day of his death, July 17, 1967, just as the six-day Newark insurrection was ending, he allegedly told Elvin Jones "If we only knew the right notes, we could eliminate all friction in the universe, and all matter would fall away from itself, nothing would hold anything together." Music that reaches this level would then both contribute to the collapse of the *present* order and eliminate friction. Quoted in a poem by David Jauss, "Hymn of Fire," in *Ask Me Now: Conversations on Jazz and Literature* [2007], p. 176.

51 For the application of this understanding of art to literature see Camille Paglia, *Sexual Personae* [1990]

52 Neil Leonard, *Jazz: Myth and Religion* [1987] and Tony Whyton *Jazz Icons* [2010] respectively.

53 I can't recall for certain, but the source for these statements might be Kasper Collins' 2007 documentary, "My Name is Albert Ayler"; there are also extensive recordings of his interviews online where it is probably located. The statement aligns Ayler with Arthur Rimbaud, the teenage poet of the later 19th century who is considered by many the greatest French poet of modern times.

54 Jeff Schwartz, *Albert Ayler* [1992]. As Schwartz pointed out to me, Wynton Marsalis, whose picture of jazz has no place of honor for Ayler, could have said something like this. Here is the the inversion by which the spirit of jazz is conceived as triumphing *over* what Ayler and Coltrane and so many others thought of spirit, for which jazz was merely the means to a greater self-opening and collective experience.

55 Classical music worshippers would agree, but they cannot extend their submission to jazz. For instance, it is an insult to human existence that Vladimir Jankelevitch, in his well-received *Music and the Ineffable*, written in 1961, could ignore all but a small portion of world music in his paean to music of feeling and spirit.

[56] Here is a taste of the kind of enthusiasm (Greek origin: "possession by a god") for this music that linked politics, spirit, and art. Sinclair: "people are going to have to get to this music sooner or later, and the sooner the better—not only for the individual musicians and bands involved, but for the good of the whole people...Because this is liberation music, self-determination music, music that will help you, inspire you to transform yourself, yourselves, and to work to bring about the transformation of the social order which keeps so many of us and so many more of our brothers and sisters, oppressed, hungry, and beaten down....the music is helping us learn about freedom." p. 34. He speaks of the "open field" of free music, of "*opening up* the possibilities inherent in the music (or in one's life), in the instruments, and in the body itself; and *realizing* those possibilities as fully as they suggest they can be realized." p. 64. "Self-Determination Music," in *Music and Politics* [1971] (italics in the original). I myself didn't read this until recently and was surprised to find the tone very similar to my own proselytizing of free improvisation in the early 80s. Saxophonist John Grundfest, living and playing free sessions in NY in the sixties, told me (email): "There was a feeling that music could change the world - we would hit a sound create a wave that could really make things better - we believed as Ayler said Music Is The Healing Force Of The Universe - now we wonder if it can save ourselves."

[57] "Free music...Get some...Free love" is the call Jefferson Airplane beamed at downtown New York before a rooftop performance in Dec. 1968, just a month after Nixon's election to the presidency and the height of sixties turmoil. Even though free music here meant free of charge, the word joined their music and sexuality as the projected triumph over repressive politics and society. The "free" culture ignored the claim of majoritarian electoral politics. (Compare to the post-election anti-Trump demos, which had no such positive, emancipatory component.) It was filmed by Jean-Luc Goddard interspersed with shots of passers-by craning their necks until cops got on the roof to stop the playing. Source online: see References "Jefferson Airplane"

[58] Garth W. Caylor, Jr., *Nineteen + Conversations with Jazz Musicians New York City 1964-1965* [2014], p. 71-2, italics in the original.

[59] Schwartz, *New Black Music*, p. 72

[60] It is this kind of playing that raised the ire of Leroy Jones (Amiri Baraka), who witnessed Greene the same year in concert and attacked him in *Downbeat Magazine* as "white, super-hip (MoDErN)" lacking soul, technique, and integrity. Baraka says Greene is unable to accomplish what he wanted, and satirizes him for "banging aimlessly at the keyboard," knocking on the wood of the piano and crawling underneath, which might be performed today by free improvisers and even a few jazz musicians. Baraka didn't mention that there were many strings missing in the middle of the piano, which pushed Greene in that direction. Greene left the country for Europe a couple years later partly because of that review, so, as Baraka might have agreed in his critique of white critics, published writers have the power to shape what music gets heard and what gets sent away. "The Burton Greene Affair," Leroy Jones, *Black Music* [1967], p. 157-160. Greene is possibly the first jazz musician to play inside the piano, also to welcome the Moog synthesizer and record with it. He started playing freeform with Alan Silva in 1962, and in California before that with Winter. Special thanks to Jeff Schwartz for his reference to this music.

What Greene was allowed to release at the time were more structured Free Jazz pieces with better known musicians (Marion Brown, alto sax, Henry Grimes, bass: *Burton Green Quartet* on ESP). This would suggest that even a maverick record company (ESP) wanted to market names that were prominent (and for commercial reasons that number had to be limited), and preferred common traits of Free Jazz over further exploration.

[61] The first quote is Willener, [1970], p. 234, italics mine. The Murray quote is from Caylor, *Nineteen + Conversations* [2014], p. 185. Willener compares Free Jazz to the events of Paris in May 1968. Both he and Jacques Attali (in *Noise* [1984]) see it as part of the widespread sixties rebellion, arousing their hope rather than despair at its evident decline. This raises the question for observers who have given something of themselves to a grand movement: at what point should they begin to say, "it's over," and start recovering, dealing with "reality," and stop chanting "Bird Lives," the resistant, sustaining hope?

Chapter 3. Collapse of the Free Jazz Movement

[62] The assumption of a dynamic of progress from avant-garde obscurity to mass acceptance recalls dependency theory, which argues that under capitalism there's a core of normative society and culture that depends on the periphery for sustenance and renewal. This theory was originally applied to the wealthy First World nations (the West) as the core and the Third World as periphery, from which wealth was siphoned off to sustain it. By this means the former will appropriate get to claim it as their achievement, included in Progress. By analogy, commercial enterprisers of normative society reject the avant-garde advances at first, which yields their low market value. They can later buy them cheap, turning them into profitable commodities, with the originators honored posthumously. Meanwhile a new avant-garde is busy creating the next innovations, renewing the cycle. This is no conspiracy, merely the way things worked for the Modernist period. This dynamic has now broken down, a complex change that has yielded a substitute avant-garde, which is in-house and institutionalized. The guardians of culture can argue that this provides the kind of innovation the unacknowledged periphery once did, without the messy situation of artists protesting and denouncing the expropriation. This would be akin to neo-colonialism as a strategy of (neo)liberalism to make it appear that crude imperialistic exploitation has been overcome.

Contrary to the analogy with dependency theory, however, the earlier 20th century avant-garde was diverse and self-conflicting, and not singular and congruent, as movements and individual modernists. The concept of one historically *leading* avant-garde first appeared in the US within painting, and was the critic Clement Greenberg's invention, who vied for his version as *the* avant-garde—formalism victorious *over* social realism, the Communist version of avant-garde art. This move was successful and pressured many artists ("here's what you should be doing to be avant-garde"), recalling the coercive politics of the 30s, when Greenberg had been a Trotskyist. The official avant-garde today is post-historical, unified under pluralism and not perceived as a field of controversy—or specific innovation, for that matter.

[63] *Time Will Tell* [2003], p. 35

[64] "Jr. Walker's music is superior to Ayler's or that that Coleman's making now, simply because of the world weariness, and corny self-consciousness (which is white life hangaround total – ie what you get for being wit dem). Jr. Walker's music existed then and now, as a force describing a purity. Ornette and Albert now describe bullshit so are bullshit....the harmonics in James Brown's voice are more 'complicated,' if that's what you dig, than Ornette Coleman will ever be. Altho, and here's the cold part, there was a time, when Ornette cdda gone straight out past Lama city, and the pyramids of black gold. His tune was that hip . . . once!! It was his life, and his commitment, as path, that changed it." p. 120, 122, *Raise Race Rays Raze: Essays Since 1965* (written presumably in 1971). It is true that both Ornette and Ayler turned away from their early

radicalism, but Baraka has no sympathy for their difficult position as musicians once Free Jazz was over. Archie Shepp, a strong follower of Baraka's direction, today says he turned back to blues because it was what people wanted to hear (at least their cultural heritage), thus confirming the problematic marriage of avant-garde and the taste of most blacks. Source online, see Shepp Interview 1990 in References.

[65] Albert Ayler's highest ranking among tenor sax players in the annual *Downbeat Magazine* polls during his lifetime was 11th for the critics' poll (1966) and 13th for readers (1967). For all the talk of opposition from critics, Ayler ranked second among critics as the "Talent deserving wider recognition" in 1966 and 1967. On the other hand, jazz *fans* (no critics voting) in 1967 ranked Ayler 31st as "Jazzman of the Year." Jeff Schwartz, *Albert Ayler* [1992]

[66] Bernard Gendron, in *Sound Commitments* [2009] For Ayler's turn, see Schwartz, *Ayler* [1992]

[67] "Milford Graves, an outspoken advocate of musicians' self-reliance and cultural integrity, was perceived as "too political" by record company executives. Ayler was asked to stop using him, and there is no record that Graves ever performed with Albert Ayler again." Schwartz, *Ayler*. "Political" would be the curse on anyone who wanted to bypass the cartel of record companies, as Graves did, and explicitly the demand for black ownership. Together with Ayler, Graves represents the spiritual side of the black cultural movement--music as a healing force.

[68] Val Wilmer, quoted in Schwartz, *Ayler* [1992] fn. 189.

[69] The major labels waited until they could imagine an upsurge of consumer interest before digging into their archives and releasing "new" material. Free Jazz recordings are more available today than during its heyday, following the rule that the most profitable worship for artists can only be achieved when they're dead and their all too human bodily existence is out of the way. Christopher Small said, concerning another classical music, for most people "a great composer is almost by definition a dead composer." (*Musicking: The Meanings of performance and Listening* [1998]. See Tony Whyton, *Jazz Icons* [2010] on the reluctance of the jazz press today to grant the status of greatness to Sonny Rollins as long as he is still living. (p. 86)

[70] Most recognized of these was Susan Sontag, who together with Hannah Arendt and Paul Goodman, were in my opinion the boldest, most incisive public intellectuals of that period. However, her *Against Interpretation* [1967] identified with the spirit of the NY white avant-garde and ignored the parallel black movement. This was no oversight; especially this hot version of jazz didn't fit Sontag's definition of contemporary art as cool, an embattled cultural term appropriated from black culture and fifties "cool jazz" before jazz was deeply confronted internally. One of her pieces, "One Culture and the New Sensibility," (1965) has cool and camp replacing fifties abstract expressionism and the beats, who idealized and absorbed the sensuality of "negro culture," thought to be the other to white America. Sontag ignored the cultural segregation just as the educated white New Left was throwing itself into civil rights and trying to break the color line on a personal level. Not long after this book Sontag was politicized by the American war against Vietnam ("What's Happening in America" of 1966 and "Trip to Hanoi") but to my knowledge she never reversed her cultural bias, which was highly Eurocentric.

The split is a crucial component to the musical situation today, where advocates of the jazz and jazz-derived avant-garde, white and black, inhabit a separate country from the inheritors of the Cagean New York School. Fred Moten puts it succinctly: "a black avant-garde exists, as it were, oxymoronically—as if black, on the one hand, and avant-garde, on the other hand, each depend for its coherence upon the exclusion of the other." (a statement he qualifies but then asserts that "avant-garde is a black thing" and that "blackness is an avant-garde thing." Read

further to find out what he means: Moten [2003] p. 32. The sixties version of this split is discussed in Benjamin Piekut's *Experimentalism Otherwise : the New York and its limits* [2011]
[71] On the divisiveness of this music see especially Leonard Feather's Blindfold Tests in *Downbeat Magazine*. In these interviews musicians often gave their frank opinion of each other; even contempt, when Miles Davis spoke. The current ethic was not yet in force, by which musicians are to avoid public criticism of each other. This is part of the repositioning of jazz within polite middle class society; interviewees are expected to promote themselves without mentioning the failings of competitors. See also Caylor [2015] and Arthur Taylor's *Notes and Tones* [1993]. Taylor, a drummer, interviewed his fellow musicians in NY during the late 60s to early 70s. The musicians voice their opinions freely to one of their own, without apparent self-promotion or caution. Admittedly Taylor interviews only established-name musicians, who at that time would not have thought promotion was their responsibility or within their competence.
[72] The "out" artist should be understood in context. In current terms this category has been formally welcomed into the marketplace, presumed to be meritocratic and pluralistic. "Marginalized" has displaced the "outside artist," many of whom were happy to have a space to work apart from the conformist mainstream. Following logic, if artists fall past marginalized into obscurity it is because they lack merit or ambition, or are willful elitists unable to accept the current requirements of career development. Rough justice for them is then justified. They are not "ahead of their time," the judgment that once patronized and flattered them as having a place in history. The outcast in visual art, meanwhile, has been replaced by the valued "Outsider Artist," which the ambitious can envy as the mark of authenticity. Against this Saidiya Hartman (scholar on the subject of slavery) says somewhere, "the right to obscurity must be respected."
[73] The phrase is from an article in the middle-brow *Saturday Review* of 1962, "The Myth of a 'Negro Literature'" anthologized in *Home: Social Essays* [1966]
[74] Tom Wolfe, *Radical Chic and Mau-Mauing the Flac Catchers* [1970]
[75] Lorenzo Thomas, "Alea's Children: The Avant-garde on the Lower East Side, 1960-1970," as quoted in Daniel Kane, *All Poets Welcome: The Lower East Side Poetry Scene in the 1960s* [2003] p. 13, the source of my information here. I have found nothing comparable to Kane's book that would investigate Free Jazz musicians as a musician community.
[76] The poet Ed Sanders gives this impression in *Tales of Beatnik Glory*, Volumes 1 & 2 [1990] and *Fug You: An Informal History* [2011], which provide first-hand descriptions of poetry readings and the lives of this East Village underground. The poets united around their common obsessions with poetry, sex, drugs, anti-commercialism, and civil rights/anti-war politics.

New York became the center of cultural radicalism thanks, inadvertently, to the federal government freeze on rents in 1943. Rent control provided the lower Manhattan underground with cheap apartments that, given its earlier cultural and political notoriety, attracted radicals to gather in one central location. The radicalism that held the sixties poets together was doomed by the lifting of censorship and academic respectability, while eighties radicals succumbed to gentrification, a material defeat compared to the earlier shift.
[77] Lionel Trilling, "On the Teaching of Modern Literature" (1961), in *The Moral Imagination to be Intelligent* [2000], p. 400. J. D. Salinger's very popular writings of the mid-fifties and sixties, centered on the introverted, arts-oriented Glass children, illustrate this. My own liberal arts education, 1960-64, and earlier spiritual concerns make me a child of this era.
[78] Op. cit., p. 395
[79] On the basis of early and later sixties recordings Archie Shepp should surely be counted among Free Jazz musicians. Yet in a 2014 interview he denied this, and felt it was a curse when he was so labeled by a record producer, blocking his chances early on. He justifies his rejection

on the basis of his cultural politics, of which free playing had been an expression. "I began to see and reflect that basically the audiences for this music were essentially white, middle-class audiences. That very few black people really listened to what I was doing...I began to think...maybe I should begin playing some of this music that people could understand." Source online, see Shepp interview 2014 in References.

[80] The bass player Sirone told Valerie Wilmer (presumably mid-70s) "'We're losing all our front-line players. I'm afraid that in five years' time we won't have any leaders left.'" As Serious As Your Life [1977], p.241). He was referring to those who turned to teaching—like the poets earlier mentioned—rather than, as she put it, "doing what the jazz musician is supposed to do—playing music." She lists all the colleges where Free Jazz musicians were accepted as teachers as of the mid-70s; all but one had previously added Black Studies courses. Those invited were Bill Dixon, Cecil Taylor, Jimmy Lyons, Andrew Cyrille, Clifford Thornton, Archie Shepp, Ed Blackwell; few held permanent positions.

[81] In 1975 Sunny Murray complained that his association with Cecil Taylor in the sixties had ruined his reputation and ability to get jobs. Wilmer [1980] p. 47. A quarter-century later he was appreciative. Any Murray interview, beginning with his first in 1965, Nineteen+ Conversations [2014], is valuable for his tone and directness, easy to locate on the web.

[82] I had many personal experiences of this but the most impactful was around 1982, after an advertised open session playing charts in NY led by sax player Jemeel Moondoc. He had come into free playing through Cecil Taylor, and had been active in the seventies loft scene, so was in a good position to know the current situation. I asked if there was anyone he knew who wanted to play free, and he told me "Composition's where it's at now, man, forget that shit." I was naïve in thinking that Free Jazz was still a going concern. When it was later resurrected Jemeel eventually became part of it.

[83] Bley said elsewhere he doesn't practice, but in the context he means not rehearsing. In the film he says he wants to play what he's never played before, but his playing for the film shows that his earlier free-form period is far behind him.

[84] John Litweiler's book of 1984 (The Freedom Principle) purports to cover Free Jazz from 1958 onward but without mentioning Loft Jazz or its participants (other than David Murray and some of the Chicagoans), who felt they were keeping the freedom principle alive. Wilmer's As Serious As Your Life [1977] is more inclusive, at least in her short biographies. The current information on Loft Jazz is minimal, but indicates its importance in laying the ground for the later free jazz revival. As of now, the best source for those involved is a comprehensive listing of William Parker gigs, which begins in 1972: Source online, see Parker in References.

Chapter 4. Free Jazz in Revival

[85] As earlier, I am focused here on New York, the crucible of modern jazz and Free Jazz, but there was an active post-Free Jazz scene also in Chicago (discussed briefly below), the Bay Area, and Los Angeles. For L.A. the source is online, see Mark Weber in References. The best source for the thoughts of (mostly) NY free jazz musicians today is a book of William Parker interviews, Conversations [2011] and Conversations II: Dialogues and Monologues [2015].

The dates I suggest indicate a curve from a long period of decline to growth of audience interest and financial support that was gradual. In 1990 Archie Shepp could still say that to play avant-garde music was not "commercially viable." The situation was changing, but Shepp would not be part of the revival. Source online, see Shepp interview

[86] http://www.artsforart.org/. I choose this rather than academic definitions because it is both defining *and* promotional, that is, it states the intentions of free jazz major champions themselves. Similar is the online Belgian-based Free Jazz Collective, which defines free as "liberated from social, historical, psychological and musical constraints." And jazz is "improvised music for heart, body and mind." http://www.freejazzblog.org /p/about-us.html

[87] Richard Gilman-Opalsky, in "Free Jazz and Radical Listening," argues that Free Jazz and free jazz are one and the same (he titles it "freejazz"), yet all his examples are from the sixties musicians. When he comes to the present he is derogatory: "the music is becoming a kind of gallery event in cities like New York and Chicago, and in posh venues overseas" but it still "comes out of explicitly radical traditions." His point is that for the conventional consumer free jazz still requires "radical listening." That is certainly true for those unfamiliar with it but not for the main audience, for whom it satisfies vital needs, whereas "radical" usually implies struggle. Sixties Free Jazz had that radical impact on him personally in the 90s, but marketed today as an historical music it is not unsettling to hear music known to be contemporaneous with one's grandfather.

[88] Classic Jazz was originally the title of a box set of six LPs commissioned by the Smithsonian Institute in 1973 and curated by jazz historian Martin Williams. He was following through on what began as a postwar project of scholar-fans to establish jazz as a narrative history. They wanted to help, which meant among other things to shape the consciousness of jazz musicians as the subjects of "jazz," (much like Clement Greenberg, as analyst and promoter of abstract expressionists) and to set the limits of jazz on a quasi-objective basis. Williams' project was useful for commercial and educational purposes, but later Classic Jazz advocates shrank the limits of that narrative. Williams had included a piece from Cecil Taylor's 1966 *Unit Structures*, performed by musicians identified with Free Jazz, and even Ornette Coleman's *Free Jazz*. Both surely challenged the large number of people introduced to jazz by this collection, but such music excised from the later version of the term.

[89] To take the word back to its roots, when applied to artists and to art, "classical" originates in 2nd century A.D. Rome, and referred to writers assessed in the highest tax bracket, as distinguished from the proletarians on the bottom, and so was a mark of class status and official recognition. "Classic Jazz" does express the wish of some to ennoble the music above the messy history of a music made by proletarians. Art distinguished as "high" still connotes the class to which it is thought to belong, no matter how much it may appropriate from those below.

[90] See the chapter by Christopher Washburne, "Does Kenny G Play Bad Jazz?: A Case Study" in *Bad Music: The Music We Love to Hate* [2005]. If jazz still provokes open conflict it is here. Most recently, Kenny G raised the hackles of Coltrane lovers by being invited to the 2016 International John Coltrane Jazz and Blues Festival.

[91] "So if you have the very elite avant garde, which a lot of what they play I don't consider to be jazz, it's more improvised music... you'll always have that, you had that before form. And a lot of people are mistaken by thinking that that's an advance." Marsalis in 2002, as quoted in *Jazz Times* http://jazztimes.com/articles/20520-wynton-marsalis-one-future-two-views

[92] The opening shot of the rebuttal to Marsalis that came from academic circles was in 1991, Scott DeVeaux, "Constructing the Jazz Tradition," reprinted in Robert G. O'Meally, *The Jazz Cadence of American Culture*, p. 483-512.

[93] The charge of recuperation intends to expose how capitalism re-purposes what it can of artistic avant-gardes as consumer items, allowing apologists of capitalism to argue that it thereby

becomes increasingly and inevitably more enlightened. It is for this reason that many today working outside the art marketplace avoid advertising themselves as avant-garde. The language used to indicate it is commonly used to market only media-approved work. Using it, they would appear to consent to terms alien to their work. On recuperation, see the introduction to McDonough, Tom ed., *Guy Debord and the situationist international: texts and documents* [2002].

94 This is the melancholic dream of Mackenzie Wark, in "The Avant-garde Never Gives Up" (Source online, see Wark in References.) Many on the cultural left today would agree with this positive take on recuperation: "I think of those who struggled in the avant-gardes of the past as comrades. One day, when I am dead too, I will join them in that past which was one endless attempt to make some present time other than this one. Some present where art and life might meet." He goes on to say that times have changed; those who identify themselves as avant-garde need to take a step back from confrontation. The response to cooptation is to close ranks and create "consistency": "As the horizon closes, perhaps the comrades who carry on in solidarity with the historic avant-gardes no longer see ourselves as disrupting, subverting, or rebelling, as those are now the slogans of the ruling class. Maybe our work is quite the opposite, a matter of creating zones of a certain consistency, endurance, commonality. Maybe in this pure war world we are the conscientious objectors." Wark is the author of the popular *A Hacker Manifesto*, and considers (avant-garde) artists to be in "the hacker class" of rebels.

95 Listen for instance to the revealing musing of William Parker looking back: "What happens to a cutting-edge musician when the edge is no longer sharp? When the cries for freedom, clusters [on piano], tone runs, and polyrhythms wear out, after 40 years of struggle in the music business we find ourselves in the same spot. Every music seems to have superseded "Great Black Music." The question is, will our day ever come?" *Who Owns Music* [2006]

96 All this is easier to see from a distance. Derek Bailey, the British guitarist who will figure prominently in later chapters, was active in the sixties, working with jazz musicians who were exploring beyond its presumed limits, including some Americans. By 1991 he perceived the transformation I have described, which he expressed in a revision to his book of the 70s: "The revolution that was free jazz is long over and a process variously described as maturing, retrenchment, rationalization, consolidation—all the usual euphemisms for a period of stagnation and reaction—has turned much of free jazz into a music as formal, as ritualized and as un-free, as any of the music against which it rebelled. Like the rest of jazz it now seems to have very little existence outside the perennial festivals at which it presents its stars demonstrating whatever it was that made them stars. But in these situations free jazz seems to fulfil a somewhat peripheral role and has never managed to integrate in any way with the main body of jazz which, after first greeting the free development with scorn and vituperation, has ever since contrived to ignore it." *Improvisation* [rev. ed. 1991], p. 56. Bailey goes on to speak at length of "black classical music" in even harsher terms, as assimilated to "white classical music," and its "retreat into academicism that, quoting Ellington, 'stinks the place up.'" Yet he singles out many who had become iconic for both jazz and free jazz, placing them far above and distinct from the fate of their genres--Steve Lacy, Cecil Taylor, and Max Roach.

97 Christian egalitarianism, invisible today, is far removed from the secular professional meritocracy, whose purpose is functionality and not redemption. The sanctified church had cultural influence beyond its specific faithful, and was a component of jazz just as much as secular modernism and commercial entertainment.

98 The reference to action painting goes back to Harold Rosenberg's coining of the term in 1952 (collected in his *The Tradition of the New* [1959]), which refers to painting as a confrontive event in

the studio of abstract expressionists, in particular Willem De Kooning. To Rosenberg these painters were metaphorical bullfighters in the arena, attacking the canvas and thereby fulfilling their passion in the spontaneous and dangerous male act. This image fit well with the postwar visual arts faced with the traumatic violence of WWII and guilt over the American dropping of the A-bomb, to which all their art tended to be a response (including John Cage's quietism). Action painting, grounded in the relation between spontaneity, modernist resistance to society, and popular existentialism of the period (the individual must decide to take action), bears upon the origins of Free Jazz. In fact, Rosenberg's essay appeared in book form the same year that Ornette Coleman recorded Free Jazz, whose cover was a Jackson Pollock "drip" painting.

[99] There was also Norbert Eisbrenner, guitarist, whose groupings with drummer Sven-Ake Johansson also had a collective character.

[100] In Denver I heard Peter Brotzmann perform a solo in the early 90s, beginning with a strong lyrical thread that approached a concrete melody, then building to a huge, sonorous climax as if released from that cage, followed by a return to the quieter melodic beginning. It dawned on me that this was classical in form: exposition, development, recapitulation, also found in some of his recorded solos.

[101] The information of this section is mostly from Mike Heffely, *Northern Sun, Southern Moon* [2005], based on his translations of extensive German texts, which make his book indispensable for Anglophone readers. For more on the political stakes involved in German Free Jazz and its funding, see Andrew Wright Hurley, *The Return of jazz: Joachim-Ernst Berendt and West German Cultural Change* [2009]

[102] For a list of invitees see http://www.fmp-label.de/freemusicproduction/projekteindex.html

[103] I witnessed this at the 1983 Wuppertal and Berlin festivals. The audience paralleled my own sixties New Left generation, had they taken Free Jazz as representing their spirit. Their uniform black dress code seemed fit for a mourning, and their presence was a statement to each other: the struggle continues!

[104] One current example is Tommy L. Lott, "When Bar Walkers Preach" pp. 99-122, in Leonard L. Brown, *John Coltrane and Black America's Quest for Freedom* [2010]

[105] "There is never any end. There are always new sounds to imagine, new feelings to get at. And always, there is the need to keep purifying these feelings and sounds so that we can really see what we've discovered in its pure state. So that we can give those who listen to the essence, the best of what we are." Coltrane, from the liner notes to *Meditations*, 1966), quoted op. cit., p. 105. Most of his interviews don't have this quality, which feels like his fully thought-out philosophy, where he had time to articulate himself adequately.

Chapter 5. The Situation for Jazz-based Music

[106] Those most aware today of the pressure to commoditize their work are not musicians but writers. And they say it, for instance Sarah Manguso: "the threat of writing to an audience becomes only more present a danger as time passes and renown increases." *Free Radicals: American Poets before their First Books* [2004], p. iv. For musicians a career is impossible without media renown, whereas writers can become even best sellers (such as David Shields, the source of the Manguso quote) *on account of* their non-fictional investigation of their problematic situation. Music is closest to poetry, never literally true as non-fiction claims to be. What gets expressed in writing *about* music (at least its commercial forms, such as free jazz) only embraces and reinforces the fiction necessary to build visibility and sustain sales.

[107] "Rock must constantly change to survive; it must seek to reproduce its authenticity in new forms, in new places, in new alliances...transforming what had been authentic into the inauthentic in order to constantly project its claim to authenticity.'" Philip Auslander, *Liveness: Performance in a Mediatized Culture* [2008], p. 83, quoting Lawrence Grossberg. This ignores the backlash against the dilution of rock when it found its way into all music, like the reaction of jazz aficionados to everything getting jazzed up in the 20s. Punk has followed the same scenario; when everything has to be punk the loyalists are offended. Hard core was not progressive, not an effort to keep rock alive with new ideas, but back-to-basics of guitar/bass/drums, stripping their music of much that technology and commerce had made possible for rock. Its strength was rebellion, something the jazz world had been more successful in shutting out of the market than rock.

[108] Contemporary Art normally refers not to art made by the vast number of contemporary artists but to art claimed to bear the most advanced truth of our civilization (the current world order) *and* is backed up by that order's most powerful institutions.

[109] For instance, Louis Armstrong, on listening back for the first time to the recording of his "West End Blues" of 1928.

[110] In the film "Imagine the Sound" [1981] Archie Shepp speaks of the first time he could "identify" his sound, which he said was "intrinsic" to him. This discovery was necessary "so that I could repeat it each time I played," where he slips into a more rational-pragmatic mode.

In general, the filmmaker chose to examine the more traditional and secular-modernist first wave of Free Jazz—Shepp, Bill Dixon, Paul Bley, and Cecil Taylor--rather than the second. Shepp had been caught between the two and eventually repudiated the second, as earlier recounted. Taylor became the most lauded figure of the fiery side of the Free Jazz period, though his poetry, dance, clear articulation on the piano, and musings on art are more continuous with the first wave than the second. More than any other he negotiated between the two and was accordingly criticized from both sides, as too orderly (European classical, intellectual) and too excessive (clusters on the piano and physicality).

[111] This information came from my horn repairman in Philadelphia, George Sarkis, who said every time Parker came through he had a different horn, which he attributed to Parker regularly selling his horn for drug money.

[112] The basic concept of signifyin' was put forward by Henry Louis Gates, Jr., *The Signifying Monkey: A Theory of African-American Literary Criticism* [1988].

[113] For instance, Parker interviewed in 1954 by Paul Desmond and radio announcer John McClellan http://www.plosin.com/MilesAhead/BirdInterviews.html#540100

[114] "Crazy" became a line in the sand through the early 70s, though the valuation was often reversed. While for Ginsberg the crazies were the true individuals, and the anti-psychiatry movement located sanity among those society labeled crazy, a public intellectual like Paul Goodman would call society crazy (*Growing up Absurd*). The epithets hurled at artists as titles meant to ridicule them, like Cubism and Fauvism (both from critic Louis Vauxcelles), indicate the specific fears of the mass public ("fauve" means "wild beast"). The artists then took a certain pride in being scorned, indeed it drew an audience that shared or identified with what was outside normative society. Without this dynamic it is hard to imagine artists ever coming to recognition by upsetting others, the thread of the Modernist/avant-garde narrative. It required a different arrangement than today, when pluralism disavows scorn on the ground that there is a place for every aesthetic, with negation in the hands of the curator and her unseen reject pile.

[115] Paul Bley (with Norman Meehan), *Time Will Tell: Conversations with Paul Bley* [2003], p. 73. The instance Bley mentions was in 1963, when for professionals, sitting in could easily be an audition and not just for fun.

[116] Kofsky, *Black Nationalism and the Revolution in Music* [1970], p. 38

[117] Tim Hodgkinson's recent book *Music and the Myth of Wholeness – Toward a New Aesthetic Paradigm* [2016] has come to my attention too late to include. From reading Howard Slater's review, "Sound Changes Sense," it might be relevant if that critique of wholeness can be applied to the artist ego, what I've called the musician persona). http://www.metamute.org/editorial/articles/sound-changes-sense

[118] The "permanent avant-garde" is a phrase of jazz historian John Szwed (biographer of Sun Ra), (cited in Gennari, *Blowin' Hot and Cool* [2006], p. 357)

[119] Baudrillard: "It is in this way, under the pretext of saving the original, that the caves of Lascaux [in which paleolithic paintings had been found] have been forbidden to visitors and an exact replica constructed 500 meters away, so that everyone can see them…It is possible that the very memory of the original caves will fade in the mind of future generations, but from now on there is no longer any difference: the duplication is sufficient to render both artificial…We need a visible past, a visible continuum, a visible myth of origin to reassure us as to our ends, since ultimately we have never believed in them." *Simulations* [1983], p. 18-20. As another analyst puts it, "How can art be the bearer of new values, when reality becomes an aesthetic hallucination?"

[120] Ishmael Reed's *To Write is to Fight* (specifically, racism) appeared just as the free jazz revival was about to begin, 1988, and the struggle was reshaped in terms that have continued to today. In the current cultural duality of conservationist tradition and cutting-edge avant-garde, "sustainability" would help to assimilate survivalism to the wider social-betterent goal.

[121] "The dead remain in danger. Of being sacrificed to the needs of the audience." Walter A. Davis, *Deracination: Historicity, Hiroshima, and the Tragic Imperative* [2001], p. 235. To speak of a period of concentrated musical creativity is valid, but a golden age is an abstraction that lops off what doesn't fit. "Back then giants roamed the earth" — the myth of a golden age was Homer's, and only major social change and the Greek philosophers would create a new one. Today's version presumes that the principle actors were putting on a show for us, when in fact they were living for themselves and performing for those who were themselves in motion. Every present is living for itself, but when it substitutes those golden others it obscures the present to those present. The real is hidden in the shadowed darkness, one of whose names is the unconscious.

[122] "Is *jazz* as we know it *dead*?" is spoken in mockery by Roscoe Mitchell on his and the Chicago Art Ensemble's *Congliptious* album. He put these words in the mouth of the critic and listener who confuses change with death. The album was released in 1968, at the tail end of the active avant-garde period, when what Ornette had promised had amassed a small corps of musicians behind it. In these titles we can see the Chicagoans committed to and continuing the challenge of the New Yorkers, though in the Art Ensemble's more compositional and performance-oriented approach, similar to Sun Ra's Arkestra. Possibly, since live NY Free Jazz rarely escaped NYC, more people heard it in the free jazz sections of their compositions performed on tour in the US than directly from the originators.

[123] By artist here I mean those whose lives are centered on actually making art, music, literature, etc., which excludes those who have become mainly producers, technicians, critics, teachers, and managers of the music world. Artists accept that the division of work and leisure cannot be overcome, and prefer their artistic work to be done in the time normally called leisure so as to keep it free of the usefulness that work demands and compensates. And a collectivity is interac-

271

tive and substantial over time, not an online list, such as Occupy Musicians. http://www.occupymusicians.com/. The preponderance there is people whose main life focus is the music world. That's fine for what it is, but it's not a collectivity of artists, and engages them for no more than a few seconds.

[124] That jazz education has been instrumental in the transformation of jazz is outside the scope of this study, but here is a tentative sketch. To my knowledge free jazz is not taught in schools, although most post-70s free jazz musicians have been initially trained there to be straight-ahead players, and don't perceive their breakaway as rebellion. The parade of Free Jazz musicians into teaching beginning around 1970 aided the shift of Black Nationalism from revolutionary project to American Dream (Black Studies programs). Both came just as jazz education was becoming a university investment, eventually educating future audience as well. The decline of jazz's commercial appeal in the late 60s, allowed the institutions to take it over as its own project. It rationalized the structure within which jazz would operate and, preparing the musicians that would populate Classic Jazz, would control the content. The trajectory of school-performance (briefly)-teaching has become the norm, with mentorship integrated into the program and master classes on which many still-performing musicians depend for income.

[125] "What has happened is that aesthetic production today has become integrated into commodity production generally: the frantic economic urgency of producing fresh waves of ever more novel-seeming goods (from clothing to airplanes), at ever greater rates of turnover, now assigns an increasingly essential structural function and position to aesthetic innovation and experimentation." Frederik Jameson, *Postmodernism, or, The Cultural Logic of Late Capitalism*, [1991] p. 4-5. True enough, but in the decades since this statement we've seen that aesthetic innovation manufactured to order (its "structural function") has little in common with its earlier models.

[126] One reference I've heard to this was in the NPR promotion for a blitz of Philadelphia concerts of free jazz musicians in June 2014, mostly well known to musicians but not to the upscale NPR public. The title possibly resulted from a decision to give free jazz a facelift by associating it with more legitimate art music rather than the more uncomfortable Dionysian, cultic image it has had.

[127] Joe Maneri Quartet, *Coming Down the Mountain*, [1997]

[128] *Perpetual Frontier: The Properties of Free Music* [2012], p. 3

[129] My categories here are partly inspired by Stephen Frosh, *Identity Crisis: Modernity, Psychoanalysis and the Self* [1991] and by the work of Walter A. Davis cited earlier. I feel tentative about this section but, for the sake of our present situation gripped in fear, it is worth trying to comprehend the relation of art, culture and psyche in their historical shifts.

[130] Hard right Republican Sen. Barry Goldwater was emblematic of the era, even prophetic. The phrase of his nominating speech in the summer of 1964 that rang a bell for many (including myself) was "Extremism in defense of liberty is no vice!…and moderation in the pursuit of justice is no virtue!" Malcolm X, whose concept of liberty and justice was far from Goldwater's, could have said something like this. Such a coincidence of opposites is the very nature of the psyche in periods of traumatic confrontation but is unsettling to normal political reasoning.

[131] In *Imagine the Sound* [1981] Bill Dixon affirmed that identity, which he struggled his whole life to maintain: "A jazz musician is a social category. It tells you who you are and what you are capable of doing, how you should do it, and what kind of money you should be getting." The public intellectual, Paul Goodman, never failed to admonish us critics in the sixties to uphold professionalism, for it was based on standards that could speak truth to power. What it relied on however was a social respect already in decline, a shift in the psyche towards a relativist, subjec-

tive truth initiated by postwar poetry and literature, which many of the radicals imported into the political, journalistic, and academic sphere.

Chapter 6. British Free Improvisation

[132] David Borgo, *Sync or Swim: Improvising Music in a Complex Age* [2005], p. 3

[133] The fact is important to remember since later the distinction between the British and German directions yielded a greater musical division. This is evident in Mike Heffely's *Northern Sun, Southern Moon: Europe's Reinvention of Jazz* [2005], the most comprehensive book in English for German free jazz. Wanting to defend free music as the reincarnation of jazz, Heffely reduces the British direction to an anomaly. He devotes only two out of 440 pages to English improvisation, with individual improvisers, notably Evan Parker and Derek Bailey, mainly viewed in relationship to continental players. In his view the German version of improvised music is the sole model, including a brief chapter on all other national groupings as of subordinate interest. They would then be included in the German *Emanzipation,* which Heffely calls "pan-European," while implying it was unified under German leadership rather than merely its influence. By contrast, written about the same time, Ben Watson's *Derek Bailey and the Story of Free Improvisation* [2004] makes no such broad European claims for Bailey's version of improvised music.

We need to remember that improvised music originated among a generation still feeling the effect of a disastrous European war. It is doubtful that the German musicians themselves, whose leftist generation sought to expose hidden Nazism, would be inclined to assert dominance for specifically German music in Europe. On the British side, resentment of their defeated enemy's economic growth, aided by American policies, compared to their own would have discouraged the Brits from welcoming a German musical invasion. Even without this, the blustery Sturm und Drang that came through strongly in German free jazz did not appeal to the British sensibility, though they produced milder versions.

[134] For this and some of the following I rely on Watson's interviews with Bailey and others (op. cit.). Watson updates and elaborates Bailey's *Improvisation* [1975 and 1992] with interviews with him as well as others associated with him. (Another useful interview is in John Corbett, *Extended Play* [1994]. Many others scattered around). The most detailed published information so far on other British free improvisers is John Tilbury's biography, *Cornelius Cardew, A Life Unfinished* [2008]. Tilbury is himself among the early improvisers and a member of the group AMM. Also, saxophonist Seymour Wright has written a Ph.D. thesis, unpublished, "The Group Learning of an Original Creative Practice: 1960s Emergent-AMM" which should be of interest as the major alternative to Derek Bailey's approach. http://seymourwright.com/#thesis) There is also a worthwhile chapter in George McKay's *Circular Breathing: The Cultural Politics of Jazz in Britain* [2005].

[135] Adorno, "Vers une musique informelle" in *Quasi Una Fantasia* [1992]. The French does not translate as "informal music" but refers to works that have their own individual form and do not participate in a form considered universal and valid for the most serious music, as the sonata form once was. His concept was consistent with his earlier analysis of Arnold Schoenberg's atonal work around 1910, which he said "denies the claim that the universal [the conventional form] and the specific are reconciled." *Philosophy of Modern Music* [1973], written in 1941, p. 40. Attention to the musical "work" as an historical concept is drawn by Lydia Goehr, *The Imaginary Museum of Musical Works* [1991], which largely ignores Adorno and the challenge to it.

[136] It is tempting to see a parallel with post-structuralism (whose public, or at least academic impact on American academe is usually dated 1967, around the same time as the British improvisers.) The task of structuralism was determinist, to perceive how cultural meanings are fixed in relation to an overarching social structure, a long-term goal of sociology to create truth following scientific standards of an unchanging Nature. Musicologists were structuralist in presuming that musical meaning was fixed within a homeostatic system of tonality and equal-temperament. Accordingly, close analysis of the text (the score) would allow reduction of the musical meaning to its analysis, apart from the affective experience of actually listening to the music. Deconstruction was the term given to the dismantling of such fixed meaning of texts. It was based on linguistic analysis that spoke of the "floating signifier." The relation of a word and its meaning would depend on differences between words rather than direct expression of essential meanings. Similarly free improvisation detached a sound from the meaning inscribed within the socially understood context of a musical form; sounds related to each other differentially rather than having a given, essential meaning. There was no way that structural analysis of an afternoon of free playing could be boiled-down to a musicological analysis from which the playing could be reconstructed.

There is an implication here (as well as in linguistic deconstruction) for proper social and vocational roles as well, specifically the musician-role. In the western conception, authentic art music is created strictly by those who can be defined as composers. Free improvisation opposed exclusive composer determination of musical meaning, which it put in the hands of each individual player and grouping. Since that time the issue has died, partly because the best known improvisers developed overall recognizable styles, a substitute for the aesthetic unity of compositions and composers' oeuvres. However, since they are technically free to ignore their given style they are unreliable for analysis and judgment, and subordinated among the far larger number structurally oriented, who can be relied upon. Furthermore, the musician as a social role that provides a needed category of culture has been undermined by the greatly weakened economic position of most professionals and the huge rise of non-career players, as we shall see.

[137] See Phillip Auslander, *Performance in a Mediatized Culture* [2008], Ch. 3, "Tryin' to Make it Real"

[138] Relating to the metaphor of factory production, in the words of Ben Watson, Bailey's approach was that of an "avant-garde from below—permanent revolution on the part of the working musician against all modes of management and crowd control, delighted evasion of the embrace of the fame-machine spectacle and its doubtful rewards, insistence on the quality of musical co-operation and absoluteness of listener attention at all times..." *Adorno for Revolutionaries* [2011] p. 49

[139] I remember this review because at the time I was on the German, free jazz side of improvised music, and "depersonalized" confirmed my musical distance from the Brits, including Bailey. For me this word conformed to the high art modernism of the poet T.S. Eliot, who in his famous essay of 1919, "Tradition and the Individual Talent" argued that the poem "is not an expression of personality but an escape from personality," which would include the expression of strong emotion. (*Selected Prose of T.S. Eliot* [1975]). By the early eighties critics still flagged Free Jazz as offensive, and I believe that Parker functioned for the reviewer as a relief from it, and perhaps also from the contemporary but lesser known Germans. Academia's attraction to Eliot in the fifties, a refusal of spontaneous emotive expression, was in part the fear of so-called mass hysteria, the rabble Edmund Burke warned against, and what scared them about both rock 'n roll fans *and* Senator McCarthy. The then-recent memory of excited Germans gone amuck was for much

of the liberal middle class homologous to the suppressed memory of contagious Negro slave uprisings that Free Jazz aroused, supposedly unable to control their emotions. The reviewer, I believe, saw Parker as saving us from all that.

Parker himself said his signature style was a response to a specific musical situation, and was nothing personal (compared to an Albert Ayler, for instance): "[Hugh Davies and Derek Bailey's] use of controlled feedback in order to sustain pitches indefinitely made it essential for me to develop the circular breathing technique. Once I had this technique under control it led to the approach which made solo playing attractive." James Saunders, *The Ashgate Companion to Experimental Music* [2009], p. 333.

Chapter 7. Free Improvisation in North America in the 80s

[140] The most lengthy investigation to date is Tom Nunn, *Wisdom of the Impulse: On the Nature of Free Improvisation* [1998], which focuses on the musical practice rather than the concrete historical community of players. Online, see Nunn in References. Nunn is a long-time improviser, instrument builder, and part of the Bay Area community of improvisers. Some excerpts are in Davey Williams' review in *The Improvisor*, http://the-improvisor.com/The_Wisdom_ofthe_ Impulse.htm. Also, two excellent intros to free improv by improvisers active from 80s to the present: Davey Williams' own book, *Solo Gig: Essential Curiosities in Musical Free Improvisation* [2011] and *Music as Adventure: The Collected Writings of Wally Shoup*, [2011] online

[141] For his initiation he was told not to bring his guitar, so he played saxophone, which he didn't know how to play. "What was really happening was these sessions - they called it Headache Music: what it amounted to was a really cathartic improvisation, informed by American free jazz and so forth." http://craignutt.com/raudelunas/russell/fredlane/davey williams.html Williams sent a tape of his and Ladonna's music to Evan Parker, who sent him a copy of *Musics*, with a strong link to an organization of players, the London Musicians Collective. These were inspirations for Davey, his partner Ladonna Smith's, and other improvisers' projects. (All issues of that magazine are now available: *Musics: A British Magazine of Improvised Music & Art* [2016])

[142] Fine's playing was close to my own at the time. It was pure accident that I found an album of his in the branch library around the corner in 1981. But motivated seekers latch onto contingent events as god-sends. I got in touch with him and in a few years we met in Minneapolis.

[143] I'd heard of free improvisation in the UK from a friend in London who sent me *Musics* in 1978, but I wasn't ready to connect that with what I was doing. I thought I was playing music but not a *kind* of music.

[144] From *Bells*, 1978, http://bells.free-jazz.net/bells-part-two/john-gruntfest/. The festival began in 1977. Henry Kuntz (a saxophonist and free improviser) published *Bells* from 1973-78. East Coast improvisers at least knew the Bay Area was home to a large free improv interest.

[145] Correspondence with Davey Williams, June, 2014.

[146] As late as the mid-80s John Zorn was still the weird, underground clarinetist, performing at a small Philadelphia concert attended by a few improvisers in 1983, where I saw him. And in 1982, when the Philadelphia audience expected to hear free improv from Eugene Chadbourne, he played his songs instead, with the explanation that he had a family to support and free improv was not doing anything to help. He was surely right about that.

[147] "Downtown" is both a musicological and geographical distinction. "Uptown" music, also called "academic," referred to serialist and other European-oriented composers whose scores were to be traditionally performed. The reference was to the upper west side, where Columbia

University and the Julliard School of Music were located. There was also Midtown, the Lincoln Center at 66th St., a stronghold of traditional Classical Music and later Classic Jazz. Downtown referred to those in the bohemias of West and East Village and just below Houston St., who were considered more radical compared to Uptown, and more likely composer-performers. None of these were sustained by the marketplace (until Downtown Minimalism hit its popular stride in the later 70s), but Uptown could count on steady institutional support, while Downtown musicians exploited the media-attractive panache of nose-thumbing artist-rebels, which then included the minimalist, Philip Glass. George Lewis has made a useful distinction between "Downtown I" of the post-Cage composers like the minimalists, and "Downtown II," what I call the popular avant-garde, and of venues such as the Knitting Factory (1987), which *were* market-dependent. (Lewis, *A Power Stronger Than Itself* [2008], p. 331)

[148] Free improvisation has possibly been more attractive to women than any other purely instrumental contemporary music (voice is treated as an instrument rather than conveyer of verbal meaning). This probably has to do with its open approach and novelty—there was no tradition of musician exclusion and hierarchy, as in the NY jazz and classical scenes. Although the hard-driving free jazz present in free improv could easily be associated with masculinity, improv was open to other options.

[149] As another example, when I was told in the mid-70s that if I was serious about music I'd have to go to music school, I thought the idea was a leftover from the fifties and no longer valid. Little did I know it would return as the basic requirement for careers.

[150] I estimate it cost about a quarter of my annual income as a handyman to put out my album in 1983 (back when livin' was easier).

[151] A chapter in Nancy Uscher's *Your own way in music: a career and resource guide* [1990] is actually titled "A Record can be your calling card," and she does refer to it as a singular product. As for reaching out, I was not alone in seeking partners among sixties Free Jazz musicians. Along with the cassettes I sent to them I said, "Please just listen to the music." I was convinced that their ears would recognize we were on the same path, but not yet aware that what I was playing was exactly what they were trying to get away from.

[152] I was most active in Philadelphia, where funded venues acted as guardians of the middle class art public's musical interest, the continuing tradition there. They balked at presenting a form of playing they considered illegitimate as music, especially coming from local musicians, who by virtue of their residence were not considered serious artists.

In our search for less discriminating venues, at times pure deception worked. In 1982 my Spring Garden Music group got a gig at a small Philly diner because the bass player had made friends with one of the staff on the basketball court, without revealing the nature of our music. As soon as we played all but one of the customers left, and eventually we took pity on the owner. The one who stayed started dancing; he was a young German guy looking for adventure. As an incipient saxophonist he soon became one of us, moved into the Spring Garden Music house, and became my major partner through the 80s—Andreas (now Max) Stehle, now living in Berlin, playing again, and organizing sessions and performances of both career and non-career players.

[153] In fact it could only have been possible after the death of the last avant-garde (in the tradition of earlier European organizations), which the Situationist International has often been called, and which ended in 1971. The SI's resistance to the spectacle could be extended to those artists the media valued as representing the culture.

[154] An article by John Rockwell in the *NY Times*, Dec. 22, 1985, "What Happened to Our Vanguard?" illustrates the situation. The "vanguard creative scene" recognized both by the *Times* and the *Village Voice* consisted of funded projects like New Music America, the Kitchen, and the "prestigious, trendy showcase" of the Next Wave Festival. This was basically the Downtown Scene (both I and II), some of which was presented in the Brooklyn Academy of Music, just over the East River. Those considered "struggling vanguard" artists were Philip Glass, Laurie Anderson, and the Talking Heads. "All we need for a renewal of new music here will be one or two commanding young composers, plus two or three farsighted young (or maybe not so young) critics, three or four bold funders and presenters and club-owners, and a new, fashionable audience." The message here is that true art is scarce; to pick out the most promising and promote the hell out of them is the music world's job.

[155] No recordings of performances that I know of are publicly available but rather a studio compilation and mix, released on vinyl in 1988 with 22 players, *Exquisite Corpses from the Bunker*. After the anarchist tenants were evicted in 1990 the music series went wandering in search of a home for several years.

[156] To trace the shift of meaning from hippie to postmodern it is well to begin with the former in its original setting of cultural rebellion. See Julie Stephens, *Anti-Disciplinary Protest: Sixties Radicalism and Postmodernism* [1998].

[157] Jim Meneses compiled and published a one-issue "The Wet Spot Magazine" after the venue closed. The Painted Bride later relented and presented two performances of local improvisers, but thereafter returned to its regular fare.

[158] By my count, based on fourteen North America tours from 1984-1989 there were seventy towns or cities where I found it possible to perform. New England: Besides Boston and NYC they were Providence, Hartford, New Haven, Worcester, Brattleboro VT, Buffalo, Rochester, Syracuse, Toronto, a major center in its own right, and Montreal. South of New England there was Philadelphia, Pittsburgh, Allentown, Baltimore, DC, Richmond VA, Greensboro NC, Chattanooga, Atlanta, Birmingham, New Orleans; Tallahassee, Gainesville, Miami, and Tampa FL. In the Midwest Cleveland, Kent, Yellow Springs, Cincinnati, Detroit, Ann Arbor, Fort Wayne, Bloomington IN; in IL, Chicago, DeKalb, Bloomington, Springfield, Champaign; Sioux City IA, Ames IA, Iowa City, Madison, Milwaukee, Minneapolis, St. Louis, Kansas City, Columbia MO, Lawrence KS, Lincoln, Minneapolis. In the southwest San Antonio, Austin, Dallas, Houston, Tulsa, Norman OK, Santa Fe, Albuquerque, Phoenix. In the West: Boulder CO, Denver, Salt Lake City, LA, Santa Barbara, San Diego, and the Bay Area: SF, Berkeley and Oakland. Later I got to Eugene, Portland OR, and Seattle.

[159]The publications I knew were *Sound Choice*, *Option* (West Coast), Brian Baker's *Gajoob* (Salt Lake City), *Factsheet Five* (Rensselaer NY), and *News of Music* (Bard College), but many more can be found in Robin James, ed. *Cassette Mythos* [1992]

[160] I myself judged most cassettes harshly. Yet once, on my way out the door for a tour, I grabbed a bag of cassettes I'd marked for the trash. As I slipped one after another into the player, without identifying the musicians (like today, many obscure musicians don't clearly label their product), I was entranced—great stuff! Their very anonymity prevented me from judging them by any aesthetic standard, a tricky business.

[161] Generally, "underground" will refer to musical forms not promoted in the mainstream press, and the collectivity of dedicated performers, and not to individuals who are merely overlooked. Much alternative or left culture today has its own media, selective for what fits the image of underground rebellion it shapes and promotes. Like the media that targets a broader demographic, it attracts those equally ambitious for attention, for whom the label "underground"

connotes acceptance into the halls of authentic radicalism. (Is there an "authentic" that some media has not authenticated?)

162 Ian MacKay of Minor Threat from the movie, *American Hardcore* 2006. Also, from Dicky Barrett in that movie, "The less it was a song the more we loved it." That is close to free improv but still tied to the song form, without which there could be no rebellion against it. Improv was no such public rebellion because there was no public for it. As a scene, hardcore had to make its point to those who needed and followed it, whereas free improv, strictly a musician community without much potential audience, was not interacting with a hungry audience.

163 Angela Rodel, "Extreme Noise Terror: Punk Rock and the Aesthetics of Badness," *Bad Music: The Music we Love to Hate*, op. cit., p. 253, fn. 23

164 For a time that claim was published in liner notes for music with merely a spirit of spontaneity or excess. This indicates the widespread use of the title, which ignored those for whom it had a more specific meaning, as it does today.

165 Coming out of my earlier engagement in radical politics, I felt improv was an implicit threat. I put it this way in 1986: "What does spontaneity have to do with this social order, with any social order, with the order of our self-socialized minds. ...Our mind moves by regret, shame, erasure, over its landscape. The contingent drifts into gray abstraction as we look towards The Model for guidance...Free improvisation is, in its idea of itself, the only music that is not tragic in this way, not searching for the end, not seeking its perfection, not repeated, not corrected. It stands at the center of music because it is the insecure void between past and future, the void of choice. It puts the immediate human at the center, and that is frightening...etc." "Free Improvisation as a Social Act," online [1986].

166 What follows is by no means a scientific survey of the press but I believe indicative. In *Cadence Magazine*, July 1980, Bay Area saxophonist/improviser Henry Kuntz was given space to reply to a review by Kevin Whitehead, now the well-known NPR jazz critic and writer, who had written about Kuntz' strange-sounding album, *Cross-Eyed Priest*. Kuntz took the reviewer to task for being unable "to 'hear' the music—either on an emotional level or, apparently, even technical," and proceeded to instruct him in detail. Another letter criticized Whitehead for his review of Charlie K. Noyes and Owen Maerck's *Free Mammals*: "All we get is a programmatic accounting of the various sounds on the record and a concluding remark about how all this stuff sounds the same these days." p. 21-22. Apparently the editor, Bob Rusch, took note and found more adequate reviewers for free improv. My record (not nearly so odd as Kuntz's) was reviewed in July 1983 positively—by another improviser and reed player, Milo Fine of Minneapolis, objective and critical of one aspect despite our personal friendship. At the time there was a bridge between consumers attracted to something strange and dismissive reviewers; the former would buy it for the very reason that a reviewer had dissed it.

167 In decline after WWII, Surrealism was renewed by a Danish painter and writer, Asger Jorn and a handful of others (COBRA, 1948-51), who saw themselves opposed to professionalism in visual art. Davey and Ladonna expanded this to non-professional musicians improvising freely. In the mid-70s Davey saw free improv as "surrealist research," " a missing link between automatism and sound-making, such as what was already fundamental to surrealist writing and visual works. That is, the music is a by-production of drawing on the intuition for source material/fuel, with *absolute disregard for what sounds are to be expected, or may be imagined*." (italics. mine)

168 In his 1924 *Manifesto of Surrealism* Andre Breton put automatic writing at the center of Surrealist practice and admired Philippe Soupault, who "opposed any effort to retouch or correct." This is of course implicit in free improvisation. To associate free improv with surrealism, stripped of

Breton's explicit cultural politics, would also put it on the more poetic-license, lighter side of the artistic avant-garde, which showed its face in the sixties.

[169] The first time I witnessed improvised movement and sound together was in the mid-80s in Philadelphia. Performers used the whole room as their space, and their imaginations seemed to expand as they played. They were obviously enjoying themselves, perhaps aided by the small size of the audience and its composition, mostly other improvisers. As for speech, a sizable Austin group I played with, Liquid Mice, did a performance where everyone read a different spiritual text at the same time, making it impossible to follow any one line of thought.

[170] The initiators were Steve Paxton and Nancy Stark Smith, and the journal *Contact Quarterly* was the vehicle of its spread. "Contact" means that some part of one's body is always touching another's. It was through this journal's listing of regular sessions that the dancer Bob Eisen was able to find venues for a tour in 1986 to sixteen cities of the Midwest, many of which I visited on tours later.

[171] http://www.the-improvisor.com/ The project grew out of Leslie Dalaba's newsletter of the Improvisors Network in NY.

[172] Bailey, noting his difference from the more discriminating Tony Oxley in the early days: "I'd play with absolutely anybody who'd turn up [at his Little Theatre gig in London in the later 60s]...What I do is not that precious." Ben Watson, *Bailey* p. 61.

[173] Attali: "The very death of exchange and usage in music...may be bringing about a renaissance. Complex, vague, recuperated, clumsy attempts to create new status for music--*not a new music but a new way of making music*--are today radically upsetting everything music has been up to this point...It is the advent of a radically new form of the insertion of music into communication, one that is overturning all of the concepts of political economy and giving new meaning to the political project." p.134, italics my own.

[174] In 1988 I wrote and circulated a booklet with a piece inspired by Antonin Artaud ("Theatre of the Moment") that dealt with the creative terror of performing a solo that can be literally anything. After finishing it I felt compelled to include a companion piece called "Against Improvisation." In this screed I critiqued the anti-disciplinary spirit, which I felt quickly reached a dead end. It was a dilemma for myself as well, since I didn't know how to combine the spontaneity of improvisation with a thoughtful approach to my own playing. Early in the decade I had asked the question, "What are we free *for*?" and couldn't come up with a satisfying answer.

[175] In a music zine I urged improvisers to experience making music in the wider world by taking their music throughout North America, but there were few takers. "It is good for our music to do it publicly at least some of the time, to get out of the artistic and private ghettoes into places where the results are unpredictable and listeners confused." "Circulate" [*Sound Choice*, 1987] Source online, see Wright in References.

Chapter 8. What Good is Free—An Excursion

[176] For more on "plastic words" see Uwe Poerksen, *Plastic Words: The Tyranny of a Modular Language*[1995]

[177] My mother attended Philadelphia Orchestra concerts in the 20s, and told me that the conductor, Leopold Stokowski, at first programed music chronologically, with contemporary music last. The audience simply walked out, so he reversed the order so they couldn't avoid it. The subject is explored in David Stubbs, *Fear of music: Why People get Rothko but don't get Stockhausen* [2009] Stubbs' quick drive through 20th century art mentions that the BBC programed modernist

music in the late 20s and 30s, thinking it "educative and elevating." To no avail; listeners reject-ed it. Finally the popular press said it was not meant for plain folk. (p. 125-7) Fifty years later postmodern populism would confirm that judgment, excluding that same music from its cata-logue as elitist. In our times music is not supposed to go beyond "a recognizable expression, [when the] chasm between recognition and unfamiliarity is too wide to be overcome by listening activity. The listener feels alienated and abandons his/her engagement." Salome Voegelin, an advocate and practitioner of sound art, as quoted favorably by Linda Kouvaras, *Loading the Si-lence, Sound Art in the Post-Digital Age* [2013] p.46.

[178] This only added to the long history of topsy-turvy mixing, with the low mocking the high (not unlike early jazz) that has roots in the medieval carnival. See Peter Stallybrass and Allon White, *The Politics and Poetics of Transgression* [1986] for the European background on this, devel-oping further the earlier work of Mikhail Bakhtin, the first modern celebrant of the carnival. As for today, artists and art institutions extend their domain by proclaiming the artistic worth of whatever they pluck out of everyday life, a move that seems never exhausted.

[179] Lonce Wyse, "Free Music and the Discipline of Sound" [2004] is the source of some of the following material. For Wyse himself "free music" refers to an emancipation for which technol-ogy is to be thanked. For him it is whatever is not in principle restricted in sound by its source material, which puts it within the broader category of sound art or "all-sound." The audience for 20th century music has lagged behind visual art, allegedly unwilling to accept inevitable pro-gress. He resolves this by positing a "technology gap" that has plagued composers; people would more likely accept avant-garde music if composers had more advanced technical means. For him the problematic public acceptance of avant-garde music is secured by the more inevita-ble advance of technology. This would invalidate any criticism of music presented as advanced, since the composers' limitations have been merely technological and not their fault. Thus it re-tains the authority scholars have conferred on modernist music. This determinism gets him off the postmodern hook of criticizing composers as elitist, more advanced than plebian opinion. Whoever has passed through the eye of critical discourse is then deemed authentically serious. Sounds made by artificial intelligence may be framed as artworks, but the sticky question of affect and reaction is deferred.

[180] Italian industrialization was largely and belatedly imported whole from Northern Europe and so had a far more severe social impact than on its predecessors. This might help explain the commonalty between the most radical Avant-gardes, Italian and Russian Futurism, both indus-trially backward countries.

[181] The above historical information is from Linda Kouvaras, *Loading the Silence* [2013], though largely concerned with Australian music.

[182] "Afrological" and "Eurological" are terms coined by George Lewis, "Improvised Music after 1950: Afrological and Eurological Perspectives" [1996] (Online, see References.) and "After-word" [2004]. They refer to methodological orientations and intentions that highlight the choices and division among musicians from at least the 1920s to today (it was of course jazz that forced the issue). The terms distinguish music from the musician's racial identity, such that each can be played by either white or black musicians. Afrological is not so bound up with identity as what Baraka calls "the black aesthetic," which seems to be something whites can only poorly imitate in their playing. White musicians and audience have obviously been susceptible to the black aesthetic, a social and affective relationship and not just the use of a different structure; other-wise popular music would be inconceivable. Lewis's terms don't deny the uniqueness of jazz improvisation, which is for the most part the creation of black musicians and derived from their

cultural heritage, even if it is more the choice of whites than blacks today. The distinction of Afro- and Eurological is useful for indicating the separated avant-gardes, and especially for how high art musicians (which Lewis calls "pan-European" and not "Western," which privileges France and Britain), have been able to exclude jazz and jazz-derived music from their conception of valid art. The distinction cannot be reduced to pop vs. art or to musicians' different orientation to a public, though these factors are involved as well.

183 Cage, an avid performer himself, was an exception to his own rule, for as a composer-performer he privately admitted to being an improviser. His tour with David Tudor in 1965 "has become an improvisation using a large library of taped material, together with short wave radios, electronic circuits, [phonograph] cartridges, and alarm devises (horns, etc.)." Letter to Edward Downes, July 15, 1965, cited in Benjamin Piekut, *Experimentalism Otherwise*, p. 16 Publicly Cage presented himself as strictly a composer performing his compositions. To admit to improvising would mean that his principles meant less to him in practice. The staged "historic" meeting of the icons in 1986—"out" jazz represented by Sun Ra and the Experimental Music tradition by Cage--was a collaborative fiasco. (If they'd first spent a week working together it might have been fantastic, but that would have spoiled the spectacle.)

184 A photographer who had quit a good job with Life Magazine, Gene Smith, rented a loft in Manhattan in the mid-50s and invited working jazz musicians to hold jam sessions there. Meanwhile he documented them on tape, including conversations, often unknown to the musicians—the whole place was bugged, a preview of the surveillance society. The sessions were neither the cutting contests of known jazz lore nor performances, but had a leisure quality to them. "Getting free" was in contrast to paid work, a chance for musicians to experiment, seen as essential to playing jazz and to the release of private tension. By the time Free Jazz became a known entity these sessions had nearly ceased to attract players, according to a remark of straight-ahead tenor saxophonist Zoot Sims in 1964. I would speculate some causality here--a tightening of jazz conventions due to the division among musicians over the implications and consequences of freeform playing. Jazz was circling its conventional wagons. Besides that, taking "free" into the real world meant a loss of the advantages of its private quality. Sam Stephenson *The Jazz Loft Project* [2009], and now a film as well. Sims' comment is on p. 232. Despite the title, the subject has nothing to do with 70s "loft jazz", which consisted of concerts, not sessions.

185 One of George Lewis' major complaints has been that composition by black musicians, especially when it involves improvisation as well, is a particularly hard pill for the Euro-centered avant-garde to swallow, or, I would add, for anyone with high art aspirations. The Eurological score is a test whether that tradition can admit to its ranks those who are equally comfortable with improvisation, considered in binary fashion to be black aesthetic turf—respected but in a minor league ball park. This is the difficulty for getting recognition and compensation for the Association for the Advancement of Creative Musicians (AACM), of which Lewis is a member.

186 To see it as discontinuous was also the view of the German free jazz musicians, who took this as a *positive* attribute, since it opened the door to their project of an independent, European construction of jazz, the Emanzipation. Also, it was the Germans, more than the French or the Americans, who thought of Free Jazz as a musicological development with significance for their own major tradition, European classical music, which would then presumably heal the Afrological/Eurological split. Heffley [2005]

187 As far as I know, in Philadelphia the black avant-garde first drew a strong following only then. They were particularly students of the more privileged and liberal private institutions—University of Pennsylvania and Haverford College, where there were concert series. That music was not featured at venues drawing from the broader middle class or the older jazz audience.

[188] This is the continuing argument. The 2009 documentary of Frank Scheffer, "In the Ocean: A Film about the Classical Avant Garde," merges the sixties NY Avant-garde (John Cage et al), 70s minimalism, Frank Zappa, and the diversity of all contemporary classical-based composition as a united front. It pleads for one huge, diverse avant-garde and this is it--jazz and other improvised musics are not included. For the iconic composer Steve Reich the motivating conception is avant-garde progress, in the tradition of American-style exceptionalism—we break absolutely with the European past but are loyal to our own. In the film he is the permanent avant-garde rebel, attacking the uptown composers in the present tense as if the sixties Establishment were still in power and blocking him. To him the Uptown composers are imitators of Europeans (whose music he was trained to create, 1958-1963), whom he addresses personally: "That's over now, when will you learn…you don't need that at all." He complains about European compositional avant-garde music as one might reprove Free Jazz: "there's no harmonic center, you couldn't whistle a tune or tap your foot." An avant-garde that includes his own Minimalism would be progressive, as with postmodernism, by becoming popular, with the elite ("you") scorned, not caring if it resonates with the populace.

In the film, diversity, another postmodernism selling-point, turns out to be carefully policed. At a crucial moment of the film pluralism is resolved by the role of curator, the art music-world expert, for whom Brian Eno speaks: "We're swamped by material, so we can appreciate people who can sort out…the group of interesting things that coheres to make one picture. That's what curators do; they 'chunk' culture together." The scrap heap of also-rans demonstrates that the "one picture" is an act of violence. To the few who are selected, the savior of the avant-garde is the hatchet-man of the many that aren't. Those who've bought into the game can't complain. How someone gets represented as *the* avant-garde of music, in this film for instance, is the behind the scenes competitive struggle to get the attention of the power brokers, here dressed up in their usual attractive attire.

[189] See Jason Baskin, "Romanticism, Culture, Collaboration: Raymond Williams Beyond the Avant-garde" [2013]

[190] That was more reasonable as a strategic position when advertised venues excluded any music they could not validate in advance by vetting the musicians' prospectus (description of the pre-structure or recording of what they will be doing) or national/cultural reputation, which was a kind of higher authority. That is of course what any bureaucracy must do if it is responsible and especially if funded and accountable. Otherwise it could be reasonably accused of allowing its space to be taken over by whatever—people with anti-social, psychopathic, criminal intent.

Chapter 9. Derek Bailey's Concept of Free Improvisation

[191]*Improvisation; Its Nature and Practice in Music* [1992] I could find no copy of the original 1975 edition, but some of the additions can be inferred by content.

[192] "…the music itself now seems capable only of looking backwards. Each successive revival sees a further mining of its history and a music once rightly described as 'the sound of surprise' is now chiefly enjoyed as a reminder of yesteryear." Bailey, *Improvisation*, p. 49. The "now" indicates this was an insertion in the 1992 revision, his verdict on Marsalis and his associates.

[193]*Minima Moralia*, [1974], p. 68.

[194] "When I was doing free jazz [before he turned to his theory-based playing called harmolodics] most people thought that I just picked up my saxophone and played whatever was going

through my head, without following any rule, but that wasn't true... People on the outside think that it's a form of extraordinary freedom, but I think that it's a limitation." "Interview with Jacques Derrida" [1997]. Source online, see Coleman in References.

[195] The most frequent reference for this distinction was Michael Nyman, *Experimental Music: Cage and Beyond* [1974]. His point was the superiority of the American over the European orientation. He was in the tradition of earlier Americanist composers, who stressed their national identity.

[196] "It is true that [experimental, avant-garde and free improvisation musics] are very often lumped together but this is probably done for the benefit of promoters who need to know that the one thing they do have in common is a shared inability to hold the attention of large groups of casual listeners...Improvisers might conduct occasional experiments but very few I think, consider their work to be experimental." Regarding the avant-garde, "There are innovations made, as one would expect, through improvisation, but the desire to stay ahead of the field is not common among improvisors. And as regards method, the improvisor employs the oldest in music-making." *Improvisation* p. 83.

[197] "Mankind's first musical performance couldn't have been anything other than a free improvisation"; however it became "a cohesive movement" only in the early sixties. *Improvisation* p. 83-84.

[198] New Music is "dressed in armour which it assumes to be more appropriate to the times. Key words now are retrenchment, repetition, retrospective, revival; other key words are usually preceded by 'neo' or 'post'; overriding all: accessibility." *Improvisation* p. 75.

[199] As far as terms are concerned, Bailey was loose, using "improvisation" for the broad practice in many cultures, yet also when he clearly meant specifically free improvisation. Later he could even dismiss "improvisation": "That's the great thing about improvisation. Or *playing—*'improvisation' has got that heavy sound to it." Interview with John Corbett, *Extended Play* [1996] p. 235. He was often playful rather than constructing a theoretic identity. In 1975 he co-founded the magazine, *Musics*, calling it an impromental experivisation arts magazine."

[200] This would follow the post-structuralist argument that a foundational essence is a fabrication. "Derrida...points out that every mental or phenomenal event is a product of difference, is defined by its relation to what it is not rather than by its essence." Philip Auslander, "Just Be Yourself: Logocentrism and Difference in Performance Theory" in *Acting Reconsidered* [2002], p. 53.

[201] Elsewhere he simply says that freely improvised music "has no stylistic or idiomatic commitment. It has no prescribed idiomatic sound." p. 83.

[202] "Gittin' To Know Y'all" [2004].

[203] Quoted in Ben Watson *Derek Bailey and the Story of Free Improvisation* [2004] p. 265. Note the scare quotes, as with Bailey's "so-called free improvisation," indicating the commonly imprecise, even possibly misleading use of the term.

[204] *Improvisation*, p. 114-115. As in identity politics, identity is a defined category seeking recognition and so tends towards purity. If I call myself a jazz musician only a certain kind of playing will be expected—a yes or no determination. The reality of actual improvisers and their playing does not follow such definitions. Just as Bailey seems to include a large number of players under his formulation (many of whom, as it turns out, reject that inclusion), so he softens the line between those of different identities. "Perhaps this is a good point at which to acknowledge that the world is not divided into improvisors, those who can, and non-improvisers, those who cannot." p. 113.

[205] Lewis argues that it is a stereotype to think jazz is "a body of received, unchanging methods, with hermetically sealed histories," yet that *does* describe its predominant form once Classic Jazz attained institutional acceptance, and not "a fluid, contested, dynamic genre with porous bor-

283

ders," which would rather typify its earlier history (both characterizations are binary exaggerations). What is missing here is a distinction of past and present tense, as in almost all critical jazz writing today. In ignoring concrete historical change (Classic Jazz, educational takeover, etc.) Lewis seems to adhere to the concept of a unified, unchanging essence of jazz, while including what Classic Jazz leaves out. Lewis is here arguing against the absolute historical distinction of free jazz and free improvisation posited by Anne Le Baron, who holds that free improv is part of a progressive postmodernist break, celebrating freedom *from* jazz rather than a more complicated dialectical relationship. In this I would agree more with Lewis. "Gitin' to Know Y'All" [2004]. And Ann Le Baron, "Reflections of surrealism in Postmodern Musics" [2002]

206 *Improvisation*, p. 89. For Carles and Comolli in *Free Jazz/Black Power*, sixties Free Jazz musicians (among whom they include whites, even Bailey) saw things much the same way, so they did not distinguish the British approach. Free Jazz rebelled against fifties jazz, which developed as a consumer choice for a middlebrow audience, especially cool jazz: "the elements that white jazz critics had believed to be specifically attached to all jazz are now systematically unhinged." p.151. The authors argued, along with many black musicians at the time, that "jazz" was a commercial construct that *denied black tradition*, which Free Jazz asserted in a polymorphic form. This directly opposes the later claims of Classic Jazz. Oxley would possibly agree that jazz is a commercial construct, and Free Jazz restored it to its roots, but that would tend to block radical experimentation. Right there is a foretaste of the distinction between the respective legacies of Free Jazz and free improvisation.

207 "...the black cultural nationalist aspect of the Art Ensemble's term, 'Great Black Music,' is often roundly criticized, while the pan-European cultural nationalism of the European free improvisors often remains uninterrogated." Lewis, op. cit. [2004] Lewis' context here is Europe. In the states, by the later 70s young liberal whites were being attracted to the black avant-garde, so its association with cultural nationalism did not hurt their attendance.

208 For a more detailed discussion of German free jazz the Brits see p. 83 ff. above.

209 See footnote 96 for the quote. Additionally, his introduction to the 1992 edition states: "The difference between the present musical climate and that of the mid-1970s...could hardly be greater. Most surveys of the intervening decade and a half tend to be lamentations on the galloping artistic cowardice, shriveled imaginations and self-congratulatory philistinism which typified the period. Other assessors, applauding the strenuous efforts evident in all areas of music to be more 'accessible' speak of a Golden Age. Either way, and significant as they are, the changes that have taken place seem to have made very little difference to improvisation." p. xiii. I assume he means here that the playing had not declined in quality but had remained the same.

Since Bailey's book is widely recognized for understanding improvised music, it is surprising that writers merging current free jazz with free improvisation have overlooked his perception of a radical decline of relation between sixties Free Jazz and resurrected free jazz and his strong judgment against the latter.

210 Lewis [2004]. Paul Helliwell says much the same: for free improvisation to be non-idiomatic "is a modernist argument on music's need to pursue its own formal autonomy. "First Cut is the Deepest," *Metamute* online [2006]

211 This is part of Lewis' argument against *any* distinction between free jazz and free improvisation on the grounds that advocates of the latter deny the historical primacy of jazz—and the significance of the AACM. This essay and his later book is, among other things, a defense of the AACM as representing that unity: "the explanatory power of both the free jazz/free improvisation and the idiomatic/non-idiomatic dialectics rests in large measure upon an erasure from the

history of improvisation of the very group whose work problematizes both dialectics – the AACM. Thus, we find an aporia in the Bailey, [Tom] Nunn, and [Anne] Le Baron texts (and many others) with respect to the AACM as a group..." However, holding different musical interests does not add up to the intention or even the effect of erasing any group from the historical record, including the AACM. Lewis, "Gitin' to Know Y'All" [2004].

[212] Watson [2004] p. 66

[213] Prévost, *Minute Particulars* [2004], p. 15

[214] The 2009 film "(Untitled)" is pertinent here. It satirizes a struggling New York composer (as well as the contemporary visual art game), and includes performances of his music. What is ridiculed is not far from scored compositions that might be expected at an art music event, *or* free improvisation; only the score and conduction by the composer would have to be removed. If one only heard the sound it would be comparable to many offerings of free improv performance. Paper is crumpled, a bucket is kicked, and glass broken, all done with such anxious precision and serious demeanor as to indicate the true object of mockery: the self-importance and seriousness with which the composer takes his work. If someone had bowed a piece of styrofoam the ridicule would even be heightened, yet one improviser, Gino Robair, has made an entire CD of just that.

Satire is directed at something known and recognized, reduced to its barest form and exaggerated. To satirize something so obscure, and widely assumed to be boring and elitist, only requires proper framing, since the music is already ridiculous to the movie audience and can be presented much as it would be in reality. (Improvisers, who can easily forget that the vast majority of the population would judge their music absurd, need to see this film, which was not made for them!) The bass clarinet is played skillfully by an actor whose character, the product of classical training, is especially true to life and not exaggerated. The non-diegetic film score itself is contemporary atonal yet would attract and not repel an audience, making evident the contrast with the parodied lead character as angry, self-indulgent, and resentful of his audience.

In the final performance the composer/conductor, as a sign of his purist scorn for the audience and patron, replaces the score with a new one consisting of nothing but rests. This is clearly a poke at John Cage's 4' 33", a rare dig at this American icon. It is the best known piece of avantgarde music, and the easy butt of jokes for people who know of it and would rather engage music as sound than be given a by now tiresome lesson.

[215] Corbett, *Extended Play* [1996], p. 235.

[216] The title of his first book indicates this: *No Sound is Innocent: AMM and the Practice of Self-Invention: Meta-musical Narratives: Essays* [1995]. American improvisers have generally been unaware of Prévost's writing; his books have been unavailable and his views have not taken root. Americans tend to respect musicians who become distinguished as soloists, whereas Prévost has chosen to present himself mainly as a member of a group, AMM, and has not been even a minor figure in the American press. Moreover, Americans tend to favor descriptive accounts, as Bailey's appears to be, and they avoid overtly prescriptive theory like Prévost's.

Prévost has done more to make improvisation available to non-professionals than anyone, through weekly workshops he has run since 1999 following the principles of AMM. In doing so he has helped to shape the approach of the present generation, taking it in a direction that has differed from Bailey's. He calls his model metamusic: "separate voices speaking at the same time, interweaving and interleaving. But each voice is not atomized or individuated. Paradoxically, it may be that individuality can only exist and develop in a collective context." Bailey [1992], interview with Prévost for the second edition, p. 129.

[217] Paul Helliwell, "First Cut is the Deepest" [2006]

[218] This dilemma led to the criticism raised at the AIM Forum in 1984 (p. 157 above), in which Prévost claimed that publication of Bailey's book gave the impression that the non-idiomatic formulation was an "'agreed objective'" when that was not the case. What's missing here is more detailed information about pressures among the early improvisers to legitimize the whole scene and present a unified concept. That struggle would have occurred when free improvisation had become not just a musician's way of experimenting but a livelihood, affected by relative prestige and the way the spectacle ("avant-garde music") treated it.

[219] I am no specialist, who would have listened to the full range of recordings of the major figures and traced their continuities over decades. However, evidence seems to point in the direction of my statement. For instance, Evan Parker's playing today does not seem to follow from what he said in liner notes to a 1970 recording, that one of the rules of free improvisation for him was "You shall investigate the unfamiliar until it has become familiar.'" (Quoted in Le Baron, "Reflections of surrealism in Postmodern Musics" p. 39). Of course what is unfamiliar can be a slight variation or a startling, perhaps troubling disjuncture.

[220] Bailey, [2004] p. 75-6. Bailey points out that in Zorn's game pieces "rehearsal is a kind of training. There's nothing specific, nobody is told what they should play, but there's a training in how to incorporate the instructions into [the musicians'] playing and an investigation of the possibilities opened up by them." Although Bailey is descriptive here, this would not be his approach, even if he might class it as non-idiomatic.

[221] *Improvisation,* p. 112 "Having no group loyalties to offend and having solo playing as an ultimate resource, it is possible to play with other musicians, of whatever persuasion, as often as one wishes without having to enter into a permanent commitment to any stylistic or aesthetic position. This might be, I think, the ideal situation for an improvisor." Elsewhere: "The essence of improvisation, its intuitive, telepathic foundation, is best explored in a group situation. And the possible musical dimensions of group playing far outstrip those of solo playing." Quoted by Anne LeBaron, "Reflections of Surrealism in Postmodern Musics," *Postmodern Music/Postmodern Thought* [2002], p. 67. It should be noted that a solo gig is often a matter of getting a fee that doesn't have to be split among partners. This isn't mercenary, merely practical, but it doesn't fit the usual music world image of the true artist.

[222] "Free improvisation, in addition to being a highly skilled musical craft, is open to use by almost anyone—beginners, children and non-musicians." *Improvisation,* p. 83. Improv in the UK was early on taken into the schools and private workshops, where improvisers became enthusiastic facilitators of adult and non-musician groups, such as organized by drummer John Stevens. No doubt this increased the audience for concerts. To my knowledge this kind of popularization has not occurred on the Continent, where the artist is more likely a distinct and protected role, enabling them to create art they are confident will be judged authentic. Continental Europeans respect themselves as the more originary home of Art, which the British have access to but are blocked by an egalitarian resistance in their culture to the unquestioned status of the artist. Despite postwar challenges to European cultural hegemony, North American culture is even more removed from the originary source of Art, and also from the rationale of "we ordinary people can create authentic art." The artist of "everyone is an artist," is not the European artist.

[223] Watson, [2004] p. 116

[224] After speaking of the advantage of being "dropped into a slightly shocking situation that you've never been in before," saxophonist Evan Parker said, "the people I've played with longest actually offer me the freest situation to work in." *Improvisation.* p. 128. Here "free" is perhaps not equated with familiarity, but does depend on it.

225 His irritation with the music world sounds like disenchantment. It apparently increased with time, leading to a criticism that dissolved the special musicology of improvisation into just "playing." In his 1992 interview with John Corbett, after substituting "playing" for "improvisation" he said, "Playing is really subversive of virtually everything. So you clamp it down, like the industry's clamped down on it. I mean they don't want improvisation, naturally. You can't make money out of this shit where you don't know what's gonna happen from one minute to another. So, the process has been, of course, to nail it all down." *Extended Play* [1996], p. 235

226 Ben Watson's critiques of recordings and performances in his book on Bailey are an exception to this; he has an uncommon ear for the collective character of free improvisation. Bailey himself was no soloist self-promoter but insisted on group playing in which the solo voice does not come through as the lead. Watson [2004] p. 159. The larger community of players, many of whom are not career-oriented, have tended towards the anti-soloist preference of Bailey, a point he held in common with Prévost. However it is difficult to resist greatness thrust upon oneself when it seems to enhance one's musical opportunities.

Chapter 10. Free Playing

227 More currently, I have been called "a dedicated representative of unconditional free playing" (ein hingebungsvoller Vertreter bedingungslosen Freispiels). What I represent to this writer is then an activity, not a genre but still a category. I do not consider myself representing anything, but the meaning is clear. *Bad Alchemy* 82, [2014]

228 For instance Paul Bley: "The way to learn how to make music is to find an audience. Anything you learn by yourself in a private room is useless." *Time Will Tell* [2003] p. 35. To seek and find an audience affirms career performers, but without the private space for exploration they are limited to what that audience will pay for, so Bley is exaggerating here.

229 The society of enjoyment is the term of Todd McGowan for a social order that has largely subverted and replaced "the society of prohibition." (*The End of Dissatisfaction Jacques Lacan and the Emerging Society of Enjoyment* [2004]). He and philosopher Slavoj Zizek argue that in today's culture it is one's duty to enjoy rather than for enjoyment to be restricted, as did institutional censorship and other prohibitions. To feel free is one expression of that. This applies especially to the entertained subject, rewarded for being dutiful in a different way--submitting to a more demanding work life. When all forms of enjoyment are available for purchase one must be dutiful to work. Musics entitled "free" must find their place in that society of enjoyment, where dissatisfaction is banished, including that of music that disturbs. However, they are reminders of that time a half-century ago when "free" was a movement that disturbed, a flag flown to gather those venturing outside the cultural perimeter. The society of enjoyment promises to eliminate the need for any such movements, leaving their memory as substitute. To rescue the joy encased in "enjoyment," I would call it the society of *mediated* enjoyment. I would also supplement it with "society of attention," where one is similarly enjoined to make oneself a consumable object of *others'* enjoyment, which is where the artist-performer fits in.

230 A "rehearsal band" does not perform, however, it plays scores or jazz tunes as if a performance is possible and sought after.

231 The concept of mimetic desire originated in the sixties with René Girard. Desire provokes imitation, leading to competitive rivalry, threatening conflict and violence. The prize sought is recognition that is effective in the world, prestige which by nature is hierarchical. Societies develop various strategies to curb this potential violence, such as the scapegoat, which Girard

elaborated on. In this game violence often results if the loser doesn't accept defeat (as Donald Trump has threatened to do in the 2016 election, raising fears of the breakdown of the political system).

[232] For my take on this thirty years ago see "Theatre of the Moment" online. Davey Williams deals with this matter extensively in his *Solo Gig* [2011], engaging musician-based issues that go beyond solo performance. Highly recommended.

[233] This is my own experience. After not performing for several weeks I will usually be fearful of audience reactions, especially if it's a solo, and I'll be glad the audience is small. Once I'm into the playing such projections disappear. Yet when I listen back to recordings and come to a quiet patch, I'll imagine a listener accusing me, "He doesn't have the energy he used to have." There is real ground for thinking this, some negative response when I was playing very sparsely in the early 00s, but not enough to warrant that recurrent voice, a deep-seated fear. I hope I never have to face a stream of approval; I'll want to duck out the back door.

In the long period of playing in the mode of forceful free jazz, I wonder what component of that was my expectation that the audience wanted to hear that. It was my bond with them, yet imaginary, since I didn't really know what they wanted. When I grew disinterested in that kind of playing I felt compelled to continue it in performance anyway, which disgusted me. To relieve myself of the fantasy of what others want and "just play," as Steve Lacy said, has often felt like a futile effort.

[234] In 1983 an Amsterdam trumpet player and I got together privately, and out of our excitement playing he suggested auditioning for a man who was producing records of improvised music. Instead of improvising together as we had done, however, the trumpeter put on a show, playing an impressive solo and not interacting. We were then not friends but mimetic rivals; I was shocked at his transformation and wasn't interested in that game. This was my introduction to the dilemma of the career-oriented musician, which I was at the time—divided between love of playing and the attempt to satisfy those who hold out the hope of a reward, which presumes they know roughly what they are looking for.

[235] On an extended stay in Germany in 1978, before I had fully committed to music, I asked my anarchist housemates if they could walk down the street funny (taking a hint from a Monty Python sketch). I was testing their anarchism, whether they could embody their disdain of social opinion. They would be aware they were lying and could be judged as falsely gaining the sympathy for the disabled. That test of resisting the moral superego I myself could not pass. When six months later I discovered free playing, music became my attempt to walk funny in public, at least half-willing to be treated as incapable of playing music, as I was on occasion. As I listen back to my earliest recording I can hear that I was not ready to go very far in that direction, and still I tend to shield myself with little signs that, yes, I am a skilled saxophonist. Part of the power of conventional musics over musicians, feeling the need to act the part of "real" musicians, is the fear of humiliation, such as jazz musicians used to bring down on the heads of any who went off the track (Ornette Coleman's experience of it was only an example of normal reactions to abnormality, which many experienced). Walking funny is socially treated as art only when properly coded and framed, the stage protecting one from being judged a crazy street person.

[236] This was recognized early in the history of free improvisation: "that such a music practice does not presuppose years of education to a virtuoso level brings up another current extra-musical viewpoint: The former extremely [elitist] position of new music is reversed into an extremely common one; almost everyone can take part in music of the present day, even actively." Erhard Karkoschka, "*Aspects of Group Improvisation*" [1971]

[237] Trust is etymologically related to "tryst," a waiting place where one trusts the lover will come.
[238] A tell-tale visual indication of free playing is when one is seen making the motion to begin a sound then withdrawing it. Either the others changed direction and the player overruled her initial impulse or she decided against it for her own internal reasons.
[239] Paul Hegarty, referring to Derek Bailey as the exemplar of free improvisation, says he "sought to get outside of all conventions of playing...While I do not think genre, style, category can be suspended except very fleetingly, the attempt is still worthwhile, and if the attempt is all we can have, then the attempt is the highest form of freedom to be aspired to, and must be maintained as an aim." Paul Hegarty, *Noise/Music: A History* [2007] p. 51. This would locate free improvisation within the avant-garde, often advanced as a noble aim to achieve freedom, which is commonly the view of advocate-critics, not Bailey's understanding.
[240] Art history, including art music, at least the popularized idea that filters to the educated public, assumes that successive generations build on each other in the competitive race-for-the-good-of-all known as progress (This is boosted by the social darwinist view that progress is natural--fact and not value. The losers in the struggle *should* be eliminated). Those lacking the motivation to be included in that scenario escape this dynamic. There is no world for them to play for when "the world" is the sum of audience numbers, on the one hand, and the art audience and its institutions on the other. The world the obscure play for can only be known and shaped by their bold and positive imagination. Their autonomy is not an act of rejection but, as Paul Goodman says, "the ability to initiate a task and do it one's own way." *Little Prayers* [1972], p.47.
[241] The philosopher Alain Badiou would see such openness as essential for an "event," which in his thinking is grounded in "the singularity of situations as such, which is the obligatory starting point of all properly human action." He is here discussing ethics, where the doctor, for instance, "is a doctor only if he deals with the situation according to the rule of maximum possibility," rather than taking into account the bureaucratic rules of the hospital, which sets explicit parameters for treatment. *Ethics* [2001] p.14-15. There is much in Badiou's philosophy that free playing would illustrate, for instance (taken from a summary by Andrew Robinson): "An Event is something akin to a rip in the fabric of being, and/or of the social order. It is traumatic for the mainstream, and exhilaratingly transformative for participants. Events are so radical as to even escape Badiou's own ontology. A lot of Badiou's discussions of the Event are negative...An event is 'supernumerary'. In other words, it is excessive over whatever is counted in the situation...It counts as nothing, in the situation's terms...Sometimes Badiou portrays the Event as purely random - an effect of chance. The word he usually uses is *hasardeux* (haphazard). It is chance in the sense of a possible encounter or dysfunction. Sometimes he portrays it as an act of creation out of nothingness." https://ceasefiremagazine.co.uk/alain-badiou-event/
[242] *Finite and Infinite Games* [1986], is a book fellow saxophonist Wally Shoup introduced to me in 1990, telling me, "Carse doesn't know it but he's really talking about free improvisation." As an aside, here's an illustration of how the social order transforms for its purposes the sixties "artistic critique," which the infinite game exemplifies. It became a model for entrepreneurial reorganization, by no means open to every option, and incorporated in the finite game of corporate success. The Generative Leadership Group uses Carse's book as required reading, summarized on their website: "One way to think of generative change is that it is the capacity of a system within an organization to create, in itself and the larger organization, change that is consistent with the future that leadership has envisioned." http://www.glg.net/pdf/Finite_Infinite_

Games.pdf For the general understanding of the artistic critique in the 90s management transformation see Boltanski/Chiapella, *The New Spirit of Capitalism* [1999/2005]

[243] Jazz tradition is possibly a more jealous, present lover for those trained in it than Mozart and
Brahms for the classically trained. A notable exception would be Joe McPhee, a saxophonist on
the far periphery of jazz, who sees himself continually attracted to new territory: "someone said
to me it's like trying to repair a car while it's rolling down a hill: dangerous and difficult but it
can be done." Interview with Stevphen Shukaitis:
http://nihilistoptimism.blogspot.com/2015/06/now-is-only-place-where-things-can.html

[244] The phrase is from *Transcendence of the Ego* [1960] p. 100. The quote, and the inspiration for
this discussion of fear in relation to art comes from Adam Phillips, *Terror and Experts* [1997].
What he's calling experts are psychoanalysts, for whom I substitute here the problematic expertise of musicians. "Protean" comes from Robert Jay Lifton, *The Protean Self—Human Resilience in
an Age of Fragmentation* [1999].

[245] In the following I apply to musical culture the thesis of Walter A. Davis' *Death's Dream Kingdom* [2006] on the psychological roots of ideology.

[246] See Russell Jacoby, *Social Amnesia* [1975], for the Americanization of Freud, which turned his
teachings in a direction he had consistently opposed.

[247] Shunyu Suzuki, *Zen Mind, Beginner's Mind* [1970] and Leo Tolstoy, "The Death of Ivan Ilyich"
[1886], available online.

[248] Phillips, op. cit., p. 56-57. The surrealists imagined themselves as poets stripped of their aura,
like ordinary people. It was as such that they turned the free association of Freudian analysis
(and of spiritualism) into the collective practice of automatic writing, which absolutely anyone
can do. In their public activities, more than the Dadaists, their subjectivity was at stake; they
wanted to shock the bourgeois only as they themselves experienced shock. They sought to come
directly from experience rather than working backwards from the audience affect that artists are
expected to deliver. The American Abstract Expressionists were similar in this, in fact nurtured
by Surrealist émigrés.

[249] Adam Phillips, *Terror and Experts* [1997], referring to Sartre's philosophy. That unpredictability, according to Peter Sloterdijk, is the key to the situation of the modern subject: "the primary
characteristic of the subject: unpredictability...freedom, or indeterminacy of action." The true
subject is an object of suspicion: "only those whom one suspects of being up to some mischief
can effectively become notable as a subject." *In the World Interior of Capital* [2013] p. 58-59.

[250] In the following I will be referencing the insights of psychologist Jacques Lacan, for whom
"Man's desire is the desire of the Other" (*Seminar XI*, p.235). This is either the immediate social
other in a performance situation or what Lacan calls the Big Other internalized as the superego.
One's own desire, Lacan is saying, is alienated in the other's desire, and to pursue it is to track it
down *there*. Applying this to the our cultural situation, entertainment is what performers do in
desiring recognition from the other—the largest number of audience—by imagining what that
other desires, including what might be hidden ("the next new thing"). Idealized serious Art, on
the other hand, is what performers do in desiring recognition from the Other known as Music,
which has a desire for what the best of them can discover and fulfill, so of course they want to be
the best. Art's scorn for entertainment would be "I pursue what is higher than the ordinary human"; the wish of entertainers for an upgrade to Art would be "I'm not just going for the fame
and fortune." Both forms of self-alienation are doomed, since we can't ever be secure in knowing what either "other" truly wants. Sales figures and institutional support (like "good works"
in Christian history) substitute for the other (audience response) and the Other (Music) respec-

tively. (Is free playing then a kind of "justification by faith alone," Luther's assertion?) What fills the gap of alienation Lacan calls "object little a" (for "autre," the other in French). That is the "it" of music, its hidden and elusive enjoyment. In-groups form around the belief that they have "it," the supposed object of envy for those who lack it and the ultimate basis of the hierarchy of visible musicians.

For artist-musicians to seek not just grants but a name that will attract customers, they must make an implicit claim to have found that gap in the Other's desire, that hidden something, which only lacks attention-getting machinery and strategy. As the artwork and name become acceptable the gap is filled in and another artist comes along the conveyor belt, making *its* differential claim. This confirms the avant-garde concept as ideological support, which rules serious art and has not been overcome by pluralism. What is called the end of Art history occurred when powerful institutions identified and rewarded the avant-garde more effectively than the artists themselves, who could never present, much less enforce, an undivided body of opinion.

[251] This is why I prefer for first time meetings to be in sessions rather than in public, to ensure undivided attention to each other. Should the meeting prove fruitful, it will more likely survive the gaze of the other.

[252] For instance, in a 2009 video, *Amplified Gesture*, guitarist Keith Rowe attributes this aim to the group AMM at its origin in 1965: "We wanted to make a form of music that had never existed ever before in the history of music." (Spoken without apparent irony. Perhaps the others in the group had no such lofty goals.) None of the other arts did this; visual artists, for instance, didn't inherit from their past the desire to shape the narrative of Art. Rowe is saying that AMM wanted to create a form that history would have to reckon with. The "history of music" is a reference not to all the music of humankind (the anthropological meaning) but specifically to that linear development of European music that was the competitive field for the high art avant-garde musician. This ambition goes beyond the common one of having one's worth considered by the music world. It is the dream of accomplishing something unique, which combines the goal of achieved Progress with possessive individualism. "Unique" has no comparative form, there is no more or less of it. The only way to reach that is to be judged from on high, the Platonic realm of spiritual truth (Music), which is far from the earthly business of sound-making. Incidentally, if it needs to be said, this is not a judgment on Rowe's playing, just an investigation of what his stated motivation entails. The video is online; see Hopkins in References.

[253] Henry Flynt is a musician and activist who repudiated the king of the hill dynamic. This came after experiencing a period of immersion in the NY avant-garde and its claimants to the title, such as John Cage and Lamont Young. See Benjamin Piekut's chapter on Flynt in *Experimentalism Otherwise*, [2011] and Piekut's interview with him at http://www.youtube.com/watch?v=4IfzftLO87E. Tony Conrad was another musician (and video) critic; he particularly accused Young of imperialism and of embracing the cult of himself as romantic hero.

[254] Davey Williams puts the matter of non-idiomatic this way in *Solo Gig* [2011]: "It turned out that this exclusionary rule was problematic, since with improvising you never know what imagery you might need to draw upon." For him that means occasional song fragments; for me it's more like the standard tone of the saxophone, a free jazz blur of notes, or some ear worm from an advertising jingle or pop song from childhood. Nothing long enough for people to sigh, "Now that's something that makes sense." Recently someone at a typical basement show mildly complained, "I thought you'd get into something but you never did." That "something" would have been a groove or clear idea that music is thought to provide.

[255] A Chicago drummer and video artist, Grant Strombeck, to whom I've dedicated this book, told me this about his "stuff," after five decades of experience: "There is no breeze. Every time I

see or hear what I have done in the past I see and hear it again. A coined phrase by Lester 'Prez' Young is 'repeater pencil' describing the act of repeating one's own past ideas. This is a problem. How does one move away from past ideas? Do I have to go on in this stuffy air? The air is stuffy. My nose is stuffy. I make stuffy art. It's all the same stuff. Hasn't the world had enough of me already?"

[256] Since I'm being personal here...This story of how to survive in the world of power I learned at the age of five or so when I saw Disney's *Song of the South*, and it's stayed with me. Br'er Rabbit was originally an African trickster, and then a figure for the American slave population, about which I knew nothing. When I find myself suddenly laughing in the middle of playing maybe it's because I'm Br'er Rabbit: "Here I am, right where I belong!" —and where the Bear can't get at me.

[257] In the early 70s Derek Bailey felt something was missing from his years of playing with others. He wanted "to have a look at my own playing to find out what was wrong with it and what was not wrong with it." His interest was to create a more "complete" language, to see "if it could supply everything that I wanted in a musical performance." *Improvisation*, p. 105 A professional musician could be expected to do this; those not aimed at and dependent on musical performance would not have this motivation.

[258] In my journal of 2003 I wrote, substituting here "playing" for "writing": "Awareness of only positive, expansive feelings is not true awareness; it is prejudiced, part of the self-boosting defense system, which by nature is one-sided. The same with playing. When I depend on motivating feeling [i.e. positive] I won't be inclined to play what is the truth for me, and I will have no right to feel confident about it. It would be as if I was trying to please myself immediately through playing, avoiding what might be disturbing, which would be the same as if I were motivated to please others." (My sister told me such radical self-doubt would drive her crazy, a response that confirmed for me that she understood what I was saying.)

[259] In the early 80s I witnessed the well-respected saxophonist Jimmy Lyons attempt to play a composition he'd just written and stop midway through in disgust. It was painful to see but to me was a model of artist behavior violating the performer contract to play through difficulty as if it didn't exist. When I tell an enthusiastic audience member of my disappointment after a performance I feel I'm letting them down by contradicting their take on it. But we both gain in learning the difference of our situations. Disappointment often comes from sensing I've lost the thread and have concentrated intensely to get it right. That focus yields what the witness receives and generates their excitement. I only come to recognize it on hearing the recording. Variations of this experience are common, at least among my partners.

Chapter 11. Free Playing and the Real World

[260] An example is Stephen Nachmanovitch, *Free Play; The Power of Improvisation in Life and the Arts* [1990], who doesn't mention that "free improvisation" or "free play" refers to a specific tradition and approach of musicians.

[261]See for instance the large catalogue of topics to which improvisation is applied in George Lewis, "Critical Responses to 'Theorizing Improvisation (Musically)'" [2013] and the two packed volumes of the Lewis and Piekut, *Oxford Handbook of Critical Improvisation Studies*, which are unavailable in libraries as of this writing. For the social implications of improvisation see also

the specialized journal of this approach, "Critical Studies in Improvisation" http://www. critical-improv.com /public/csi/index.html.

[262] From 1997 to 2013 Pete Gershon's *Signal to Noise* was a US print publication widely available to musicians and listeners, and covered free improvisation as well as many other musics on the left side of music culture. It too succumbed to the internet and publication costs, while the audience for the musics covered grew.

[263] "The bulk of freely improvised music, certainly its essential part, happens in either unpublicized or, at best, under-publicised circumstances: musician-organised concerts, ad hoc meetings and private performances...the more conducive the setting is to freely improvised music, the less compatible it is likely to be with the kind of presentation typical of the music business." *Improvisation*, p. 141.

[264] We might rather call what artists make "art events" rather than works. This would take art away of analysts and give it back to the artists (or those who want it), making a painting more likely an event than a thing. A symphony becomes a work on condition that the composer is absent, off doing something else or dead, unable to interfere. If artworks are events, the spectator is a point of awareness in a specific moment in time. And free playing, most obviously an event and not a thing, would draw all artists to get in touch with how it's done.

[265] I was surprised to read a review sometime in the 90s of another sax player described as "post-Jack Wright." I was delighted and amused that my playing had been raised to the level of a musical form for someone else and was presumed so established and well-known that it could be taken for granted, imitated and surpassed. My playing was suddenly marked as History, which means past and done with, yet elevated to the known, official lineage of saxophonists. Others would be dared to come up with something more advanced—the old legend versus the young upstart. For a musician this is not only helpful for a career but almost like being loved! I would presumably be post-Evan Parker, parallel to John Butcher. This review would probably sound ludicrous to most today, a period of post-linear development and the permanent avant-garde, not to mention the huge shift from critical reviewing to promotion.

[266] For abstract expressionism the value placed on spontaneity had to overcome the principle that quick work cannot yield art. From there to "everyone an artist" was a quick slide the art world had to outwit in order to maintain Art as an activity that doesn't contradict the social value of work. The genius might work fast but will pay a price (the suffering artist motif).

[267] Some artists distrust recordings as "the best" they have done, despite media hype. Asked for recommendations of recordings, John Coltrane said "some of the best wasn't recorded. Recordings always make you tighten up just a little bit." Quoted in Leonard L. Brown, *John Coltrane and Black America's Quest for Freedom* [2010]. That "always" is a strong critique of what is considered his oeuvre.

[268] A reviewer paid me a compliment some might call backhanded: "These tracks are pure spontaneous improvisation in which the players allow anything to happen. As a result, *there are none of the familiar elements that most folks associate with music.*" (italics mine) Don Seven, "Baby Sue" review of myself and percussionist Ben Bennett on the CD "Tangle" http://www.babysue. com/2014-June-LMNOP-Reviews.html#anchor620033. As a social and artistic value, spontaneity depends on the reassuring "familiar elements" of music in the background.

[269] By embracing the present as the fullness of time, art today conceals its nostalgia for the time when past, present, and future were conceived linearly. That was once the task of the European imagination, scientific as well as artistic, faced with the unscaleable wall of icons known as the Ancients, from the Dark Ages through Modernism. Enlightened heroism was to be undaunted in the face of what was rock-hard and unmovable, to find cracks in solid tradition through

which flowers (or weeds) of the human spirit would grow, eventually levelling the wall. It was the meaning of Progress and the debate that extended through the Cold War—which side has truly broken with "the way things are," which is in the grip of the past. That imagination is now walled in by the spectacle. Instead of statues that can be toppled, the icons are projected on all the walls of the cave and the cracks interpreted as part of the desired image. It's as if John Coltrane and John Cage have betrayed their own continual advances upon earlier work and will permit no one to stand on their shoulders and see beyond them.

[270] In Russia before the Soviet collapse all art was feared by the authorities, above all poetry. This they censored it heavily, which only kept the language obscure and metaphorical Readers were attached as to a crossword puzzle whose solution would relieve their oppression. American censorship was untroubled by this, only selected words presented social danger. Today's art is thought to "make a difference" if its message is as prosaic and unambiguous as possible.

To my knowledge the most poetic *and* insightful reviewer of the free musics is an Italian, whose imaginative use of the English language exceeds any American reviewers. Massimo Ricci reviews practically everything sent to him with gusto and care. https:// touchingextremes .wordpress.com/ Unlike other reviewers, he does not hesitate to be negative at times. This irritated one established British improviser, criticized for mediocrity of his latest output. In today's situation musicians expect reviewers to be on their side against society's supposed indifference. They are to serve as unpaid promoters needed to sustain the worship of the faithful. Beneath the glowing promo, all professional art music today is survivalist: "we need all the help we can get." Criticism that suggests a recording is not up to the level of those previous is apparently not helpful to the musician; they might already know that.

[271] A useful study would compare the procedures for "deciderization," as David Foster Wallace calls it, of the different art fields in the Age of Information glut of art product. Wallace was given the job of guest editor, something like a curator, for an anthology of essays in 2007. He had to read through 100 essays and select 20, but the series editor had already culled that number (Wallace assumes) from "a vast pool of '06 nonfiction—every issue of hundreds of periodicals, plus submissions' from [the series editor's] network of trusted contacts all over the United States." *Both Flesh and Not: Essays* [2012], p. 306. The series editor really did all that?

For music the fantasy that the music world is a responsible curator is upheld without an enabling myth backing it. For instance, does anyone imagine that the music world employs people who listen to at least a bit of all the tiny labels and make an evaluation? "Music is a mystery" once again comes to the rescue. Musicians know how to get reviewed in print, where it counts: a considerable outlay of cash to those politely called "publicists" or very elaborate and calculated schmoozing.

[272] In Philadelphia, Spring Garden Music (myself, basically) organized the East Coast Free Music Festival in 1984 and 1985, so far the only such festivals focused on the music alone in that city. The second one received an arts council grant of $500, split between fifteen musicians. It included local and other musicians--Steve Hunt from Chicago, Chris Cochrane, Borbetomagus, William Parker and Joe McPhee from NY, and Roger Turner from Britain. I didn't know that applicants were expected to ask for twice what they needed, which the agency would then cut in half, and to get corporate sponsorship, both of which I would have refused to do anyway.

[273] As for public arts funding in general after neoliberal cutbacks, according to Joni Maya Cherbo US government support is "commonly referred to as an 'arms-length' paradigm." Cherbo, Joni Maya; Stewart, Ruth Ann, and Wyzomirski, Margaret Jane, eds. *Understanding the Arts and the Creative Sector* [2008], "Towards an Arts and Creative Sector," p.18. The government

has no program to directly support artists at a regular income level or to provide enough funding for venues to pay musician fees adequate for living costs, as in Northern Europe and Switzerland. Instead it provides occasional short-term grants and tax concessions to the middlemen (non-profit organizations), and requires organizers to find corporate sponsors, which of course prefer conventional art. Since the late 90s arts administrators at the policy level, in the interest of neoliberal restructuring, have pressured non-profits to perceive themselves as a sector of the economy (the "Creative Sector"). They must reorganize themselves so as to contribute to the local economy and support the arts according to the bottom line of cost effectiveness. There is little reason to believe that the already minimal funding for small-audience arts will be increased, even for school-credentialed musicians. For those lacking credentials the situation is still more tenuous. By contrast, through the 80s in Philadelphia, for instance, a noblesse oblige spirit encouraged a small funded gallery to make its space available for free improvisation. When that ended it was a coop gallery, without funding but with members themselves supportive of free improvisation. Now through gentrification that gallery has closed its doors, and no venue can be counted on steadily without a rental fee.

274 Advice to would-be professionals urges them to win an audience, contradicting earlier conceptions of the artist that marked that as betrayal. The terms of artistic correctness are familiar throughout higher education. Specifically, new music is defined as "any music that employs innovative, unexpected sounds or forms *with the intention of challenging audiences to examine their assumptions about music, performance, and the consumption of musical experiences.*" (italics mine) Sam Himler, "Audience Cultivation in American New Music" http://www.newmusicbox.org /articles /audience-cultivation-in-american-new-music/. Himler wants musicians to join forces with liberals as a market strategy. "Bigger audiences for new music mean greater impact of progressive ideologies." However, "challenging audiences" would be counterproductive if they are alienated, so there is a calculable limit to sound that is "unexpected." Since "new music" means composed, improvised music is not in his catalogue; it falls outside the bracket of contemporary grant-funded music. The article correctly outlines the contemporary sociology of performance, distinguishing between the concert and the (DIY) show, the appropriate behavior for each, how audiences react, and how musicians should operate for maximum effect. Thanks to Evan Lipson for pointing me to this article.

275 *Sync or Swim: Improvising Music in a Complex Age* [2005], p. 3, quoted in full, p. 113. Another example would be Iain Anderson, *This is Our Music* [2007], who apparently sees no significant difference between the two free musics, using "free improvisation" to refer to sixties Free Jazz.

276 To my knowledge, those who read the more popular-aimed literature on free playing, such as Stephen Nachmanovitch's *Free Play; The Power of Improvisation in Life and the Arts,* aren't likely show up at music concerts under that title. This would confirm that people do not expect the American self-help/humanist philosophy of free improvisation to be realized as a specific form of music but an extension of what already exists publicly.

277 Scott Thomson's "The Pedagogical Imperative of Musical Improvisation," [2007], appeared in an online Canadian academic journal (http://www.criticalimprov.com/article/view/353). Thomson, a Canadian improviser and organizer, speaks of "collective improvisation." That might be correctly understood by some Canadian readers, despite the rarity of discourse concerning actual playing experience and the paucity of attendance at such events by non-players.

278 Both economic and psychological reasons might help understand Evan Parker's musicological turn to his distinctive solo, tour de force circular breathing, on which his name and identity have been based since at least the late 70s. He defended it on musical grounds but it probably paid the bills better than his ability to improvise in groups. In the 80s some peers dismissed it as

a stunt, hearing about that alone and endlessly from transfixed audiences and media, but even then his dexterity in groups should have been obvious.

[279] The following anecdote passed around among musicians captures the essence. In 1968 composer/pianist Frederick Rzewski asked Steve Lacy to describe the difference between composition and improvisation in fifteen seconds. He said: "...in composition you have all the time you want to decide what to say for fifteen seconds, while in improvisation you have fifteen seconds." The full, extemporaneous answer took exactly fifteen seconds. Found in Derek Bailey, *Improvisation*, p. 141

[280] Not long ago, men who played this way would hesitate to let a woman they were interested in know what music they did, since it would typically scare her away. That is possibly changing. But only recently a partner musician's relatives came to a performance of his and were shocked to think that anyone would pay for even a single concert. It is akin to a parent hearing their child is on drugs and needs help. No wonder so many musicians eventually abandon or modify their youthful dreams in the face of the near-universal judgment that they have wasted their time and talent and are putting off the need to think realistically about their lives.

There is no active myth of unique talent and posterity to console ambitious young musicians, as there was for the writer Delmore Schwartz (1913-1961), for instance. His stories in *The World is a Wedding* [1948] illustrate the collision of the 19th century cursed poet legend and the spectacle, which ultimately triumphed. The only escape is total exorcism of the dream that someday the artist will reach deep inner satisfaction with what they do *and* be socially recognized and rewarded for it. It might indeed happen, but the dream blocks it. Schwartz and so many others died trying. They were the innocents; a half-century hence we have no excuse.

[281] This understanding of the everyday from Kristin Ross, *The Emergence of Social Space: Rimbaud and the Paris Commune* [1988], p. 19.

[282] "Gravity for example, does not reveal itself through thought or descriptions. Only by releasing our human grasp on some thing and entering into the space of unknowing can an object fall and gravity be revealed." Rachel K. Ward, "Radical Thinking," essay on Jean Baudrillard. http://www.ctheory.net/articles.aspx?id=685

Chapter 12. Resurgence of Free Improvisation and the Present Situation

[283] October 28, 1998

[284] This is my conjecture based on touring around the country and checking list-servs. I first knew of Phiba, which I posted to in April 1997, and soon after discovered the others. As for New York, perhaps because of the continuity of free improv there it lacked the novelty that founded listservs elsewhere. Also, NY held the aura of cultural leadership and career-driven music, and the list-servs were peopled with those outside that range. However, by the early 00s both gigs and sessions thrived in NY and Brooklyn, as we shall see.

Due to the lack of income for this music, the East and West Coasts have largely separate histories, with little touring and few player contacts between them. The story of improv in the Bay Area has yet to be written. The venues and communal support there hasn't weakened over the past thirty years. It is the region most likely to have an old guard from the mid-80s, when it began to pick up again after a short decline. As with all high-cost cities, gentrification is taking its toll. It still has possibly the largest and most stable number of improvisers in the US that one could call organized--see the extensive list at .bayimproviser. com/artists.asp. Accordingly, as in Europe the next generation lacked the same sense of itself as independent discoverers, while for many of the older players free playing has been eclipsed by interest in composition and structured forms.

Seattle has had a continuous community (by which I mean players available to each other, not just numbers), with the oldest and longest-running free improvisation festival in the US, beginning in 1985 (http://www.earshot.org/event/31st-seattle-improvised-music-festival/). Initial participants were largely countercuturals who would improvise only on that occasion. In 1998 a new leadership under 80s-veteran saxophonist Wally Shoup took over, inviting only experienced and committed improvisers, to the chagrin of the regular invitees. This move at least shows Seattle displaying some of the signs of resurgence present on the East Coast. Chicago on the other hand had always been a strong jazz-entertainment town, and musics enabling careers dominate the others, as in New York.

[285] The first degree program in improvisation was at San Jose State in California (1991), but there were non-degree pedagogies for improvisation earlier, summarized in Tom Nunn, *Wisdom of the Impulse* [1998] (online). The most prominent was that of Pauline Oliveros, a musician-composer-educator who was also closely involved with academic institutions. Like Davey Williams and Ladonna Smith before her, her approach transcended the musician identity and welcomed non-musicians. Calling her workshops and approach Deep Listening, she continued the John Cage experimental tradition of environmental listening, both nature or man-made. Unlike the player-based initiative of Davey and Ladonna, however, she aimed at a specific aesthetic — meditative, long tones and acoustic reverberation, an admixture of mostly quiet electronics, which prefigured the aesthetic of reductionism soon to come. It was an experience of sound for some who had no interest in becoming musicians, a philosophy outside music school education.

[286] For instance the Autumn Uprising festival (1997-2002), organized by Dave Gross, Boston reed player, at first included free jazz players in an eclectic mix, and was popular enough to draw a varied audience. Later, taste would become more differentiated into specific scenes.

[287] Maneri, quoted earlier (p. 107), was one of the few who crossed the border between jazz-based improvisation and the experimental, compositional tradition, in particular microtonalism. Microtonalism spanned the continent (Harry Partch and Ivor Dareg on the West Coast), though to my knowledge it only took hold with improvisational performers in Boston. The counterpart of the NEC on the West Coast is Mills College.

[288] The European version, reductionism, more openly threatened the key figures there. I myself was closely engaged with it for several years, was a touring partner of Rainey's, and worked with reductionists in Berlin, perhaps the only "old guard" American to do so. I was not interested in the overall aesthetic project but in techniques, like playing quietly and working with breath and sound, and generally doing the opposite of all I had known.

[289] Erstquate was the project of Abbey, whose Erstwhile Records was the main support for American lowercase music, and Tim Barnes, percussionist, who ran the venue Quakebasket. Barnes now lives in Louisville KY and runs a venue there that welcomes all kinds of improvised music, and Abbey continues to release electro-acoustic improvisation and new composition on his label. For a list of shows Abbey produced go to http://www.erstwhilerecords.com/ live.html

[290] Ty Cumbie: "I started my series with [percussionist Lucas] Ligeti on August, 2003. Although there is still a scene existing the best times were probably over by 08 or 09."

[291] "The Volunteer's Collective (VC) was initiated in Baltimore in 1989 by 'no one in particular.' The idea was to form a utopian-minded, open-ended, conceptually generic enfeeble [sic!] that would take on projects which were outside of the value-system or perceptual/social regimenta-

tion of the prevailing culture that required or benefited from a large group. In principle, anyone could take up this collective banner and use it as a context for their activities or for organizing a large group without restriction, for whatever that was worth. The value of having a repeated generic context was to build a history and sense of decentralized continuity in the dark, as it were. Also, to simply encourage people to feel their power in relation to this kind of activity, and to encourage it." —John Berndt, http://www.johnberndt. org/vc/index.html

[292] http://redroom.org/series/

[293] At one High Zero I was grouped with four drummers in a line, such that I had to maneuver awkwardly and couldn't find a position where I could hear them equally and feel I was playing with them all. When I complained later Neal Feather, one of the collective, explained with a grin, "We thought that if anyone could handle it, you could." To me at the time it was more spectacle than musically interesting, yet I could see how it mocked my usual seriousness and that of conventional festivals, which are designed to enhance the aura around the players and disallow any possible difficulty and negative judgment.

[294] Now only the capitols, the other being L.A., get to determine and crown the national culture stars. They then go forth to reap the reward by displaying it to the rest of the world, which lacks the power to bestow it on anyone. If the ultimate American success story is not money in itself but stardom, then to achieve success it makes sense to take the road to the capitol.

[295] A series that included avant-garde jazz began in 1970 in an Episcopal church on the University of Pennsylvania campus in West Philadelphia. It was named Geno's Empty Foxhole after its founder, Geno Barnard, and the title of one of Ornette Coleman's albums. It included a few living in Philadelphia--bagpiper Rufus Harley and saxophonist Byard Lancaster—otherwise all NY musicians--Cecil Taylor, Charles Mingus, the Sun Ra Orchestra (then in NY), Roland Kirk, and the Chicago Art Ensemble, then more resident in NY. http://www.sas.upenn.edu/music /west phillymusic/jazz/webchristman1.html It paralleled NY Loft Jazz even though it included some more conventional jazz musicians. There was once a thriving jazz scene in Philadelphia, strongest in neighborhood clubs on "the strip" of 52nd St. in West Philadelphia and in Germantown, and a tradition of Philadelphia saxophonists and others who moved on to NY.

[296] Bowerbird was reminiscent of the Open Mouth poetry series of the early 80s, with a couple open readings per week (no featured reader, as is today's norm) at a large variety of venues. The Bowerbird list covering the first two years is at http://www.bowerbird.org /newsite/events /feb2006_aug2008.php For the earliest shows scroll to the bottom. Eugene Lew's shows are at http://www.hungrymonsters.net/goodfridays/then.htm

[297] The quote is from a Facebook post of Hurt's responding to mine in late August 2014, in which I argued that Philadelphia has a two-tier art culture, with local musicians, including free improv and punk (in the 80s), on the lower tier, ignored as illegitimate music. I compared Philadelphia to other major cities, which have fostered local artist-based scenes and become noted for them. Following Hurt's dissing I presented a critique of Bowerbird and his investment in it, which drew respondents lining up on one side or the other. The most vociferous counterattack to that came from a musician recipient of a $60k Pew Fellowship grant (Pew has been the major funder of Bowerbird). One supporter of my view was a relatively small-scale producer of events who told me he had to stay silent because of a pending application. The $60K Pew grant for the Bowerbird project was for a relatively unknown black composer, Julius Eastman (1940-1990). http://www.pcah.us/ grants/9818_in_search_of_eastman

[298] A reporter covering the 2016 Republican Convention in Cleveland for *Harper's Magazine*, Walter Kirn, by some twist of fortune ended up at a session of what would be either free jazz or

free improv, "a local underground-music scene—the psychedelic trap" he calls it, and devoted over two columns to it. He was first impressed that these folks did not fit his stereotype, for they assessed national politics with reasonable judgment. Then they played: "It's outlandish, it's loud, and it follows no straight lines. If you can think you can hear where it's going, that's you, not it. That's you, feeling lost, anxious for a groove. But it is not anxious. Lost is where it lives," an excellent description of free playing from an innocent listener's viewpoint. He got a souvenir CD of this uprooting experience, apparently more provocative than the convention itself. Listening to it later, and concluding his piece: "It's unsparingly berserk. No through-lines, no verses, no strong melodies, but if you really get your head inside it, really lose yourself, you'll hear something true. You'll hear what's going on." Here's the middle class journalist, introduced to a world truly off the cultural radar, in an era that proclaims that everything of significance is visible and readily available. Kirn didn't run away, instead allowing his new-journalist vulnerable self to engage and tell the truth of his experience. [*Harper's Magazine*, Oct. 2016]

299 The quoted words are from a Facebook post, dissing a band accused of an offhand un-p.c. comment by one of its members, which was then banned from a show. Elsewhere I've heard of the banning of male musicians who play "harsh noise" (with which some free improv could be classed), not for artistic reasons but because they are said to typify male acting-out behavior. The Philadelphia A-Space (Anarchist) requires musicians to police themselves and the audience: "Anyone organizing an event within the space is expected to ensure the event is not authoritarian, pro-state, capitalist, patriarchal, white supremacist, cissexist, ableist, or otherwise in line with any ideology that fosters domination." http://a-space.org/booking/. Traditionally, anarchists rejected the Stalinist correct political line as well as moralism; today many anarchists have their own political correctness, recalling the government loyalty oath of postwar anticommunism. The fear of being disrupted by art has found a new rationale, appropriate to a time when art and entertainment both are policed for positive effect on and response from audiences.

300 Given my focus on North America I am obliged to ignore European reductionism, whose main period was late 1990s-2002. American lower-case arose roughly simultaneously from a parallel cultural turn against music of obvious emotive engagement. It was encouraged by the Europeans; to choose one's aesthetic is a hallmark of European avant-garde art, and association with Europe is a plus for white middle-class American artist-musicians. The sourcebook containing the varying views of participants is Burkhard Beins, *Echtzeit Berlin: Selbstbestimung einter Szene / self-defining a scene*, in German and English. An overview more accessible in the states is Marta Blazanovic's dissertation, "Berlin Reductionism--An Extreme Approach to Improvisation Developed in the Berlin Echtzeitmusik-Scene" http://edoc.hu-berlin.de/dissertationen/blazanovic-marta-2012-11-12/PDF/blazanovic.pdf

301 Paul Goodman, "Little Prayers and Finite Experience [1972], p. 39

302 Instead of adding devices I chose to play extensively with electronicists, following my interest in lower case. My new sounds come partly from imitating electronics, or mocking it if you will, which sometimes confuses audiences as to who was making what sound. I've jokingly called my music "post-electronic saxophone." For me if acoustic and electronics compete it should be playful, strongly affecting each other. I don't partner with those who set up a sequencer or drone and walk away from the instrument, or are too engaged with their devices to interact. Recently I've experimented with the keyboard synthesizer, which as a piano player I find great fun, a relief from my high skill level on the saxophone and the weight of seriousness. However, at present satisfaction comes too quickly for my taste; the saxophone gives more to push against, as does the acoustic piano. Sooner or later I need the physicality of the acoustic instrument, more directly responsive to the body's touch. Playing a wind instrument is hand and mouth working

together; the longing of the artist hand to make and the poet's mouth to speak are united, the proverbial bringing of life into art.

[303] The phrase is from Fredric Jameson, *Postmodernism* [1991] p. 10, though Jameson, unlike more traditional Marxists, is at least ambivalent about many aspects of postmodern culture.

[304] In 2004 I did a tour with two Berlin musicians, my first one coast-to-coast since 1988, playing within lower case parameters. We had warm receptions, and some received us with great attention and curiosity in the Midwest.

[305] http://www.springgardenmusic.com/no-net.html. The first grouping was nine by accident, a recording project I put together in the Bay area with the help of guitarist John Shiurba while on tour with Bhob Rainey in 2000. Later that spring he organized the earlier-mentioned BSC, which took the form of a band rather than the No Nets, which had different invitees each time and were more workshops than performance-oriented.

[306] http://www.museumfire.com/events.htm

[307] The Impermanent Society is at http://www.impermanentsociety.com/

[308] The only print publication in English covering "alternative, underground and non-mainstream musics," including free improvisation, is *The Wire Magazine*. It has reviewed High Zero Festival but not XFest, nor have XFest organizers sought to get the press to cover it.

[309] From the founder of the 24-hour Day of Noise, KZSU DJ Voice of Doom: "Noise is the liberation of sound from the narrow rules of conventional music, calling a project noise frees you up to include any kind of sound in the artwork. The Day of Noise event has always been about the freedom of non-commercial radio to deviate from the standardized conceptions of what the audience wants or needs." http://kzsu.stanford.edu/dayofnoise/ The list of groups draws from a range of musics that includes free improv, experimental composition, and free jazz.

I am avoiding the larger issue of noise as a concept developed first by Jacques Attali (1985) and then Paul Hegarty, *Noise/Music: A History* [2007]. Hegarty has insights into free improvisation and free jazz, some of which coincide with my own, but he considers noise a form of musical product and the approaches and interests of the players more my concern.

[310] *Noise and Capitalism* joins free improv with noise music, together with all intentional soundmaking that "locates itself self-reflexively at the limit of what can be accepted as music," including eai, free jazz, music concrète, and avant-garde composition. This 2009 publication edited by Mattin and Anthony Iles contains articles by academics, musicians, and music writers who derive radical political meaning from these musics, with most articles seeing them as at least potentially anti-capitalist. Herding musicians into genres, then finding common cause between them, it attempts to resurrect the image of an intentionally trouble-making avant-garde, politically a kind of popular front. To declare it radical and anti-capitalist ignores that the European avant-garde (with the possible exception of noise) would evaporate without state support. It performs in comfortable settings for predictably agreeable paying audiences.

Finding music politically significant is a good excuse for avoiding spontaneous response to the music itself. At any rate, when significance presumes public presence, as does *Noise and Capitalism* we are far from the American situation of free improv. Its conjuncture with noise music is a marriage of convenience, for it does not share the aim of symbolic dissent.

[311] Tim Hodgkinson, British composer and well-known improviser, considers free improvisation to be threatened with extinction, much as jazz and free jazz have been: "*if* free improvisation is to survive, it is only by feeling its way forwards, taking this and rejecting that, according to what works best within this aesthetic process that defines it as a practice." (Nov. 2010) (http://www.acousticlevitation.org/doesfree.html.) Free improvisation would then have the character of a

substantial "it," with a life that is subject to its fate in the public sphere. Doesn't survival here imply public visibility? Survival is of no concern to the non-career musicians who will go on playing regardless of what happens to "it." Hodgkinson here is speaking for the genre and its market position, which ordinary players may cheer on but only name musicians depend on.

[312] An example of the experimental mix would be the Austin-based No Idea Festival. It presents separate sets of musicians with individualized aesthetics, sound artists (a title distinct from musician), composers playing their own pieces, and some focused on free improvisation. "No Idea" suggests radical openness, but whatever experimenting composers and soloists have done in preparation has come to an end before being presented to the audience. noideafestival.com/

[313] I discussed avant-garde as a term in an earlier footnote (20) and elaborate here briefly. The word is problematic because it refers to various concrete movements, where it is a noun asserted by the artists, and also an adjective applied to all "advanced" art. The adjective in the past few decades has itself become a noun referring to the official avant-garde, whose permanence is secured and necessary to the social order. That use of avant-garde absorbs the first in the belief that art is summed up as a universal, progressive history contributing to History itself. This is a concept of non-artist critics and academics and not the artists themselves. Artists are then not for-themselves but have created for the sake of this history, advancing one on the other in continuous succession. To be progressive (and the political is included here) then requires the dismissal of the actuality of those producing art, traditionally workers, in favor of the needs of History. (This is the error of most Marxism, by the way, which confines artists to the camp of their patrons and interpreters.) This efficient economy absorbs the conflicts between artists, for a Rimbaud and a Mallarmé are both treated as avant-garde but had strongly opposed interests. Such division is the reality of artists. (They also don't get to make the selection of who is worthy and who is not—is there a survey that shows whether those treated as geniuses even cared about such things?) When their descendants are also put in the same boat it looks like Rimbaud agreed with Mallarmé's aestheticism, since that view triumphed in 20th Century formalist criticism. Today formalism is heavily critiqued, but the picture of a phalanx of artists all marching together, however many self-interested petty quarrels they had, remains. I have Kristin Ross [1988], p.64-65, to thank for this.

[314] As for manifestoes and declamatory statements from that era, the British publication of the 1970s, *Musics: A British Magazine of Improvised Music & Art* [2016], recently collected and republished, will confirm that the avant-garde spirit was alive and strong among the originary free improvisers. They did not hesitate to create institutions under their authority and should not be considered alternative culture, which diminishes any such project.

Ch. 13. Conclusion

[315] "Stop and think," the injunction of both Hannah Arendt and Slavoj Zizek, means for me "I can't stop thinking, and no printed book I've authored can make me." A book is material reality; thinking is the spirit in motion, crystalizing rather than crystalized. As in Zeno's paradox, I am ever coming to conclusions but never getting to a place known as *there*. Only in death is that achieved and the improvisation finished. For more writing go to http://www.springgardenmusic.com/the.free.musics.appendix.htm#postpublication.

[316] Quoted in Ross Posnock, *Renunciation: Acts of Abandonment by Writers, Philosophers, and Artists,* [2016] p. 240.

References

Adorno, Theodor, *Introduction to the Sociology of Music*, Seabury Press, NY, 1976
_____, *Minima Moralia*, Verso, London, 1974 (Germany 1951)
_____, *Quasi Una Fantasia* , London/NY Verso, 2011, written in 1961
Aldington, Robert, ed. *Sound Commitments: Avant-garde Music and the Sixties*, Oxford U. Press, NY, 2009
Anderson, Iain, *This is Our Music*, U. of Pennsylvania Press, Philadelphia 2007
Attali, Jacques, *Noise, the Political Economy of Music*, University of Minn. Press, 1985, first published in France in 1977
Atlas, James, *Delmore Schwartz: The Life of an American Poet*, Farrar, Straus and   Giroux, NY, 1974
Auslander, Philip, "Just Be Yourself: Logocentrism and Difference" in Phillip B. Zarilli, ed., *Acting (Re)considered: A Theoretical and Practical Guide*, Routledge, London/NY, 2002
_____, *Liveness: Performance in a Mediatized Culture*, 2nd. ed., Routledge, Abingdon (UK) and NY, 2008
Bad Alchemy 82, review of *If Anything Could be the Same*, 2014, http://www.badalchemy.de/   no download of this issue presently available.
Badiou, Alain, *Ethics: An Essay on the Understanding of Evil*, Verso, London, 2001 (1993)
Bailey, Derek, *Free Improvisation: Its Nature and Practice in Music*, Da Capo Press, NY, 1992 (revised; first published edition 1975)
Baraka, Amiri (Leroy Jones before 1967), *Blues People, Negro Music in White America*, William Morrow, NY, 1963
_____ , *Black Music*, Morrow, NY, 1967
_____, *Home: Social Essays*, Morrow, NY, 1966
_____, *Raise Race Rays Raze: Essays Since 1965*, Random house, NY, 1971
Baskin, Jason, "Romanticism, Culture, Collaboration: Raymond Williams Beyond the Avant-Garde." *Cultural Critique* 83 (Winter 2013)
Baudrillard, Jean, *Simulations*, Semiotext(e), New York, 1983
Beins, Burkhard, *Echtzeit Berlin: Selbstbestimung einer Szene / self-defining a scene*, Wolke Verlag, Hofheim, 2011
Belgrade, Daniel, *The Culture of Spontaneity: Improvisation and the Arts in Postwar America*, Univ. of Chicago Press, 1998.
Benedetti, Paul and Dehart, Nancy, eds., *Forward Through the Rearview Mirror: Reflections on and by Marshall McLuhan*, MIT Press, Cambridge MA, 1997
Blazanovic, Marta, *Berlin Reductionism--An Extreme Approach to Improvisation Developed in the Berlin Echtzeitmusik-Scene*, Ph.D. thesis, http://edoc.huberlin.de/dissertationen/blazanovic-marta-2012-11-12/PDF/blazanovic.pdf
Bley, Paul (with Norman Meehan), *Time Will Tell: Conversations with Paul Bley*, Berkeley Hills Books, Berkeley CA, 2003
Borgo, David, *Sync or Swim: Improvising Music in a Complex Age*, Continuum, NY, 2005
Brown, Leonard L., *John Coltrane and Black America's Quest for Freedom*, Oxford U. Press, NY, 2010

Carle, Philippe and Comolli, Jean-Louis, *Free Jazz/Black Power*, original publication in French 1971, now translated, U. of Miss. Press, Jackson MS, 2015

Carse, James P., *Finite and Infinite Games*, The Free Press, NY, 1986

Caylor, Garth W. Jr., *Nineteen + Conversations with Jazz Musicians* New York City 1964-1965, Create Space, NY, 2014

Cherbo, Joni Maya; Stewart, Ruth Ann, and Wyzomirski, Margaret Jane, eds. *Understanding the Arts and the Creative Sector*, Rutgers University Press NJ, 2008

Chusid, Irwin, *Songs in the Key of Z: The Curious World of Outsider Music*, A Cappella Books, Chicago, 2000

Coleman, Ornette, interview in "Jacques Derrida interviews Ornette Coleman," http://theendofbeing.com/2013/03/06/jacques-derrida-interviews-ornette- coleman-the-others-language/

Corbett, John, *Extended Play: Sounding Off from John Cage to Dr. Funkenstein*, Duke Univ. Press, Durham NC, 1994

Crary, Jonathan, *24/7: Late Capitalism and the Ends of Sleep*, Verso, London, 2013

Davis, Walter A., *Deracination: Historicity, Hiroshima, and the Tragic Imperative*, SUNY Press, Albany, 2001

_____, *Death's Dream Kingdom: The American Psyche Since 9-11*, Pluto Press, London/Ann Arbor MI, 2006

DeVeaux, Scott, "Constructing the Jazz Tradition," 1991, reprinted in Robert G. O'Meally, *The Jazz Cadence of American Culture*, Columbia U. Press, NY, 1998

Douglas, Ann, *Terrible Honesty, Mongrel Manhattan in the 1920s*, Farrar, Straus and Giroux, NY, 1993

Eliot, T.S., *Selected Prose of T.S. Eliot*, Harcourt Brace, NY, 1975

Feinstein, Sascha, ed., *Ask Me Now: Conversations on Jazz and Literature*, Indiana U. Press, Bloomington, 2007

Frosh, Stephen, *Identity Crisis: Modernity, Psychoanalysis and the Self*, Routledge, London, 1991

Gabbard, Krin, *Jazz Among the Discourses*, Duke University Press, NY, 1995

Gennari, John, *Blowin' Hot and Cool, Jazz and its Critics*, Univ. of Chicago Press, Chicago, 2006.

Gendron, Bernard, "After the October Revolution: The Jazz in New York, 1964-65" in Robert Aldington, *Sound Commitments*, above

_____, "'Moldy Figs' and Modernists: Jazz at War 91942-1946)" in Krin Gabbard, ed., *Jazz Among the Discourse*, above

Gilman-Opalsky, Richard, "Free Jazz and Radical Listening," *Fifth Estate* Summer/Fall 2009

Gioia, Ted, "Where Did Our Revolution Go? Free Jazz Turns Fifty" http://www.jazz.com/jazz-blog/2008/2/25/where-did-our-revolution-go-free-jazz-turns-fifty-years-old

Goehr, Lydia, *The Imaginary Museum of Musical Works*, Oxford: Clarendon Press, Oxford, 1992

Guilbaut, Serge, *How New York Stole the Idea of Modern Art : Abstract Expressionism, Freedom, and the Cold War*, Univ. of Chicago Press, Chicago, 1985

Haden, Charlie, Interviews, http://www.charliehadenmusic.com/media/interviews

Hamilton, Andy, *Lee Konitz: Conversations on the Improviser's Art*, Univ. of Michigan Press, Ann Arbor, 2007

Hegarty, Paul, *Noise/Music: A History*, Continuum, New York/London, 2007

Heffely, Mike, *Northern Sun, Southern Moon: Europe's Reinvention of Jazz*, Yale University Press, New Haven, 2005

Helliwell, Paul, "First Cut is the Deepest," *Metamute*, Oct. 12 2006, http://www.metamute.org/editorial/articles/first-cut-deepest

Himler, Sam, "Audience Cultivation in American New Music"
http://www.newmusicbox.org/articles/audience-cultivation-in-american- new-music/

Hopkins, Phil, *Amplified Gesture: An Introduction to Free Improvisation: Practitioners and their Philosophy*, (DVD) Samadhisound, 2009 http://www.ubu.com/film/hopkins_amplified.html

Hurley, Andrew Wright, *The Return of Jazz: Joachim-Ernst Berendt and West German Cultural Change*, Berghahn Books, NY, 2009

The Improvisor: The International Journal of Free Improvisation, Birmingham AL, http://www.the-improvisor.com/

James, Robin, ed., *Cassette Mythos*, Autonomedia, Brooklyn NY, 1992

Jameson, Frederik, *Postmodernism, or, The Cultural Logic of Late Capitalism*, Duke University Press, Durham, NC, 1991

Jankelevitch, Vladimir, *Music and the Ineffable*, Princeton U. Press, Princeton, 2003

Jauss, David, "Hymn of Fire," in *Ask Me Now: Conversations on Jazz and Literature*, ed. Sascha Feinstein, Indiana U. Press, Bloomington, 2007

Jefferson Airplane, Jean-luc Goddard film,
https://www.youtube.com/watch?v=WAJJE5Wo_OY

Jenkins, Todd S., *Free Jazz and Free Improvisation: An Encyclopedia*, 2 vols., Greenwood Press, Westport, CT, 2004

Jorn, Asger, *The Natural Order and Other Texts*, Aldershot /Ashgate, Burlington VT, 2002

Jost, Ekkehard, *Free Jazz*, Da Capo Press, NY, 1995 (originally published 1975)

Kane, Daniel, *All Poets Welcome: The Lower East Side Poetry Scene in the 1960s*, U. of California Press, Berkeley, 2003

Karkoschka, Erhard, "*Aspects of Group Improvisation*" 1971
http://www.erhardkarkoschka.de/artikel.html

Kaufmann, Vincent, *Guy Debord: Revolution in the Service of Poetry*, U. of Minn. Press, Mpls., 2006 [original French edition 2001]

Kofsky, Frank, *Black Nationalism and the Revolution in Music*, Pathfinder Press, NY, 1970

Linda Kouvaras, *Loading the Silence, Sound Art in the Post-Digital Age*, Adgate Publ., Surrey (UK), 2013

Kuntz, Henry, *Bells*, published 1973-78, specifically on John Grundfest,
http://bells.free-jazz.net/bells-part-two/john-gruntfest/

Lacy, Steve, *Conversations*, Duke U. Press, Durham NC, 2006

Le Baron, Anne, "Reflections of surrealism in Postmodern Musics" in *Postmodern Music/postmodern Thought*, ed. Judy Lochhead and Joseph Auner, Routledge, NY-London, 2002

Leland, John, *Hip: The History*, Harper, NY, 2005

Leonard, Neil, *Jazz: Myth and Religion*, Oxford Univ. Press, NY, 1987

Levin, Robert, "The free jazz revolution of the 60s," 2010, http://www.allaboutjazz. com/free-jazz-the-jazz-revolution-of-the-60s-by-robert-levin.php?page=1

Lewis, George E., *A Power Stronger Than Itself, the AACM and American Experimental Music*, U. of Chicago Press, Chicago, 2008

_____, " Improvised Music after 1950: Afrological and Eurological Perspectives" 1996.http://artsites.ucsc.edu/faculty/abeal/4classes/George%20Lewis%20article.pdf

_____, "Gittin' To Know Y'all: Improvised Music, Interculturalism, and the Racial Imagination," http://www.criticalimprov.com/article/view/6/14, 2004

_____, "Afterword to 'Improvised Music after 1950": The Changing Same" in Daniel Fischlin and Ajay Heble, eds., *The Other Side of Nowhere: Jazz, Improvisation, and Communities in Dialogue*, Wesleyan Univ. Press, Middletown, 2004

_____,"Critical Responses to 'Theorizing Improvisation (Musically)'" http://www.mtosmt.org/issues/mto.13.19.2/mto.13.19.2.lewis.php

_____, and Benjamin Piekut, *Oxford Handbook of Critical Improvisation Studies*, Oxford U. Press, NY, 2016

Litweiler, Jon, *The Freedom Principle : Jazz after 1958*, William Morrow, New York, 1984.

Lopes, Paul, *The Rise of a Jazz Art World*, Cambridge U. Press, Cambridge, 2002

Manguso, Sarah, and Davis, Jordan, *Free Radicals: American Poets before their First Books*, Sub press, 2004

Mann, Ron, *Imagine the Sound* , Canadian film, 1981

Mattin, and Iles, Anthony, eds., *Noise and Capitalism*, Arteleku Audiolab, San Sebastian (Spain), 2009

McClure, Daniel Robert, "New Black Music or 'anti-jazz': Free jazz and America's cultural de-colonization in the 1960s" https://www.academia.edu/621042/New_Black_Musicoranti-jazz_Free_jazz_and_Americas_cultural_de-colonization_in_the_1960s

McDonough, Tom ed., *Guy Debord and the situationist international : texts and documents*, MIT Press (October Book), 2002

McGowan, Todd, *The End of Dissatisfaction Jacques Lacan and the Emerging Society of Enjoyment*, SUNY Press, Albany, 2004

McKay, George, *Circular Breathing: The Cultural Politics of Jazz in Britain*, Duke Univ. Press, 2005.

Morris, Joe, *Perpetual Frontier: The Properties of Free Music*, Riti Pub., Stoney Creek CT, 2012

Moten, Fred, *In the Break: The Aesthetics of the Black Radical Tradition*, U. of Minnesota Press, Minneapolis, 2003

Nachmanovitch, Stephen, *Free Play; The Power of Improvisation in Life and the Arts*, Jeremy P. Tarcher, Los Angeles, 1990

Musics: A British Magazine of Improvised Music & Art, Ecstatic Peace Library, London?, 2016

Nunn, Tom, *Wisdom of the Impulse: On the Nature of Free Improvisation*, 1998, online in two parts
http://intuitivemusic.dk/iima/tn_wisdom_part1.pdf
http://intuitivemusic.dk/iima/tn_wisdom_part2.pdf

Nyman, Michael, *Experimental Music: Cage and Beyond*, Schimer Books, NY, 1974

Paglia, Camille, *Sexual Personae: Art and Decadence from Nefertiti to Emily Dickenson*, Random House, NY, 1990

Parker, William, *Conversations*, Rogue Art, Paris, 2011

_____, *Conversations II: Dialogues and Monologues*, Rogue Art, Paris, 2015

_____, *Who Owns Music: Notes from a Spiritual Journey*, Buddy's Knife, Jazzedition, Cologne, 2007

_____, Discography, http://www.bb10k.com/PARKER. disc.html

Phillips, Adam, *Terror and Experts*, Harvard U. Press, Cambridge, 1997

Piekut, Benjamin, *Experimentalism Otherwise, The New York Avant-Garde and its Limits*, U. of Calif. Press, Berkeley, 2011

Poerksen, Uwe, *Plastic Words: The Tyranny of a Modular Language*, Pennsylvania State U. Press, University Park, Pa. 1995

Posnock, Ross, *Renunciation: Acts of abandonment by Writers, Philosophers, and Artists*, Harvard U. Press, Cambridge MA/London, 2016

Prévost, Eddie, *Minute Particulars*, Copula, Matching Tye, 2004
_____,"Eddie Prévost: Master of Disorientation," interview, 2001,
http://www.monastery.nl/bulletin/prevost/prevost.html
_____, *No Sound is Innocent: AMM and the Practice of Self-Invention: Meta-musical Narratives: Essays*, Copula (Matchless Press), Harlow UK, 1995
Rockhill, Gabriel, *Radical History and the Politics of Culture*, Columbia Univ. Press, NY, 2014
Rockwell, John, *NY Times*, Dec. 22, 1985, "What Happened to Our Vanguard?"
Rosenberg, Harold, *The Tradition of the New*, Horizon Press, NY, 1959
Ross, Kristin, *The Emergence of Social Space: Rimbaud and the Paris Commune*, Verso, London 1988
Sanders, Ed, *Tales of Beatnik Glory: Volumes 1 & 2*, Citadel Underground, NY, 1990
Saunders, James, *The Ashgate Companion to Experimental Music*, Ashgate, Farnham England, Burlington VT, 2009
Sartre, Jean-Paul, *Transcendence of the Ego*, Hill and Wang, NY, 1960 (1937)
Schiller, Friedrich, *Naïve and Sentimental Poetry and On the Sublime*, tr. Julius A. Elias, Frederick Ungar Publishing Co., NY, 1966
Schwartz, Delmore, *The World is a Wedding*, New Directions, NY, 1948
Schwartz, Jeff, *Albert Ayler: His Life and Music*, 1992,
http://www.reocities.com/jeff_l_schwartz/ayler.html
_____, dissertation, unpublished
_____, *New Black Music: LeRoi Jones(Amiri Baraka), Bill Dixon, and the Making of Free Jazz*, draft copy, Jan. 2014
Shepp, Archie, interview 2001, http://jazztimes.com/articles/20207-archie-shepp-the-sound-and-the-fury
_____, interview 1990,
http://www.archieshepp.net/manage_content.php?cat_id=4&item_id=34
_____, interview 2014, http://daily.redbullmusicacademy.com/2014/08/archie-shepp-interview
Sheffer, Frank, "In the Ocean: A Film about the Classical Avant Garde," 2009,
https://www.youtube.com/watch?v=h0NwiTHIhGM
Shoup, Wally, *Music as Adventure*, nine muses, 2011, http://users.speakeasy.net/~ wal lyshp/wshoup/ music%20as%20adventure%20digital%20version.pdf
Sinclair, John, "Self-Determination Music," in Sinclair and Levin, Robert, *Music and Politics* (originally published in "Jazz & Pop"), World Pub. Co., NY, 1971
Sloterdijk, Peter, *In the World Interior of Capital: For a Philosophical Theory of Globalization*, tr. Wieland Hoban, Polity Press, 2013 (2005)
Small, Christopher, *Musicking: The Meanings of performance and Listening*, Wesleyan U. Press, Middletown CT, 1998
Spellman, A. B., *Four Lives in the Bebop Business*, Pantheon Books, NY, 1966
Stallybrass, Peter and White, Allon, *The Politics and Poetics of Transgression*, Cornell U. Press, Ithaca, 1986
Stephenson, Sam, ed., *The Jazz Loft Project : Photographs and Tapes of W. Eugene Smith from 821 Sixth Avenue, 1957-1965* , Knopf, New York, 2009
Sontag, Susan, *Against Interpretation*, Eyre & Spottiswoode, London, 1967
Stephens, Julie, *Anti-Disciplinary Protest: Sixties Radicalism and Postmodernism*, Cambridge Univ. Press, Cambridge UK, 1998
Stubbs, David, *Fear of music: Why People get Rothko but don't get Stockhausen*, O Books, Win chester UK, 2009

Suzuki, Shunyu, *Zen Mind, Beginner's Mind*, Walker/Weatherhill, NY, 1970

Taylor, Arthur, *Notes and Tone: Musician-to-Musician Interviews*, Da Capo Press, NY, 1993

Thomas, Lorenzo, "Alea's Children: The Avant-Garde on the Lower East Side, 1960-1970," *African American Review* 27, no. 4 (1993), 94.

Tilbury, John, *Cornelius Cardew, A Life Unfinished*, Copula, London, 2008

Thomson, Scott, "The Pedagogical Imperative of Musical Improvisation," *Critical Studies in Improvisation*, vol. 3 no.2 (2007) http://www.criticalimprov.com/article/view/353

Trilling, Lionel, *The Moral Imagination to be Intelligent: Selected Essays of Lionel Trilling*, Farrar, Strauss, Giroux, NY, 2000

Uscher, Nancy, *Your Own Way in Music: A Career and Resource Guide*, St. Martin's Press, NY, 1990

Varèse, Edgard, http://www.ubu.com/sound/varese.html

Voegelin, Salome, *Listening to Sound and Silence: Towards a Philosophy of Sound Art*, Continuum, London, 2010

Wallace, David Foster, *Both Flesh and Not: Essays*, Little, Brown and Co., NY, 2012

Warburton, Dan, "Interview with Burton Green," *Paris Transatlantic interview*, 2003, http://www.paristransatlantic.com/magazine/interviews/greene.html.

Wark, Mackenzie,"The Avant-garde Never Gives Up" http://www.lanaturnerjournal.com/print-issue-7-contents/the--never-gives-up

Washburne, Christopher J. and Derno, Maiken, eds. *Bad Music: The Music We Love to Hate*, Routledge, NY, 2004

Watson, Ben, *Derek Bailey and the Story of Free Improvisation*, Verso, London, 2004

_____, *Adorno for Revolutionaries*, Ukant Publishers, London, 2011

Weber, Mark, "The Early LPs of the Free Jazz Scene in LA" http:// markweber.free-jazz.net/2012/01/24/the-early-lps-of-the-free-jazz-scene-in-los-angeles/

Whyton, Tony, *Jazz Icons: Heroes, Myths and the Jazz Tradition,*   Cambridge University Press, Cambridge UK, 2010

Willener, Alfred, *The Action-image of Society; On Cultural Politicization*, Pantheon Books, Lon don, 1970

Williams, Davey, *Solo Gig: Essential Curiosities in Musical Free Improvisation*, Birdfeeder Editions, Birmingham AL, 2011

Wilmer, Valerie, *As Serious as Your Life: The Story of the New Jazz,* Allison & Busby, London, 1980

Wolfe, Tom, *Radical Chic and Mau-Mauing the Flac Catchers*, Farrar, Straus & Giroux, New York, 1970

Wright, Jack, "Circulate" *Sound Choice*, issue no.8, May-June 1987 http://www.springgardenmusic.com/essays.html

_____, "Free Improvisation as a Social Act," 1986, http://www.springgardenmusic.com/essays.html#freesocialact

_____, "Theatre of the Moment" and "Against Improvisation," 1988, http://www.springgardenmusic.com/essays.html#theatreofthemoment

_____, "You Know the Story," 1989, http://www.springgardenmusic.com/ youknow_files/you_know_the_story.jack.wright.compressed.pdf

_____, William Parker/Jack Wright Duo https://springgardenmusic.bandcamp.com/track/william-parker-duo-ny-1985

Wyse, Lonce, "Free Music and the Discipline of Sound" 2004, http://journals.cambridge.org/article_S1355771803000219

Made in the USA
Columbia, SC
27 April 2020